FIFTH EDITION

US GOVERNMENT AND POLITICS

for A-level

Anthony J. Bennett

SERIES EDITOR:
Eric Magee

DYNAMIC LEARNING

HODDER
EDUCATION
AN HACHETTE UK COMPANY

Hachette UK's policy is to use papers that are natural, renewable and recyclable products and made from wood grown in sustainable forests. The logging and manufacturing processes are expected to conform to the environmental regulations of the country of origin.

Orders: please contact Bookpoint Ltd, 130 Park Drive, Milton Park, Abingdon, Oxon OX14 4SE. Telephone: (44) 01235 827720. Fax: (44) 01235 400454. Email education@bookpoint.co.uk

Lines are open from 9 a.m. to 5 p.m., Monday to Saturday, with a 24-hour message answering service. You can also order through our website: www.hoddereducation.co.uk

ISBN: 978-1-4718-8936-3

© Anthony J. Bennett and Eric Magee 2017

First published in 2017 by

Hodder Education
An Hachette UK Company
Carmelite House
50 Victoria Embankment
London EC4Y 0DZ

www.hoddereducation.co.uk

Impression number   10 9 8 7 6 5 4

Year   2021 2020 2019 2018

Photos reproduced by permission of: **p. 2** digidreamgrafix/Fotolia; **p. 5** PAINTING/Alamy Stock Photo; **p. 7** Stock Connection Blue/Alamy Stock Photo; **p. 10** nickjene/Fotolia; **p. 11** Bettmann/Getty; **p. 13** REUTERS/Alamy Stock Photo; **p. 15** MediaPunch Inc/Alamy Stock Photo; **p. 18** mrallen/Fotolia; **p. 22** Stock Connection Blue/Alamy Stock Photo; **p. 25** Granger Historical Picture Archive/Alamy Stock Photo; **p. 28** Lebrecht Music and Arts Photo Library/Alamy Stock Photo; **p. 30** Kristoffer Tripplaar/Alamy Stock Photo; **p. 31** Everett Collection Historical/Alamy Stock Photo; **p. 32** dpa picture alliance/Alamy Stock Photo; **p. 33** Granger Historical Picture Archive/Alamy Stock Photo; **p. 37** (left) Ian G Dagnall/Alamy Stock Photo; **p. 37** (right) World History Archive/Alamy Stock Photo; **p. 40** Peter Horree/Alamy Stock Photo; **p. 41** Jackson/AP/REX/Shutterstock; **p. 42** Everett Collection Historical/Alamy Stock Photo; **p. 46** B Christopher/Alamy Stock Photo; **p. 48** WPA Pool/Pool/Getty; **p. 50** MCT/Getty Images; **p. 52** LH Images/Alamy Stock Photo; **p. 53** Sean Pavone/Alamy Stock Photo; **p. 54** ANDY BUCHANAN/Stringer/Getty; **p. 58** Brooks Kraft LLC/Corbis via Getty Images; **p. 60** ddp USA/REX/Shutterstock; **p. 65** ZUMA Press, Inc./Alamy Stock Photo; **p. 66** ZUMA Press, Inc./Alamy Stock Photo; **p. 68** Bill Clark/CQ Roll Call/Getty; **p. 72** REUTERS/Alamy Stock Photo; **p. 74** White House Photo/Alamy Stock Photo; **p. 78** DOD Photo/Alamy Stock Photo; **p. 85** dpa picture alliance/Alamy Stock Photo; **p. 89** Mark Reinstein/Getty; **p. 91** Danita Delimont / Alamy Stock Photo; **p. 96** (left) US Senate/Alamy Stock Photo; **p. 96** (right) Ed Zurga/Epa/REX/Shutterstock; **p. 101** eye35.pix/Alamy Stock Photo; **p.104** Fotolia; **p. 105** Todd Taulman/Fotolia; **p. 110** Fotolia; **p. 112** Pool/Getty Images; **p. 115** Charles Agholan/Fotolia; **p. 116** (top) ZUMA Press, Inc./Alamy Stock Photo; **p. 116** (bottom) wolterke/Fotolia; **p. 120** MediaPunch Inc/Alamy Stock Photo; **p. 128** Judie Long/Alamy Stock Photo; **p. 130** Everett Collection Inc/Alamy Stock Photo; **p. 132** REUTERS/Alamy Stock Photo; **p. 133** MICHAELREYNOLDS/EPA/REX/Shutterstock; **p. 136** NICHOLAS KAMM/Staff/Getty; **p. 139** WDC Photos/Alamy Stock Photo; **p. 141** Fox Photos/Stringer/Getty Images; **p. 143** Diana Walker/Getty Images; **p. 148** Stacy Walsh Rosenstock/Alamy Stock Photo; **p. 153** Granger Historical Picture Archive/Alamy Stock Photo; **p. 154** vario images GmbH & Co.KG/Alamy Stock Photo; **p. 156** WDC Photos/Alamy Stock Photo; **p. 163** rich lasalle/Alamy Stock Photo; **p. 165** REUTERS/Alamy Stock Photo; **p. 172** Fotolia; **p. 175** SAUL LOEB/Staff/Getty Images; **p. 176** Xinhua/Alamy Stock Photo; **p. 184** DENNIS COOK/AP/REX/Shutterstock; **p. 187** Reuters/Alamy Stock Photo; **p. 192** Verkouteran/AP/REX/Shutterstock; **p. 195** Drew Angerer/Getty Images; **p. 198** Andrew Harnik/AP/REX/Shutterstock; **p. 201** PJF Military Collection/Alamy Stock Photo; **p. 206** Dan Kitwood/Getty; **p. 212** Bloomberg/Getty; **p. 214** Granger Historical Picture Archive/Alamy Stock Photo; **p. 216** Jim West/Alamy Stock Photo; **p. 222** Science History Images/Alamy Stock Photo; **p. 232** 3desc/Fotolia; **p. 238** Sandy Huffaker/Stringer/Getty Images; **p. 243** ZUMA Press, Inc./Alamy Stock Photo; **p. 247** Ron Jenkins/Stringer/Getty; **p. 250** Anadolu Agency/Getty Images; **p. 251** 3D Stock Illustrations/Alamy Stock Photo; **p. 254** Reuters/Alamy Stock Photo; **p. 259** Reuters/Alamy Stock Photo; **p. 266** Bettmann/Contributor/Getty Images; **p. 268** Xinhua/Alamy Stock Photo; **p. 280** ZUMA Press, Inc./Alamy Stock Photo; **p. 287** Francis Specker/Alamy Stock Photo; **p. 291** Jonny White/Alamy Stock Photo; **p. 294** Patrick Rolands/Fotolia; **p. 305** WorldFoto/Alamy Stock Photo; **p. 307** REUTERS/Alamy Stock Photo; **p. 314** ZUMA Press, Inc./Alamy Stock Photo; **p. 318** RICHARD ELLIS/Staff/Getty Images; **p. 326** Sarah Vaughan/Alamy Stock Photo; **p. 333** Bill Clark/Getty Images; **p. 337** Allan Tannenbaum/Getty Images; **p. 343** PAUL J. RICHARDS/Getty Images; **p. 345** David Grossman/Alamy Stock Photo.

Cover photo reproduced by permission of Marina Riley/Alamy Stock Vector

Typeset by Aptara, India

Printed in Italy

A catalogue record for this title is available from the British Library.

Get the most from this book

Special features

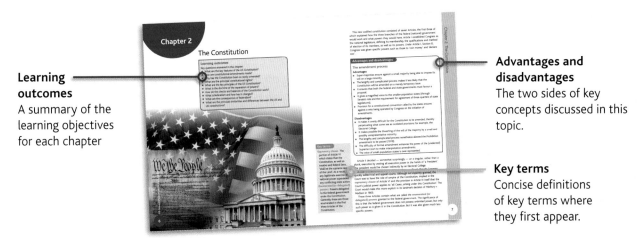

Learning outcomes
A summary of the learning objectives for each chapter

Advantages and disadvantages
The two sides of key concepts discussed in this topic.

Key terms
Concise definitions of key terms where they first appear.

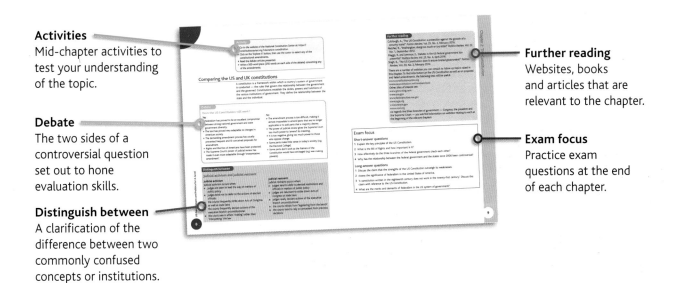

Activities
Mid-chapter activities to test your understanding of the topic.

Debate
The two sides of a controversial question set out to hone evaluation skills.

Distinguish between
A clarification of the difference between two commonly confused concepts or institutions.

Further reading
Websites, books and articles that are relevant to the chapter.

Exam focus
Practice exam questions at the end of each chapter.

About this book

US Government and Politics is written specifically for students studying the A-level specifications in Politics offered by Edexcel and AQA. This fifth edition has been substantially rewritten, updated and rearranged for use with the new politics specifications for teaching from September 2017, as well as covering the developments in US politics surrounding the 2016 elections and the Trump administration.

As the two awarding bodies are examining students using different types of questions, at the end of Chapters 2–7 there are boxes containing sample questions relating to each awarding body.

Other resources

It is my hope that American politics is a subject in which you will become genuinely interested. This textbook will give you a grounding in the subject, but in such an ever-changing subject you will need to be constantly updating your knowledge of what is going on in Washington. Hodder Education, which publishes this textbook, also publishes *Politics Review*, a magazine written exclusively for A-level Politics students. It is published four times each academic year. Hodder Education also publishes the *US Government & Politics Annual Update*. This book, published in January each year, keeps you updated on what has happened in Washington over the previous 12 months. It is full of up-to-date examples, tables and anecdotes for you to use in your essays, and is written exclusively for A-level Politics students. It is also well worth visiting some of the following websites:

- www.washingtonpost.com
- www.nytimes.com
- www.realclearpolitics.com

You will find more specific website information at the end of each chapter in the Further Reading box.

Exam specifications

The table below shows you how you can use this book in conjunction with the Edexcel and AQA specifications.

Chapter	Edexcel	AQA
1 An overview		
2 The Constitution	The US Constitution and federalism	The constitutional framework of US government
3 Congress	US Congress	The legislative branch of government: Congress
4 The presidency	US presidency	The executive branch of government: President
5 The Supreme Court and civil rights	US Supreme Court and civil rights	The judicial branch of government; civil rights
6 Elections	US democracy and participation	The electoral process and direct democracy
7 Political parties and pressure groups	US democracy and participation	Political parties; pressure groups

The US/UK comparative element of each section of the specification is fully covered within each related chapter.

Contents

Chapter 1

US and comparative politics: an overview

Learning outcomes

Key questions answered in this chapter:

- What are the key facts about the USA?
- How did it all start?
- What were the Articles of Confederation?
- How do the three branches of government fit together?
- What is representative democracy?
- What is popular sovereignty?
- Why hold elections?
- Why are parties and pressure groups important?
- What are the three theoretical approaches we will use in our study of comparative politics?

Introduction

The USA is a vast country. The entire UK would fit into the state of Oregon (see Figure 1.1). The 48 mainland states cross four time zones. At midday in New York, it is 11 a.m. in Chicago, 10 a.m. in Denver, and just 9 a.m. in Los Angeles. It takes just under 6½ hours to fly from London to Boston on America's east coast. But it takes another 6½ hours to fly from Boston to Los Angeles on America's west coast. If you took a train from Boston to Los Angeles, it would take you just over three days.

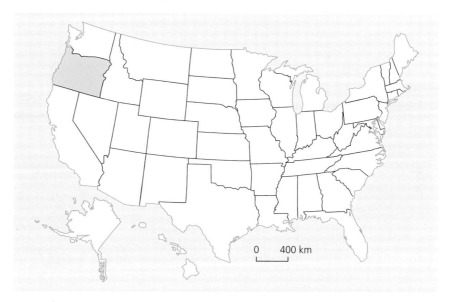

0   400 km

Figure 1.1 The state of Oregon (highlighted) is the geographic size of the UK

The USA is also a very diverse country. There is the tropical landscape of Florida but also the frozen Arctic wastes of Alaska. There are the flat prairies of Kansas but also the Rockies of Wyoming and Colorado. There are the deserts of Arizona but also the forests of New Hampshire and Maine. It is diverse in its landscape, its climate, its economy and its people. The USA is also 'the hyphenated society', in which people think of themselves as African-Americans, Hispanic- and Latino-Americans, Asian-Americans, Irish-Americans, Polish-Americans, or even Native-Americans. American society has been described as a 'melting pot' — a great cauldron filled with people from diverse lands, cultures, languages and religions.

This diversity gives rise to Americans' need for symbols of unity — most notably in their attachment to the American flag. While flag waving is still regarded as something of an oddity in the UK — generally associated with football supporters or the Last Night of the Proms — countless families in rural and suburban America go through the daily ritual of raising and lowering the flag outside their homes each morning and evening. Public buildings in the USA display the flag as a matter of course. Each day begins in most American schools with children standing to face the flag at the front of the classroom and reciting the Pledge of Allegiance (see Box 1.1). There is even a day each year — 14 June — designated as Flag Day.

> **Box 1.1**
>
> ### Pledge of Allegiance
>
> 'I pledge allegiance to the flag of the United States of America and to the Republic for which it stands, one nation, under God, indivisible, with liberty and justice for all.'

These characteristics of size and diversity have important political implications too. Size brings with it the need for decentralisation — for the federal system of government established by the country's Founding Fathers in 1787. Diversity comes in the form of laws that differ between states about such matters as elections, crime and punishment. Different regions of the country have discernibly different ideological characteristics. The 'conservative' South stretches from Texas to Virginia (see Figure 1.2). The 'liberal' Northeast includes such states as Massachusetts and Rhode Island. The west coast, too, is liberal leaning, especially in the Californian cities of Los Angeles and San Francisco. All this has implications for governing, as well as for political parties and for elections.

Figure 1.2 The 48 contiguous states of the USA

The historical setting of the Constitution

How did it all start? Students of US government and politics need to know something of the origins of the country. The 13 original British colonies were strung out along the eastern seaboard of America from Maine in the north to Georgia in the south. Some were the creations of commercial interests, others of religious groups. All had written charters setting out their form of government and the rights of the colonists. Democracy was limited. Although each colony had a governor, a legislature and a judiciary, each also had a property qualification for voting from which women and black people were excluded. And then, of course, there was slavery. Yet, despite their shortcomings, the colonies provided a blueprint of what was to come.

In the view of the British government, the American colonies existed principally for the economic benefit of the mother country. The colonists were obliged to pay tax to Britain, but they had no representation in the British Parliament. This led to a growing resentment. Bostonian patriot James Otis declared: 'Taxation without representation is tyranny!' As Britain tried to tighten its grip on the colonies' economic affairs in the 1770s, revolution became inevitable. The War of Independence began in April 1775.

> **Box 1.2**
>
> ### Extract from the Declaration of Independence
>
> 'We hold these truths to be self-evident, that all men are created equal, that they are endowed by their Creator with certain unalienable Rights, that among these are Life, Liberty and the pursuit of Happiness.'

The Declaration of Independence stated that 'all men are created equal' (see Box 1.2). But what did it mean for Jefferson and his co-authors to say this and, what was more, to claim that this was a 'self-evident' truth? Because the Declaration had talked only of 'men', and because most blacks in the about-to-be-created nation were held in slavery, and the poor were to be denied voting rights, then perhaps it could be argued that the Declaration was assuming, to quote George Orwell, that 'some are more equal than others'. Was it not self-evident that the framers of the Declaration were saying that only white wealthy men were endowed with these rights?

But they were saying no such thing, for two very good reasons. First, it is easily forgotten that until comparatively recently the words 'man' or 'men' were used interchangeably to refer to human beings in general with no reference to gender. It really is not that long ago when most people talked of the principle of 'one man, one vote' to mean that every adult — regardless of gender — should have the right to vote. Furthermore, the Declaration of Independence uses the words 'men' (twice) and 'people' (eight times) synonymously.

John Trumbull's painting *Declaration of Independence*

Second, it is important to distinguish between asserting a right and claiming that everyone is already enjoying it. The denial of a right in practice is surely not the denial of a right in principle. As Abraham Lincoln would later explain just before he became president, the authors of this document 'did not mean to assert the obvious untruth, that all were then actually enjoying that equality, nor yet, that they were about to confer it immediately upon them, but they meant simply to declare the *right*, so that the *enforcement* of it might follow as fast as circumstances should permit'.

Jefferson then went on to announce some of the rights that all citizens should enjoy. This was clearly not meant as a comprehensive list, for the three mentioned — life, liberty and the pursuit of happiness — are preceded with the phrase 'among these are'. Because all are entitled to these rights simply by virtue of being human, they are often referred to as natural rights. Yet even in a democratic society, the government must regulate these natural rights through law. Thus, the right to life does not give one the right to use deadly force against any person who breaks into your home. The right of liberty would doubtless include the right to travel, and while no democratic government would prohibit its citizens from travelling within its borders, it does regulate that freedom through the laws it enacts regarding such matters as speed limits, traffic lights and car licensing requirements.

While Jefferson was announcing these high principles, the less well-remembered Richard H. Lee was offering his 'plan of confederation' for post-colonial government. The Articles of Confederation were eventually ratified by the 13 independent states by March 1781, although the hostilities with Great Britain were not formally concluded until the Treaty of Paris in 1783. These articles set up a confederacy — a 'league of friendship', a loose collection of independent states — rather than a national government. Having just fought for — and won — their independence from Great Britain, the Virginians, New Yorkers and the rest were not going to give it away again to some new centralised government. Virginians wanted to govern Virginia. New Yorkers wanted to govern New York. The national government was a feeble affair with no executive branch, no judiciary and a legislature that was little more than a talking shop. The most significant fact about the government created by the Articles of Confederation was that it was weak. Thus, the ex-colonists had succeeded in gaining their independence but had failed to form a nation, and by this failure they almost turned their victory into defeat. What ensued was a shambles.

Many of the leaders of the Revolutionary War, such as George Washington and Alexander Hamilton, believed that a strong national government was essential. As the states squabbled over currency, commerce and much else, they began to fear the reappearance of the British and the loss of all they had so remarkably achieved. A small group of men with such fears met at Annapolis, Maryland, in September 1786. Attendance was poor, so another meeting was called in Philadelphia in May 1787 with the declared purpose of strengthening the Articles of Confederation. That might have been their purpose, but four months later the attendees had scrapped the articles, written an entirely new Constitution and become the Founding Fathers of the United States of America.

The Philadelphia Convention was made up of 55 delegates representing 12 of the 13 states. (Rhode Island, suspicious of what was planned, refused to send any delegates.) In those four stifling hot months of the summer of 1787 they wrote a new form of government. They quickly concluded that a confederacy was structurally flawed and hopelessly weak, but they saw from political history that stronger forms of government led to the trampling underfoot of citizens' rights and liberties. Thus they would have to create an entirely new form of government — one that had a strong centre while still preserving states' rights and individual liberties. The answer was a federal constitution, a bill of rights and an intricate set of checks and balances between the different levels and branches of government.

The convention initially considered two plans: one put forward by New Jersey, the other by Virginia. The New Jersey Plan — favoured by the states with smaller populations — was designed merely to strengthen the Articles of Confederation. The Virginia Plan — favoured by the states with larger populations — was much more radical. But with support equally divided, the convention was deadlocked.

The impasse was broken with what became known as the Connecticut Compromise. The stroke of genius came in the plan's recommendation that the new national legislature should be made up of two chambers. In the lower house (the House of Representatives) the states would be represented proportionally to their population, but in the upper house (the Senate) the states would be represented equally, regardless of population. Other compromises followed, concerning such matters as the method of electing the president. A new **constitution** was born — a constitution we shall study in detail in Chapter 2. But before we do that, we take an overview of the government and politics of the United States.

> **Key term**
>
> **Constitution** The basic political and legal structures prescribing the rules by which a government operates. It may take the form of a codified document.

The machinery of government

Maybe the best way to get an overview of the machinery of government in the United States would be to visit the nation's capital — Washington DC — and take in the buildings that stand on the 16 blocks of Pennsylvania Avenue between Capitol Hill and Lafayette Square. Our first stop would be at the midway point — number 700 of that famous avenue — at the National Archives Building. Even on the hottest and most humid days of a Washington summer, you will see an orderly, and surprisingly hushed, line of American tourists waiting to enter. As they do, shirts are put on and baseball caps removed.

Looking west down Pennsylvania Avenue from Capitol Hill

Not much in America causes such reverential behaviour. But this is the building that houses the Constitution of the United States of America. Americans are not known for queuing, and they are certainly not known for quietness, but the Constitution demands both.

The Constitution laid out the machinery of government and provided for three branches of the federal government — the legislature (to make the laws), the executive (to carry out the laws), and the Supreme Court (to enforce and interpret the laws) (see Figure 1.3). Walk from the National Archives up Pennsylvania Avenue and you will reach Capitol Hill where stands the Capitol — the building where Congress meets to make America's laws. Here sit the 435 members of the House of Representatives and the 100 members of the Senate. In terms of law making, their powers are pretty much co-equal — though the Senate has other powers that give it greater prestige.

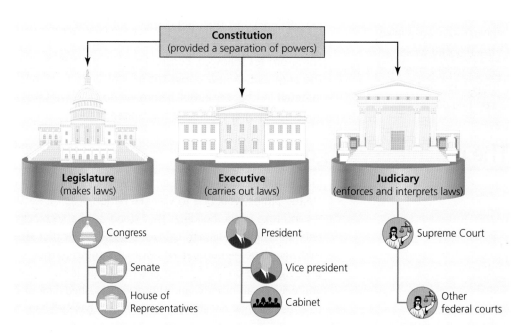

Figure 1.3 The three branches of the US government

From Capitol Hill, look 15 blocks back down Pennsylvania Avenue and you will see the grand building that houses the United States Department of the Treasury — one of the 15 departments that make up the executive branch of government. And just behind that is the White House — the hub of the executive branch of government. The White House is both the official residence of the president and — in the West Wing — the president's workplace. Here also we find the vice president, the room where the president's cabinet meets from time to time, as well as all the offices for the president's closest aides and advisers.

Standing just across the road from the Capitol is the building that houses the Supreme Court. Here nine justices, chosen by the president but confirmed by the Senate, rule on whether the laws that Congress passes and the president signs are compatible with the Constitution. Over recent decades, the Court has found itself having to rule on such issues as gender rights, the rights of racial minorities, restrictions on the ownership of firearms, freedom of speech, freedom of religion, President Obama's healthcare reforms (see Box 1.3), and even who had won the presidential election in 2000 between George W. Bush and Al Gore.

Box 1.3

Obama's healthcare reform (2010)

To see how the three branches of the federal government — Congress, the president and the Supreme Court — are all required to play a part in the governance of the United States, let's see how President Obama's landmark healthcare reform (otherwise known as 'Obamacare') became law, and what happened once it did.

First, both houses of Congress had to pass the healthcare reform bill, in identical forms. This is because both houses have equal legislative power. After almost a year of trying, this finally occurred on 21 March 2010.

Now, in order for this bill to become law, the President needed to sign it. So, just two days later, on 23 March, President Obama signed healthcare reform into law. It was now the job of the executive branch of government to carry out the law by rolling out the provisions it made for healthcare and healthcare insurance.

So thus far, Congress had passed the law and the President had signed it. But some opponents of the new law thought it was unconstitutional — in other words, that part of it was not permitted by the United States Constitution. Resolving that dispute was the job of the courts, and ultimately the United States Supreme Court.

So almost exactly two years after the law became effective, lawyers from both sides argued their case before the nine justices of the Supreme Court. Then, on 28 June 2012, the Court announced its decision, essentially upholding the law's provisions.

Looking at these separate buildings can be somewhat misleading, for it gives the impression that Congress, the president and the Supreme Court are politically separate. True, they are entirely separate when it comes to membership. No one is allowed to be simultaneously a member of more than one branch of government. Thus when in November 2008 senators Barack Obama and Joe Biden were elected respectively president and vice president, both had to resign from the Senate. It would be like the British prime minister having to resign from parliament before taking up residence at 10 Downing Street.

But politically, these three institutions are not separate. As Richard Neustadt famously remarked, they are 'separate institutions, *sharing* powers'. So as Box 1.3 shows, for the Patient Protection and Affordable Care Act — otherwise known as 'Obamacare' — to become, and remain, law, all three branches of government had to be in agreement, for each of them has *shared* power. And what's true for law making is true for pretty much everything else. It can make the exercise of political power somewhat problematic, but then that's what the framers of the Constitution wanted. Given their experience of rule from Great Britain, they had learned to distrust unchecked political power. As Thomas Cronin put it: 'Leadership [in America] is difficult precisely because the Framers of the Constitution wanted it to be so.' The Constitution is a power-averse document.

Democracy and participation

In 1787, the American nation's founders chose to set up what they called a republic — what today we call **representative democracy**. In a representative democracy — sometimes called a participatory democracy — the people elect officials who perform the functions of government on their behalf and are periodically accountable to them. This raises the question as to whether these 'elected officials' are merely the people's puppets — mandated always to act in such a way as to gain the approval of those who elected them. In *The Federalist Papers* — a series of essays published by James Madison and Alexander Hamilton in 1787 and 1788 in order to urge acceptance of the new Constitution — Hamilton had this to say on the relationship between these elected officials and the people. They would sometimes, said Hamilton, have to defend the people 'against their own temporary errors and delusions'. It would indeed be important that they were not swayed by every passing fad and fancy of the people, even one supported by a majority. At such times, said Hamilton, elected officials have 'a duty to withstand the temporary delusion in order to give [the people] time and opportunity for more cool and sedate reflection'.

But such a situation would be temporary. For the United States was about to become the first modern nation to base itself on the principle of **popular sovereignty** — the principle that all political power derives from the people. As the Declaration of Independence famously states: 'Governments are instituted among Men, deriving their just Powers from the Consent of the Governed.'

Box 1.4

Preamble to the US Constitution

'We the People of the United States, in Order to form a more perfect Union, establish Justice, insure domestic Tranquility, provide for the common defence, promote the general Welfare, and secure the Blessings of Liberty to ourselves and our Posterity, do ordain and establish this Constitution for the United States of America.'

It was this principle that was enshrined in the opening words of the Preamble to the Constitution (see Box 1.4) — 'We the People.' And some seven decades and more later, it was the same principle that was elaborated in those famous words of Abraham Lincoln in his Gettysburg Address (1863) that democracy is 'government of the people, by the people, and for the people'. Thus two essential elements of a representative democracy based on the principle of popular sovereignty are elections and political parties.

The Gettysburg Address, Lincoln Memorial, Washington DC

Elections and voting

Why have elections at all? We have already partly answered this question. There are four main reasons:

- To provide a way for the people to control their government and hold their elected officials to account.
- To elect people to office, as James Madison wrote in *Federalist* no. 57, who have 'the most wisdom to discern, and most virtue to pursue, the common good of society'. What Madison would have made of the elections of 2016 in this regard is a troubling thought.
- To foster the participatory principle of representative democracy by giving people a chance to campaign, attend rallies, donate money, and — these days — join their candidate's Facebook group.
- To stimulate public debate on those policy issues of most pressing importance. Such debate might be corporate or individual, spoken or electronic, supportive or critical.

Elections are much more widespread in American politics than they are in British politics. Both houses of Congress are elected directly by the people — the House of Representatives every two years, and the Senate every six years with one-third of the senators being up for re-election every two years. Thus every two years there are congressional elections for all 435 members of the House and one-third of the 100 senators. Furthermore, these elections are preceded by primary elections in which ordinary voters can have a say as to whom they wish to see as the party candidates in the upcoming general election.

Jimmy Carter campaigning in 1976

Then, once every four years, Americans elect their president. It is the presidential election that receives so much attention from the world's media. Again, this election is preceded by a series of state-based primary elections, allowing ordinary voters to have a say in who the major parties' candidates should be.

Thus Americans have numerous opportunities to vote — both to choose candidates for an upcoming election, and then to choose between the candidates at the election. How and why voters exercise their democratic rights is another aspect of interest to students of politics. I can still recall an incident while campaigning for Jimmy Carter in the Democratic primary in New York in 1976. Outside his home state of Georgia, Carter was a total unknown at the start of the campaign, and he was up against other Democrats who had a much higher national profile. On the streets of Midtown Manhattan we had to ascertain whether or not voters would support Carter in the upcoming primary, and if possible to discover the reason for their decision. An elderly black woman told me she would be voting for Governor Carter. I — unwisely — asked why. 'I know too much about the others,' came back her matter-of-fact reply.

Political parties

The leaders of the former Soviet Union often boasted that they held fairly frequent elections. That was indeed true, but the reason why most observers in the West would not have considered their political system a democracy was because voters were offered no genuine choice between competing political parties.

It is worth remembering that the USA's Founders disliked political parties, describing them as 'factions' motivated by ambition and self-interest. This was understandable. After all, the success of the newly born nation was still to be guaranteed and Britain was waiting in the wings to take advantage of any internal squabbling. (We did, after all, try to win back the old colonies in the ill-fated — for us — War of 1812.) So it is slightly ironic that today America has what are probably the oldest political parties in the world. One of them, the Republican Party, is even affectionately known as the GOP — the Grand Old Party.

For most of its history, America has had two major competing political parties. From Abraham Lincoln (1861–65) to Barack Obama (2009–17), America had 28 different presidents — 18 Republicans and 10 Democrats. During the same period, these two parties alternated in their control of Congress. Indeed, it has been unusual for anyone who was not either a Democrat or a Republican to be even elected to Congress. So in this sense at least, America really does have a two-party system.

In terms of ideology and policy priorities, the Democratic Party in the United States would be similar to a cross between the Liberal Democrats and 'New Labour' in the UK, while the Republicans look very similar to the UK Conservative Party. Both American parties have become more ideologically cohesive over the past two decades.

Pressure groups

In a participatory democracy, many citizens also belong to groups that attempt to exert influence on those who hold office — in any of the three branches of government. These groups are distinct from political parties because they do not participate directly in elections. They do not seek to win power, merely to influence those who do. Hence they are collectively known as pressure groups or, in America, as 'interest groups' because they represent a specific 'interest'.

Pressure groups seek to:
- broaden citizen participation in politics
- engage in public education on issues that affect their members
- influence the policy agenda of politicians both during and between elections

Pressure groups come in a great many different shapes and sizes. There are economic groups such as business associations and trade unions (in America referred to as labour unions). There are policy groups, political action committees (PACs), Super PACs, think-tanks and foundations. Pressure groups have played, and continue to play, a very significant role in many policy areas including women's rights, gender equality, rights of ethnic minorities, Americans with disabilities, the environment, gun control, healthcare and seniors (the elderly).

The methods they use — including direct lobbying, election-time campaigning, legal action and protest — are sometimes questioned as to whether they are always compatible with the ideals of representative democracy. Their huge discrepancy in size, wealth and influence also causes much debate, as does the clash between what may be in the special interest of a particular group and what may be in the wider interest of society as a whole.

Comparative politics

Two representative democracies

Throughout this book we shall also be considering some of the key similarities and differences between the government and politics of the United States and those of the United Kingdom. It is probably true to say that when American government courses are taught in American schools and universities, there are more comparative references to British government than to that of any other country. Likewise, when in this country we teach courses on the government of the United Kingdom, there are more comparative references to US government than to that of any other country. So why is this?

First, as we saw earlier in this chapter, the two nations have close historical and cultural ties. Anyone who visits America from this country will almost certainly have noticed many Americans' fascination with a wide range of so-called 'English customs' and their seemingly insatiable interest in our Royal Family. Once when I happened to be attending a conference in Philadelphia at the same time as Queen Elizabeth II was visiting the city, I was introduced as 'the Queen's representative' and asked detailed questions about the well-being of both Her Majesty and her extended family.

Queen Elizabeth II and President Barack Obama

Second, the governmental and political systems of these two nations are both markedly different but also complementary; hence our focus will be on both similarities and differences. Indeed, I have found it to be the case that, to begin with, students tend to regard the two systems as well-nigh identical. It is only as they learn more about how the two systems actually work that the differences become more apparent. For although both systems are based on the democratic principle, the way they apply this principle is quite different.

Britain has what we call **parliamentary government**. In a parliamentary system, the people vote for their representatives to the law-making body (although in the UK, only to the House of Commons). Whichever party gains a majority in the legislature, its leader — often called the prime minister — becomes head of the executive branch of government, usually referred to as 'the government'. Other legislators from the prime minister's party make up the cabinet and run the executive departments. Thus there are literally dozens of public officials who serve both in the legislature and in high-level executive positions at the same time. The UK, along with many other European countries, has a parliamentary system as do other large democracies such as India, Japan and Australia.

The United States, on the other hand, has **presidential government**. In a presidential system, the chief executive — the president — is independently elected and cannot be dismissed by the legislature. This means that different parties may run the executive and legislative branches at the same time. Furthermore, no public official is allowed to serve in more than one branch at any one time. The president's cabinet is therefore drawn from outside the legislature, or serving legislators who accept a cabinet post must resign from the legislature. Most countries in central and southern America, as well as some in Asia and Africa, have a presidential system.

When studying politics comparatively, we will be focusing on similarities and differences. You need to ask yourself questions such as:

- Why do these similarities/differences exist?
- What are the consequences of any differences?
- Which (of, for example, the two institutions) is more or less powerful?
- Which (of, for example, the two processes) is more straightforward or complicated?
- Which (of, for example, the two systems) is more or less effective?
- What are the possible advantages/disadvantages of these differences?
- Which is more/less democratic?
- Which is more in need of reform?

Indeed, these will doubtless be the way examiners will frame their questions in the end-of-course examination. This means that you will need to go beyond the simple statement that 'X is different from Y', to analyse both the possible underlying *causes* as well as the possible *consequences* and *implications* of these differences.

Three theoretical approaches

Finally, it will be necessary to have a basic knowledge and understanding of three of the different theoretical approaches that we can adopt in our study of comparative politics. These are summarised in Box 1.5 on page 16.

The structural approach

The approach most widely adopted by scholars of comparative politics is called the *structural approach* and focuses on *the institutions* in a political system and the processes within them. A structural approach suggests that political outcomes are largely determined by the formal processes laid out within the political system. Structures create particular relationships, such as between the government and the governed, between employers and employees, between the party establishment and party members, or between pressure groups and their members. As a consequence, the lives of individuals and groups within a society are largely determined by their position within a structure.

As institutions are such an important part of representative democracies, any study of comparative politics focusing on the USA and the UK must in large part be a comparative study of institutions. In its narrowest meaning, an **institution** is 'any formal organisation whose members interact on the basis of the specific roles they perform' (Hague and Harrop, 2010). Hence, in this narrow sense, a study of comparative politics through an institutional approach would focus on legislatures, executives and judiciaries. But in a wider sense, a structural approach to comparative politics would also focus on such things as constitutions, class structures, electoral systems, political parties, pressure groups and the media as being important 'structures' and 'processes' within a representative democracy.

Theresa May and Donald Trump meet at the White House, January 2017

The rational approach

A second possible approach is what political scientists call the *rational* or *rational choice approach*. This approach focuses not on institutions but on *individuals*. It assumes that individuals act in a rational, logical way in order to maximise their own self-interest. They choose what rationally will be best for themselves — hence the term 'rational choice'. This approach presumes that each individual has their own set of political goals — be they social, economic, cultural, environmental, or whatever — and they will make decisions based on the best way to achieve those goals. A rational approach suggests that individuals will act rationally, choosing to act in a particular way so as to give them the most beneficial outcome.

This approach seems especially appropriate in studying voting behaviour and the way people operate within political parties and pressure groups. When Ronald Reagan in his televised debate with President Jimmy Carter in 1980 posed the question to voters, 'Are you better off than you were four years ago?' he was appealing to their rationality. Reagan knew that most Americans did not feel they had become better off under Carter's four years in office and so that question would focus voters on their self-interested need for change. That said, this approach is not without its critics, who believe that it overestimates human rationality — take, for example, the woman in New York voting for Jimmy Carter — and ignores the difficulty of the ordinary individual gaining the accurate information required to make such 'rational' choices.

The cultural approach

A third possible approach is called the *cultural approach* and focuses neither on institutions nor on individuals, but on *ideas*. Thus a study of comparative politics through a cultural approach focuses on the prevailing political, social, economic and religious ideas within each nation. **Culture** can be defined as a shared, learned and symbolic system of values, beliefs, ideas and attitudes that shapes and influences people's perceptions and behaviour. It tells us who we are collectively, what is important to us, and how we should behave — as Americans or as citizens of the UK. Culture must be collective; there is no such thing as a culture of one. By definition, culture is shared among members of a community. So a cultural approach to politics suggests that shared ideas, beliefs and values often determine the actions of individuals and groups within them.

But again, this approach has some rather obvious pitfalls. While we can usually identify the *majority* view of these national values and expectations, we must realise that any country as large and as socially complex as the USA or

---

Box 1.5

Summary of the three theoretical approaches

Structural approach
- Focuses on *institutions* in a political system and the processes within them.
- Suggests that political outcomes are largely determined by the formal structures and processes laid out within a political system.
- Suggests that the lives of individuals and groups within a society are largely determined by their position within a structure.
- *Especially relevant when comparing legislatures, executives, judiciaries and constitutions, but also electoral systems, political parties and pressure groups.*
- For example, the structural differences between the US and UK constitutions, being respectively codified and uncodified, lead to differences of outcome.

Rational approach
- Focuses on *individuals* within a political system.
- Suggests that individuals act rationally, choosing to act in a particular way out of self-interest, and as a way to give themselves the most beneficial outcome.
- Suggests that individuals have a set of political goals and that they will make decisions based on the best way to achieve those goals.
- *Especially relevant when comparing legislators, members of the executive branch, voters, as well as members of political parties and pressure groups.*
- For example, the different choices made by the affluent and the poor when voting in elections — each attempting to achieve their desired policy goals.

Cultural approach
- Focuses on shared *ideas* within a political system or group.
- Suggests that these shared ideas, beliefs and values of a group within society often determine the actions of that group.
- Culture tells us who we are collectively, what is important to us, and how we ought to behave.
- For example, the different relationships between the state and organised religion in the USA compared with UK being accounted for by the cultural history of each nation.

the UK will contain a number of sub-cultures that will be much more difficult to identify. There must therefore be a danger that 'culture' becomes something of a set of sloppy generalisations — the kind of thing one might read in a tourist book about what 'Americans' are like and how they behave. There is also a debate about whether or not culture is shaped — and announced — by the nation's elite and therefore merely reflects the cultural ideas of those elite groups. In the main, the United States was originally the creation of White Anglo-Saxon Protestants (WASPS). As a result, a view of American culture arose that equated 'Americanism' with the values of WASPS. Blacks, Catholics, Jews and later Hispanics were seen as sub-cultures. But even among the majority American community, there are significant differences with regard to American culture. Take, for example, views on such issues as pornography, homosexuality, right to life, or prayer in public (i.e. state-run) schools. Hence, during the 1990s, we had what were often referred to as the 'culture wars', in which Americans disagreed profoundly and angrily about what constituted American culture.

But culture can explain why individuals and societies act and behave in certain ways. It can explain how they react to safeguard what they see as the fundamental rights and liberties of their nation — to safeguard 'their way of life'. It can explain why people vote in a certain way, take to protest marches or movements, or fight for causes. Culture has a power to motivate people and to shape society, to create far-reaching change or to preserve the status quo.

So to summarise, comparative politics is rooted in *institutions*. It stresses the role institutions and processes play in shaping and constraining the behaviour of individuals. Indeed, the fundamental idea in comparative politics is that institutions and processes matter. The rational choice approach, on the other hand, assumes that *individuals* are out to maximise self-interest and engage in political action to receive benefits — for themselves — at a minimal cost. And although cultural explanations of politics are often vague, *ideas* also matter — both shared ideas that shape a nation's self-portrait and underpin its society, and shared ideas within a group that underpin its actions and beliefs. So the study of comparative politics is the study of the 'three Is' — institutions, individuals and ideas.

References

Hague, R. and Harrop, M., *Comparative Government and Politics: An Introduction*, Palgrave Macmillan, 2010.

Chapter 2

The Constitution

Learning outcomes

Key questions answered in this chapter:

■ What are the key features of the US Constitution?
■ How are constitutional amendments made?
■ Why has the Constitution been so rarely amended?
■ What are the principal constitutional rights?
■ What are the key principles of the US Constitution?
■ What is the doctrine of the separation of powers?
■ How do the checks and balances of the Constitution work?
■ What is federalism and how has it changed?
■ What are the consequences of federalism?
■ What are the principal similarities and differences between the US and UK constitutions?

Introduction

What's your first thought when you see this chapter title — 'The Constitution'? I guess you think of old, musty-smelling documents, archaic rules, old-fashioned language that is largely incomprehensible, and eighteenth-century men dressed in leather breeches and wigs. That's quite understandable. But the American Constitution is a far more dynamic document than those words and phrases would lead you to believe. After all, consider the following questions:

- Who decides on the racial balance permitted in America's schools and universities?
- Who decides on the rules under which campaign finance operates?
- Who decides what rights Americans have to own guns?
- Who decides on the rights of arrested persons?
- Who decides on the operation of the death penalty in America?
- Who decides on what rights women have in the matter of abortion?
- Who decides on whether same-sex marriages are permitted within America?
- Who decides on matters of freedom of speech?
- Who decides whether or not you have a right to burn the American flag?
- Who decides on whether the president or Congress has exceeded their powers?

The answer to those questions — and to many more — is, ultimately, the United States Supreme Court. But how do they arrive at these decisions? By interpreting and applying what the United States Constitution has to say on these matters. Yes, the Constitution is America's ultimate handbook. And although you won't find any mention of abortion, marriage or flag burning in this document, you will find all the principles from which decisions on these and other matters can, and must, be arrived at.

And there's more. Why could President Barack Obama not run for re-election in 2016? Answer: because the Constitution limits a president to two terms in office. Why did Jeff Sessions have to resign from the Senate when he became attorney general (head of the Department of Justice) in 2017? Answer: because the Constitution forbids someone being a member of the legislature and the executive at the same time. Why are elections to the House of Representatives held every two years? Answer: because the Constitution says so. Why do all those over 18 have the right to vote? Answer: because the Constitution says so. Why do Americans have such feeble gun control laws? Answer: because the Constitution states that 'the right of the people to keep and bear arms shall not be infringed'.

So, as we study the Constitution, forget the musty-smelling museum exhibit, and think instead of the most important eighteen pages of printed matter that are to be found anywhere in the United States. It really is the stuff of everyday life, now, in the twenty-first century.

The nature of the Constitution: three key features

On 17 September 1787, the task of writing the new Constitution was complete. When the delegates emerged from their self-imposed silence in Independence Hall in Philadelphia, it is said that a woman approached Benjamin Franklin and asked: 'Well, Doctor, what have we got — a republic or a monarchy?' Replied Franklin: 'A republic, if you can keep it.'

A codified constitution

Key term

Codified constitution A constitution that consists of a full and authoritative set of rules written down in a single text.

There are three key features that we need to understand about the nature of the United States Constitution. First, it is a **codified constitution**. A code is a systematic and authoritative collection of rules. So, for example, the Highway Code is the collected and authoritative set of rules for all road users. In much the same way, the United States Constitution is the collected and authoritative set of rules of American government and politics. By definition, a codified constitution is also a written constitution, though as we shall see later, not everything about the ordering of American government and politics is to be found in the Constitution.

> **Box 2.2**
>
> ### The nature of the Constitution
>
> 1 It is a codified constitution.
> 2 It is a blend of specificity and vagueness.
> 3 Its provisions are entrenched.

Key terms

Supremacy clause The portion of Article VI which states that the Constitution, as well as treaties and federal laws, 'shall be the supreme law of the Land'.

Enumerated (or delegated) powers Powers delegated to the federal government under the Constitution. Generally these are those enumerated in the first three Articles of the Constitution.

This new codified constitution consisted of seven Articles (see Box 2.1), the first three of which explained how the three branches of the federal (national) government would work and what powers they would have. Article I established Congress as the national legislature, defining its membership, the qualifications and method of election of its members, as well as its powers. Under Article I, Section 8, Congress was given specific powers such as those to 'coin money' and 'declare war'.

Article II decided — somewhat surprisingly — on a singular, rather than a plural, executive by vesting all executive power in the hands of 'a President'. The president would be chosen indirectly by an Electoral College.

Article III established the United States Supreme Court, though Congress quickly added trial and appeal courts. Although not explicitly granted, the Court was to have the role of umpire of the Constitution, implied in the **supremacy clause** of Article VI and the provision in Article III itself that the Court's judicial power applies to 'all Cases...arising under this Constitution'. The Court would make this more explicit in its landmark decision of *Marbury* v *Madison* in 1803.

These three Articles contain what are called the **enumerated (or delegated) powers** granted to the federal government. The significance of this is that the federal government does not possess unlimited power, but only such power as is given it in the Constitution. But it was also given much less specific powers.

A blend of specificity and vagueness

This brings us to our second feature of the United States Constitution — that it is a blend of both specificity and vagueness. So far we have focused on the specifics. But not everything in the Constitution is quite so cut and dried. We need to be aware of what are known as implied powers — powers of the federal government that the Constitution does not explicitly mention, but that are reasonably implied from the delegated powers. So, for example, the power to draft people into the armed forces may be implied from Congress's enumerated power to raise an army and navy. Congress was also given the power to 'provide for the common defence and general welfare of the United States'. From this was implied that Congress had the power to levy and collect taxes to provide for the defence of the United States.

Many of the implied powers are deduced from what is called the necessary and proper clause of Article I, Section 8. This is often referred to as the 'elastic clause' of the Constitution because, by it, the powers of the federal government can be stretched beyond the specifically delegated or enumerated powers. So in this sense, although some parts of the Constitution are very explicit, there are other parts where it is very vague and the Constitution has therefore been able to adapt to the ever-changing circumstances of the nation. As we shall see in Chapter 5, much of this adaptation has been done by the Supreme Court.

We have seen, therefore, that the Constitution delegated certain powers to the federal government alone. The Constitution also includes what we call reserved powers — that is, powers that are reserved to the states alone or to the people. This provision is found in the Tenth Amendment (see Box 2.3), added to the original Constitution in 1791. This again limits the power of the federal government by stating that all the powers not delegated to the federal government, or prohibited to the states, 'are reserved to the States, or to the people'. Then there are also the concurrent powers of the Constitution — those powers shared by the federal and state governments, such as collecting taxes, building roads and maintaining courts.

Key terms

Implied powers Powers possessed by the federal government by inference from those powers delegated to it in the Constitution (see also 'Necessary and proper clause').

Necessary and proper clause The final clause of Article I, Section 8, which empowers Congress to make all laws 'necessary and proper' to carry out the federal government's duties.

Reserved powers Powers not delegated to the federal government, or prohibited by it to the states, are reserved to the states and to the people.

Concurrent powers Powers possessed by both the federal and state governments.

Box 2.3

The Tenth Amendment

'The powers not delegated to the United States by the Constitution, nor prohibited by it to the States, are reserved to the States respectively, or to the people.'

Alongside the specific granting of powers there is the supremacy clause of Article VI, mentioned earlier. This enshrines into the Constitution a key principle of American government that asserts the supremacy of national law. In this clause, the Constitution provides that the laws passed by the federal government under its constitutional powers are the supreme laws of the land. Therefore any legitimate national law automatically supersedes any conflicting state law.

Its provisions are entrenched

So far we have been introduced to two important features of the Constitution — that it is codified, and that it is a blend of specificity and vagueness. But there is

Entrenchment The application of extra legal safeguards to a constitutional provision to make it more difficult to amend or abolish it.

a third important feature which we call **entrenchment**. And that leads us into a consideration of the process for amending the Constitution.

Perhaps the best way to help us understand what the word 'entrenchment' means is to remember its non-political meaning. In the time, say, of the First World War, an entrenchment was the establishment of a military force in trenches (hence the word) or other fortified positions so as to protect against enemy attack. So when we say that various governmental or political provisions are entrenched, it means that they are, as it were, protected from enemy attack — from those who would wish to change or abolish them. The way this is done is to insist upon some kind of complicated system, as well as on super-majorities, in order to make amending such provisions exceedingly difficult, thereby affording them special protection. In the United States Constitution, entrenchment is provided through the complex amendment process.

Frieze depicting the signing of the Constitution

Amendments to the Constitution

The amendment process

The Founding Fathers, while realising the likely need to amend the Constitution, wanted to make doing so a difficult process. Thus, it was to be a two-stage process requiring super-majorities of more than 50%, such as two-thirds or a three-quarters majority (see Table 2.1). The process is laid out in Article V. Stage 1 is the proposal and stage 2 is the ratification. Constitutional amendments can be proposed either by Congress or by a national constitutional convention called by Congress at the request of two-thirds of the state legislatures. All constitutional amendments thus far have been proposed by Congress. No national constitutional convention has ever been called, although by 1992, 32 state legislatures had petitioned Congress for a convention to propose a balanced budget amendment — just two states short of the required two-thirds.

Table 2.1 The amendment process

	Proposed by	Ratified by	How often used?
1	Two-thirds of the House and Senate	Three-quarters of the state legislatures (38)	26 times
2	Two-thirds of the House and Senate	Ratifying conventions in three-quarters of the states	Once (Twenty-First Amendment)
3	Legislatures in two-thirds of the states calling for a national constitutional convention	Three-quarters of the state legislatures	Never
4	Legislatures in two-thirds of the states calling for a national constitutional convention	Ratifying conventions in three-quarters of the states	Never

During the presidency of Bill Clinton (1993–2001), there were 17 votes on proposed constitutional amendments, an unusually high number. All these votes occurred during the six-year period when the Republicans controlled both houses of Congress — 1995–2001. A proposal to amend the Constitution requires a two-thirds majority in both houses to be successful. During this period, the House of Representatives agreed to a balanced budget amendment (1995) and a flag desecration amendment (1995, 1997 and 1999). However, the Senate agreed to neither of these, although it was only one vote short of the two-thirds majority required to pass the balanced budget amendment in 1997 and four votes short of passing a flag desecration amendment in 2000.

During the presidency of George W. Bush (2001–09), there were six further attempts to amend the Constitution. But only three of these six votes — the three in the House of Representatives to ban the desecration of the American flag — received the required two-thirds majority. This means that the House has now voted on this amendment six times since 1995. Almost every time, the number of 'yes' votes has declined. When the Senate voted on the amendment in June 2006, the vote was 66–34, just one vote short of the required two-thirds majority. But with the Democrats retaking control of both houses of Congress in the 2006 midterm elections, passage of the amendment became much less likely as it is mostly Republicans who vote 'yes' on banning the desecration of the flag. This is the reason why these votes took place when the Senate and House of Representatives were controlled by the Republicans. Democrats tend to vote 'no' on such proposals.

At the start of the 113th Congress in January 2013, bills to amend the Constitution were introduced on a range of subjects, including amendments to:

- require a balanced federal budget
- ban flag desecration
- reverse recent Supreme Court decisions on campaign finance
- guarantee equal rights for men and women
- introduce congressional term limits

In November 2016, outgoing Democratic senator Barbara Boxer of California introduced a bill to abolish the Electoral College in the aftermath of the presidential election result earlier in the month that saw Democrat Hillary Clinton win the popular vote but lose in the Electoral College.

Once an amendment has been successfully proposed, it is sent to the states for ratification. An amendment can be ratified either by three-quarters of the state legislatures or by state constitutional conventions in three-quarters of the states. Of the 27 amendments added to the Constitution, only one has been ratified by state constitutional conventions — the Twenty-First Amendment, which repealed the Eighteenth Amendment and thus ended the prohibition of alcohol. Of the 33 amendments passed to them for ratification by Congress, the states have ratified 27. Thus, once an amendment has been successfully proposed by Congress, it stands a good chance of finding its way into the Constitution.

Only six amendments have failed at the ratification stage in over 210 years. The most recent was the District of Columbia voting rights amendment, which would have granted the District — the federal capital — full representation in Congress as if it were a state. Only 16 states — rather than the 38 required — had voted to ratify this amendment when it expired in 1985. Three years earlier, the equal rights amendment for the rights of women had fallen just three states short in the ratification process.

The Bill of Rights and later amendments

Of the 27 amendments to the Constitution, the first ten were proposed together by Congress in September 1789 and were ratified together by three-quarters of the states by December 1791. Collectively, they are known as the Bill of Rights (see Box 2.4). Many states had somewhat reluctantly signed up to the new federal Constitution with its potentially powerful centralised government. The Bill of Rights was designed to sugar the constitutional pill by protecting Americans against an over-powerful federal government.

Box 2.4

Selected amendments to the Constitution

Amendments I–X: the Bill of Rights (1791)

I	Freedom of religion, speech, the press, and assembly
II	Right to keep and bear arms
III	No quartering of troops in private homes
IV	Unreasonable searches and seizures prohibited
V	Rights of accused persons
VI	Rights of trial
VII	Common-law suits
VIII	Excessive bail, and cruel and unusual punishments prohibited
IX	Un-enumerated rights protected
X	Un-delegated powers reserved to the states or to the people

Some later amendments

XIII	Slavery prohibited (1865)
XIV	Ex-slaves made citizens — including 'equal protection' and 'due process' clauses (1868)
XVI	Federal government granted power to impose income tax (1913)
XVII	Direct election of the Senate (1913)
XXII	Two-term limit for the president (1951)
XXV	Presidential succession and disability procedures (1967)
XXVI	Voting age lowered to 18 (1971)

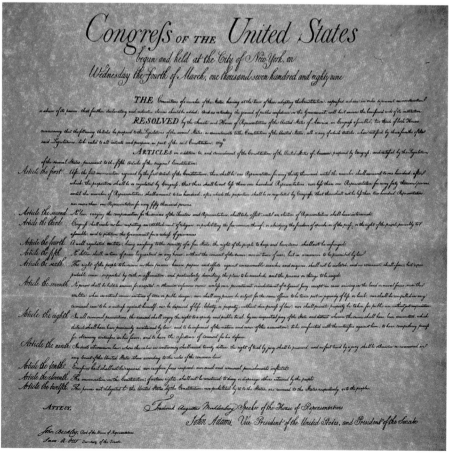

The United States Bill of Rights

Seventeen further amendments have been passed since the Bill of Rights. The Twelfth Amendment (1804) revised the process for electing the president and vice president. The Thirteenth (1865), Fourteenth (1868) and Fifteenth (1870) Amendments were proposed and ratified immediately after the Civil War to end slavery and guarantee rights to the former slaves. The Fourteenth Amendment, as we shall see later, has become increasingly important in American society through its 'equal protection' and 'due process' clauses. The Sixteenth Amendment (1913) is of crucial importance in understanding how the federal government's power increased during the twentieth century. It allowed the federal government to impose an income tax. The Seventeenth Amendment (also 1913) provided for the direct election of the Senate. Previously, senators were appointed by their state legislatures. The Twenty-Second Amendment (1951) limited the president to a maximum of two terms in office. The Twenty-Fifth Amendment (1967) dealt with issues of presidential disability and succession, which had come to the fore following the assassination of President Kennedy four years earlier. The Twenty-Sixth Amendment (1971) lowered the voting age to 18.

Why has the Constitution been amended so rarely?

With only 27 amendments passed, and only 17 of those in the last 210 years, the question is raised as to why so few amendments have been passed. There are four significant reasons.

- The Founding Fathers created a deliberately difficult process. The need for both Congress and the states to agree, and the need for super-majorities, make the amendment process difficult. Hundreds of amendments have been initiated, but very few have made it successfully through the process.
- The Founding Fathers created a document that was, at least in parts, deliberately unspecific and vague, such as Congress's power 'to provide for the common defence and general welfare' of the United States. This has allowed the document to evolve without the need for formal amendment.
- The most important reason, the Supreme Court's power of judicial review, is considered in Chapter 5. Suffice it to say here that this power allows the Court to interpret the Constitution and thereby, in effect, change the meaning of words written over two centuries ago — to make what one might call 'interpretative amendments' rather than formal amendments. Thus, for example, the Court can state what the phrase in the Eighth Amendment, which forbids 'cruel and unusual punishments', means today.
- Americans have become cautious of tampering with their Constitution. They hold it in some degree of veneration. In the early decades of the last century, they got themselves into difficulties by amending the Constitution to prohibit the manufacture, sale and importation of alcohol. Fourteen years later, 'Prohibition' was discredited and the offending amendment was repealed. This experience proved to be an important lesson for subsequent generations.

Activity

- Go to the website of the National Constitution Center at: **https:// constitutioncenter.org/interactive-constitution**.
- Click on the 'Explore it' button, then use the cursor to select any of the constitutional amendments.
- Read the debate articles presented.
- Write a 500-word piece (250 words on each side of the debate) concerning any of the amendments.

Constitutional rights

Chapter 2 The Constitution

Key term

Constitutional rights
Fundamental rights guaranteed by the Constitution, including freedom of speech and religion, and freedom from arbitrary arrest.

The Constitution guarantees certain fundamental **constitutional rights**. Just listing rights in a constitution does not, in itself, mean that these rights are fully operative. The government — be it federal, state or local — must take steps to ensure that these rights are effectively protected. As we shall see later, all three branches of the federal government — the legislature (Congress), the executive (the president) and the judiciary (the courts, and especially the Supreme Court) — play an important role in trying to ensure that these constitutional rights are effective for all Americans. So what rights are granted by the Constitution?

The First Amendment guarantees the most basic and fundamental rights: freedom of religion; freedom of speech; freedom of the press; freedom of assembly. Debates such as those concerning prayers in public (i.e. state) schools, pornography on the internet, flag burning and press censorship all centre upon First Amendment rights. The Second Amendment guarantees that 'the right of the people to keep and bear arms shall not be infringed'. It is on this amendment that the debate about gun control focuses. The Supreme Court weighed in with a major decision on the meaning of this amendment in 2008. The Fourth Amendment guarantees the right against unreasonable searches — either of your person or of your property. You might well have heard of Americans 'pleading the Fifth Amendment' — the right to silence, protecting the individual from self-incrimination. The Eighth Amendment, which states that 'cruel and unusual punishments' shall not be inflicted, is the focus of the death penalty debate. The Tenth Amendment tends to be an article of faith of the modern Republican Party, in standing up for states' rights over the increasing power of the federal government in Washington DC.

Later amendments have been added to guarantee other fundamental rights and liberties. Voting rights were guaranteed to women by the Nineteenth Amendment in 1920 and to those over 18 years of age by the Twenty-Sixth Amendment in 1971. Voting rights were also guaranteed to previously discriminated minorities — notably black voters — by the Twenty-Fourth Amendment passed in 1964. It is largely up to the courts, especially the United States Supreme Court, to ensure that these rights are effective. We shall examine this in Chapter 5.

The principles of the Constitution

The Constitution is based on three key principles — fundamental and foundational ideas — that form its very core and basis: namely, the separation of powers, checks and balances, and federalism. Linked with the first two is another principle, that of bipartisanship, and linked with federalism is the principle of limited government. The following sections will consider each of these principles.

Key term

Separation of powers A theory of government whereby political power is distributed among the legislature, the executive and the judiciary, each acting both independently and interdependently.

Separation of powers

The first key principle is the **separation of powers**. This is a theory of government whereby political power is distributed among three branches of government — the legislature, the executive and the judiciary — acting both independently and interdependently. This framework was put in place by the Founding Fathers because of their fear of tyranny. The framers of the Constitution were influenced by the writings of the French political philosopher Montesquieu (1689–1755). In his book *De L'Esprit des Loix* (*The Spirit of the Laws*), published in 1748, Montesquieu argued for a separation

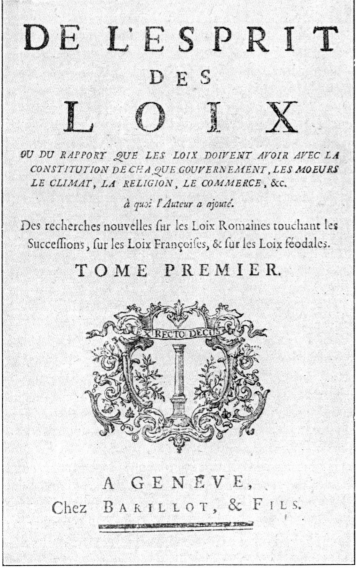

Title page to *De L'Esprit des Loix* by Montesquieu

of powers into legislative, executive and judicial branches in order to avoid tyranny. 'When the legislative and executive powers are united in the same person...there can be no liberty,' he wrote.

The Founding Fathers had the idea that each of these three independent yet co-equal branches should check the power of the others. It was decided that no person could be in more than one branch of the federal government at the same time — what we might call 'the separation of personnel'. When, in 2008, Senator Barack Obama was elected president, he had to resign from the Senate, as did his newly elected vice president Senator Joe Biden. In this sense, the three branches — the institutions of government — are entirely separate.

However, the term 'separation of powers' is misleading, for it is the *institutions* that are separate, not the *powers*. Professor Richard Neustadt was the most helpful in clearing up this potential confusion. Neustadt (1960) wrote: 'The Constitutional Convention of 1787 is supposed to have created a government of "separated powers". It did nothing of the sort. Rather, it created a government of separated institutions *sharing* powers.' Quite right. So the concept is best thought of as the doctrine of 'shared powers'. And those 'shared powers' are what checks and balances are all about, for the Founding Fathers set up an intricate system whereby each branch of the federal government would check and balance the other two. This is especially important in terms of the legislature and the executive, which Professor S.E. Finer (1970) described as being 'like two halves of a bank note — each useless without the other'.

Checks and balances

The second key principle of the Constitution is **checks and balances**. This principle gives each branch of the federal government — the legislature, the executive and the judiciary — the means to partially control the power of the other branches, largely to resist encroachments on its own powers and to maintain democratic government. The main checks and balances exercised by each branch are detailed in Box 2.5. We shall look at these in turn.

Box 2.5

Checks and balances: how they work

Because the Constitution creates a system of separate institutions that share powers, each institution (or branch) can check the powers of the others. The major checks possessed by each branch are as follows.

President
1 Can check Congress by vetoing a bill it has passed
2 Can check the federal courts by nominating judges and by the power of pardon

Congress
1 Can check the president by:
   - amending/delaying/rejecting the president's legislative proposals
   - overriding the president's veto
   - the power of the purse
   - refusing to approve the president's appointments (Senate only)
   - refusing to ratify the president's treaties (Senate only)
   - using the impeachment and trial powers to remove the president from office
2 Can check the federal courts by:
   - proposing constitutional amendments to overturn a judicial decision
   - refusing to approve a person nominated to the federal courts (Senate only)

Federal courts
1 Can check Congress by declaring a law unconstitutional
2 Can check the president by declaring the president's actions — or the actions of any of the president's subordinates — unconstitutional

As well as these formal checks, there are also informal checks, such as Congress's check of investigation through its committee system.

Checks by the president on Congress

The president is given the power to recommend legislation to Congress. They do this formally in January of each year in what is known as the **State of the Union Address**. Presidents use this set-piece speech, delivered to a joint session of Congress — as well as cabinet members, the justices of the Supreme Court, and other invited guests — before a nationwide audience on primetime television. It is the president's main opportunity to lay out their legislative agenda, in effect saying to Congress, 'this is what I want you to debate and pass into law'. President Obama used his State of the Union Address in January 2010 to focus on his healthcare reform proposals, urging Congress: 'Let's get it done!' Two months later, Obama signed the bill into law.

In addition, the president has the power to **veto** bills passed by Congress. During his eight years in office, President Obama used the regular veto on 12 occasions including, in 2016, his veto of a bill that would have rescinded parts of his healthcare reform legislation.

Key terms

State of the Union Address An annual speech made by the president to a joint session of Congress, setting out his proposed legislative programme for the coming year.

Presidential veto The president's power under Article II of the Constitution to return a bill to Congress unsigned, along with the reasons for his objection.

President Barack Obama delivering his 2011 State of the Union Address

Checks by the president on the courts

Here the president has two significant checks. First, the president nominates all federal judges — to the trial courts, appeal courts and Supreme Court. It is the last that are the most important. During his first term, President Barack Obama was able to make two appointments to the Supreme Court — Sonia Sotomayor (2009) and Elena Kagan (2010). By choosing justices whose judicial philosophy matches their own, presidents can hope to mould the outlook of the Court for years to come.

Second, the president has the power of pardon. This has become controversial in recent times. In 1974, President Ford pardoned his predecessor — President Nixon — for any crimes that Nixon might have committed in the so-called Watergate affair. On the final day of his presidency, President Clinton pardoned 140 people, including Mark Rich, a notorious tax fugitive. President Obama pardoned 142 people during his final three weeks in office.

Checks by Congress on the president

The Founding Fathers were most anxious about the possible power of the singular executive they had created — the president. As a result, they hedged this branch of government with the most checks. Congress exercises eight significant checks on the president.

- Congress can amend, block or even reject items of legislation recommended by the president. In 2010, it passed — but in a significantly amended form — President Obama's healthcare reform bill. But Congress blocked Obama's attempt at immigration reform and rejected every proposal he made regarding meaningful gun control legislation.

- Congress can override the president's veto. To do this, it needs to gain a two-thirds majority in both houses of Congress. During President George W. Bush's two terms, Congress overrode four of his 11 regular vetoes, including his vetoes of the 2007 Water Resources Development Bill and the 2008 Food Conservation and Energy Bill. It was not until the last four months of his eight years in office that Congress first overrode one of President Obama's vetoes — his twelfth. In September 2016, Obama vetoed the Justice Against Sponsors of Terrorism Act that would have allowed American families of the victims of the September 11 terrorist attacks to sue the government of Saudi Arabia for any role they played in the plot.

- Congress has the significant power that is referred to as 'the power of the purse'. All the money that the president wants to spend on the president's policies must be voted for by Congress. Its refusal to vote for this money will significantly curtail what the president can do — be it in domestic or foreign policy. In 2007, the Democrat-controlled Congress attempted to limit President George W. Bush's spending on the military operations in Iraq.

President Franklin D. Roosevelt signs the declaration of war on Japan, 8 December 1941

- In the field of foreign policy, Congress has two further checks on the president. Although the Constitution confers on the president the power to be 'commander-in-chief' of the armed forces, it confers on Congress the power to declare war. Although this power seems to have fallen into disuse — the last time Congress declared war was on Japan in 1941 — Congress has successfully forced presidents since then to seek specific authorisation before committing troops to situations in which hostilities are likely or inevitable. In October 2002, President George W. Bush gained specific authorisation from Congress to use military force in Iraq. The House approved the use of troops in Iraq by 296 votes to 182, while the vote in the Senate was 77 votes to 23.

- The Senate has the power to ratify treaties negotiated by the president. This requires a two-thirds majority. In 2010, the Senate ratified the new START Treaty with Russia by 71 votes to 26. In 1999, the Senate rejected the Comprehensive Test Ban Treaty by 48 votes to 51 — that is, 18 votes short of the 66 votes required to ratify it. This was the first major treaty to be rejected by the Senate since the rejection of the Versailles Treaty in 1920. Five minor treaties had been rejected in between. Then in December 2012, the Senate rejected the Convention on the Rights of Persons with Disabilities by 61 votes to 38 — just five votes short of the two-thirds majority required to ratify it.

- Another check exercised by Congress over the president is an important power held by the Senate alone — the power to confirm many of the appointments that the president makes to the executive branch and all the appointments he makes to the federal judiciary. Executive appointments subject to Senate confirmation include such high-profile posts as cabinet members, ambassadors and heads of important agencies such as the Central Intelligence Agency (CIA) and the Federal Bureau of Investigation (FBI). Only a simple majority is required for confirmation. Rejections are unusual, but only because presidents usually consult informally with key senators before announcing such appointments, naming only those for whom confirmation is a fair certainty. In 1987, the Senate rejected (42–58) President Reagan's nominee, Robert Bork, for a place on the Supreme Court (see Chapter 5). In 1989, the Senate rejected (47–53) John Tower as secretary of defense. In October 2005, Harriet Miers withdrew as a nominee to the Supreme Court following widespread criticism by Republican senators of her lack of qualification and conservative credentials. When in March 2016 President Obama nominated Judge Merrick Garland to the Supreme Court to replace Justice Antonin Scalia who had died the previous month, the Republican-controlled Senate refused to proceed with confirmation hearings on Judge Garland, claiming that the nomination should await the new president who would take up office in January 2017.

President Obama nominates Judge Merrick Garland to the Supreme Court, March 2016

- Two further important checks on the president are given to Congress. The first is the power of investigation: Congress — usually through its committees — may investigate the actions or policies of any member of the executive branch, including the president. Following a terrorist attack on the American diplomatic compound in Benghazi, Libya, in September 2012, in which the American ambassador Christopher Stevens was killed, no fewer than seven congressional committees held hearings on the events that had led up to it and the way both President Obama and then secretary of state Hillary Clinton had handled the matter.

- Finally, in the most serious circumstances, investigation may lead to impeachment — the ultimate check that Congress holds over the executive. Congress may impeach any member of the executive branch, including the president. Two presidents — Andrew Johnson (1868) and Bill Clinton (1998) — have been impeached by Congress. It is the House of Representatives which has the power of impeachment. In 1998, it passed two articles of impeachment against President Clinton — for perjury (228–206) and obstruction of justice (221–212). Just a simple majority is required. Once the House has impeached, the Senate then conducts the trial. If found guilty by a two-thirds majority, the accused person is removed from office. In President Clinton's case, the Senate found him not guilty on both articles of impeachment — the votes being 45–55 on perjury and 50–50 on obstruction of justice, respectively 22 and 17 votes short of the required two-thirds majority. In the 1860s, President Johnson escaped conviction by the Senate by just one vote. In 1974, President Nixon resigned rather than face near certain impeachment by the House and conviction by the Senate. Thus, through impeachment — what someone has described as 'the political equivalent of the death penalty' — Congress can remove the president. This is the ultimate check. The president holds no similar power — he cannot remove Congress.

> **Key term**
>
> **Impeachment** A formal accusation of a serving federal official by a simple majority vote of the House of Representatives.

The New York Times announces President Nixon's resignation

Checks by Congress on the courts

Congress has two important checks on the courts. First, there is again the power of impeachment, trial and removal from office. In the space of three years (1986–89), Congress removed three federal judges from office — Harry Claiborne for tax evasion, Alcee Hastings for bribery, and Walter Nixon for perjury. In March 2010, the House of Representatives impeached federal judge Thomas Porteous for corruption, and following guilty verdicts in the Senate on four counts, Judge Porteous was removed from office later that year.

A more subtle but still significant check is that Congress can propose constitutional amendments to — in effect — overturn a decision of the Supreme Court. When in 1896 the Supreme Court declared federal income tax to be unconstitutional, Congress proposed the Sixteenth Amendment granting Congress the power to levy income tax. It was ratified and became operative in 1913. Congress has more recently attempted unsuccessfully to reverse Supreme Court decisions on such issues as flag burning and prayer in public schools. Following a controversial ruling by the Supreme Court on the subject of campaign finance in 2010, Senator Tom Udall (Democrat, New Mexico) introduced a proposed constitutional amendment to reverse the effects of this decision. But the amendment got no further than an unsuccessful vote on the Senate floor.

Checks by the courts on Congress

The judiciary — headed by the Supreme Court — possesses one very significant power over Congress: the power of judicial review. This is the power of the court to declare Acts of Congress to be unconstitutional and therefore null and void. In the 1997 case of *Reno* v *American Civil Liberties Union*, the Supreme Court declared the Communications Decency Act (1996) unconstitutional. In 2013, in the case of *United States* v *Windsor*, the Court declared the Defense of Marriage Act (1996) unconstitutional.

Checks by the courts on the president

The courts have the same power of judicial review over the executive branch. Here the power of judicial review is the ability to declare actions of any member of the executive branch to be unconstitutional. In *United States* v *Richard Nixon* (1974), the Court ordered President Nixon to hand over the so-called White House tapes and thereby stop impeding investigation of the Watergate affair. Nixon obeyed, handed over the tapes and resigned just 16 days later, once the tapes showed his involvement in an intricate cover-up. In the 2006 case of *Hamdan* v *Rumsfeld*, the Supreme Court declared unconstitutional the military commissions set up by the administration of President George W. Bush to try suspected members of Al Qaeda held at Guantánamo Bay in Cuba. Then in 2014, in *National Labor Relations Board* v *Noel Canning*, the Court ruled that President Obama had acted unconstitutionally in making three appointments to the National Labor Relations Board without the approval of the Senate. In 2017, in the case of *State of Washington* v *Donald J. Trump*, the federal courts placed a temporary restraining order on President Trump's executive order that banned people from seven Muslim-majority countries from entering the United States.

Bipartisanship

The checks and balances between the three branches of the federal government — especially those between the legislature and the executive — have important consequences for US politics. The framers of the Constitution hoped to encourage a spirit of **bipartisanship** and compromise between the president and Congress. Laws would be passed, treaties ratified, appointments confirmed and budgets fixed only when both branches worked together. President George W. Bush managed to achieve his education reforms in 2001–02 because he worked with leading congressional Democrats such as Senator Edward Kennedy. The trouble is that gridlock can result. Most recent presidents have accused the Senate of either rejecting or blocking their judicial nominations for partisan reasons. As a consequence, a large number of posts in both the federal trial and appeal courts remain unfilled for months, even years, slowing down the work of the courts.

This raises the issue of **divided government**, a term used to refer to the situation in which one party controls the presidency and the other party controls one or both houses of Congress. Of late, this has become the norm. The 48 years between 1969 and 2016 have seen 35½ years of divided government, and for 24 of those years the president's party controlled neither house. For only 12½ years of this period did one party control the presidency and both houses of Congress: 1977–81 (Jimmy Carter) and 1993–95 (Bill Clinton) for the Democrats; January–June of 2001 and 2003–07 (George W. Bush) for the Republicans; and 2009–11 (Barack Obama) for the Democrats. It is worth noting, too, that divided government has not always been the norm. In the previous 48 years — from 1921 to 1969 — there was divided government for only ten years.

Does divided government make the checks and balances between Congress and the president more or less effective? There are arguments on both sides. Some think that divided government leads to *more* effective government. Bills are scrutinised more closely, treaties checked more carefully and nominees questioned more rigorously in the confirmation process. There is some evidence that when Congress and the president are of the same party, legislation, nominations, budgets, treaties and the like are nodded through without as much careful scrutiny as there should be. Not since 1935 has the Senate rejected a treaty of a president of its own party. Only twice in the last 50 years has Congress overridden a veto of a president of its party. In 1964, Democrat President Johnson managed to persuade a Congress with Democrat majorities in both houses to pass the Tonkin Gulf Resolution which authorised him to take whatever action was deemed appropriate in South Vietnam. During the years of Republican control from 2003 through 2006, Congress was fairly feeble in exercising its oversight function of Republican president George W. Bush's war in Iraq.

Others, however, think that divided government leads to *less* effective government. Examples such as the treatment of Republican Supreme Court nominees Robert Bork (1987) and Clarence Thomas (1991) by a Democrat-controlled Senate, and the impeachment proceedings conducted against Democrat President Bill Clinton by a Republican-controlled Congress (1998–99) seem poor advertisements for effective checks and balances. We shall see what happens under the return of united government from January 2017 as a Republican president governs with his own party in the majority in both houses of Congress.

Key terms

Bipartisanship Close cooperation between the two major parties to achieve desired political goals. In the US system of government, it may be crucial for political success.

Divided government When the presidency is controlled by one party, and one or both houses of Congress are controlled by the other party.

Does the US Constitution still work?

Yes

- Federalism has proved to be an excellent compromise between strong national government and state government diversity.
- The text has proved very adaptable to changes in American society.
- The demanding amendment process has usually prevented frequent and ill-conceived proposals for amendment.
- Rights and liberties of Americans have been protected.
- The Supreme Court's power of judicial review has made it even more adaptable through 'interpretative amendment'.

No

- The amendment process is too difficult, making it almost impossible to amend parts that are no longer applicable or to add parts that a majority desires.
- The power of judicial review gives the Supreme Court too much power to 'amend' its meaning.
- It is too negative, giving too much power to those who oppose change.
- Some parts make little sense in today's society (e.g. the Electoral College).
- Some parts don't work as the framers of the Constitution would have envisaged (e.g. war-making powers).

Federalism A theory of government by which political power is divided between a national government and state governments, each having their own areas of substantive jurisdiction.

Limited government A principle that the scope of the federal government should be limited to that which is necessary for the common good of the people.

Popular sovereignty The principle, inherent in both the Declaration of Independence and the Constitution, that ultimate political authority rests with the people.

Federalism

The third key principle of the Constitution is **federalism**. 'We the People of the United States, *in order to form a more perfect Union...*' So began the preamble to the new Constitution. Certainly, the first attempt at union was weak and almost disastrous. The Articles of Confederation showed just about how far the newly independent peoples of America were prepared to go in the formation of a national government — not very far; but the experience of confederacy had been educative. The compromise between a strong central government and states' rights was to be federalism. It was what James Madison called 'a middle ground'.

Limited government

The framers of the Constitution wanted **limited government**, whereby government would do only what was essential, leaving the citizens' fundamental rights and freedoms as untouched as is possible in an organised and orderly society. The seventeenth-century English philosopher John Locke had grounded the case for limited government on the twin foundations of individual rights and **popular sovereignty**.

At the Philadelphia Convention, there was considerable disagreement between those who wanted the states to remain sovereign and others who wanted to create a more centralised, federal arrangement. In order to bring about agreement between the anti-federalists and the federalists, the delegates agreed on a compromise by which the power of the new federal government would remain limited in its reach. The Founding Fathers had not thrown off one tyranny in Great Britain in order to create another nearer home.

Thus the principle of limited government remains central to political debate today about the proper scope of the federal government. One sees it today in debate over the federal government's role in such issues as healthcare provision, education, immigration and gun control legislation.

James Madison, writing later in *The Federalist Papers*, put the debate this way:

If men were angels, no government would be necessary. If angels were to govern men, neither external nor internal controls on government would be necessary. In framing a government which is to be administered by men over men, the great difficulty lies in this: you must first enable the government to control the governed; and in the next place oblige it to control itself.

Federalism involves a degree of decentralisation, which has proved suitable for a country as large and diverse as the USA has become. As Benjamin Franklin knew at the signing of the Declaration of Independence, a certain level of national unity was vital: 'We must all hang together, or, most assuredly, we shall all hang separately.' Thus, out of the disunity of the Articles of Confederation came the *United* States of America — *E Pluribus Unum* — 'Out of Many, One'.

Under the Articles of Confederation, America had a confederacy, a loose league of friendship among the states. But the Articles soon ran into trouble, as we saw in Chapter 1, mainly because there was only a very weak central government. But Americans had fought a long war against the strong central power of the British government. They were not about to exchange a foreign tyranny for one of their own making. To the framers of the Constitution, their newly devised federal system avoided both extremes — the extreme of disunity under the Articles and the extreme of over-centralisation under Britain. As James Madison wrote, dividing power between the federal and state levels meant a 'double security' for the people. 'The different governments', he wrote, 'will control each other, at the same time that each will be controlled by itself.'

Nowhere is the word 'federal' or 'federalism' mentioned in the Constitution. How, then, was it written into the document? First, it was written into the enumerated powers of the three branches of the federal government — Congress was 'to coin money', the president was to 'be commander-in-chief' and so on. Second, it was included in the implied powers of the federal government. These are the powers that flow from, for example, the 'elastic clause' of the Constitution. Third, the federal government and the states were given certain concurrent powers: for example, the power to tax. Furthermore, the Tenth Amendment reserved all remaining powers 'to the states and to the people'. Finally, the Supreme Court was to be the umpire of all disagreements between the federal and state governments. As Chief Justice Charles Evans Hughes wrote in 1907: 'We are under a Constitution, but the Constitution is what the judges say it is.'

Benjamin Franklin (1706–90)

James Madison (1751–1836)

The changing federal–state relationship

Federalism is not, however, a fixed concept. It is ever changing. As America has changed, so has the concept of federalism. During the latter part of the nineteenth century and the first two-thirds of the twentieth century, a number of factors led to an increased role for the federal government.

- **Westward expansion.** From 13 colonies clustered up and down the Atlantic coast, settlement spread westwards across the Appalachian mountains, over the plains of the Midwest, across the Rockies and all the way to the Pacific coast.
- **The growth of population.** Simultaneously, the population grew from just under 4 million in 1790, to 76 million by 1900, and 322 million by 2016. A growing nation required management by a growing government.
- **Industrialisation.** This brought the need for government regulation — the federal executive Department of Commerce and Labor was formed in 1903 before being split into two separate departments just ten years later.
- **Improvements in communication.** While the nation grew in size, it shrank in terms of accessibility as modern methods of communication gradually developed. Journeys that had taken weeks eventually took only days or hours as roads, railways and aircraft opened up the nation. Radio, followed by television, brought instant communication and a feeling of national identity. People could communicate with others thousands of miles away, first by telephone and now by Twitter and e-mail.
- **The Great Depression.** Events influenced the federal–state relationship, too. When the Great Depression hit the USA in 1929, the states looked to the federal government to cure their ills. The state governments did not possess the necessary resources to reverse the huge levels of unemployment, launch vast public works schemes or rescue agriculture from the effects of the dust bowl conditions. It was Franklin Roosevelt's New Deal, with its ambitious schemes to build roads and schools and provide hydroelectric power, which helped get the USA back to work.
- **Foreign policy.** With the onset of the Second World War, the USA stepped out as a world superpower and the federal government — with exclusive jurisdiction over foreign policy — found its role enhanced significantly.
- **Supreme Court decisions.** Political changes occurred to alter the federal–state relationship. Decisions made by the Supreme Court — especially between 1937 and the 1970s — further enhanced the power of the federal government through their interpretation of the implied powers of the Constitution. This was possible through the Court applying a more expansive meaning to the powers allocated to Congress in Article I, Section 8 of the Constitution, especially the 'necessary and proper clause', the 'common defense and general welfare clause' and the commerce clause. From the mid-1980s, under the chief justiceships of William Rehnquist (1986–2005) and more recently John Roberts (2005–), the Court has sometimes taken a more restrictive view of these clauses, thereby limiting the role of Congress in particular and the federal government as a whole. This was most clearly seen in the 2012 decision of *National Federation of Independent Business* v *Sebelius*, in which the Court declared that President Obama's Healthcare Reform Act could not be justified under the commerce clause, but only under Congress's power to levy taxes.

Key term

Commerce clause The clause in Article I, Section 8 of the Constitution empowering Congress to regulate commerce with foreign nations and among the states.

■ **Constitutional amendments.** One of the three post-Civil War amendments, the Fourteenth, changed dramatically — although not immediately — the federal government's relationship with the states. For the first time, the Constitution had been amended to impose prohibitions directly on state governments. Two requirements of the Fourteenth Amendment in particular have, over time, revolutionised the federal–state government relationship. These requirements — referred to as the 'due process' and the 'equal protection' provisions — are found towards the end of Section 1 of the Amendment. They read: 'Nor shall any State deprive any person of life, liberty, or property, without due process of law; nor deny to any person within its jurisdiction the equal protection of the laws.'

These provisions of the Fourteenth Amendment have been used by the Supreme Court to invalidate state laws requiring public (i.e. state) school segregation and other forms of racial discrimination. Moreover, the Supreme Court has employed them to outlaw a wide array of other state laws, ranging from certain restrictions on abortion, to Florida's attempt to order a recount in the 2000 presidential election between George W. Bush and Al Gore.

Equally importantly, the passage of the Sixteenth Amendment (1913) allowed the federal government to impose an income tax. This gave the federal government the means to launch all the grand programmes that would flourish from Roosevelt's New Deal through the presidencies of Truman, Kennedy and Johnson to the late 1960s.

Phases of federalism

In the period from the 1780s to the 1920s, the individual state governments exercised most political power. The focus was very much on states' rights. But following the devastating effects of the Wall Street Crash and the Great Depression, the period from the 1930s to the 1960s saw a significant increase in the power and scope of the federal government. During this period, the federal government made increasing use of categorical grants — schemes by which it was able to stipulate how federal tax dollars were used by the states.

During the final three decades of the twentieth century, however, there was a discernible movement towards decentralisation — what President Nixon called **new federalism**. This era saw the rise of block grants — money given to states by the federal government to be used at their discretion within broad policy areas. This change in the federal–state relationship coincided with the administrations of four Republican presidents: Richard Nixon, Gerald Ford, Ronald Reagan and George H.W. Bush. But in some ways, the states did not benefit much from these new trends in federalism. As the federal deficit increased in the 1980s, federal programmes were cut. This gave rise to a new term — the **unfunded mandate** — by which the federal government would legally require states to perform some function without providing any money with which to fund it.

By the mid-1990s, however, with a new Republican majority in both houses of Congress, Washington was once again talking of devolving power back to the states. One might therefore refer to these decades as an era of 'zigzag federalism', for during this period, while in some policy areas states gained greater flexibility and autonomy to experiment with new policy approaches, in other areas Washington exercised stricter control. This kind of inconsistency was to be seen during the second Bush presidency, and especially after the events of 11 September 2001.

Key terms

New federalism An approach to federalism characterised by a return of certain powers and responsibilities from the federal government to the states.

Unfunded mandate A federal law requiring states to perform functions for which the federal government does not supply funding.

Map of the USA in state licence plates

Federalism under George W. Bush (2001–09)

Key term

Great Society Democratic president Lyndon Johnson's programme of economic and social reforms and welfare schemes — announced in May 1964 — to try to solve America's problems of poverty, malnutrition, poor housing and access to medical care.

When George W. Bush arrived in Washington in January 2001, one would have presumed that as a Republican president he would continue the moves towards shrinking the size of the federal government and of decentralisation. But one of the most unexpected facts about the administration of George W. Bush was that he presided over the largest overall increase in inflation-adjusted federal government spending since Lyndon Johnson's **Great Society** programme of the mid-1960s. Total federal government spending grew by 33% during Bush's first term (2001–05). The federal budget as a share of the economy grew from 18.4% of gross domestic product (GDP) in 2000, Clinton's last full year in office, to 20.5% in 2008 — Bush's last full year in office. Four policy areas accounted for this expansion of the federal government under George W. Bush — education, Medicare, homeland security along with national defence, and finally the economy and jobs following the Wall Street and banking collapse of 2008.

Education

As governor of Texas, George W. Bush had focused on education as one of the most important areas of policy and he brought the same focus to Washington in 2001. Education had been a cornerstone of George W. Bush's 2000 election campaign with its slogan of 'No child left behind'. Now, as president, Bush wanted to use the re-authorisation of the 1965 Elementary and Secondary Education Act as a vehicle for his education reforms. The No Child Left Behind Act, signed into law by President Bush in January 2002, ushered in the most sweeping changes in federal education policy since the 1960s. In what was a major expansion of the federal government's role in education, the new law mandated that the states test children annually in grades 4 to 8 (equivalent to Years 3 to 7 in the UK) using, in part, a uniform national test. It required that children in failing schools be moved to successful ones and provided for a 20% increase in funding for the poorest, inner city schools. It tripled the amount of federal funding for scientifically based reading programmes. For Bush, this was the federal government as enabler. At the bill-signing ceremony at the White House, he declared:

> The federal government will not micromanage how schools are run. We believe strongly the best path to education reform is to trust the local people. And so the new role of the federal government is to set high standards, provide resources, hold people accountable, and liberate school districts to meet these standards.

Significant questions remain as to the effectiveness of Bush's much-trumpeted education reforms. But whatever else the No Child Left Behind Act was, it signalled a whole new approach to federal–state relations for a Republican president.

George W. Bush's No Child Left Behind Act ushered in sweeping changes in federal education policy

Medicare

Key term

Medicare A federal government scheme, introduced in 1965, to provide America's over-65s with basic health insurance to cover medical and hospital care.

Medicare is a federal government healthcare programme for the over-65s introduced in 1965 by Democrat president Lyndon Johnson. In December 2003, George W. Bush signed a major Medicare expansion bill into law which included a new prescription drug benefit. The measure was estimated to cost $400 billion in its first ten years and was written to benefit American seniors. That a Republican president should preside over the modernisation and expansion of Medicare was certainly something of an irony. But a number of conservative Republicans were critical of the price tag of the reforms as well as of the fact that a Republican president was supporting such a huge expansion of a federal government programme. In the House, 25 Republicans voted 'no' on its final passage, as did nine Republicans in the Senate.

Homeland security and defence

Between 2001 and 2009, spending by the Department of Defense increased from $290 million to $651 million, an increase of 125%. Between 2001 and 2006, spending on homeland security increased from just $13 million to $69 million — more than a five-fold increase in five years. Both these increases were, of course, the direct result of the events of 11 September 2001, and the subsequent military operations in both Afghanistan and Iraq, as well as the 'war on terror' and the push to increase homeland security significantly. Defence spending rose during the George W. Bush years from 15% of the federal budget to 21%; homeland security from less than 1% to just shy of 3%.

Aerial view of damage caused at the Pentagon (Department of Defense), 11 September 2001

Economy and jobs

There was yet another extraordinary example of big-government Republicanism in September 2008 when President Bush authorised Secretary of the Treasury Henry Paulson to take control of two troubled privately owned but government-sponsored mortgage companies — the Federal National Mortgage Association, known as Fannie Mae, and the Federal Home Loan Mortgage Corporation, known as Freddie Mac. Together Fannie Mae and Freddie Mac owned or guaranteed about half of the $12 trillion US mortgage market and had suffered huge losses with the collapse of the housing market. 'In Crisis, Paulson's Stunning Use of Federal Power', headlined *The Washington Post*'s front page the day after Paulson's announcement. 'Not since the early days of the [Franklin D.] Roosevelt administration, at the depth of the Great Depression, has the federal government taken such a direct role in the workings of the financial system,' wrote the *Post*'s Steven Pearlstein in the related article. This was followed by the Bush administration's sponsorship of a $700 billion so-called 'bail-out' package for Wall Street to alleviate the effects of the credit crunch. Again, this looked more like the policies of a New Deal Democrat than of a conservative Republican. The package was passed through Congress by mostly Democrat votes.

Federalism under Barack Obama (2009–17)

Whereas the Bush administration concentrated in its second term on war and terrorism, the Obama administration was more focused on domestic policy as a way of delivering his 'change' agenda as announced during his 2008 presidential campaign. This had a profound effect on the relationship between Washington and the states. War and security against terrorism are conducted exclusively by the federal government; domestic policy is increasingly the domain of the states. As a result of Obama's first-term policies, a number of changes in the federal–state relationship were observed.

By 2012 the ratio of state and local government employees to federal employees was the highest since before President Roosevelt's New Deal in the 1930s. Federal government assistance to the states increased from 3.7% of gross domestic product (GDP) in the last year of the Bush administration (2008) to 4.6% of GDP in the first year of the Obama administration (2009). Similarly, money from the federal government, which accounted for 25% of state government spending in 2008, accounted for 30% of such spending in 2009. Whereas under Bush's economic stimulus package (2003) just $20 billion went to the states, under Obama's stimulus package (2009) $246 billion went to or through the state governments. This significant increase in federal money going to the states between 2005 and 2010 (see Figure 2.1) came partly as a result of such programmes as: the re-authorisation of the State Children's Health Insurance (S-CHIP) programme in 2009; the expansion of Medicaid (a health insurance programme for the poor); and over $4 billion invested in the Race to the Top programme to boost education in the states, as well as programmes like the Pell Grants for university education.

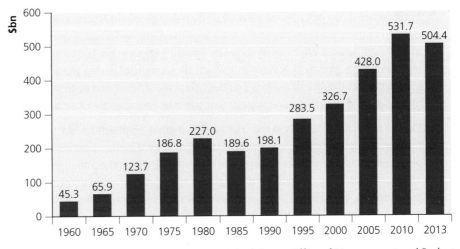

Source: United States Office of Management and Budget

Figure 2.1 Federal grants to states and localities, 1960–2013 (in billions of 2005 dollars)

But the aspect of Obama's legislative programme which came in for most criticism regarding its implications for the federal–state relationship was his healthcare reform legislation. Many Republicans saw the passage of this programme in 2010 as 'the end of federalism' and there were those in the Tea Party movement who accused Obama of being more of a socialist than a federalist. The argument centred on the provision in the law whereby those Americans who could not afford to buy health insurance would be covered by an expansion of the federal–state Medicaid programme. States had to participate in this expansion of Medicaid or lose all their federal funding for Medicaid, the federal government's largest grant programme.

A number of states sued, arguing that this was a violation of the principles of federalism and was therefore unconstitutional. Their contention was that this provision in the law amounted to coercion rather than persuasion. In *National Federation of Independent Business* v *Sebelius* (2012), the Supreme Court agreed with this argument and struck down the Medicaid provision in the law — a victory for the states. Thus Obama's expansive view of the federal government was somewhat curbed by the Supreme Court's decision. Although most of the Affordable Care Act was allowed to stand by the decision, the philosophical argument underpinning the decision was clearly based on a more limited role of the federal government than President Obama and the Democrats in Congress had claimed.

By the close of the Obama presidency, Americans' views on the federal government were decidedly negative. Exit poll data in the 2016 presidential election showed that only 29% of voters were either enthusiastic about or satisfied with the federal government, while 69% were either dissatisfied or angry. Furthermore, by a narrow margin, more thought that the government was 'doing too much' (50%) than that thought it 'should do more' (45%).

Activity

Read the following article and then answer this question:

Is Washington doing too much or too little?

Give reasons for your answer.

Thomas Paine wrote in *Common Sense* in 1776: 'Government, even in its best state, is but a necessary evil; in its worst state, an intolerable one.' The line helped to inflame the American Revolt against British government then, but it would today describe the view taken by many people in America. Conservatives have always been more inclined to think that government is not a legitimate engine for social change. Politicians have been campaigning and running 'against Washington' for years. Ronald Reagan in his 1981 inauguration speech said: 'It is time to check and reverse the growth of government which shows signs of having grown beyond the consent of the governed.' In recent years this line of thinking has become more strident and aggressive with the emergence of the Tea Party and associated groups, questioning not just the laws as passed by Obama, but even his entitlement to office.

On the other hand, liberals in the USA have laid great emphasis on 'elastic clauses' in Article 1, Section 8: the implied powers clause and the interstate commerce clause. Liberals have never questioned the role of government as a vehicle for change, and it is under Democratic administrations — in the New Deal era, and the 1960s — that federal government has grown to include new departments and agencies, tasked with regulating the economy, controlling the environment, tackling social problems. As is often the case, the left has been in awe of the populist appeal and rhetoric of the right, and Clinton felt obliged to promise in 1996 that 'the era of big government is over', but he could not have foreseen the events that were to follow.

During the George W. Bush administration:

- Federal grants to the states reached unprecedented levels, growing from $318 billion to $407 billion in the first term alone, largely as a result of 9/11 and Bush's No Child Left Behind education reforms.
- State initiatives in such policy areas as assisted suicide, medical use of marijuana and same-sex marriage were overridden by the federal government.
- The country's two largest mortgage companies — Fannie Mae and Freddie Mac — were effectively nationalised.

During the Obama administration:

- The American Recovery and Reinvestment Act (2009) provided $275 billion in economic aid in such areas as transportation, energy, public safety and IT provision.
- The Patient Protection and Affordable Care Act (2010) — commonly known as Obamacare — cost the federal government $938 billion over ten years.
- The American Jobs Act (2011) provided $140 billion in federal government grants for modernising schools and repairing roads.

- The President signed an Executive Order — Deferred Action for Childhood Arrivals (2012) — that conferred non-immigrant legal status on around 1.7 million illegal immigrants who came to the United States before their 16th birthday, were under 31 years of age, had completed high school, and had no serious criminal record.

- The President signed an Executive Order — Deferred Action for Parents of Americans (2014) — offering temporary legal status to millions of illegal immigrants, along with an indefinite reprieve from the threat of deportation.

So is Washington doing too much or too little? The answer to this question will depend on how Americans feel about the economic and social developments since 2008. If the person asked is left-leaning, or has one of the jobs created by the stimulus package, or newly has health insurance, or may benefit from changes in immigration policy, or is alert to the economic difficulties of the global financial crisis, then they will likely think favourably of the federal government. On the other hand, if one starts from a position of fiscal conservatism, worried about the deficit, worried about paying it back, paranoid that the federal government will introduce gun controls, opposed to immigration reform, and fearful that it also promotes activities considered immoral, then the answer will be very different. One thing is for certain — the debate is a potent one, and strong feelings are held on both sides.

Source: an abridged and updated version of an article by Robert Fletcher, *Politics Review*, Vol. 22, No. 1, September 2012

Consequences of federalism

Federalism has consequences throughout US government and politics.

- **Legal consequences.** There is tremendous variety in state laws on such matters as the age at which people can marry, or can drive a car, or have to attend school. Laws vary on drugs and whether the death penalty is used. There are both federal and state courts.

- **Policy consequences.** The states can act as policy laboratories, experimenting with new solutions to old problems. Of late we have seen this in such areas as healthcare provision, immigration reform, affirmative action programmes and environmental policies. Healthcare reform in Massachusetts and immigration reform in Arizona have both received considerable national attention, though much of the latter was declared unconstitutional by the Supreme Court in 2012.

- **Consequences for elections.** All elections in the United States are state-based and run under state law. Even the presidential election is really 50 separate state-based elections with the outcome decided by a state-based Electoral College. Each state decides such matters as: how candidates will be chosen for elections in their state; the procedures for getting a candidate's name on the ballot paper; what mechanisms are used in polling stations — punch cards or touch-screen computers. Arizona has experimented with on-line voting while both Washington State and Oregon have moved to an entirely postal ballot.

- **Consequences for political parties.** It is important to realise that political parties in America are essentially decentralised, state-based parties. Texas Democrats are more conservative than Massachusetts Democrats; Vermont Republicans more liberal than South Carolina Republicans. One can see the effects of federalism in the United States Congress with its state-based representation. The consequences of federalism were highlighted in the 2016 presidential nomination contest when Republicans in Colorado, North Dakota and Wyoming decided not to hold either a primary or a caucus, but to choose their national convention delegates through a state party convention, much to Donald Trump's chagrin. There was nothing the national Republican Party could do about it.

The Affordable Care Act ('Obamacare') significantly expanded federal funding of Medicaid and was widely opposed by Republicans.

- **Economic consequences.** These are seen not only in the huge federal grants going to the states, but also in the complexity of the tax system in America. Income tax is levied by both the federal government and some state governments, different property taxes are levied by the state governments, and sales taxes vary between cities.
- **Regionalism.** The regions of the South, the Midwest, the Northeast and the West have distinct cultures and accents, as well as racial, religious and ideological differences. There is a distinct difference between the conservatism of the Deep South and the liberalism of the Northeast. What plays well in 'the Bible Belt' may not be popular in 'New England'.

When all is said and done, federalism has proved to be an appropriate system of government for the United States. It has adapted itself to the ever-changing nation. Despite its frustrations, there are few who question its future. Some Americans may think the federal–state relationship has at times got out of kilter, but most believe that its strengths far outweigh its weaknesses.

Debate

Does federalism work today?

Yes
- It permits diversity.
- It creates more access points in government.
- It provides a 'double security' for individual rights and liberties.
- It makes states 'policy laboratories', experimenting with new solutions to old problems.
- It is well suited to a geographically large and diverse nation.

No
- It can mask economic and racial inequalities.
- It can frustrate the 'national will'.
- It makes problem solving more complicated.
- The relationship between federal and state governments can become a source of conflict and controversy.
- It is overly bureaucratic — and therefore costly to run and resistant to change.

Comparing the US and UK constitutions

A constitution is a framework within which a country's system of government is conducted — the rules that govern the relationship between the government and the governed. Constitutions establish the duties, powers and functions of the various institutions of government. They define the relationship between the state and the individual.

The origins of the two constitutions

'If the British Constitution developed in the mists of time, the American Constitution emerged in the mists of gunpowder smoke, the creature of a revolution' (Walles, 1988). Thus the two constitutions are partly shaped by their origins — the British Constitution by evolution, the American Constitution by revolution. The American Constitution burst onto the political stage in 1789 almost fully grown. The British Constitution has emerged piecemeal over centuries. Both constitutions are therefore partly a product of the culture and societies that shaped them. The kind of national and political upheaval seen in America in the late eighteenth century has not been seen in Britain since the Norman Conquest of the eleventh century. The English Civil War of the seventeenth century failed to have similarly long-lasting effects as the monarchy was quickly restored and the evolutionary development continued. Even the so-called Glorious Revolution of the 1680s, accompanied as it was by the drawing up of a Bill of Rights, failed to give birth to any new formal statement of governmental relationships.

The differences in their origins, and the differences in the two cultures from which they grew, shape the two constitutions. The US Constitution is largely shaped by the expectations, fears and culture of America in the late eighteenth century. It is shaped by the expectations for such ideas and beliefs as liberty, individualism, equality, representative democracy, limited government, states' rights and the rule of law. These form the core values of America's political culture. The Constitution is shaped by a society that had broken free from a distant and autocratic monarchy, and that was largely accepting of slavery, fearful of state-organised religion, and deferential to fundamental rights and liberties, including gun ownership. All these — and many other — characteristics of late eighteenth-century American society can be found in the original seven Articles and the first ten Amendments. We can see these cultural and societal norms in such constitutional provisions as:

- the federal system of government
- the strict separation of personnel between the three branches of the federal government
- the First Amendment requirement that 'Congress shall make no law respecting an establishment of religion'
- the Second Amendment's provision that 'the right of the people to keep and bear arms shall not be infringed'

And as American society and culture changed, so the Constitution was further amended to reflect these changes, such as:

- the Thirteen, Fourteenth and Fifteenth Amendments following the Civil War and the emancipation of the slaves
- the Eighteenth and Twenty-First Amendments reflecting the era of Prohibition
- the Nineteenth Amendment reflecting the emancipation of women
- the Twenty-Fourth Amendment reflecting the civil rights movement

The British Constitution, on the other hand, is different largely because it is the product of a different culture. It has been shaped by and has evolved within a society and culture dominated by a belief in a constitutional monarchy, a deferential class system and an established church. We can see these effects of British society and culture in:

- the role and power of the monarchy
- the presence of hereditary peers in the House of Lords (although now in much-reduced numbers)
- the inclusion of the two archbishops and 24 of the bishops of the Church of England in the House of Lords

Archbishop of Canterbury, Justin Welby, in the House of Lords

In these and others ways, these two sharply different constitutions reflect the sharp differences between the cultures of the two nations they serve.

The nature of the two constitutions

The constitutions of the USA and the UK are fundamentally different not only in their origin but in their nature. They are structurally different. Whereas the USA — like the vast majority of democracies — has a codified constitution, the UK has an uncodified constitution. A codified constitution is one in which most of the rules concerning the government of the nation are drawn together in one document. The United States has a single document running to no more than 7,000 words which contains most of the country's constitutional arrangements. However, even a codified constitution often contains parts that are uncodified. For example, the US Constitution contains no mention at all of such important matters as primary elections, congressional committees, the president's cabinet, or the Executive Office of the President, nor even of the most significant power of the Supreme Court — judicial review.

Convention can become part of the constitution even in a codified arrangement. When President George Washington declined to seek a third term of office in 1796, he put in place the convention of a two-term limit on the presidency — a convention that held for well over a century until broken by Franklin Roosevelt in 1940. It was only after Roosevelt had been elected to a third (1940) and a fourth (1944) term that the convention was formalised in the codified document as the Twenty-Second Amendment (1951).

> ### Advantages and disadvantages
>
> ## The codified constitution
>
> ### Advantages
> - All the constitutional provisions can be found easily in one document.
> - The provisions within the constitution are entrenched and therefore protected from arbitrary change.
> - It provides more significant and effective checks and balances between the various branches of government.
> - It can be made surprisingly flexible by judicial interpretation.
>
> ### Disadvantages
> - It tends to elevate the importance of unelected judges over elected officials.
> - It can be inflexible and therefore fail to change as society changes.
> - The enumeration of rights and liberties does not necessarily mean that those rights and liberties are safeguarded in reality.
> - It tends to be less 'evolutionary'.

Similarly, although the UK is said to have an uncodified constitution, it is certainly not entirely unwritten. Indeed, much of the UK Constitution is written down — for example, in Acts of Parliament, Common Law, and works of authority such as those by Erskine May (1815–86) and Walter Bagehot (1826–77). It is simply not collected together into a document called 'a constitution'.

Another important difference relates to the matter of entrenchment (see page 22). Entrenchment is a feature of most written constitutions that makes amendment deliberately difficult. The reason for this is a belief that the specific rights and provisions that are enshrined in the constitution should not be subject to change by a passing whim, even if the change is supported by a majority of the electorate. Indeed, entrenchment means that not only is the process for amending a constitution a difficult one, but it must be supported by a super-majority. Two examples will illustrate this point.

Under Article I of the United States Constitution, the length of terms for members of the House of Representatives and the Senate is fixed at two and six years respectively. So to change the length of those terms of office would require a constitutional amendment with the necessary super-majorities in both houses of Congress and among the state legislatures. The length of terms for members of the UK House of Commons is fixed at five years. But this is fixed merely by an Act of Parliament — the Fixed-Term Parliaments Act (2011). So all that would be required to change the length of that term of office would be another Act of Parliament — passed by simple majorities in both houses of Parliament. In the United States the provision for legislators' terms of office is entrenched, while in the UK it is not.

The United States Constitution also entrenches a number of rights and liberties, including the Second Amendment right to 'keep and bear arms'. But in the United Kingdom, the rights of gun owners have no such entrenched protection and can be changed simply by Act of Parliament. Following the Dunblane Massacre in 1996 in which 16 children and a teacher were killed, Parliament passed the Firearms (Amendment) (No. 2) Act (1997) banning

The US Supreme Court chamber

high-calibre handguns. Here again we see the difference in the cultures of the countries. Whereas in the United States a culture enshrining belief in individualism is careful to protect the right of individuals to own firearms, in Britain where the culture is quite different such a liberty is regarded by most as a weird anachronism bordering on extremism and paranoia.

Democracy and sovereignty in the two constitutions

Here again, the US and the UK constitutions differ significantly. Although both constitutions can be said to be based on the principle of democracy, the two have evolved at different speeds to different conclusions. In the USA, as a result of the culture of the nation, the concepts of direct democracy and popular sovereignty are — and always have been — more in evidence. So, although both constitutions are based on democracy, the shared ideas and beliefs that shaped them are different.

The US Constitution allows Americans a much greater role in the electoral processes of their nation than does the UK Constitution for people in Britain. Between the 1780s and the 1880s, the US House of Representatives was elected on a far wider franchise than the UK House of Commons. The Senate has been directly elected since 1914 whereas Britain's second chamber still has no elected members at all. The election of the US president has evolved from an indirect to a virtually direct election. The significant growth of the direct primary through the twentieth century allows ordinary voters to participate in candidate selection for elections at all levels of government. Moreover, in the states, the initiative, referendum and recall procedures allow a high level of direct participation. The Tenth Amendment clearly sets out where power resides — with the people.

By contrast, the UK Constitution emphasises representative democracy and parliamentary sovereignty. British citizens — who are, strictly speaking, 'subjects of the Crown' — have fewer opportunities for democratic participation than their American counterparts. Again, this reflects the cultural heritage of the UK. They can elect members of only one of the two houses in Parliament and the UK prime minister is not subject to any direct election. The second chamber is still appointed and the hereditary monarch and Parliament remain sovereign, not the people. A recent innovation, however, has been the use of referendums, of which there have now been 13 since 1973, but only three of these (in 1975, 2011 and 2016) have been nationwide.

The provisions of the two constitutions

Despite these significant differences, the two constitutions make some very similar broad provisions. Both provide for systems of government that could be described as representative democracies. Both provide for national governments divided into three branches — a legislature, an executive and a judiciary. Both provide for a bicameral legislature. Both — now — provide for a Supreme Court, for fixed-term elections (with some wiggle room in the UK) and for sub-national governments: state governments in the USA, and devolved governments for Scotland, Wales and Northern Ireland in the UK.

But those similarities mask a host of differences. Both constitutions provide for three branches of government, but the way in which they share power, and the way in which their personnel are either separate (in the USA) or fused (in the UK) makes a substantial difference to the way things work. Both provide for bicameral legislatures, but the US Senate bears little resemblance in selection, membership or powers to the UK House of Lords. The two supreme courts may share the same name, but if one were to allow canine illustrations, the one in the United States is a mastiff compared to the UK's chihuahua. From 2011, the UK House of Commons was subject to fixed-term elections, but as we discovered in April 2017, the terms were not that fixed. When Prime Minister Theresa May announced her intention to call an early election — in June of that year — all she required was a two-thirds majority vote in the House of Commons as laid down in the 2011 Act. The vote was 522–13. May then announced at the launch of the Conservative Party manifesto that if returned to government, it was their intention to repeal the Act. Furthermore, the relationship between London and the devolved governments in Scotland, Wales and Northern Ireland is in no way the same as that between Washington and the states. Thus although the provisions of the two constitutions may be superficially similar, they are marked by significant differences. We shall now proceed to consider these differences in three important areas: separation/fusion of powers, checks and balances, and federal/devolved systems.

Separation/fusion of powers

The US Constitution is said to be based on the doctrine of the separation of powers. But as we have seen, this is better understood as the doctrine of shared powers. This is especially important when considering the relationships between the legislature and the executive under each constitution. Under the US Constitution, both these branches are entirely separate. Neither the president, nor the vice president, nor any of the department or agency heads can be serving members of the legislature, nor may any serving member of Congress hold any executive office. The president cannot prematurely end a Congress and call new elections, and neither can Congress remove members of the executive branch, except for 'high crimes and misdemeanours' by impeachment. And even were the president to be removed from office, the vice president would immediately and automatically take over. There would be no new elections.

The UK Supreme Court in London, with a statue of Abraham Lincoln in the foreground

But under the UK Constitution there is said to be a fusion of powers. British ministers operate in both the executive and legislative branches, heading government departments at the same time as being members of Parliament. As MPs they pass legislation and as members of the executive they are also responsible for its implementation. The prime minister is both head of the executive branch as well as leading their party in the House of Commons. Parliament can cause the downfall of an entire government through a No Confidence vote, as occurred to the Labour government of Prime Minister Jim Callaghan in 1979. Until the setting up of the UK Supreme Court in 2009, the Law Lords in the House of Lords served concurrently in both the legislature and the judiciary, and the Lord Chancellor served in all three branches, being also a member of the cabinet. These differences are largely the product of the structural differences between the two systems of government, reflecting the cultural differences at work in the two countries.

But this is only one side of the coin. The other side is what we call checks and balances, and this is especially pertinent when it comes to relations between the executive and the legislature.

Checks and balances

Checks and balances is the principle that gives each of the three branches of government the means to partially control the power exercised by another branch. This principle runs like a seam through the US Constitution and it speaks eloquently of the fears of the Founding Fathers — fears of executive power, and the tyranny of the government over the people. 'Ambition must be made to counteract ambition,' wrote James Madison. By an intricate series of checks and balances, 'a double security arises to the rights of the people,' he continued. So, once more, we see that constitutional differences between the USA and the UK reflect cultural differences between the two nations as they developed. To put it somewhat crudely, the US Constitution was written to protect the rights of the governed; the UK Constitution evolved to protect the powers of the government. Checks and balances were the means by which the rights and freedoms of Americans would be protected. They would limit the power of government. The end result is diffusion of power and the obstruction of strong government. But give it a more contemporary name, and one often ends up with gridlock.

Under the UK Constitution, things are quite different. The prime minister draws up legislative proposals which their ministers then introduce into and shepherd through Parliament with a (virtually) guaranteed parliamentary majority. The prime minister is leader of the largest (usually the majority) party in the House of Commons. The five-yearly general election decides both the make-up of the House of Commons and the identity of the prime minister. The end result is concentration of power and the promotion of strong, usually one-party government. But the danger — certainly to the eyes of American observers — is of an overly autocratic government that is careless of the rights of individuals and minorities.

Federalism/devolution

The USA has a federal system of government in which political power is divided between a national government and state governments, each having its own area of substantive jurisdiction. Americans think of themselves as Floridians, Virginians, New Yorkers or whatever. Federalism is very appropriate to a country as large and diversified — in race, culture, language and economy — as the USA. It also adds yet another layer of checks and balances, and thereby further limits governmental power.

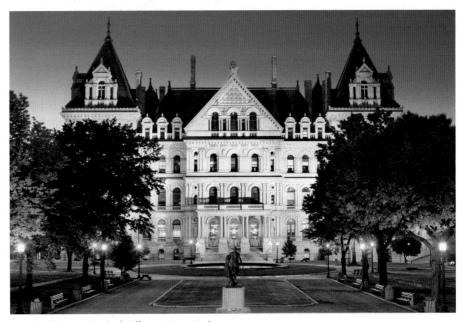

New York State Capitol, Albany, New York

Key term

Devolution The statutory granting of powers from the central government to a sub-national government.

For centuries, the UK could be described as a unitary system of government with all political power emanating from the central government in London. But nowadays it can best be described as a devolved form of government in which certain powers are the prerogative of the central government while the exercise of other powers is devolved to the principalities of Scotland, Wales and Northern Ireland. Once again, the differences emanate from the structural differences between the two systems of government as well as the cultural differences which were at work as the two nations developed their respective systems of government.

But federalism and devolution are two quite different political animals. In a federal system, certain powers are granted solely to the national government, other specific and substantive powers are granted solely to the state governments, and some powers are shared. The states are not subservient to the national

The chamber of the Scottish Parliament

government. Diagrammatically, the states are not *below* the national government but *alongside* it, sovereign in their own areas of substantive jurisdiction.

But in a devolved system such as exists in the UK, the national government is sovereign. All devolved governmental power exists only with the agreement of the national government. It may cede more powers to the devolved government. Equally, it may reclaim them. In 1972, the UK government suspended the Northern Ireland Parliament at Stormont and replaced it by direct rule from the Westminster Parliament. Devolution is essentially no more than decentralisation on a grander scale within a unitary system of government.

That said, both federalism in the USA and devolution in the UK seek to serve the same purpose — to give power and legitimacy to local communities in the nation and to give voice to growing regional or, as in the case of Scotland, nationalist pressures. They are both mechanisms for answering calls for government to be 'nearer to the people' and to attempt to overcome a feeling of distant alienation from those furthest from the centre of national power.

Both systems also encourage a debate as to how much autonomy the subnational governments should be granted. In the USA, this has been seen in a debate between the centralising tendencies of the first half of the twentieth century as the Democrats' programmes sought to increase the power and economic clout of Washington at the expense of the states, as compared with moves towards more decentralisation and 'states' rights' by Republican presidents such as Richard Nixon and Ronald Reagan. Likewise in the UK, there was a lengthy debate during the second half of the last century as to whether devolved powers should be granted to Scotland and Wales. But since these principalities were granted their own legislative and executive powers, there has been a continuing debate — especially in Scotland — as to how much these powers should be increased. Devolution has also led to calls by some for Scotland to become an independent nation, showing another significant difference between federalism and devolution within a unitary system.

References

Finer, S.E., *Comparative Government*, Penguin, 1970.

Neustadt, R., *Presidential Power and the Modern Presidents*, John Wiley & Sons, 1960.

Walles, M., *British and American Systems of Government*, Philip Allan, 1988.

Further reading

Colclough, A., 'The US Constitution: a protection against the growth of a security state?' *Politics Review,* Vol. 25, No. 3, February 2016.

Fletcher, R., 'Washington: doing too much or too little?' *Politics Review,* Vol. 22, No. 1, September 2012.

Maggs, R. and Lemieux, S., 'Debate: Is the US federal government too powerful?' *Politics Review*, Vol. 25, No. 4, April 2016.

Singh, R., 'The US Constitution: does it ensure limited government?' *Politics Review,* Vol. 23, No. 3, February 2014.

There are a number of websites you can consult to follow up topics raised in this chapter. To find information on the US Constitution as well as on proposed and failed amendments, the following sites will be useful:

www.constitutioncenter.org

www.usconstitution.net/constam.html

Other sites of interest are:

www.governing.com

www.usa.gov

https://fedstats.sites.usa.gov

www.nga.org

www.census.gov

www.ncsl.org

As regards the three branches of government — Congress, the president and the Supreme Court — you will find information on websites relating to each at the beginning of the relevant chapters.

Exam focus

Edexcel

Section A (Comparative)

1 Examine the extent to which the US and UK constitutions adhere to the doctrine of the separation of powers. *(12)*

2 Examine the provision of checks and balances in the US and UK constitutions. *(12)*

Section B (Comparative)

In your answer you must consider the relevance of at least one comparative theory.

1 Analyse the significant differences between the US and UK constitutions. *(12)*

2 Analyse the differences between federalism in the US Constitution and devolution in the UK Constitution. *(12)*

Section C (USA)

In your answer you must consider the stated view and the alternative to this view in a balanced way.

1 Evaluate the extent to which the checks and balances of the US Constitution are still effective today. *(30)*

2 Evaluate the extent to which the process for amending the US Constitution works well. *(30)*

3 Evaluate the extent to which the US Constitution is now past its 'use-by' date. *(30)*

4 Evaluate the extent to which the US federal government nowadays does too much. *(30)*

AQA

Section A (USA)

1 Explain and analyse three ways in which Congress can check the president. *(9)*

2 Explain and analyse three ways in which the concept of federalism influences US government. *(9)*

Section A (Comparative)

1 Explain and analyse three ways in which structural theory could be used to study the constitutions of the UK and the USA. *(9)*

2 Explain and analyse three ways in which cultural theory could be used to study the constitutions of the UK and the USA. *(9)*

Section B (USA)

The US Constitution: still working well, or out of date?

It is now over 225 years since the Founding Fathers drew up in essence what we know today as the US Constitution. But does it still work? There are a number of areas in which the answer to that question appears to be 'no'. When it comes to the war-making powers, the president is commander-in-chief but Congress has the power to declare war as well as the power of the purse. The result has often been that Congress has had little or no say in major foreign policy decisions. In the area of appointments to the executive and judiciary, the president has the power to nominate, but the Senate has the power 'to advise and consent'. But the whole process has become deeply politicised. The Electoral College is seen as a hopeless anachronism that has failed badly twice in the last two decades. The Second Amendment makes meaningful gun control legislation almost impossible.

But there are counter-arguments. The amendment process has kept the USA from frequent and ill-conceived amendments. Many of the checks and balances work just how the Founding Fathers wanted — to guard against executive tyranny. And the Supreme Court, through its power of judicial review, has constantly updated the Constitution, not through formal amendment but by judicial interpretation.

Adapted from 'Is the US Constitution past its use-by date?' in Anthony J. Bennett, *US Government & Politics Annual Update 2012*, Chapter 8.

Analyse, evaluate and compare the arguments in the above passage for and against how well the US Constitution works. *(25)*

Section C (Comparative)

In your answer you should draw on material from across the whole range of your course of study in Politics.

1 'The US Constitution is not as flexible as the UK Constitution.' Analyse and evaluate this statement. *(25)*

2 'Checks and balances work better in the US Constitution than in the UK Constitution.' Analyse and evaluate this statement. *(25)*

3 'The US Constitution allows for a greater degree of decentralisation than the UK Constitution.' Analyse and evaluate this statement. *(25)*

Congress

Introduction

A bumper sticker I once saw on a car in Albuquerque, New Mexico, read, 'WHAT'S THE OPPOSITE OF PROGRESS? **CONGRESS!**' And to many Americans, that sums up their negative attitude to the law-making arm of the federal government — that Congress is unproductive and obstructionist, and has, as one academic put it, 'a built-in negative bias'. And when, like the people in New Mexico, you're nearly 2,000 miles — a 28-hour drive across ten states — from Washington DC, Congress seems very remote and its failings seem all the more magnified. 'After all,' many Americans ask, 'what *has* Congress ever done for us?' One is tempted to reply that, apart from Medicare, Medicaid, affordable health insurance, education, irrigation, interstate highways, public order, national defence and security, the protection of civil rights, a minimum wage, social security and a good deal more, what *has* Congress done for America? Yet a Gallup Poll in July 2016 found that a mere 13% of Americans approve of the job Congress is doing, with 83% saying they disapprove. Indeed, in 2013, the polling organisation Public Policy found Congress to be more unpopular than used car dealers, lice, traffic jams and cockroaches!

So Congress is thought to be unproductive and is therefore unpopular. But as we study Congress, we need to keep in mind that there are at least two paradoxes hidden behind these facts and figures. One paradox is that, while on the one hand Americans disapprove of Congress, they approve of — and consistently re-elect — their own members of Congress. Another is that, while many Americans call for Congress to 'do more', many of them also believe in the principle of limited government, which states that Congress — as well as the other branches of the federal government — should be limited in what it can do, that in many ways the *fewer* laws it passes, and the *less* it interferes in the lives of ordinary Americans, the better. The state motto of New Hampshire is 'live free or die', but that belief spreads well beyond the borders of one small state.

The structure of Congress

Congress is bicameral: it is made up of two houses — the House of Representatives and the Senate. This arrangement for the legislative branch of government was one of the compromises devised by the Founding Fathers at the Philadelphia Convention. Some delegates to the convention had wanted the states to be equally represented in the legislature, while others had wanted representation to be proportional to population. The compromise was to have a two-chamber structure. In the lower house (the House of Representatives) the states would be represented proportionally to their population, but in the upper house (the Senate) the states would be represented equally. This kept both the states with large populations and those with small populations content.

Table 3.1 Membership of Congress in outline

House of Representatives	Senate
■ lower house	■ upper house
■ 435 members	■ 100 members
■ represent a congressional district	■ represent entire state
■ serve two-year terms	■ serve six-year terms
■ must be at least 25 years old	■ must be at least 30 years old
■ must be a US citizen for at least seven years	■ must be a US citizen for at least nine years
■ must be resident of state they represent	■ must be resident of state they represent

Furthermore, some delegates wanted to see the legislature directly elected by the people, while others thought the legislators should be indirectly elected. In another compromise, the Founding Fathers decided that the House of Representatives would be directly elected but the Senate would be indirectly elected — appointed by the state legislatures. This arrangement for the Senate continued until 1914 when, as a result of the Seventeenth Amendment, the first direct elections for the Senate were held. The whole of the House is elected every two years. Senators serve six-year terms with one-third of the Senate being up for re-election every two years. Thus in the congressional elections held every two years, the whole of the House and one-third of the Senate are up for re-election.

Today, the House of Representatives is made up of 435 members — referred to either as representatives or congress(wo)men. Each state has a certain number of members proportional to its population. The number of representatives for each state is reapportioned after each ten-yearly census, which is held in the zero-numbered years (e.g. 2000, 2010, 2020). Some states gain House seats, while others lose them. For example, following the 2010 census, the Texas House delegation rose from 32 to 36, while New York's fell from 29 to 27 and Ohio's fell from 18 to 16. Except in states that have just one representative, each member represents a sub-division of the state known as a congressional district.

With 50 states in the Union and each state having two senators, there are today 100 members of the Senate.

The composition of Congress

Congresswoman Lisa Blunt Rochester (D–Delaware) is one of the few women in Congress

The Constitution lays down certain qualifications to become a senator or representative (see Table 3.1). To be a senator, one must be at least 30 years old and have been a US citizen for at least nine years. To be a representative, one must be at least 25 years old and have been a US citizen for at least seven years. Members of both houses must be resident in the state they represent. So much for the constitutional requirements, but what does Congress look like in terms of gender and race?

Women have been persistently under-represented in Congress. In 1992, the Democrats tried to focus on this issue and declared 1992 'the Year of the Woman'. The title might have struck some as contrived, but the effect was dramatic, virtually doubling the number of women in Congress in just one election. Gains in the last decade have been rather more modest, as Table 3.2 shows. The majority of the women in both houses are Democrats — the party that tends to attract the female vote. Following the 2016 elections the number of women in Congress remained the same at 104: 83 in the House and 21 in the Senate. This means that women still make up only 19% of the House and 21% of the Senate, which, needless to say, is hardly representative of American society as a whole. In this sense, Congress certainly does not 'look like America'.

Table 3.2 Congressional membership by gender and race, 1979–2017

Years	Women		African-Americans		Hispanics/Latinos	
	House	Senate	House	Senate	House	Senate
1979–80	16	0	16	0	6	0
1981–82	19	1	17	0	7	0
1983–84	21	2	21	0	10	0
1985–86	22	2	20	0	10	0
1987–88	23	2	23	0	10	0
1989–90	25	2	24	0	9	0
1991–92	28	2	25	0	9	0
1993–94	47	7	38	1	18	0
1995–96	48	8	38	1	18	0
1997–98	51	9	38	1	18	0
1999–2000	56	9	35	0	19	0
2001–02	59	14	36	0	18	0
2003–04	59	14	38	0	22	0
2005–06	64	14	41	1	24	2
2007–08	71	16	40	1	23	3
2009–10	75	17	39	1	23	2
2011–12	72	17	42	0	24	2
2013–14	78	20	41	1	31	3
2015–16	84	20	44	2	32	4
2017–18	83	21	46	3	34	4

Of the 83 women elected to the House in 2016, 62 were Democrats and only 21 Republicans. In the Senate, of the 21 women, 16 were Democrats, just 5 Republicans. One of the problems in trying to increase the representation of women in Congress is that women are also under-represented in the pool of recruitment from which members of Congress are commonly drawn, namely state legislatures. In 2017, just 24.8% of state legislators were women, higher than in the US Congress but significantly below the figure in the population at large. In only 13 states do women make up 30% or more of state legislators — Nevada at just under 40% having the highest proportion of women. But there are 16 states — ten of them in the South — in which women make up less than 20% of state legislators. In Wyoming in 2017, a mere 11% of state legislators were women.

Representation by race is much better in the House of Representatives than in the Senate because the federal courts have allowed states to draw congressional district boundaries to create districts that are likely to return a Representative from an ethnic minority group. These so-called 'majority-minority districts' are often geographically distorted as they attempt to group together sometimes scattered pockets of minority voters. Figure 3.1 shows North Carolina's 12th Congressional District, which links small towns scattered for 100 miles along Interstate 85. The district is currently represented by African-American Democrat Alma Adams. The redrawing of district boundaries following the 1990 census clearly boosted African-American representation in the House, as Table 3.1 shows. By 2017, all the African-American representatives were Democrats. Between 2005 and 2008, Barack Obama of Illinois was the only African-American senator. After he had resigned following his election

Figure 3.1 North Carolina's 12th Congressional District

to the presidency, another African-American, Roland Burris, was appointed to complete the remaining two years of Obama's six-year term, but he did not seek election in his own right when the term expired in 2010, leaving the Senate with no African-American members in January 2011. However, by January 2017, there were three African-American senators.

Again, as with women, there is an issue about the low levels of representation in state legislatures — the main pool of recruitment for Congress. In 2015, in only 15 states did African-Americans make up more than 10% of state legislators. The state with the highest percentage of African-American state legislators is Mississippi with 28%. That said, currently five of Mississippi's six-member congressional delegation are white.

Table 3.2 shows the Hispanic-American representation in Congress over the past three decades or so. At the start of the 115th Congress (January 2017), 21 of the 34 Hispanic House members come from California (10), Texas (6) and Florida (5). Two of New Mexico's three House members are Hispanic. Of those 34 Hispanic house members, 25 are Democrats and just 9 Republicans. At the same time, four states were represented in the Senate by a Hispanic-American — Florida (Republican Marco Rubio), New Jersey (Democrat Bob Menendez), Texas (Republican Ted Cruz) and Nevada (Democrat Catherine Cortez Masto). These four states all have a Hispanic-American population above the 16.3% national average. Altogether, Hispanics make up only 8% of the House membership and just 4% of the Senate.

In terms of prior occupations of members of Congress, politicians, business people, bankers and lawyers predominate in both houses. Around 60% of both houses in the 114th Congress (2015–16) had previously served as politicians. Members with a previous career in business or banking accounted for 53% of House members and 42% of senators, while 40% of House members and 60% of senators had been lawyers. This is hardly a representative cross-section of America.

Table 3.3 Religious affiliation of members of Congress (2017) compared with US population

	House (%)	Senate (%)	US population (%)
Protestant	55.4	58	47
Catholic	33.1	24	21
Jewish	5.1	8	2
Mormon	1.6	6	1.6
Muslim	0.5	0	0.9
Buddhist	0.5	1	0.7
Hindu	0.7	0	0.7
Others/Unaffiliated	2.0	3	23

In terms of religious faith, Congress is rather more Christian than the nation as a whole (see Table 3.3). This is especially marked in terms of Catholics, who make up 33% of the House and 24% of the Senate but only 21% of Americans as a whole. People of Jewish faith are over-represented in both chambers, as are Mormons in the Senate. There are three Buddhist and Hindu members of Congress, as well as two Muslims. If they were represented in Congress as per the American population as a whole, there would be around four members of each religious group.

Both houses of Congress are dominated by the Republican and Democratic parties. In January 2017, all members of the House and all bar two members of the Senate are members of one of the two major parties. The exceptions are Senator Bernie Sanders of Vermont and Angus King of Maine who sit as independents, though they almost always vote with the Democrats and Sanders actually competed in their 2016 presidential primary contest. In terms of party control of each house, between 1993 and 2017 the House of Representatives has been controlled by the Democrats for 14 years and by the Republicans for 10 years. During the same period, the Senate has been controlled by the Republicans for 12½ years and by the Democrats for 11½ years. We shall have more to say about parties in Congress later in this chapter.

The powers of Congress

Law making

Article I of the Constitution begins with these words: 'All legislative Powers herein granted shall be vested in a Congress of the United States.' Notice the phrase 'herein granted' — for here is another example of the way the Constitution provides for what we call limited government (see Chapter 2). Congress has only those legislative powers granted by the Constitution. When it comes to legislation, both houses of Congress are equal in the sense that all bills must pass through all stages in both houses. Neither house can override the wishes of the other. Both houses must agree to the proposed law in exactly the same form before it can be sent to the president for his consideration.

The Constitution does, however, grant one special law-making power to the House of Representatives, in that only the House can begin the consideration of money bills — that is, bills raising revenue (tax bills). This is because at the beginning of the nation's history only the House was directly elected and the Founding Fathers believed that the people's directly elected representatives should have the first say in matters concerning the people's money. But the Senate must also pass — and may amend — such bills, so this special power of the House is really not all that significant. We shall consider the details of the legislative process later in this chapter.

Overseeing the executive branch (investigation)

While the Constitution makes no explicit statement concerning Congress's power of oversight, it is implied by the powers granted to it in Article I, Section 8, where it is said that a legislative body may investigate any subject that is properly within the scope of its legislative powers. Moreover, the fact that Congress establishes and votes on the budgets of all the executive departments and agencies of the federal government implies that Congress has oversight of these departments and those who run them. Congress's oversight of the executive branch occurs almost exclusively in the committee rooms, exercised by the congressional standing and select committees. We shall consider the details of congressional oversight later in this chapter.

Overriding the president's veto

Related to Congress's law-making powers, both houses must vote — by two-thirds majorities in each — to override the president's veto of a bill. In 2007, Congress overrode President Bush's veto of the Water Resources Development Bill. The vote in the House was 381–40, which was 100 votes over the 281 required for a two-thirds majority. The vote in the Senate was 81–12, which was 19 votes over the 62 votes required. Congress overrode four of Bush's 12 vetoes during his eight years in office.

During Barack Obama's eight years in office, Congress overrode just one of his 12 vetoes. In September 2016, they overrode his veto of the Justice Against Sponsors of Terrorism Act that would have allowed families of victims of the September 11 terrorist attacks to sue the government of Saudi Arabia for any role they may have played in the plot. The Senate voted 97–1 to override Obama's veto and the House followed later the same day with a vote of 348–77.

Confirming appointments

The Constitution grants to the Senate alone the power to confirm — by a simple majority — many appointments made by the president. These include all the president's appointments to the federal judiciary and a great many — though not all — of the appointments to the executive branch. As a result, whenever the president wishes to fill a vacancy in the trial, appeal or supreme courts of the federal government, the Senate must give its consent. When Justice John Paul Stevens retired in 2010, President Obama's nominee Elena Kagan was confirmed by the Senate by 63 votes to 37.

Similarly, whenever a vacancy occurs in a senior executive branch post, the president must seek the Senate's approval for replacement appointments. In 2013, when Secretary of State Hillary Clinton resigned, President Obama had to gain the approval of the Senate to appoint John Kerry to replace her. The Senate voted 94–3 to confirm him. An informal agreement called 'senatorial courtesy' allows a president to confer with any senator of their own party from a particular state before they make a nomination to fill a vacancy for a federal office affecting that state. This is important when it comes to appointments that the president makes to the federal trial courts.

Elena Kagan is sworn in at the start of her confirmation hearings before the Senate Judiciary Committee, June 2010

Ratifying treaties

The Senate also has the sole power to ratify — by a two-thirds majority — all treaties negotiated by the president. This means that the president needs to keep the Senate fully informed throughout treaty negotiations, to avoid concluding treaties that the Senate is unlikely to ratify. In December 2010, the Senate voted by 71 votes to 26 to ratify the new Strategic Arms Reduction Treaty (START) negotiated by President Obama with his Russian counterpart Dmitry Medvedev.

Initiating constitutional amendments

The two houses are also co-equal when it comes to initiating constitutional amendments. A constitutional amendment must be approved by a two-thirds majority in both houses before it can be sent to the states for their ratification (see Chapter 2).

Impeaching and removing public officials

Another important power that the Constitution (Article II, Section 4) grants to Congress is the power to impeach and remove from office 'all civil Officers of the United States' for 'Treason, Bribery, or other high Crimes and Misdemeanours'. As one can see, this is a two-stage process and each house performs one of the stages. The House of Representatives has 'the sole Power of Impeachment'. Remember that to impeach someone is to formally accuse and charge them with an offence serious enough to warrant removal from office. The House has used this power 19 times since 1789, the most recent concerning federal judge Thomas Porteous in 2010 on charges that included corruption and perjury. In 1998, the House impeached President Clinton on two counts — perjury and obstruction of justice.

The Senate has 'the sole Power to try all Impeachments'. This Senate trial is to determine whether the person is guilty of the offence, or offences, of which they have been accused by the House. If they are found guilty by a two-thirds majority, the person is immediately removed from office. In December 2010, Judge Thomas Porteous was found guilty and removed from office by the Senate, but the Senate acquitted President Clinton on both counts in 1999.

In 1998, Bill Clinton was impeached on counts of perjury and obstruction of justice

Because members of Congress are not considered 'officers of the United States', but rather representatives of the people, they cannot be impeached and removed from office in this way. Nevertheless, under a separate power (Article I, Section 5), each chamber may expel a member for 'disorderly Behaviour' by a two-thirds majority vote. The most recent example was the expulsion by the House of Democrat James Traficant of Ohio after his conviction in a federal court on charges including bribery and filing false tax returns.

Confirming an appointed vice president

The Twenty-Fifth Amendment (1967) gave to both houses the power to confirm a newly appointed vice president. But note carefully that this power relates only to a vice president who is appointed, not to those who are elected. The Twenty-Fifth Amendment gave the president the power to fill a vacancy in the vice presidential office should the vice president become president, resign or die in office. This has occurred twice. In 1973 Vice President Spiro Agnew resigned and President Nixon appointed Gerald Ford to succeed him. Ford was confirmed by both the Senate (92–3) and the House (387–35). The following year President Nixon resigned and Ford became president. Ford then appointed Nelson Rockefeller to succeed him as vice president. The votes on that occasion were 90–7 in the Senate and 287–128 in the House.

Declaring war

Both houses must concur in a declaration of war. This has occurred on only five occasions — the last one being 1941, when America declared war on

Japan in the Second World War. Since the mid-twentieth century, Congress has found itself either sidelined by presidential war making — in Korea or Vietnam, for example — or merely being asked to sanction military action that the president has already decided to take, for example in Iraq.

Electing the president and vice president if the Electoral College is deadlocked

If in the presidential election no candidate wins an absolute majority of Electoral College votes (see Chapter 6) then the House of Representatives is charged with electing the president, and the Senate with electing the vice president. This power has been used only twice — in 1800 and 1824.

Comparing the House and the Senate

It is often suggested that the Senate is more powerful and prestigious than the House. House members often seek election to the Senate. Indeed in 2016, 12 House members ran for Senate seats. In 2017 there were 50 former House members in the Senate but no ex-senators in the House of Representatives. There are some significant reasons why this may be the case.

Table 3.4 Powers of Congress in outline

Joint powers of both houses	Sole powers of the Senate	Sole powers of the House
■ law-making ■ overseeing the executive branch (investigation) ■ overriding president's veto ■ initiating constitutional amendments ■ impeaching and removing public officials ■ confirming an appointed vice president ■ declaring war ■ electing president and vice president if Electoral College deadlocked	■ confirming appointments ■ ratifying treaties	■ beginning consideration of money bills

While House members represent only a congressional district, senators represent the entire state. For example, Representative Henry Cuellar represents only the 28th Congressional District of Texas, but Senator John Cornyn represents the entire state of Texas. He also enjoys a six-year term in the Senate, whereas Cuellar has only a two-year term in the House. Senator Cornyn is one of only 100 in the Senate whereas Congressman Cuellar is one of 435 in the House. Because of the smaller size of the Senate, a senator is likely to gain a leadership position more quickly than a member of the House. Indeed Senator Cornyn was elected as Senate Majority Whip in January 2015. Congressman Cuellar, meanwhile, was only 18th in seniority among the 21 Democrats serving on the House Appropriations Committee of which he is a member. Yet he was elected to the House only two years after John Cornyn was elected to the Senate.

The Senate is seen as a launching pad for a presidential campaign. Presidents Harry Truman, John Kennedy, Lyndon Johnson, Richard Nixon and Barack Obama were all former members of the Senate. Five senators launched campaigns for the 2016 presidential race: Republicans Ted Cruz, Rand Paul, Marco Rubio and Lindsey Graham as well as Democrat Bernie Sanders. There were also three former senators running for the presidency in 2016: Democrats

Hillary Clinton and Jim Webb, plus Republican Rick Santorum. The Senate is also seen as a recruitment pool for vice presidential candidates. Walter Mondale, Dan Quayle, Al Gore and Joe Biden — four of the last seven vice presidents — were either former or serving members of the Senate when elected vice president. Indeed, the Democrats have nominated a senator or former senator as their vice presidential candidate in every election since 1944, except for 1984 — that is, in 16 out of the last 17 elections.

Senator John Cornyn speaks to reporters, March 2015

Senators enjoy significant exclusive powers — especially those concerned with the confirmation of appointments and the ratification of treaties (see Table 3.4). Many of them also enjoy greater name recognition outside their state. However, when it comes to the passage of legislation, senators and

Debate

Is the Senate more prestigious than the House?

Yes
- Senators represent the entire state.
- Senators serve longer terms.
- Senators are one of only 100.
- Senators are more likely to chair a committee or sub-committee or hold some other leadership position.
- The Senate is seen as a recruiting pool for presidential and vice presidential candidates.
- Senators possess significant exclusive powers.
- House members frequently seek election to the Senate, but not the other way around.

No
- Both houses have equal power in the passage of legislation — Congress's key function.
- Both houses must approve the initiation of constitutional amendments.
- Both houses conduct oversight of the executive branch.
- Both houses fulfil a representative function.
- Members of both houses receive equal salaries.

representatives enjoy equal powers, and the same goes for most of the other constitutional powers of Congress. Finally, it is worth noting that members of both houses receive the same salary — in January 2017, $174,000.

The committee system

Writing in 1885, Woodrow Wilson — 28 years before becoming president — said this about Congress:

> The House sits, not for serious discussion, but to sanction the conclusions of its committees as rapidly as possible. It legislates in its committee rooms; not by the determination of majorities, but by the specially-commissioned minorities [the committees]; so that it is not far from the truth to say that Congress in session is Congress on public exhibition, while Congress in its committee rooms is Congress at work.

Table 3.5 Congressional committees in outline

Type	Function
Standing committees	■ Legislation and scrutiny of the executive branch (both houses) ■ Begin confirmation of appointments (Senate only)
House Rules Committee	Timetabling of legislation in House of Representatives
Conference committees	Reconciling differences in legislation (joint)
Select committees	Special, ad hoc, investigative committees (both houses, or joint)

The most important types of congressional committee are: standing committees, the House Rules Committee, conference committees and select committees (Table 3.5). The committee system of Congress is both extensive and highly important.

Standing committees

Standing committees exist in both houses of Congress (see Table 3.6). They are permanent, policy-specialist committees. Most standing committees are divided into sub-committees, examples of which are shown in Table 3.7. A typical Senate standing committee comprises around 18 members, while a typical House standing committee is made up of around 30–40 members. The party balance in each standing committee is in proportion to that which exists within the chamber as a whole. At the beginning of the 115th Congress (January 2017), the Republicans were the majority party in both houses. Thus, all congressional standing committees had a Republican majority.

House and Senate members seek assignments on committees that are closest to the interests of their district or state. For example, both of North Dakota's senators, Republican John Hoeven and Democrat Heidi Heitkamp, are members of the Senate Agriculture Committee. Re-elected members are routinely reappointed to their former committees unless they have asked for a new assignment. Some committees — for example, Judiciary, Armed Services and Appropriations — are more prestigious than others. New members might have to wait some years to get assigned to these more sought-after committees.

Key term

Standing committee
A permanent, policy specialist committee of Congress playing key roles in both legislation and investigation.

Table 3.6 Congressional Standing Committees

Senate standing committees	House standing committees
Agriculture, Nutrition and Forestry	Agriculture
Appropriations	Appropriations
Armed Services	Armed Services
Banking, Housing and Urban Affairs	Budget
Budget	Education and the Workforce
Commerce, Science and Transportation	Energy and Commerce
Energy and Natural Resources	Financial Services
Environment and Public Works	Foreign Affairs
Finance	Homeland Security
Foreign Relations	Judiciary
Health, Education, Labor and Pensions	Natural Resources
Homeland Security and Governmental Affairs	Oversight and Government Reform
Judiciary	Rules
Rules and Administration	Science, Space and Technology
Small Business and Entrepreneurship	Small Business
Veterans' Affairs	Transportation and Infrastructure
	Veterans' Affairs
	Ways and Means

Table 3.7 Examples of congressional sub-committees

Committee	Sub-committees
House Science, Space and Technology Committee	■ Energy ■ Environment ■ Oversight ■ Research and Technology ■ Space
House Transportation and Infrastructure	■ Aviation ■ Coastguard and Maritime Transportation ■ Economic Development, Public Buildings and Emergency Management ■ Highways and Transit ■ Railroads, Pipelines and Hazardous Materials ■ Water Resources and Environment

Functions of standing committees

Standing committees have two functions in both the House and the Senate, and a third function in the Senate only.

Conducting the committee stage of bills

The first function of standing committees in both houses is to conduct the committee stage of bills in the legislative process. This involves holding 'hearings' on the bill at which 'witnesses' appear. These witnesses might be:

- other members of Congress
- members from the relevant executive departments or agencies, or even from the White House
- representatives from interest groups or professional bodies likely to be affected
- ordinary members of the public

Witnesses make prepared statements in front of the committee and are then subjected to questioning from committee members. The length of such hearings is determined largely by the length of the bill itself and the level of controversy that it engenders. Short, non-controversial bills attract short hearings lasting no more than a few hours. But long, controversial bills are given hearings that might last — on and off — for weeks or even months. At the conclusion of these hearings, a vote is taken by the committee on whether or not to pass the bill on to the full chamber for debate and votes — the next stage in the legislative process.

Conducting investigations

The second function of standing committees in both houses is to conduct investigations within the committee's policy area. This enables Congress to fulfil its oversight function. Such investigations are often launched into perceived problems, crises or policy failures. They attempt to answer such questions as 'Why did this happen?', 'Is current legislation proving effective?' and 'Is new legislation required?' The format is much the same as for legislative hearings, with witnesses being summoned and questions asked. We shall consider this function in more detail when we study Congress's oversight function of the executive branch of government.

Confirming presidential appointments

In the Senate, standing committees have a third function: to begin the confirmation process of numerous presidential appointments. The two committees that are particularly busy in this regard are the Senate's Judiciary and Foreign Relations committees. The former must hold hearings on all the federal judicial appointments made by the president; the latter holds hearings on all ambassadorial appointments. It was the Republican-controlled Senate Judiciary Committee that refused to hold hearings on President Obama's Supreme Court nominee Judge Merrick Garland in 2016. Other Senate standing committees oversee appointments made within their particular policy areas.

Hearings are held at which supporters, and possibly critics, of the nominee are heard from before a vote is taken. The vote is not decisive — only recommendatory — but it is a very important clue to the likely outcome of the nomination. Because these committees are regarded as the policy specialists in their particular areas, their recommendations are rarely overturned. An overwhelming — possibly unanimous — 'yes' vote by the committee indicates that the nominee will receive easy passage on the floor of the Senate, but a close vote will indicate problems ahead. Should the majority of a committee vote 'no', the nomination is certain to be defeated, if it even gets to the Senate floor (see Table 3.8).

Table 3.8 Senate standing committee and floor votes on selected presidential nominees

Nominee	Post	President	Committee vote	Senate floor vote
Robert Bork	Supreme Court	Ronald Reagan	5–9	42–58
John Tower	Secretary of Defense	George H.W. Bush	9–11	47–53
Clarence Thomas	Supreme Court	George H.W. Bush	7–7	52–48
Ruth Bader Ginsburg	Supreme Court	Bill Clinton	18–0	96–3
Betsy DeVos	Secretary of Education	Donald Trump	12–11	51–50*

*Vice president Mike Pence cast the tie-breaking vote.

The standing committees of Congress have considerable power to help the parent chambers manage their huge workloads, but there are limits to their power. As congressional scholar Burdett A. Loomis (2004) points out:

Committees are powerful but not all-powerful: they cannot legislate; they cannot require the executive to comply with their wishes; they cannot implement policies once they have been approved.

House Rules Committee

The House Rules Committee is one of the standing committees of the House of Representatives, but it performs a different function from the others. It is responsible for prioritising bills coming from the committee stage on to the House floor for their debate and votes. Because there is a huge queue of bills waiting to be considered on the House floor, the Rules Committee has a vital legislative role to play. Its name comes from the 'rule' it gives to a bill, setting out the rules of debate by stating, for example, whether any amendments can be made to the bill at this stage. There are three basic types of rules:

- open rules that permit unlimited amendments, provided they are relevant to the bill
- modified (or restrictive) rules that limit the total number of amendments, what sections of the bill can be amended, and who can propose them
- closed rules that forbid any amendments

House Rules Committee chair Pete Sessions (left) at an early-morning committee meeting on healthcare legislation, 2017

The Rules Committee is unusual in that its membership is much smaller and more skewed to the majority party than other standing committees. In 2017, the House Rules Committee had just 13 members — nine Republicans and only four Democrats — chaired by Pete Sessions of Texas. Chair of the House Rules Committee is considered one of the most influential posts in Congress.

Conference committees

Conference committees are required because of two important characteristics of the legislative process in Congress. First, both houses have equal power. Second, bills pass through both houses concurrently, rather than consecutively. As a consequence, there are often two versions of the same bill — a House version and a Senate version. By the time the bill has passed through each house, the two versions are likely to be different. If, after being passed by each house, the two versions of the bill are different, and if these differences cannot be reconciled informally, then a conference committee is set up.

All conference committees are ad hoc — set up to consider only one particular bill. The members, known as 'conferees', are drawn from both houses.

Their sole function is to reconcile the differences between the House and Senate versions of the same bill. Once a conference committee has come up with an agreed version of the bill, this version must be agreed by a vote on the floor of each house. If agreement is not forthcoming, the same conference committee may be reconvened. Another compromise will be drawn up and sent to the floors of both houses. Should that be unacceptable to one or both chambers, the bill will be sent back to the *standing* committees that first considered it.

Conference committees are important because they are likely to draw up what will become the final version of the bill. Their power is checked, however, by the ability of the House and Senate to refuse to sign up to their compromise version. But, as we shall see when we consider the legislative process in detail, conference committees are used much less frequently nowadays. The House and Senate leadership have found other ways to resolve differences in the versions of bills passed by their respective chambers.

Select committees

Select committees are sometimes known as 'special' or 'investigative' committees. Nearly all are ad hoc, set up to investigate a particular issue. Most of them are constituted within just one chamber, but sometimes a joint select committee is set up with members drawn from both houses. But why are select committees needed when, as we have already seen, the standing committees have an investigative function? A select committee is set up when the investigation either: does not fall within the policy area of one standing committee; or is likely to be so time consuming that a standing committee would become tied up with it, thus preventing the standing committee from fulfilling its other functions.

In 2014 the then Speaker of the House John Boehner set up the House Select Committee on Events Surrounding the 2012 Terrorist Attack in Benghazi that had resulted in the deaths of the American ambassador to Libya, Christopher Stevens, and three other Americans. Hearings began in September 2014 but it was not until October 2015 that Hillary Clinton, who at the time of the attack was serving as secretary of state (foreign secretary), appeared before the committee for 11 hours of questioning. The committee published its final report in June 2016.

There are also a few permanent select committees: in the Senate there are four, on Aging, Ethics, Indian Affairs, and Intelligence; in the House there is just one, on Intelligence.

Committee chairs

Those who chair standing committees are always drawn from the majority party in that house. Thus, in the 115th Congress (2017–18), all the standing committees are chaired by Republicans. The **seniority rule** states that the chair of the standing committee will usually be the member of the majority party with the longest continuous service on that committee. The same usually applies to what are called the 'ranking minority members' of each committee.

However, the Republicans in both the House and the Senate have amended the seniority rule by adopting term limits for committee chairs when they are in the majority. Republicans in both houses now have a three-term limit — that is six years — on committee chairs. Furthermore, when they are in the majority, House Republicans use their leadership-dominated Steering Committee to play a key role in determining who will be awarded committee chairs rather than relying solely on seniority.

Key term

Seniority rule A 'rule' that the chair of a congressional standing committee is the member of the majority party with the longest continuous service on that committee.

Those who chair standing committees have a number of important powers. They:

- control the committee's agenda
- decide when the committee will meet
- control the committee's budget
- influence the membership, meetings and hearings of sub-committees
- supervise a sizeable committee staff
- serve as spokesperson on the committee's policy area within Congress, to the White House and in the media
- make requests to the House Rules Committee (in the House) and the party leadership (in the Senate) for scheduling of legislation on the House floor
- report legislation to the floor of their respective chamber on behalf of the full committee

Chairing a congressional committee brings power, perks and publicity. For many, this is the pinnacle of their congressional career.

Congress and legislation

The legislative process in Congress is best thought of in six stages:

1 Introduction
2 Committee stage
3 Timetabling
4 Floor debate and vote on passage
5 Conference committee (*optional*)
6 Presidential action

To be successful, all bills must pass through stages 1–4 and 6. Stage 5 — the conference committee — may be avoided if both houses pass the bill in the same form or if any differences can be resolved informally. To be successful, a

The chamber of the House of Representatives as President Trump presents his first Address to Congress, 28 February 2017

bill must pass through all these stages during a Congress — that is, two years. So, for example, the 115th Congress runs from January 2017 until December 2018. Any bills not completed in one Congress must start the process again at the beginning of the next Congress.

Introduction

The introduction is a pure formality. There is no debate and no vote. In the House, it involves nothing more than placing a copy of the bill in a 'hopper' — a tray — on the clerk's desk. In the Senate, the introduction involves reading out the title of the bill on the Senate floor. Bills are then numbered, printed, circulated and sent on to the appropriate standing committee.

The most important fact to comprehend at this stage is the sheer volume of legislation that is introduced in Congress. As Table 3.9 shows, in a typical Congress, anything between 10,000 and over 14,000 bills are introduced. Of these, only around 2–4% actually make it into law. The process explains largely why this percentage is so small. The 112th Congress (2011–12) was the least productive in terms of legislation of any recent Congress, with only 284 of the 12,299 bills introduced becoming law.

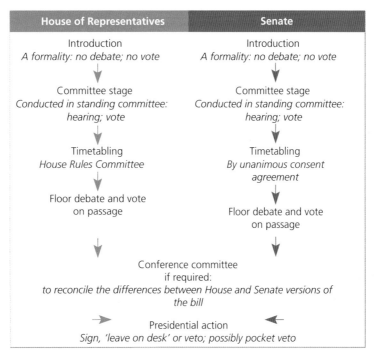

Figure 3.2 Legislative process in Congress

Table 3.9 Percentage of bills introduced that were enacted into law, 2001–16

Years	Bills introduced	Laws enacted	Percentage of bills enacted
2001–02	10,789	383	3.5
2003–04	10,669	504	4.7
2005–06	13,072	483	3.7
2007–08	14,042	460	3.3
2009–10	13,675	385	2.8
2011–12	12,299	284	2.3
2013–14	10,637	296	2.8
2015–16	12,063	328	2.7

Source: www.govtrack.us/congress/bills/statistics

Committee stage

This is the most important stage. Far more bills fail here than at any other stage. Hundreds of bills are referred to each of the standing committees in both chambers in each Congress. This is far more than they can handle. A significant number are pigeon-holed — put to one side, with no action taken on them at all, no hearings and no vote. It is those with a good deal of support — from members of Congress, the White House, the administration or interest groups, for example — that are given hearings. The hearings may be either in the full committee or in the relevant sub-committee.

There are other reasons why this stage is so important. The committee stage comes very early in the legislative process — *before* the debate in the chamber. The full House and Senate have not yet debated the bill. The standing committee members are regarded as the policy specialists in their policy area and they have the full power of amendment — anything can be added to and anything removed from the bill at this stage. Professor Vile (1999) stated that 'it is difficult to exaggerate the importance of these [standing] committees, for they are the sieve through which all legislation is poured, and what comes out, and how it comes out, is largely in their hands'.

Once the hearings have been completed, the committee holds a mark-up session — making the changes it wishes — before reporting out the bill, effectively sending it on to its next stage. The report written by the committee does four things: states the main aims of the bill; reviews the amendments made by the committee; estimates the cost of implementation; and recommends future action to be taken by the full chamber.

Timetabling

By the time Congress has been in session for a few months, a huge number of bills will be waiting to come to the floor of both chambers for debate and vote on passage. While there are dozens of committee and sub-committee rooms, there is only one floor in each house. Something of a legislative traffic jam develops, with bills queuing for their turn on the House and Senate floors. Each house has its own procedure for dealing with this potential problem.

The Senate deals with it through what is called a **unanimous consent agreement**. This is, in effect, an agreement between the Senate majority and minority leaders on the order in which bills will be debated on the Senate floor.

The House of Representatives deals with it through the House Rules Committee. The 'prioritising' role of the House Rules Committee makes it a kind of legislative 'gatekeeper' or 'traffic cop' — allowing some bills through but holding others back. If the Rules Committee fails to give a rule to a popular bill, House members may resort to the discharge process. A discharge petition must be signed by an absolute majority of House members — 218. Once that demanding requirement has been fulfilled, the bill is discharged from the Rules Committee and comes automatically to the House floor for debate. This process was used successfully in 2002 on the Bipartisan Campaign Reform Act, and in 2015 to force a vote on a bill to re-authorise America's Export-Import Bank, the official export credit agency of the federal government.

Floor debate and vote on passage

This is the first opportunity for the full chambers to debate the bill. In the House, most bills are first considered at this stage in the Committee of the

Whole House, which allows for as many members to take part in the debate as possible. In both houses, further amendments can usually be made. Votes are taken both on amendments and on the whole bill at the end of the debate. Simple majorities are required. Votes can be either by voice vote or by recorded vote. In the former, members merely call out 'aye' or 'no': this is used mostly for non-controversial bills. In a recorded vote, a record of each member's vote is made. In the House this is done electronically; in the Senate by a roll-call vote with the clerk alphabetically calling the roll of the 100 Senators. Both procedures take 15 minutes.

In the Senate, there is the possibility of a **filibuster** taking place, by which senators exercise their right of unlimited debate to delay a bill. Stamina is more important than relevance in conducting a filibuster. Senators have been known to read out extracts from the Constitution, the Declaration of Independence, the Bible and even the telephone directory. In 1957, Strom Thurmond conducted a filibuster against a civil rights bill that lasted for over 24 hours. On 10 December 2010, independent senator Bernie Sanders of Vermont spoke on the Senate floor against a tax deal which President Obama was trying to work out with congressional Republicans. Sanders spoke from 10.25 in the morning until just before 7 o'clock that evening, a total of just over 8½ hours. Then on 24 September 2013, Senator Ted Cruz of Texas spoke non-stop for just over 21 hours on the Affordable Care Act — making this the fourth longest filibuster in the Senate's history. Following the mass shooting at an Orlando night club in June 2016, senators Chris Murphy of Connecticut, Ben Sasse of Nebraska and Pat Toomey of Pennsylvania launched a filibuster of just short of 15 hours to press for tighter gun control legislation. These days it is just as likely that a filibuster will be conducted by a group of senators as by one individual.

A filibuster can be ended by a procedure known as 'closure' (or 'cloture'). To be successful, a closure petition must be signed by 16 senators and then voted for by at least three-fifths (60) of the entire Senate. Until the 1970s, filibusters and cloture motions were relatively unusual events. For example, in the 91st Congress (1969–70) only 7 cloture motions were presented with 6 of those being voted on. Thirty years later in the 104th Congress (1999–2000), there were 71 cloture motions presented with votes on 58 of them. But by the 110th Congress (2007–08) a record 139 cloture motions were presented with votes on 112. The figures fell only slightly in the next two congresses. As a result of this huge increase in filibusters, Senate Majority Leader Harry Reid and Minority Leader Mitch McConnell reached a deal in January 2013 to try to limit the use of filibusters, but the next two years saw another huge rise in the use of the cloture (Figure 3.3). Later the same year, the Senate Democrats passed what is often referred to as 'the nuclear option' to require only a simple majority vote to end filibusters of certain executive and judicial branch nominations, though this did not include nominations to the Supreme Court. When the Republicans returned to the majority in the Senate in 2015, they kept these reforms in place. Then in 2017, in order to secure the confirmation of Neil Gorsuch to the Supreme Court, the Senate rules were changed yet again — this time by the Republicans — forbidding the filibustering of Supreme Court nominations.

Key term

Filibuster A device by which one or more senators can delay action on a bill or any other matter by debating it at length or by other obstructive actions.

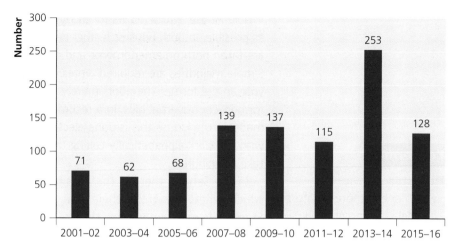

Figure 3.3 Number of cloture motions filed per Congress, 2001–16

After the debate and the approval of any amendment, each chamber votes either to pass or to defeat the bill. (In the House, the Committee of the Whole House 'rises and reports' and then the chamber in normal session votes on the measure.) Having come through this process in each house, the House version and the Senate version of the bill are likely to be different. If the differences are relatively minor, the two houses may just agree informally — among the leadership — to adjust the bills to make them identical. But if the differences are significant, then a conference committee may be set up to reconcile the differences.

Table 3.10 Differences between the legislative process in each chamber

House of Representatives	Senate
Two-year terms give greater sense of urgency	Six-year terms give less sense of urgency
House members have only one major committee assignment; thus tend to be more policy specialists	Senators serve on two or three major committees; thus tend to be more generalists
Referral of bills to standing committee done by the Speaker and is difficult to challenge	Referral of bills to standing committee is easier to challenge
Discharge process limits power of standing committees to refuse to report out a bill for consideration by the whole house	No discharge process — enhances standing committees' power to block bills
Timetabling from committee stage to the floor is controlled by the majority party through the House Rules Committee	Timetabling from committee stage to the floor is generally agreed between the majority and minority leaders
All revenue bills have second reading in Committee of the Whole House	No similar procedure in the Senate
Debate usually limited to one hour, and strict limit on length of speeches controlled by bill managers	No limits on speeches allows opportunity for delay and filibustering; difficult to end with cloture motion
Hard to amend a bill because most bills given a closed rule	Amendments to bills are easier to achieve
435 members: more difficult to keep a tally of likely voting intentions	100 members: easier to keep tally of likely voting intentions
Recorded votes are by electronic device	Recorded votes are by the Clerk calling the roll and each member responding in person
In the case of a tied vote on final passage, a bill is defeated	In the case of a tied vote on final passage the vice president (as President of the Senate) has a casting vote

Conference committee

Conference committees have declined in use over the past 20 years. In the 104th Congress (1995–97), 37 conference reports were adopted, but by the 113th Congress (2013–15) that number had fallen to just two.

The decline in the use of conference committees began soon after the Republicans took control of both houses of Congress in 1995. In place of the formalised, bicameral conference committees, the Republicans began to use a more ad hoc, leadership-driven approach whereby one chamber was simply asked to endorse the legislation passed by the other chamber, in a system not dissimilar to what occurs in the UK Parliament. Indeed, the same somewhat derogatory term began to be used for the procedure — 'ping ponging' — where the bill from one chamber is offered on a take-it-or-leave-it basis to the other chamber. The result of this is to greatly reduce the possible input from minority party members and thereby further to increase the partisanship seen in Congress.

There are quite a number of mainly quite subtle differences in the legislative process between the two chambers (see Table 3.10). But once a version of the bill has been agreed by both houses — with or without the offices of a conference committee — the bill is ready to be sent to the president.

Presidential action

The president always has three options as to what to do with a bill. At times, he has a fourth.

Signing the bill into law

First, he will sign into law bills he fully supports and for which he wishes to claim some credit. An example of this is the March 2010 signing by President Obama of the Patient Protection and Affordable Care Act. A bill-signing ceremony is arranged, usually at the White House, where a number of key House and Senate members who have supported the bill through its passage are present for a photo opportunity with the president. This is an opportunity for both credit claiming and political thank-yous. The president may also decide to sign bills out of political expediency. In this category would come the March 2002 signing by President Bush of the Bipartisan Campaign Reform Act.

President Obama signs into law a bill to overhaul the Department of Veterans' Affairs as members of Congress and war veterans look on, August 2014

Leaving the bill on his desk

The president may decide to 'leave the bill on his desk'. He does this for bills upon which he takes no position at all, or which he would like to veto but knows his veto would be overridden. These bills will become law without his signature within ten congressional working days.

Regular veto

The president may veto the bill using a regular veto. He does this to bills that he strongly opposes. Presidents use the threat of a veto as a bargaining tool with Congress. The president hopes that the threat of the veto will cause Congress to make the changes in the bill which the president has demanded. To veto the bill, the president must act within ten congressional working days of receiving it, sending it back to its house of origin with a message explaining his objections. He must veto the whole bill, not just parts of it.

Congress then has three options. It can put right the 'wrongs' identified by the president in his veto message and return the bill for his signature: this is unlikely, as members of Congress will have been well aware of his objections during the bill's passage. The second option is to attempt to override the veto. This requires a two-thirds majority in both houses — a demanding and difficult requirement that is rarely achieved. Third, Congress may realise that it does not have the votes necessary to override the veto, and may accept that the president has won. The last is by far the most likely option.

In the 228 years between 1789 and the end of Barack Obama's second term in January 2017, presidents have used the regular veto 1,508 times, and of those just 111 have been overridden by Congress. That gives the president a 92% success rate. There are two main reasons for this. First, the cards are stacked so much against Congress. The president needs only 34 supporters in the Senate to win. Second, the president will study the final passage votes of bill. If it has passed by huge majorities in both houses on final passage or on the conference report, then he will rarely veto. If, however, the majorities have been small, he can veto with confidence, knowing that he will prevail. In July 2008, Congress overrode President George W. Bush's veto of the Medicare Improvements Bill by votes of 383–41 in the House and 70–26 in the Senate. It was Bush's fourth defeat in 11 vetoes in eight years.

Pocket veto

The president may have a fourth option — to use a **pocket veto**. If the bill is awaiting the president's action when the legislative session ends, the bill is lost: this is a pocket veto and cannot be overridden by Congress. A late rush of bills may arrive on the president's desk just as the legislative session ends, so this can be a significant power. President Clinton was the last president to use a pocket veto — on the Consumer Bankruptcy Overhaul Bill in December 2000. George W. Bush claimed to have used the power in December 2007 when he killed the National Defense Authorisation Bill, but House Speaker Nancy Pelosi rejected this, saying that the House was technically still in session at the time. In early 2008, Congress passed the bill again in a slightly amended form and the President signed it into law.

> **Key term**
>
> **Pocket veto** A veto power exercised by the president at the end of a legislative session whereby bills not signed are lost.

Assessing Congress's effectiveness in legislation

> The cards are stacked against action by Congress. As a result, those who seek action in Congress face a far more difficult task than those whose purpose is negative. (Carr, 1974)

It is difficult to get bills passed through Congress successfully. There are seven specific reasons for this:

■ A vast number of bills are introduced. This immediately makes the process crowded.

■ The process itself is complicated. Professor R.V. Denenberg (1976) describes Congress as a 'bastion of negation', the process of passing laws as a 'legislative labyrinth' and the legislative process as having 'a built-in negative bias'. Box 3.1 shows how complicated the process was to enact President Obama's healthcare reform legislation in 2010. There had to be seven separate votes — four in the House and three in the Senate.

■ There is the need at some stages for super-majority votes: a three-fifths majority to stop a legislative filibuster in the Senate, as in the 21 December 2009 vote on Obama's healthcare reform; a two-thirds majority in both houses to override the president's veto.

■ Power in Congress is decentralised. Much power resides with the standing committees and especially with those who chair them. Party leaders have limited powers — former Senate majority leader Bob Dole once described himself as the 'majority pleader'.

■ The fact that both houses possess equal power makes the process more difficult. If, as in the UK Parliament, one house can virtually override the wishes of the other, legislation is generally more easily accomplished.

Box 3.1

Healthcare reform legislation, 2009–10

2009

January–July	House committees on Energy and Commerce, Education and Labor, and Oversight and Government Reform draw up proposed legislation.
July	House Speaker Nancy Pelosi unveils proposed House bill (Affordable Healthcare for America Bill), which is an amalgam of the bills drawn up by the three House committees.
9 September	President Obama addresses joint session of Congress on healthcare reform.
13 October	Senate Finance Committee reports out the Senate bill (Patient Protection and Affordable Care Bill) by a vote of 14–9.
7 November	House passes its healthcare bill by 220–215 (D: 219–39; R: 1–176).
18 November	Senate Majority Leader Harry Reid introduces Senate healthcare bill for floor debate.
15 December	President meets with Senate Democrats to urge passage of healthcare bill.
21 December	Senate votes to end Republican filibuster of bill by 60–40 (D: 60–0; R: 0–40).
24 December	Senate passes its healthcare bill by 60–39 (D: 60–0; R: 0–39). But the two houses have not passed identical pieces of legislation.

2010

27 January	President uses his State of the Union Address to urge final passage of healthcare bill.
21 March	House passes the Senate's bill by 219–212 (D: 219–34; R: 0–178). House immediately passes Reconciliation Bill (amendments to Senate bill) by 220–211 (D: 220–33; R: 0–178).
23 March	President holds bill signing ceremony at the White House to sign Patient Protection and Affordable Care Act into law.
25 March	Senate passes amended version of House Reconciliation Bill by 56–43 (D: 56–3; R: 0–40). House passes the same bill by 220–207 (D: 220–32; R: 0–175).
30 March	President signs the Healthcare Reconciliation Act into law

- Between 1981 and 1987, from June 2001 to December 2002, and from January 2011 to January 2015, these two equal houses were controlled by different parties. In the 1980s, the Republicans controlled the Senate, but the Democrats controlled the House. In the two more recent examples, it has been the other way around.
- Even if the two houses of Congress are controlled by the same party, it may not be the president's party. He is therefore likely to find it difficult to pass the bills he wants.

Some critics suggest that open rules are now so rarely used that ill-considered and poorly crafted legislation is likely to be rammed through the House by the majority party. As Figure 3.4 shows, the balance between open and closed rules has changed significantly over the past 20 years, leading to much frustration on behalf of the minority party — the Democrats through much of this period.

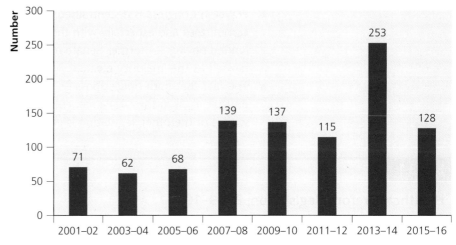

Figure 3.4 Open and closed rules in the House of Representatives, 1995–2015 (%)

Another criticism of the legislative process is the dramatically declining use of conference committees to reconcile House and Senate bills. Important legislation needs the benefit of a conference committee to ensure greater member participation, which generally leads to a more effective process and better legislation. Without a conference committee, the final version of the bill is often decided by just a handful of members, mostly drawn from the leadership of the majority party.

So just how effective is Congress as a legislative body? During the last 25 years, Congress has certainly passed some significant pieces of legislation (see Box 3.2). It has addressed some of the big political issues facing America during this period, including gun control, trade, education, the economy and healthcare. To take a more focused and more recent snapshot, between January 2015 and the end of March 2016, Congress passed 139 pieces of legislation. That sounds quite impressive and hardly a reason to be critical of Congress. And some of these Acts of Congress were indeed significant pieces of legislation (see Box 3.3). But of those 139 Acts, 22 were passed merely to rename a local facility after some distinguished local citizen: 16 post offices, three courthouses, one federal building, one highway, and one arboretum! Others were passed to:
- allow the Postal Service to issue a stamp to raise money for breast cancer research
- award congressional gold medals to participants of the civil rights march in Selma, Alabama in 1965
- require the secretary of the treasury to mint coins to commemorate the centenary of Boys Town (a children's charity)
- establish a ten-year term for the Librarian of Congress

> ## Box 3.2
>
> ### Ten significant laws passed by Congress since 1990
>
> - Americans with Disabilities Act (1990)
> - Brady Handgun Violence Protection Act (1993)
> - North American Free Trade Agreement (1993)
> - No Child Left Behind Act (2002)
> - Bipartisan Campaign Finance Reform Act (2002)
> - Emergency Economic Stabilization Act (2008)
> - Children's Health Insurance Program (2009)
> - American Recovery Reinvestment Act (2009)
> - Patient Protection and Affordable Care Act (2010)
> - Wall Street Reform and Consumer Protection Act (2010)

> ## Box 3.3
>
> ### Selected laws passed by Congress, January 2015–March 2016
>
> - Medicare Access and CHIP Reauthorization Act
> - Department of Homeland Security Appropriations Act
> - Disaster Relief Act
> - Iran Nuclear Agreement Review Act

Hardly matters of great national importance. Yet when the Republicans won control of both houses of Congress in January 2015, they promised to rewrite and simplify the United States tax code; replace the healthcare law with what they called 'patient-centred' care; overhaul the criminal justice system; expand free trade; and put the federal government on the path towards a balanced budget. While there was time to pass laws to rename 16 post offices, there was a complete blank on any those five declared promises. No wonder many Americans think that Congress is ineffective. As to the reasons for this ineffectiveness, we shall come to those later in this chapter.

> ### Activity
>
> For more information on the legislative process in Congress, go to the Center on Congress website at **centeroncongress.org**.
>
> - Click on 'Learn about Congress'.
> - Click on 'How Does Congress Work?'
> - Under the heading 'Interact', click on 'The Dynamic Legislative Process'.
> - Then follow the on-screen instructions.
> - This will allow you to follow a presentation which will further explain how a bill becomes a law in Congress.
>
> To watch live coverage of the House and Senate chambers when in session (remember that Washington DC is five hours behind UK time) go to **www. congress.gov**.
>
> - Click on one of the Live Video windows.
> - Then click on 'Watch Live Floor Proceedings'.

Congress and oversight

Having studied Congress's legislative function, we now turn to a second important function of Congress, that of **oversight** of the executive branch. The Constitution does not explicitly grant Congress oversight responsibility. But it does give Congress the power to make laws, and over the years oversight of the executive branch has come to be seen as an implied power of Congress. Members of Congress have to know what is going on in order to make the laws, see how the laws they have passed are working, and amend the laws. And to carry out this oversight, Congress has given itself a number of significant powers: to subpoena documents and testimony; to hold individuals in contempt if they fail to comply with Congress's demands for information; and to make it illegal to lie to Congress. Congressional oversight also includes the Senate's power of confirmation of numerous presidential nominations as well as its power to ratify treaties.

We have already touched on Congress's oversight function when we were considering the work of congressional committees, for it is in the committee rooms of Congress that most of the oversight takes place. The reason for this is fundamental — the absence of the executive branch from the chambers of Congress. It is only in the committee rooms that members of the executive branch can be questioned. And we have also seen that because the standing committees of Congress are permanent policy specialist bodies, they can wield a considerable degree of clout. Some examples of recent committee oversight hearings are given in Table 3.11. But activity is not always the same as achievement. So the question arises as to whether congressional oversight is effective. Does Congress act as a watchdog or merely as a lapdog?

Table 3.11 Examples of standing committee oversight hearings during 2016

Committee	Investigation
House Homeland Security Committee	ISIS in the Pacific: assessing terrorism in Southeast Asia
House Armed Services Committee	US strategy for Syria and Iraq
Senate Judiciary Committee	The need for a Balanced Budget Amendment to the Constitution
Senate Foreign Relations Committee	US–China relations: strategic challenges and opportunities
Senate Commerce, Science and Transportation Committee	The future of self-driving cars

There is quite a bit of agreement — as well as much evidence to support the theory — that congressional oversight of the executive is only really effective when Congress is not controlled by the president's party. Exhibit A in this argument is the fact that almost all modern-day examples of the Senate's rejection of presidential nominations, whether to the executive or judicial branches, have come when the president's party has not controlled the Senate. It was a Democrat Senate in 1987 which rejected Republican president Ronald Reagan's nomination of Robert Bork to the United States Supreme Court. The same was true of the Senate's 1989 rejection of George H.W. Bush's nomination of John Tower to be secretary of defense. In reverse, it was a Republican Senate which, in 1999, rejected both Bill Clinton's nomination of Ronnie White to be a federal trial court judge and his Nuclear Test Ban Treaty.

Exhibit B would be the relationship between Congress and President George W. Bush during his eight-year term. Throughout most of the first six years (2001–06), Bush's Republican Party controlled both houses of Congress. There was a brief 18-month period between June 2001 and December 2002 when the Democrats controlled the Senate, but by only one vote, and much of this period coincided with the President's sky-high approval ratings following the attacks on New York and Washington on 11 September 2001. During these years, congressional oversight was light, if not at times almost non-existent. Democrat Congressman Steny Hoyer pointed out that oversight activity during this period was low even by the standards of other periods of united government. So, for example, in 1993 and 1994 when Democrats controlled Congress during Democrat Bill Clinton's first two years, there were 135 oversight hearings held. In contrast, in 2003 and 2004 the Republican-controlled Congress held only 37 oversight hearings.

But that all changed following the Republicans' loss of control in both houses in the 2006 midterm elections. Indeed, some Republicans even conceded that, had they done a better job of oversight when they held the majority, they might not have been so severely punished by the voters. Once the Democrats took control on Capitol Hill in January 2007, the President found himself facing some very feisty committee chairs. 'We are not a potted plant, watching the administration function,' commented the House Foreign Affairs Committee chairman Tom Lantos. The Senate Appropriations Committee chairman Robert Byrd told the secretaries of state and defense, and the chairman of the Joint Chiefs of Staff in February 2007: 'Congress is not a rubber stamp or a

Former Secretary of State Hillary Clinton prepares to give evidence to the House Select Committee on Benghazi, 22 October 2015

presidential lapdog, obedient and unquestioning. Oversight, oversight, oversight is among our most important responsibilities, and oversight, oversight, oversight has been lacking for far too long.'

Assessing Congress's effectiveness in oversight

So how effective is congressional oversight? To some, congressional oversight — especially at times of **divided government** — is just a polite phrase for trying to embarrass the president and his administration. Republican Senator Jim DeMint of South Carolina described Democrats' oversight of George W. Bush in 2007 as 'political posturing and demagoguing' which 'hasn't really changed anything'. Five years later, the boot was on the other foot when House Republicans organised hearings in no fewer than six committees on the terrorist attack in Benghazi, Libya, in September 2012. Two Senate committees also held hearings. It was estimated that in total, these eight committee hearings interviewed 252 witnesses, published 13 separate reports running to nearly 2,000 pages, and asked over 3,000 questions. The main reason for all this apparent oversight activity — although few Republicans would openly admit it — was that Hillary Clinton, who was serving as secretary of state when the attack took place, was the front-runner in the race to become the Democratic Party's presidential candidate in 2016.

It is worth asking whether all this oversight activity by Congress ultimately produces wiser policies and more effective implementation. According to congressional scholars Norman Ornstein and Thomas Mann (2007), 'While the constitutional arsenal of Congress is powerful, it has limited ability to quickly reverse the course set upon by a determined president.' But, they continue: 'Oversight keeps an administration on its toes; the lack of oversight, and the expectation that there will be none, leads to complacency, arrogance and maladministration.' Ironic, therefore, that the congressional Republicans might be held responsible for some of the failings of George W. Bush's Republican administration, and likewise that congressional Democrats could be blamed for some of Obama's failures, simply because they didn't criticise enough.

The effectiveness of Congress in its oversight role also depends on a number of variables. We have already seen that party control is one such variable. Watch out for the degree to which Republicans in Congress use their oversight powers on the administration of President Trump. Another is the relative popularity of Congress as compared with that of the incumbent president. Over recent years, Congress's standing in the eyes of the public has reached historic lows. This lessens its chances of acting as an effective check on the executive branch. As the president's approval rating ebbs and flows over a four- or eight-year period, this too affects the relationship between Congress and the White House. Congress finds it much easier to curb the actions of an unpopular president than of a popular one. The size of the president's mandate at the last election is therefore another relevant factor. A president who wins by a landslide (Ronald Reagan in 1984) is much less vulnerable than a president who has won with only a minority of the popular vote (Bill Clinton in both 1992 and 1996), or one who actually lost the popular vote, like Donald Trump. Finally, a national crisis — such as 9/11 — will usually strengthen the president's hand at Congress's expense.

Congress and representation

Key term

Representation Either *how* legislators represent their constituents; or *who* the legislators are and whether they are 'representative' of constituents in terms of, for example, gender and race.

The third function of Congress is that of **representation**. First of all, we need to be aware that the term 'representation' can be used in two different ways. When we considered the composition of Congress, we saw that it is not very representative of America in terms of gender or race. This is to use the term 'representative' in terms of *who* represents the electorate. This is called the resemblance model of representation and considers the extent to which the people's representatives resemble them in matters such as gender, race, age, occupation and religion. When considering the composition of Congress we saw that, in this sense, Congress is not very representative of America as a whole. Women are still significantly under-represented in Congress, and Congress is also whiter, older, more professional and more Christian than the nation as a whole.

But one must then ask, 'Why is any of this important? Does it matter if women or other societal groups are not fairly represented?' The short answer is 'Yes, it does matter' — and for two significant reasons. First, fair representation in government and politics upholds the democratic values of fairness and representative democracy. To quote Bill Clinton from 1992, America's government should 'look like America'. And second, it has significant policy implications. Academic studies have shown, for example, that women in government are much more likely to raise and tackle issues concerning civil rights and liberties, education, health and the workplace than are men. Different groups see issues differently. It is not that older people cannot represent the young, or lawyers cannot represent truck drivers, or Catholics cannot represent Muslims. It is just that they will not see the issues in quite the same light, and may indeed differ on what issues they consider worthy of consideration.

Models of representation

Having said all that, however, here we are mainly using the term 'representation' in terms of *how* legislators represent their constituents. In this sense, there are two contrasting models of representation — the delegate model and the trustee model (see Box 3.4). The delegate model would require legislators merely to follow their constituents' preferences, while the trustee model allows legislators to follow their own judgement. Any theory of representation requires us to hold these two seemingly contradictory principles in some sort of creative tension.

House and Senate members place a high premium on representing the interests of their constituents — and with good reasons. First, the Constitution states that they must be residents of the state they represent, so this gives them a good understanding of what 'the folks back home' are saying. Second, a number of states go further by insisting — through the 'locality rule' — that House members reside in the congressional district that they represent. Third, typical House or Senate members do not just reside in the state or district; they will have been born, raised and educated and will have worked there. Fourth, House members are especially careful about constituents' views because they have to face the electors every two years.

Two models of representation

Trustee model

In the trustee model of representation, as advocated by James Madison and Edmund Burke, the legislator (representative) is vested with formal responsibility for making decisions on behalf of others. Such representation is said to be based on 'mature judgement'. This tends to fit well with how most members of Congress see their role. One member of Congress told me: 'I believe in the Burkean model of representation and agree with the Founding Fathers that "the passions of the day should be dampened".' But critics of this model see it as being overly elitist.

Delegate model

A delegate is someone who is chosen to act on behalf of others. They are therefore not a free agent and can exercise little if any private judgement. Legislators who follow this model would base their decisions solely on the wishes of their constituents. This model is therefore linked to the principle of popular sovereignty, in which the people are sovereign. The holding of referendums fits well with this model, for in a referendum the people decide and the representatives merely follow those instructions.

Engagement with constituents

There are various methods by which members of Congress can find out about their constituents' views. While they are in Washington DC, members of Congress keep in touch by phone and e-mail with their offices back in the state or district. They read the local newspapers — these days, usually online. They receive visits, phone calls, letters and e-mails from constituents. They discover what their constituents want by making regular visits back home. The frequency depends on how far 'home' is from Washington DC. Congressman Dan Newhouse (D – Washington), for example, represents a district nearly 3,125 miles (5,000 kilometres) from the nation's capital. A flight from Washington DC to Seattle — the nearest large airport — takes 6–7 hours, the equivalent of flying from London to Boston. Newhouse therefore makes use of the longer recess periods — for example, around Christmas, Easter, Memorial Day (May) and Independence Day (July).

Back home, House and Senate members have a variety of engagements, including:

- holding party and 'town hall' meetings
- conducting 'surgeries' with individual constituents
- making visits around the state/district
- appearing on local radio phone-in programmes
- interviews with representatives of the local media
- addressing groups such as chambers of commerce, professional groups and charity lunches
- visiting local schools, hospitals and businesses

On most issues, constituents' views are likely to be divided, with some in favour and others against. Through town hall meetings and constituency mail, the views of the discontented are more likely to be heard than those of the content. One Democrat Congressman described his constituency mail as 'what

Senator Jerry Moran (left) holds a town hall meeting in Emporia, Kansas, in July 2015

folks don't like from the folks who don't like it'. It is usually not a representative cross-section of constituency opinion. Furthermore, members of Congress are meant to be more than just 'delegates' of their constituents and may need to balance other factors as well as the national good against what is perceived as being merely locally popular or electorally expedient.

Fulfilling the representative function

How do members of Congress fulfil their representative function? There are a number of ways in which they can do this, including through:

- voting on legislation on the floor of the chamber
- membership of standing committees of particular interest to their constituents
- lobbying executive departments and agencies on relevant policies
- performing constituency casework, helping constituents with all kinds of federal matters such as student loans, passport and visa issues, and receipt of federal benefits
- trying to gain money and projects to benefit their states or districts (so-called pork barrel politics)

Key term

Pork barrel A term used to refer to funds provided for superfluous projects in a member of Congress's state or district.

Pork barrel politics was something over which ordinary voters always had ambivalent and somewhat contradictory views. When their own members of Congress engaged in it, they praised it as good constituency service. But when other members of Congress indulged in it, they criticised it as wasteful government spending. Having peaked in 2006, pork barrel politics has tailed off to virtually zero in recent years.

As pork barrel politics was fading, what one might call 'e-democracy' was increasing. Members of Congress now make frequent use of online communication tools to stay in touch with their constituents, including televised town hall meetings, video conferencing, posting films of their activity on YouTube, and blogging with constituents. You will also find many members nowadays taking to Facebook, Twitter and Instagram to show a more personal side to constituents — in some unfortunate cases, rather too personal.

It would be wrong to think that members of Congress perform these tasks merely to enhance their chances of re-election or to reduce the chance of receiving a challenger in the congressional primary. Many, if not most, members of Congress are motivated by a deep commitment to public service and genuinely want to do all they can to improve the lives of their constituents.

Assessing Congress's effectiveness in representation

We have already seen that Congress is not all that effective at representation in terms of the resemblance model. It's certainly more effective in this sense than it used to be, but it still has some way to go to fulfil its representative function in this sense.

How effective is Congress in terms of *how* members of Congress represent their constituents? Certainly on issues that significantly affect a majority of their constituents, members of Congress will be very assiduous in performing their representative function. This is especially true for House members, whose two-year terms of office mean such frequent elections. Constituents may have short memories — but not that short. But it also needs to be remembered that on most issues, members of Congress will have people on both sides of the argument among their constituents. And even finding out what the majority opinion of one's constituents is on any given issue will often be something of a challenge.

> ### Key term
>
> Gridlock Failure to get action on policy proposals and legislation in Congress. Gridlock is thought to be exacerbated by divided government and partisanship.

Debate

Is Congress the 'broken branch'?

Yes

- In terms of legislation, too often characterised by gridlock and inaction
- Lack of bipartisanship and compromise
- Senate action often frustrated by filibustering or the threat of it
- Confirmation of presidential appointments often degenerates into partisan point scoring
- Too many uncompetitive seats pushes parties to ideological extremes
- Foreign policy checks on the president often ineffective (e.g. declaring war)

No

- Congress passes hundreds of laws each year
- Strong on constituency representation and looking after 'the folks back home'
- Congress alone does not cause gridlock in government
- Polarisation in Congress is merely reflective of a polarised country
- Has successfully called presidents and their administrations to account
- Slowness in Congress is often because of what the Founding Fathers wrote in the Constitution

Voting in Congress

One way in which members of Congress fulfil their representative function is in the votes they cast on the floor of the House or the Senate. House and Senate members are called upon to cast a large number of votes each year (see Table 3.12). Indeed, in 2007, members of the House of Representatives voted 1,186 times, beating the previous high of 885 set in 1995. In just four days between 5 and 8 May 2008, members of the House of Representatives were asked to vote on the floor 66 times, including 28 times on one day — 7 May. Having said that, votes in the Senate in 2016 fell to a remarkably low figure (163) as the Republican majority sat on its hands and President Obama's second term wound its way through its lame duck period.

Table 3.12 Recorded votes in Congress, 2007–16

	2007	2008	2009	2010	2011	2012	2013	2014	2015	2016
House	1,186	690	991	664	949	659	641	564	705	622
Senate	442	215	397	299	235	251	291	366	339	163

When they do vote, members of Congress might be voting on budgets, amendments to bills, final passage of bills, bills from conference committees, constitutional amendments or — in the Senate — on treaties or appointments made by the president. They will probably be rushing to the floor to cast their vote, having just broken off a committee hearing or a meeting with constituents or staff.

Part of the vote tally board above the press gallery in the House of Representatives

Recorded votes in the House of Representatives are nowadays taken 'by electronic device', where members have 15 minutes to cast their votes. These were introduced to cut down the time it took to read out the names of the 435 members, which is how the recorded votes used to be carried out in the House. Entering the House chamber, each member places an electronic card into a small machine affixed to the back of the bench. As the member votes by pressing one of the buttons on the machine, a coloured light — green for 'yes', red for 'no', orange for 'present' — appears next to their name on the tally board displayed on the wall above the press gallery.

What factors affect voting in Congress?

There are six factors to consider. We have already considered the role played by constituents, so here we take a look at the other five. The relative importance of each factor varies from one member of Congress to another and from one vote to another. It may also be true that a congress(wo)man or senator's vote might be the result of multiple factors.

Political party

Political party is one of a number of determinants of voting in Congress. For some members, on some issues, it may be the most important determinant. A party unity vote — often simply called a party vote — sometimes occurs in Congress when the issue is a contentious, ideological matter, such as civil liberties, taxation, gun control, abortion or school prayers. An example is given in Box 3.5. In this particular vote all except two Republicans voted 'yes' and all except four Democrats voted 'no' — clearly a party vote.

The parties have few 'sticks' or 'carrots' to encourage party voting. Sticks such as the threat of de-selection do not work in a system in which voters decide on candidates in primary elections. Carrots such as executive branch posts do not work in a system of 'separated institutions', in which posts in the executive and legislature do not overlap.

Box 3.5

Example of party (unity) vote in the House of Representatives

Federal Information Systems Safeguard Act (2016)
This bill established government operations and personnel laws concerning the security of federal information systems, restrictions on access to websites, probationary periods, the senior executive service, employee use of official time, and the maintenance of Internal Revenue Service records.

- Vote on final passage in House of Representatives, 7 July 2016
- Yes: 241; No: 181
- Republicans: 237–2
- Democrats: 4–179

Despite this very low threshold for qualifying as a party vote, around 15 years or so ago only around 45 to 50% of votes in each chamber were party votes. But the last decade has seen a significant increase in party votes in Congress. In 2010, the Senate recorded its highest percentage of party votes in over half-a-century — 78.6% — and the following year the House of Representatives recorded its highest ever percentage of party votes at 75.8%. In 2013 both houses recorded party voting in just under 70% of all recorded votes. This shows that party cohesion has certainly increased significantly since 2002, when both houses recorded figures in the low 40s.

It is important to remember, however, that party labels do not necessarily mean voting together. Conservative Democrats, like Congressman Jim Cooper of Tennessee and Senator Heidi Heitkamp of North Dakota, often vote with Republicans. Likewise, moderate Republicans, such as Congressman Frank LoBiondo of New Jersey and Senator Susan Collins of Maine, often vote with Democrats. Although the ideological spread within each party is not as wide as it used to be three or four decades ago, both parties in both houses do still include both ideological and more centrist members. We shall have more to say about the role of parties in Congress later in this chapter.

The administration

The term 'the administration' refers to members of the executive branch, including the president. Much legislation voted on in Congress has been initiated by the administration.

Cabinet members — the heads of the 15 executive departments — have a keen interest in the passage of legislation affecting their policy areas. So members of the administration — from the departments and agencies as well as the White House itself — keep in contact with members of Congress through phone calls as well as meetings in an attempt to persuade them to cast their votes in certain ways. They talk with members of the relevant committees as well as with staff on Capitol Hill. Often the White House gets involved through the Office of Legislative Affairs as well as directly in the person of the president (see Chapter 4).

Any persuasion needs to be regular, reciprocal and bipartisan. It is important that members of Congress are approached not only just before an important vote comes up. It is important, too, that those from the departments and the White House are willing to do favours in return, offering a two-way street of mutual cooperation. All this needs to be done with members from both parties. For an administration to talk only with members of its own party is usually a recipe for disaster. Success tends to occur in Congress when there is a bipartisan coalition.

Pressure groups

Pressure groups use a number of different ways to try to influence how members of Congress vote (see Chapter 7). They make direct contact with members as well as with their staff. They attempt to generate public support for their position. They make visits and phone calls, provide evidence to committees, organise rallies, demonstrations and petition drives, and engage in fundraising and campaigning. Money raised is used to fund politicians who support their cause and to seek to defeat those who do not. Certain policy areas have seen significant pressure group activity in recent years, including the environment, abortion, gun control, healthcare and welfare reform.

Colleagues and staff

Because of the huge numbers of votes that members of Congress have to cast, they cannot personally know the details of all of them. They therefore rely on others to help them make a decision on a vote.

Other colleagues can be helpful. A congressman might turn to fellow members of the same chamber and of the same party who share the same philosophy and views. Some senior members act as mentors to newer members, offering advice and suggestions on votes. In the House, one could look out fellow members of the state delegation, especially those from neighbouring districts. Members of the relevant committee can be a help — especially those who chair committees or who are the ranking minority members.

Senior staff members — the chief of staff or legislative director — at the weekly staff meeting in a Capitol Hill office of a Republican House member, might be heard telling their Congressman: 'You'll want to support this', or 'This plays well in the district'. One Republican House member talked thus of the importance of his senior staff:

> You can always tell those who don't know how things work here on Capitol Hill. When they leave my office after a meeting, they thank me and then hand me copies of all their papers so that I can follow up on whatever it was we were talking about. They don't know how things work. Those who *do* know how things work thank me and then give the papers to *my staff*. I remember getting an invitation from someone in the [Bill] Clinton administration and the invitation stated: 'Members only. No staff.' Who do they think it is that I talk with just before I make a decision on how to vote?

Personal beliefs

On certain votes, House or Senate members may vote according to their own personal beliefs. Issues such as abortion, capital punishment, taxation (increases or cuts), federal subsidies and defence spending are likely to bring a member's own personal philosophy to the fore. There are, for example, members of Congress who will never vote for a federal subsidy to any industry or group, while others will never vote to deny life to a fellow human being, whether through capital punishment or war.

Activity

- Go to the Center on Congress website at **centeroncongress.org**.
- Click on 'Learn About Congress'.
- Click on 'How Does Congress Work?'
- Under the heading 'Interact', click on 'How a Member Decides to Vote'.
- This will allow you to simulate the steps towards a vote in the House of Representatives on a Flag Desecration Amendment to the US Constitution. Follow the on-screen instructions to participate in the simulation.

Parties in Congress

Party leadership

Party leadership in Congress is affected by the constitutional principles of separation of powers, federalism and bicameralism. Separation of powers means that party leaders in Congress may hold little sway down the other end of Pennsylvania Avenue — in the White House — even when the president is a member of their party. Federalism means that party leaders in Congress have little or no control over what is going in the 50 state parties across the country. Bicameralism means that party leaders operate only within their own chamber and may not always be singing from the same song sheet as their counterpart in the other chamber.

In both chambers, the members of each party elect a leader who is designated as majority leader or minority leader depending on the party's status in that chamber. But in the House of Representatives there is also the Speaker, who is elected by the entire house. For obvious reasons, the Speaker is always drawn from the majority party and hence the House majority leader serves as the Speaker's top lieutenant, running the chamber's day-to-day business. The Speaker meanwhile operates as a partisan as well as an organisational figure with such powers as referring bills to committees, appointing the majority members of the House Rules Committee, interpreting and enforcing the rules of the House, and appointing select committee and conference committee chairs. When the Speaker is not from the president's party, they may become a kind of 'leader of the official opposition', acting as a spokesperson for the party not currently controlling the White House. Republican Speaker Paul Ryan found himself playing this role to Democratic president Barack Obama throughout 2016.

In the Senate, there is also the post of president pro tempore, a figurehead position that by custom goes to the longest-serving member of the majority party. Their main role is to preside over the Senate when the vice president is not present. But in practice, the most junior members of the majority party are usually to be seen presiding over the Senate's daily business.

Standing committee chairs, party whips and chairs of various party, policy and campaign committees would also be loosely regarded as part of the party leadership in Congress.

Increased partisanship

Partisanship in Congress is a relatively recent phenomenon. The conventional wisdom about political parties in Congress used to be that they were 'like two bottles with different labels, both empty' (Lord Bryce, 1910). But writing just a decade ago, Ronald Brownstein (2007) had this to say of the new era of what he termed 'hyper-partisanship' in US politics:

> The defining characteristics of this age are greater unity **within** the parties and more distinct conflicts **between** them. On almost every major issue, the distance between the two parties has widened, even as dissent within the parties has diminished.

Votes in Congress used frequently to involve one group of Democrats and Republicans voting against another group of Democrats and Republicans. Looking at this more closely, votes often comprised Republicans joining with conservative Democrats on one side, with liberal Democrats and moderate Republicans on the other side. But over the past decade, conservative Democrats and moderate Republicans — the centrists of Congress — have become increasingly rare breeds. Look what happened in the 2010 midterm elections. Of the nine centrists in the Senate whose seats were up for re-election in 2010, four chose to retire, two were defeated in primaries, a further two were defeated in the general election, and the other — Robert Byrd of West Virginia — died before Election Day. It was much the same in the House of Representatives. Of the 60 most conservative Democrats in

Senators Kirsten Gillibrand (D–NY) and Pat Roberts (R–KS) — respectively the most liberal and most conservative members of the Senate in 2015

the House during the 111th Congress (2009–10), 37 (62%) lost in the 2010 midterms, and of the five most moderate House Republicans, only one was re-elected.

One of the simplest ways to understand what has happened to the parties in Congress is to take two snapshots of the US Senate: in 1982 and 2015. Back in 1982, one of the most liberal Senate Democrats was Ted Kennedy of Massachusetts. Meanwhile, the most conservative of the Senate Democrats was Ed Zorinsky of Nebraska. They rarely voted together, yet they were both Democrats. Among Republicans in the Senate in 1982, the most liberal or 'moderate' Republican was Lowell Weicker of Connecticut. In the same party was arch-conservative Strom Thurmond of South Carolina. Again, Weicker and Thurmond had little in common — except they were both Republicans. Between Weicker (the most liberal Republican) and Zorinsky (the most conservative Democrat) were 35 Democrats and 23 Republicans. In other words, 35 Democrats were more conservative than Weicker and 23 Republicans were more liberal than Zorinsky. Republican Strom Thurmond was more likely to vote with Democrat Ed Zorinsky than with fellow Republican Lowell Weicker. Likewise, Democrat Ted Kennedy was more likely to vote with Republican Lowell Weicker than with fellow Democrat Ed Zorinsky. As Figure 3.5 shows, there was a huge ideological overlap between the two parties. The differences *within* the parties were far greater than the differences *between* them.

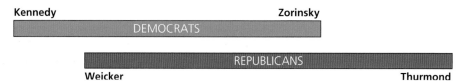

Kennedy   Zorinsky

DEMOCRATS

REPUBLICANS

Weicker   Thurmond

Figure 3.5 Ideological overlap in the Senate, 1982

In 2015, the most liberal Senate Democrat was Kirsten Gillibrand of New York and the most conservative of the Senate Democrats was Heidi Heitkamp of North Dakota. Among Republicans in the Senate in 2015, the most liberal Republican was Susan Collins of Maine and the most conservative of the

Senate Republicans was Pat Roberts of Kansas. Between Collins (the most liberal Republican) and Heitkamp (the most conservative Democrat) there was not a single senator. In other words, all 54 Republicans were more conservative than Heidi Heitkamp and all 45 Democrats were more liberal than Susan Collins. As Figure 3.6 shows, there was absolutely no ideological overlap at all between the two parties. The differences *between* the parties are now greater than the differences *within*. Both parties have become more ideologically cohesive and distinct: the Democrats have become a more distinctly and cohesive liberal party; the Republicans have become a more distinctly and cohesive conservative party. It is hardly surprising that, as a result of this ideological sorting of the parties in Congress, there has been an increase in partisanship and polarisation.

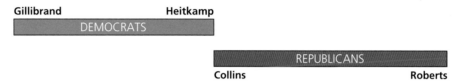

Figure 3.6 Ideological separation in the Senate, 2015

A factor which has led to the increased partisanship in Congress has been the disappearance of the centrist members of both parties: that is, members whose voting is more towards the political centre — conservative Democrats and liberal Republicans. It isn't just that the same people are voting in different ways, although there may be some of that, but that the people in Congress are different — more ideological, more partisan. Again, this is most clearly seen in the Senate. Over the past few election cycles, both parties in the Senate have lost prominent centrists and their places have been taken by far more ideological members. So, for example, in 2010 a centrist Democrat (and former moderate Republican) Arlen Specter of Pennsylvania was replaced in the Senate by conservative Republican Pat Toomey. The American Conservative Union, which awarded Specter a 43% rating for his voting record in the Senate in 2010, awarded his replacement Pat Toomey a 93% rating.

Debate

Do parties play an important role in Congress?

Yes
- Leadership in Congress is run by the parties.
- Committees in Congress are organised by the parties.
- With increased partisanship, party discipline is much stronger in Congress than it used to be.
- Party is an important determinant of voting in Congress.
- It is almost impossible to be elected to Congress without being a major party candidate.

No
- Views of constituents can often outweigh party considerations — especially for House members.
- Parties have no control over candidate selection.
- Both parties are made up of ideological factions that compete with party cohesion.
- The executive branch has few 'sticks or carrots' with which to incentivise party discipline.
- Congressional leadership, likewise, is fairly impotent in the face of opposition.

In the House of Representatives, partisanship has also been increased by the way district boundaries have been redrawn. This occurs after each ten-yearly census. In many states, it is the state legislators who are the main players in this redistricting process. What they have done in many states is to draw up districts which are safe seats for one or other party. Take California, for example. Until 2011, redistricting was controlled by the state legislators. In the 2010 midterm elections in California, the average vote for winners of the state's 53 House seats was 66%. The politicians in the state legislature deliberately drew the boundaries so as to bring about these results. If one defines a competitive district as one in which the margin of victory is 10 percentage points or less, then only 4 of the 53 California House races were competitive in 2010. The other 49 California House members therefore had little or no incentive to talk or vote in a bipartisan fashion. All they had to do was vote in a way to please their own party supporters. Hence they voted in a highly partisan fashion. After California voters took away the redistricting power from state legislators in 2011 and gave it to an independent commission, House races in California became more competitive. In 2012 the number of competitive races in the state went up from 4 to 12.

Congressional caucuses

Strictly speaking there are just four congressional caucuses — the House Republican caucus, the House Democratic caucus, and the two parallel caucuses in the Senate. In this sense a congressional caucus is the collection of members of either major party elected to either the House or the Senate. The Democrats in both chambers refer to their groups as the Democratic caucus; the Republicans' name is the Republican Conference. It is these groups that, for example, elect the majority and minority leaders and the party whips in each house. They perform organisational functions as well as meeting regularly to formulate legislative strategy.

But these four party caucuses are not monolithic. Over time, and especially in the House with its larger membership, other groups or caucuses — officially called congressional member organisations — have grown up to represent smaller but cohesive groups within each chamber, often based on ideological, regional, ethnic or economic interests (see Box 3.6). In this sense, these congressional caucuses are a growing rival to the parties' formal leadership and have increasingly become a cue in congressional voting.

Congressional caucuses have three main functions:

- Educational — caucuses provide information to members on proposed legislation and may offer policy briefings as well as publishing briefing papers.
- Agenda setting — caucus members may work together to boost the chances of their particular issue getting on to the congressional legislative agenda. They might co-sponsor legislation, circulate 'Dear Colleague' letters to drum up support, meet with the party leadership to press their cause, or lobby relevant committee members.
- Encouraging support for their proposals in votes on the floor of each chamber.

Box 3.6

Examples of congressional caucuses

Blue Dog Coalition

- A group of mainly southern House Democrats who are fiscally conservative
- Formed 1995 in the wake of significant Republican gains
- Gives a voice to conservative, moderate, centrist Democrats
- Influential in passing welfare reform (1995–96)
- From 37 members in 2003–04, had fallen to just 18 in 2017–18

Congressional Black Caucus

- Formed in 1971 exclusively for African-American members of both houses
- Originally had 13 members
- In 2017–18 had 47 members — 2 Senate Democrats, 44 House Democrats, 1 House Republican (Mia Love, Utah)
- Although it claims to be bipartisan, only five black Republicans have ever joined the CBC
- Currently Senator Tim Scott (R-SC) is not a member

Congressional Hispanic Caucus

- Formed in 1976 to support policies that benefit the Hispanic and Latino communities
- Began as a bipartisan group, but the Republican members left in the late 1990s and formed their own caucus — the Congressional Hispanic Conference

House Freedom Caucus

- Founded in 2015 as a group of around 40 conservative House Republicans
- Many also belong to the Republican Study Committee, a much larger conservative Republican caucus in the House with over 170 members
- Supports 'limited government, the Constitution and the rule of law, and policies that promote the liberty, safety and prosperity of all Americans'
- Closely allied with the Tea Party movement
- Members of the caucus were at the centre of the movement to force House Speaker John Boehner to resign in September 2015
- Paul Ryan announced his willingness to stand to replace Boehner as Speaker only after the Freedom Caucus officially endorsed him

The Tuesday Group

- A group of around 50 moderate House Republicans
- Founded in 1995 following the Republican takeover of the House and to counter-balance a large number of conservative Republicans who were newly elected to the House in the 1994 midterm elections
- Its predecessor was called the Wednesday Group, which was founded in the early 1960s
- Closely allied with another caucus — the Republican Mainstream Partnership — of moderate Republicans drawn from both chambers
- In 2007, the group set up its own political action committee (PAC) to help members improve their chances of re-election

Comparing Congress with the UK Parliament

Structural differences

The fundamental difference between a presidential and a parliamentary system is the relationship between the legislature and the executive. So the best way to understand the differences between the US Congress and the UK Parliament is to start with the geography of Washington and London.

- In Washington, the Capitol — the building that houses the Senate and the House of Representatives — and the White House are both imposing buildings that stand just over a mile apart on the same thoroughfare. The

White House is just 16 blocks down Pennsylvania Avenue from Capitol Hill. Commentators often refer to the president and Congress as being at 'both ends of the Avenue', although strictly speaking Pennsylvania Avenue stretches well to the east of the Capitol and well to the west of the White House.

■ In London, the Palace of Westminster — a grand term if ever there was one — which houses the House of the Lords and the House of Commons, dominates the Westminster scenery. The prime minister's residence and office space at 10 Downing Street is no more than a fairly modest terraced house in a Whitehall cul-de-sac. What this tells us is that while in Washington Congress is an equal partner in a system of 'separated institutions sharing powers', in London Parliament dominates in a system based on the doctrine of parliamentary sovereignty.

There are therefore some fundamental structural differences between Congress and Parliament. Members of Congress are constitutionally prohibited from simultaneously holding office in the executive branch. Likewise, the president and vice president are selected independently of Congress for fixed terms of office and are removable by Congress only by impeachment. All other executive branch members, including the president's cabinet, are entirely separate from Congress. This means that the administration cannot fall because the president loses a vote in Congress. Even were the president to be impeached by the House and then found guilty by the Senate and removed from office, the vice president would automatically step up to replace him. This means that members of Congress from the president's party do not feel under any obligation necessarily to support the president's policies.

As Cal Jillson (2016) expresses it:

> Because the separation of powers system is designed to uncouple the fate of executives and legislators, divided government is not just possible, it is common, [and] in the minds of many Americans, is not a bad thing. Rather it is just another way to separate, check and balance political power.

In contrast, in the UK 'the stability of the government hinges on the strength and cohesion of the majority party or coalition' (Jillson, 2016). The government can fall by a vote in the House of Commons. These are important structural differences between Washington and Westminster that account for many of the contrasts between Congress and Parliament.

Composition of Congress and Parliament

The composition of Congress and Parliament can be understood by seeing how the two institutions reflect the different cultural backgrounds of the two countries. Congress is very much a reflection of its federal system of government. Representation is based on the 50 states — in the Senate, by equal representation regardless of population; in the House, by representation proportional to each state's population. But every constituency bears the name of a state. In the Senate, Ben Sasse is the senator from Nebraska; in the House Adrian Smith is the member for the third district of Nebraska.

But in Parliament, MPs represent constituencies based mostly around the historic counties, cities and towns of the UK — with MPs, for example, representing South Suffolk, Birmingham Edgbaston, and Colchester. The Suffolk town of Ipswich, for example, has sent a representative to Parliament since 1386. Meanwhile, the House of Lords still reflects the culture of a nation that dates back centuries to a time when lords, barons, earls and knights — and bishops of the Church of England — held considerable sway over vast swathes of the country, and when the hereditary principle, and the established church, were dominant. Thus Congress and Parliament still reflect the two significantly different cultures of the two nations.

Lincoln, the oldest constituency in the UK having been established in 1265, returned Karen Lee, Labour, as its MP in 2017

Powers and functions of Congress and Parliament

Legislation

In terms of their legislative powers, whereas the two houses in Congress enjoy equal power, in Parliament it is the House of Commons that dominates (see Table 3.13). Whereas in Congress both houses must agree on the final version of a bill before it is passed to the president for signing, in Parliament the House of Lords can propose amendments to legislation but in the end the Commons will usually get its way. And if needed, the House of Commons can use its power under the Parliament Act of 1949 to override the objections of the Lords.

Table 3.13 Legislative function of Congress and Parliament compared

Congress	Parliament
No government programme of legislation exists	A government programme of legislation dominates the agenda
Level of party discipline is lower	Higher levels of party discipline
Thousands of bills are introduced in any one session	A limited number of bills are introduced in any one session
Individual members introduce numerous pieces of legislation	Individual members introduce few pieces of legislation
Few of these bills are passed into law	Most bills are passed into law
Committee stage comes before the floor debate	Committee stage comes after the second reading
Standing committees are permanent and policy specialist	Standing committees are non-permanent and non-specialist
Bills are usually considered by both houses concurrently	Bills are considered by the two houses consecutively
The two chambers have equal powers	The lower chamber dominates
The president has a significant veto power	The royal assent is no longer withheld

Furthermore, because of the structural differences we have just outlined, Congress is a *real* legislature while Parliament is not. According to Philip Norton (1985), Parliament merely 'legitimises legislation'. Or to paraphrase Andrew Heywood (2002): legislation is passed *by* Congress, but it is merely passed *through* Parliament. In the view of the former clerk of the House of Commons Robert Rogers, bills in Parliament 'are not "draft legislation", they are what the government wants — the government's shopping list'. In Congress, the president's administration can afford no shopping lists, just wish lists. In Parliament, the Queen's speech — written for her by her government — states that 'My government will...'. In Congress, the president's State of the Union Address *asks* Congress if it would be good enough to *consider* his ideas.

Oversight

The differences between Congress and Parliament in their oversight of the executive branch are largely a consequence of the structural differences between the two systems of government. In the USA, Congress and the executive are entirely separate; in the UK, Parliament and the executive are intertwined. In the USA, the administration survives regardless of anything that does — or does not — occur in Congress. In the UK, the survival of the government usually depends on its maintaining the support of the House of Commons.

The extent of oversight is also affected by the structural differences between the two systems. So, for example, the fact that the Senate has oversight of all judicial and numerous executive appointments within the federal government gives Congress a reach in oversight quite unknown to the UK Parliament. Likewise, the Senate's power to ratify treaties gives another significant extension of its oversight powers that Parliament does not have. In addition, the House of Representatives' power to impeach any public official within the federal government, and the Senate's power to try such cases of impeachment, gives yet another arm of oversight unknown to Parliament. Congress also has more control over the budget than does Parliament.

Finally, Congress has the specific power to declare war, although this has not been used in over seven decades. In the UK, the power to commit armed troops to conflict abroad is one of the remaining royal prerogatives — that is, powers that are derived from the Crown rather than from Parliament. But under David Cameron's premiership, the power of Parliament in this area was significantly enhanced and it would now be politically very difficult for future governments to take any significant military action without prior specific approval from Parliament.

Table 3.14 Methods of oversight in Congress and Parliament compared

Congress	Parliament
Standing committee hearings	Question Time (including Prime Minister's Question Time)
Select committee hearings	Select committee hearings
Confirmation of appointments (Senate)	Liaison Committee hearings
Ratification of treaties (Senate)	Correspondence with ministers
Impeachment, trial, removal from office	Tabling of early day motions
	Policy debates
	Office of the Ombudsman
	Votes of no confidence

But not only do the structural differences between the two systems affect the extent of oversight; they also determine the different methods by which such oversight is conducted (see Table 3.14). Because of the strict separation of powers between the legislature and the executive, there can be no face-to-face oversight of the executive branch conducted on the floor of either the House or the Senate. There is, therefore, no congressional equivalent to Parliament's Question Time for the simple reason that there would be no executive members present to give the answers.

All such face-to-face oversight can take place only in the committee rooms of Congress. That is where executive branch officials are summoned to appear to answer questions of either standing or select committee members. But even then it is a tradition that presidents are not summoned to appear before congressional committees because they are not answerable to them. In a presidential system, the president is answerable directly to the people — those who elected him. Only three incumbent presidents have chosen to give evidence in person to a congressional committee (see Table 3.15), the last being President Gerald Ford on 17 October 1974.

Table 3.15 Incumbent presidents who have given testimony to congressional committees

President	Year	Committee	Subject of testimony
Abraham Lincoln	1862	House Judiciary Committee	Premature leak to the press of his State of the Union Address
Woodrow Wilson	1919	Senate Foreign Relations Committee*	Treaty of Versailles and the League of Nations
Gerald Ford	1974	Subcommittee on Criminal Justice, House Judiciary Committee	Reasons for his pardon of former president Richard Nixon

*Testimony taken at the White House

In Parliament, opportunities for oversight abound. These opportunities have been significantly strengthened and extended with the development of a robust select committee system over the past two decades. MPs also have quite a galaxy of oversight methods which they can use (see Table 3.14). But activity does not always equal effectiveness. Most observers conclude that Parliament is controlled by the government more than government is controlled and checked by Parliament.

Representation

When it comes to members of Congress and members of Parliament fulfilling their representative functions, then the rational choice approach helps us to understand the subtle differences between the two and to see the way self-interest goes some way to shaping the way legislators in the two systems fulfil their representational function.

Gaining re-election is obviously an important priority for any elected official — unless they hold on to their job, they will not be able to achieve any of their desired policy objectives. So who controls the electoral destiny of legislators in Washington and at Westminster? In Congress, constituents play a much more important role than party. Indeed, one could argue that party plays little or no role at all, other than providing a voting cue by virtue of the party label. It will be disgruntled constituents who might decide to back a challenger to the incumbent member of Congress in a congressional primary, as voters in Florida's third congressional district did in 2016 and thereby unseated 12-term Democrat Corrine Brown. But for members of the UK House of Commons, it is the party that performs the function of candidate selection. Before the 2015 general election, Conservative Party members in the South Suffolk constituency deselected their sitting MP Tim Yeo, who had represented the constituency for over 30 years. So whereas Brown was felled by her constituents, Yeo was felled by his party.

Legislators in both Congress and Parliament will also be mindful of the frequency with which they will face their constituents. This is another structural difference. Therefore members of the US House of Representatives who have to face their voters every two years will probably need to be more attentive to their constituents than members of the UK House of Commons or their Senate colleagues who respectively serve five- and six-year terms. In January 2010, the House Majority Whip James Clyburn criticised his colleagues in the Senate, saying that 'they tend to see themselves as a House of Lords and don't seem to understand that those of us who go out there every two years stay in touch with the American people, and we tend to respond to them a little better'.

Comparing each of the two houses

Both Congress and Parliament are bicameral. But one could say that this is about as far as the similarities go. Whereas Congress is composed of two mostly equal chambers — although, as we saw earlier, the upper house (the Senate) might be regarded as more powerful and prestigious — Parliament is dominated by the lower house, the House of Commons. Of course, this has not always been the case and until the passage of the 1911 Parliament Act both houses enjoyed equal power. Indeed, for roughly three-quarters of the nineteenth century, the prime minister was drawn from the House of Lords. But with the extension of the franchise in both countries through the nineteenth and early twentieth centuries, both nations had to face the issue of how much power it was still appropriate for an unelected second chamber to hold. The different ways in which they solved this problem tell us a good deal about the impact that a nation's culture — its shared beliefs and attitudes — can have on its government and politics.

In the UK system, Parliament is dominated by the House of Commons

The bicameral system under which the UK is governed today dates back to medieval times when knights representing the shires and boroughs — in the House of Commons — began to meet separately from the church hierarchy and nobles — in the House of Lords. The House of Lords was initially the more powerful house, but that changed after the Civil War and the country's 11 years without a monarch. After the hereditary House of Lords thwarted the will of the elected House of Commons over the 1909 budget, Asquith's Liberal government set about removing significant powers from the upper house by the 1911 Parliament Act. Three decades later, Attlee's Labour government went even further. The hereditary peers remained, but they lost a good deal of their power. A century later, 92 hereditary peers and 26 bishops of the Church of England still remain as members of the House of Lords.

The US Constitution begins with the words 'We the People'

But the USA dealt with the problem in the opposite way. Rather than having its powers stripped away, the indirectly elected Senate was given a directly elected mandate by the passage of the Seventeenth Amendment in 1913. The following year saw the first direct elections to the Senate. The solution was the one you would expect in a nation whose culture embraces the concept of popular sovereignty, and whose Constitution not only begins with the words 'We the People' but also contains a prohibition on 'titles of nobility'. A directly elected Senate and an appointed, and still partly hereditary, House of Lords provide one of the clearest illustrations of the different cultures of these two democracies.

Table 3.16 Comparing strengths and weaknesses of the lower chambers

US House of Representatives	UK House of Commons
Strengths	**Strengths**
■ Has initiative power on all money bills	■ Powers
■ Draws up articles of impeachment	■ Presence of the executive
■ Power of standing committees	■ Power of backbenchers
■ Strong constituency links because of two-year term	■ Select committees
	■ Prime Minister's Question Time
Weaknesses	**Weaknesses**
■ Executive branch members can appear only in committees, not on the floor	■ Party strengths unreflective of votes at general election
■ President rarely if ever gives direct evidence	■ 'Punch and Judy' politics, especially at Question Time
■ Shares legislative power with the Senate	■ Overly dominated by the government
■ Short election cycle	■ Unrepresentative in terms of gender
■ Gridlock, partisanship and possibility of divided government	■ Strong parties can mean weak constituency representation

Table 3.17 Comparing strengths and weaknesses of the upper chambers

US Senate	UK House of Lords
Strengths	**Strengths**
■ Exclusive power over confirmation of appointments ■ Exclusive power over treaty ratification ■ Sole power to try cases of impeachment ■ Regarded as recruitment pool for the presidency and vice presidency ■ Six-year terms ■ Equal power in legislation with the House	■ Membership is in some ways more representative of UK society ■ Expertise and experience of members ■ Lack of strict party discipline ■ Quality of debate ■ Members not subject to the whim of constituency pressures ■ Continuity
Weaknesses	**Weaknesses**
■ Executive branch members can appear only in committees, not on the floor ■ President rarely if ever gives direct evidence ■ Shares legislative power with the House ■ Gridlock, partisanship and possibility of divided government	■ Lack of a democratic mandate ■ Has mostly only delaying powers regarding legislation ■ Seen as a chamber of political failures and retirees ■ Government often lacks a majority ■ Presence of Anglican bishops

Table 3.18 Comparing Congress and Parliament: similarities and differences

Similarities	Differences
Both are bicameral	Congress: both houses elected; Parliament: only one house elected
Different parties may control each house	Congress: two equal houses; Parliament: lower house dominates
President/prime minister's party may not control both houses	Congress: only two parties represented; Parliament: multiple parties, especially in the House of Commons
Both houses in both institutions have a role in passing legislation and in oversight of the executive	Congress: executive branch excluded; Parliament: executive branch included
Much work done away from the chambers in committees	Terms of office: 2 years in House of Representatives; 5 years in House Commons; 6 years in Senate; lifetime in House of Lords
Oversight function conducted by the standing committees in Congress and by the select committees of the House of Commons	Size of upper houses: Senate — 100; House of Lords — around 800 (lower house also significantly larger in UK)
All elections are on first-past-the-post system	Senate has oversight powers unknown to the House of Lords (e.g. confirmation of appointments)
	Each American has three representatives in Congress (two in the Senate, one in the House); each British person has only one representative in Parliament

When comparing the strengths and weaknesses of the respective lower and upper chambers (Tables 3.16 and 3.17), it is important to remember that some factors may be argued as being both potential strengths and weaknesses. For example, it is doubtless a strength of the Senate that it has the power to confirm numerous presidential appointments, but the partisan way that process often occurs is a weakness. It is doubtless a strength of the House of Commons that it can call the prime minister to account in person on a weekly basis, but the fact that Prime Minister's Question Time often descends into what could be described as 'Punch and Judy' politics is a weakness.

The Senate and the House of Lords have at least one element in common: each includes a significant number of former members of the lower house. But the reasons for the movement from the lower to the upper houses are quite different. In Congress, moving from the House to the Senate is a much-sought-after promotion. At each election cycle, a significant number of House members seek election to the Senate. Indeed, former House members make up around half the membership of the Senate. But in Parliament, movement from the Commons to the Lords indicates either political retirement or failure — or both. Most self-respecting MPs try to avoid it for as long as possible. The difference in status between the two chambers in their respective systems is shown by this curious statistic, that only once — in 1880 — was an incumbent member of the House of Representatives elected as president, and that's even longer ago than when the last peer served as UK prime minister.

It is often suggested that the office of the British prime minister has, over recent decades, been 'presidentialised'. This is a highly contentious claim that we will examine in the following chapter. But in one important respect, it would be possible to say that the UK Parliament has been 'congressionalised' by the introduction and development of a powerful set of department-related select committees in the House of Commons. In their oversight role, they have come to mirror in both expertise and political clout the standing committees of Congress.

So to conclude, Congress illustrates the dispersed power within the American political system. In Congress, power is dispersed between the two chambers and, within each chamber, among the multitudinous committees. Parliament, on the other hand, illustrates the concentration of authority within the British political system. As Malcolm Shaw (2013) concluded, 'Parliamentary authority is concentrated in one chamber, on one side of that chamber, on the front bench of that side, and to an increasing extent in one man [or woman] on that bench — the prime minister.'

References

Brownstein, R., *The Second American Civil War: How Extreme Partisanship Has Paralyzed Washington and Polarized America*, Penguin, 2007.

Carr, R.K., *Essentials of American Democracy*, Dryden Press, 1974.

Denenberg, R.V., *Understanding American Politics*, Fontana, 1976.

Heywood, A., *Politics*, Palgrave Macmillan, 2002.

Jillson, C., *American Government: Political Development and Institutional Change*, Routledge, 2016.

Loomis, Burdett A., *The Contemporary Congress*, Thomson/Wadsworth, 2004.

Norton, P., *Parliament in the 1980s*, Blackwell, 1985.

Ornstein, N. and Mann, T. (2007) 'The Hill Is Alive with the Sound of Hearings', www.aei.org, 21 March.

Shaw, M., *Anglo-American Democracy*, Routledge, 2013.

Vile, M.J.C., *Politics in the USA*, Routledge, 1999.

Further reading

Ashbee, E., 'Congress: An obstacle to effective government?' *Politics Review*, Vol. 22, No. 2, November 2012.

Bennett, A.J., 'Congress: Why is it so unpopular?' *Politics Review*, Vol. 24, No. 2, November 2014.

Bennett, A.J., 'Is Congress overly dysfunctional and partisan?' *Politics Review* Vol. 26, No. 1, September 2016.

Hamal, R. and Baker A., 'Is Congress "the broken branch"?' *Politics Review*, Vol. 23, No. 4, April 2014.

There are a number of websites you can consult to follow up topics raised in this chapter. The best place to start would be the websites of the two houses of Congress:

www.house.gov

www.senate.gov

These sites have information on such things as members, leadership, committees, legislation and votes.

Another good website from which to follow the work of Congress is www.rollcall.com. Its video collection is especially worth looking through (click on 'Video' on the home page).

Exam focus

Edexcel

Section A (Comparative)

1 Examine the ways in which the US House of Representatives and the UK House of Commons are different. *(12)*

2 Examine the methods of oversight of the executive in the US Congress and the UK Parliament. *(12)*

Section B (Comparative)

In your answer you must consider the relevance of at least one comparative theory.

1 Analyse the differences in the way legislation is passed in the US Congress and the UK Parliament. *(12)*

2 Analyse the strengths and weaknesses of the upper chambers in the USA and the UK. *(12)*

Section C (USA)

In your answer you must consider the stated view and the alternative to this view in a balanced way.

1 Evaluate the extent to which Congress is a representative body. *(30)*

2 Evaluate the extent to which political parties play an important role in Congress. *(30)*

3 Evaluate the extent to which the real work of Congress occurs in committees rather than in the chambers. *(30)*

4 Evaluate the extent to which Congress can check the power of the executive branch. *(30)*

AQA

Section A (USA)

1 Explain and analyse three ways in which Congress can check the power of the executive branch. *(9)*

2 Explain and analyse three ways in which committees play an important role in Congress. *(9)*

Section A (Comparative)

1 Explain and analyse three ways in which rational choice theory could be used to study how members of the US House of Representatives and members of the UK House of Commons work. (9)

2 Explain and analyse three ways in which structural theory could be used to study the legislative process in the US Congress and the UK Parliament. (9)

Section B (USA)

Is Congress the 'broken branch'?

Here is a paradox: public opinion polls regularly find very low levels of satisfaction with Congress, and yet voters regularly re-elect their own congressmen and senators. There are a number of reasons why Congress might be regarded as 'broken'. Gridlock abounds. Major legislation languishes in both houses. Significant policy concerns remain unaddressed. Bipartisanship is dead; partisanship abounds. And yet the Founders wrote the Constitution in such a way that demands compromise and cooperation if it is to work. Especially in the House, the majority of races are uncompetitive which merely pushes politicians further to the ideological extremes.

And yet, Congress does pass hundreds of pieces of legislation in every two-year Congress. Compared with other legislatures, members are very diligent in the way they represent their constituents' views. What is more, while it is true that Congress is often fairly unproductive, 'limited government' is one of the cornerstone principles upon which the Constitution was built. And there are fifty state legislatures around the country churning out legislation year by year. Blaming Congress for partisanship is rather like blaming a mirror for the image it reflects. It is the country that is polarised — a polarisation that Congress merely reflects.

Analyse, evaluate and compare the arguments in the above passage for and against the view that Congress is the 'broken branch'. (25)

Section C (Comparative)

In your answer you should draw on material from across the whole range of your course of study in Politics.

1 'The US Congress is a more powerful legislature than the UK Parliament.' Analyse and evaluate this statement. (25)

2 'The committees in the US Congress are more effective than the committees in the UK Parliament.' Analyse and evaluate this statement. (25)

3 'Parties play a less important role in the US Congress than in the UK Parliament.' Analyse and evaluate this statement. (25)

The presidency

Introduction

> I, Barack Hussein Obama, do solemnly swear that I will faithfully execute the Office of President of the United States, and will to the best of my ability, preserve, protect and defend the Constitution of the United States. So help me God.

With these words, Barack Obama became the 44th president of the United States at (just after) 12 noon eastern standard time on Tuesday, 20 January 2009. Unfortunately, between them, Chief Justice John Roberts, who was administering the oath, and the President-elect (as he still was), fluffed their lines in front of a crowd of over one million. So the following day, at 7.35 p.m., the Chief Justice dropped by the White House to meet up with the President (as he now was) to do it again! And this time there was no crowd, no family, no television cameras — and no fluffing of lines. Was it necessary to do it again? Probably not. But the White House commented that the oath was repeated 'out of an abundance of caution'.

Caution is not a word many people associated with Mr Obama's predecessor, George W. Bush. But the office of the US president is often misunderstood by casual observers for two reasons. First, they tend to see the president as a one-man band when in fact he is part — though admittedly an important part — of an orchestra. Hence, this chapter is entitled 'The presidency' rather than 'The president', drawing to our attention the organisation rather than simply the person. Second, they tend to think of the president as 'the most powerful man in the world'. True, the president does have a considerable amount of power, more in foreign policy than in domestic policy. Whereas in foreign policy the president can use his formidable commander-in-chief powers, when it comes to domestic policy, he is far more limited — hedged around with numerous checks and balances, especially from Congress. President Johnson was once heard to remark: 'The only power I've got is nuclear, and I'm not allowed to use that.'

The US presidency is therefore something of a paradox: power and weakness. The president has to be both commander-in-chief and 'bargainer-in-chief'. He has considerable formal powers, but there are formidable limits on his use of those powers. To run the federal bureaucracy, mould public opinion and get on with Congress, the president needs to be an effective administrator, communicator, persuader, facilitator and leader.

The creation of the presidency

The Founding Fathers created a president who would be both head of state and head of the government. This is important to remember. The US president is not just another politician; he — and perhaps one day, she — is the personification of the nation. 'I am both king and prime minister,' remarked President Theodore Roosevelt. The arrival of the president at a formal, public function is greeted by a military band playing 'Hail to the Chief'. The White House may not have the grandeur of Buckingham Palace, but it is certainly a good deal more imposing than 10 Downing Street.

Second, the Founding Fathers created a singular executive. 'The executive power shall be vested in a president of the United States of America' are the opening words of Article II of the Constitution. It is important to remember this when considering the president's cabinet, for it is not — and cannot be — a decision-making body. President Truman had on his Oval Office desk a sign that read simply: 'The buck stops here.'

Table 4.1 Presidents since 1961

President	Party	Years in office
John F. Kennedy	Democrat	1961–63
Lyndon B. Johnson	Democrat	1963–69
Richard M. Nixon	Republican	1969–74
Gerald R. Ford	Republican	1974–77
Jimmy E. Carter	Democrat	1977–81
Ronald W. Reagan	Republican	1981–89
George H.W. Bush	Republican	1989–93
William J. Clinton	Democrat	1993–2001
George W. Bush	Republican	2001–09
Barack H. Obama	Democrat	2009–17
Donald J. Trump	Republican	2017–

Third, they created an indirectly elected president. The president was to be chosen by the Electors — the great and the good — in an Electoral College. As Chapter 6 will explain, this system has been adapted into a direct election, although the mechanism of the Electoral College still survives.

Finally, they created a limited — a checked — president. The Founding Fathers feared tyranny, and especially they feared tyranny by the executive branch. As a result, they hedged the president with a host of checks and balances (see Chapter 2). Thomas Cronin and Michael Genovese (1998) have written:

> The men who invented the presidency did not wish to create a ruler. Instead they hoped to create conditions where leadership might from time to time flourish. A ruler commands; a leader influences. A ruler wields power; a leader persuades.

Students of the US presidency need to understand that the office is often a limited and, for its main occupant, a frustrating one.

Five presidents in the Oval Office: (left to right) George H.W. Bush, Barack Obama, George W. Bush, Bill Clinton, Jimmy Carter

The formal powers of the president

The powers of the president are his tasks, functions or duties. They are laid out in Article II of the Constitution. Essentially, they have been the same for every president — from George Washington to Donald Trump, and all the 42 presidents in between. It all makes for a very presidential daily schedule (see Table 4.2).

Table 4.2 The President's schedule, 12–14 September 2016

12 September	
11.00 a.m.	President receives Presidential Daily Briefing
4.10 p.m.	President meets with Congressional Leadership, Oval Office
13 September	
10.00 a.m.	President and Vice President receive Presidential Daily Briefing
12.05 p.m.	President departs White House
1.00 p.m.	President arrives Philadelphia, Pennsylvania
1.45 p.m.	President delivers remarks at a Hillary for America campaign event
3.05 p.m.	President participates in a Democratic National Committee event
4.30 p.m.	President departs Philadelphia
5.10 p.m.	President arrives JFK Airport, New York
7.05 p.m.	President delivers remarks and takes questions at a Democratic Congressional Campaign Committee event
8.40 p.m.	President departs New York
9.50 p.m.	President arrives at White House
14 September	
10.30 a.m.	President and Vice President receive Presidential Daily Briefing
11.20 a.m.	President holds bilateral meeting with State Counsellor Aung San Suu Kyi of Burma
12.45 p.m.	President meets Vice President for lunch, Private Dining Room
4.00 p.m.	President meets with Secretary of the Treasury Jack Lew, Oval Office

Propose legislation

Article II of the Constitution states: '[The president] shall from time to time give to the Congress information of the State of the Union, and recommend to their consideration such measures as he shall judge necessary and expedient.' This gives the president the power to propose legislation to Congress, which he may do through the annual State of the Union Address. But the president can propose legislation at any time by, for example, calling a press conference or making an announcement at a public event. At the start of his second term in 2013, President Obama used his State of the Union Address to promote his policy proposals on job creation, deficit reduction, immigration reform, gun control and increasing the federal minimum wage.

Submit the annual budget

The budget is really just another piece of legislation, but it is potentially the most important. The Office of Management and Budget (OMB) draws up the annual federal budget for the president. The OMB is part of the president's own bureaucracy, which is known as the Executive Office of the President (EXOP). The president then submits the budget to Congress. This is followed by a lengthy bargaining process between the president and Congress — especially lengthy if the presidency and Congress are controlled by different political parties. We shall consider this in more detail later in this chapter.

Sign legislation

Once bills have been passed through a lengthy and complicated legislative process in Congress (see Chapter 3), they land on the president's desk. He has a number of options, but the most likely is that of signing the bill into law. He will do this to bills for which he wishes to take some credit. Elaborate bill-signing ceremonies are often held, attended by House and Senate members who have been particularly supportive, relevant members of the administration, as well as interested parties who will be affected by the new legislation.

At the bill-signing ceremony at the White House for the Patient Protection and Affordable Care Act in March 2010, President Obama invited not only the Democratic Party leadership in Congress but also the widow of the late senator Edward Kennedy, who had made healthcare reform one of his life's ambitions. Also present was 11-year-old Marcelas Owens of Seattle, who became an advocate for reform after his mother died without health insurance.

Veto legislation

As well as signing bills into law, the president has the option of vetoing them. The *regular veto* is a much-used presidential weapon. Even the threat of it can be an important bargaining tool. Altogether, from George Washington to George W. Bush, presidents have used just over 1,500 regular vetoes. Congress may attempt to override the president's veto, but is rarely successful. George W. Bush's 63.6% success rate with vetoes was the third lowest of any president.

The president may have the power of *pocket veto* at his disposal, too, but this can be used only at the end of a congressional session. Pocket vetoes cannot be overridden by Congress. President George H.W. Bush used 15 pocket vetoes, while both Bill Clinton and George W. Bush used just one each. During his two terms, Barack Obama used 12 regular vetoes. Congress failed to override the first 11 but succeeded on the twelfth. This was in September 2016 when President Obama vetoed the Justice Against Sponsors of Terrorism Act which would have allowed families of victims of the September 11 terrorist attacks to sue the government of Saudi Arabia for any role they played in the plot. In his veto message to Congress, Obama said that the legislation would 'undermine core US interests' and 'create complications' in diplomatic relations with other countries. The congressional override would not have come as any surprise to the President as the legislation had passed through both houses on near unanimous voice votes.

Act as chief executive

The opening 15 words of Article II of the Constitution grant the president all executive power. Thus, the president is chief executive — in charge of running the executive branch of the federal government. This, as explained later in the chapter, is a huge job and much of the day-to-day running is delegated to those who run the federal government's principal departments and agencies. Modern presidents have needed their own bureaucracy — EXOP — to help them to coordinate the work of the federal government.

The Oval Office

Nominate executive branch officials

The president has the power to nominate hundreds of officials to the executive branch of government. An incoming president — such as Donald Trump in 2017 — has a host of such posts to fill. The most important of these are the heads of the 15 executive departments, such as the Treasury, State and Agriculture. In addition, there are lower-level officials in all these departments, as well as ambassadors, agency heads and members of regulatory commissions. The Senate must confirm all these appointments by a simple majority vote. Appointments continue to be made throughout the president's term of office.

Nominate all federal judges

Nomination of judges involves the president in making hundreds of appointments. The president must fill vacancies not only on the federal Supreme Court, but also on the federal trial (district) and appeal (circuit) courts. All judicial appointments are for life and therefore assume a special importance. They must be confirmed by a simple majority vote in the Senate.

Act as commander-in-chief

This power was particularly important for presidents in office from the 1940s to the 1980s. Whether it was Franklin Roosevelt fighting the Second World War, Harry Truman in Berlin and Korea, Kennedy in Cuba, or Lyndon Johnson and Richard Nixon in Vietnam, presidents were seen as playing a highly significant role as commander-in-chief. Then came the demise of the Soviet Union and the break-up of the communist bloc in eastern Europe during the presidencies of Reagan and George H.W. Bush. It was the same Bush who successfully fought the Persian Gulf War in 1991.

The post-Cold War era saw a diminution of the president's commander-in-chief role. The decade from 1991 to 2001 brought no significant foreign policy engagement by a US president — nothing on the scale of Korea, Vietnam or

the Gulf War. The events of 11 September 2001 changed all that, however, and George W. Bush found himself thrust into the role of a wartime president. During his eight years in office, Barack Obama found himself drawn into foreign crises in Iraq, Afghanistan, Libya and Syria, as well as managing highly sensitive relationships with Israel, Russia and Cuba.

In this area, Congress's checks are more questionable. The Constitution gives Congress the power to declare war, but that power has not been used since 1941. The president now asks Congress to 'authorise' his use of troops. Congress passed the Gulf of Tonkin Resolution in 1964, giving President Johnson the power 'to take all necessary measures' in Vietnam. Congress passed authorising resolutions in 1991 and 2002 before US troops were used in Kuwait and Iraq respectively. Congress also has the 'power of the purse' with which to check presidential war making, but this has not always proved effective.

Whenever the president travels away from the White House a specially modified briefcase — known as the nuclear 'football' — is carried by a military officer so that the president has immediate access to the nuclear codes should that prove necessary. This is a stark reminder of the president's commander-in-chief role.

A military officer carries the nuclear 'football' (left) from Air Force One

Negotiate treaties

The presidential seal of office

The president's seal of office shows an eagle clutching a bundle of arrows in one claw, symbolising the commander-in-chief role, and an olive branch in the other to symbolise his peace-making role. Modern-day presidents have used this power to negotiate such treaties as the Strategic Arms Reduction Treaty (Ronald Reagan), the Chemical Weapons Ban (George H.W. Bush) and a nuclear arms treaty with Russia (Barack Obama).

The president's power is checked by the Senate, which must ratify treaties by a two-thirds majority. During the twentieth century the Senate rejected seven treaties. The first and last were significant in that they were major treaties. In 1920, the Senate rejected the Treaty of Versailles which President Woodrow Wilson had negotiated on behalf of the United States. Then, in 1999, President Clinton failed to gain even a simple majority for the Comprehensive Test Ban Treaty, let alone the two-thirds majority required.

Pardon

Presidents possess the power of pardon and use it with varying degrees of frequency. In 1974, President Ford pardoned his predecessor, Richard Nixon, over all Watergate-related matters. President Clinton caused a storm on his final day in office in January 2001 when he pardoned 140 people including fugitive Mark Rich, whose former wife had made large monetary donations to Clinton's election campaigns and had given expensive personal gifts to the President and First Lady. In contrast with Clinton's 140 pardons in one day, George W. Bush pardoned only 189 people in eight years. Barack Obama was even more restrained in his first seven years in office, pardoning just 70 people. But he then pardoned a further 142 in his last month in office for a total of 212.

Head of state

Not only do presidents perform all these formal constitutional functions, but also they must perform the role of head of state. This is most clearly seen at times of national tragedy when the president takes on the role of comforter-in-chief, sometimes of mourner-in-chief. President George W. Bush played this role in the weeks following the attacks on the United States on 11 September 2001. It was the President who addressed the nation that night from the Oval Office, and he did so again at the prayer service in the Washington National Cathedral three days later, seeking to bind the nation's wounds and lift its fallen spirits. More recently we saw President Obama play this role following the devastation caused by Hurricane Sandy in October 2012, as well as in the aftermath of the killing of 20 children and 6 adults at Sandy Hook Elementary School in Newtown, Connecticut, in December of the same year.

The vice president

Under normal circumstances, the vice president is elected as part of a joint ticket with the president. In 2016, voters were offered a choice of Clinton and Kaine or Trump and Pence. But since 1967 and the passage of the Twenty-Fifth Amendment, there are circumstances under which the vice president may be appointed rather than elected. Should the vice presidency become vacant, the president has the power to appoint a new vice president, who must be confirmed by a simple majority vote of both houses of Congress. This has occurred twice.

■ In 1973, Vice President Spiro Agnew resigned, having pleaded 'no contest' to a charge of income tax evasion. President Nixon then appointed Congressman Gerald Ford as vice president. Ford was duly confirmed by votes of 92–3 and 387–55 by the Senate and House of Representatives respectively.

■ Less than a year later, Nixon resigned from the presidency over the Watergate affair. Vice President Ford therefore became president. He then appointed the former governor of New York, Nelson Rockefeller, as the new vice president. Rockefeller was confirmed by congressional votes of 90–7 and 287–128.

Table 4.3 Vice presidents since 1981

Vice president	Party	Years in office
George H.W. Bush	Republican	1981–89
J. Danforth Quayle	Republican	1989–93
Albert A. Gore	Democrat	1993–2001
Richard B. Cheney	Republican	2001–09
Joseph R. Biden	Democrat	2009–17
Michael R. Pence	Republican	2017–

The Constitution originally gave four powers to the vice president.

■ He is the presiding officer of the Senate, but this is a function that the vice president rarely performs. The Senate usually deputes junior members of its chamber to chair debates.

■ The vice president is granted the power to break a tie in the Senate. Indeed, it is only to perform this function that a vice president will usually attend the chamber. Dick Cheney cast a tie-breaking vote in April 2001 to protect President Bush's $1.6 trillion tax cut. In the 24 years between January 1993 and January 2017, vice presidents were called upon to break tied votes on 12 occasions — four by Al Gore (1993–2001) and eight by Dick Cheney (2001–09). Joe Biden (2009–17) never used this power, thus becoming the first vice president to serve two full terms and never cast a tie-breaking vote. In contrast, Mike Pence cast his first tie-breaking vote within a month of taking office.

- The vice president is given the task of counting and then announcing the result of the Electoral College votes. Thus in January 2001, outgoing Vice President Gore had to announce his own defeat in the previous November's election, and in January 2013 Vice President Biden announced his own successful re-election along with that of President Obama.

- The first three powers are either of little importance or occur rarely — or both. It is the final power that gives the office of vice president its potential importance. The vice president becomes president upon the death, resignation or removal of the president from office. This has occurred on nine occasions: four times following the assassination of the president; four times following the natural death of the president; and once following the resignation of the president (President Nixon in August 1974). The insignificant powers of the office, coupled with this potential importance, led the first vice president, John Adams, to remark of the post: 'In this I am nothing; but I may be everything.'

More recently, the vice president has acquired a fifth power: to become acting president if the president is declared, or declares himself, disabled. This is another provision of the Twenty-Fifth Amendment. The power has been used three times: on 13 July 1985, when President Reagan was hospitalised briefly; and on 29 June 2002 and 21 July 2007, when President George W. Bush required sedation in order to undergo a colonoscopy. On these two occasions, Cheney was acting president for just over two hours.

As the workload of the president mushroomed during the middle decades of the last century, presidents realised that the vice president could be a significant player in the White House, a role begun by Vice President Richard Nixon during the presidency of Dwight Eisenhower (1953–61) and continued by almost all of his successors. Al Gore, Dick Cheney and Joe Biden all played important roles in their respective administrations.

The cabinet

Key term

Cabinet The advisory group selected by the president to aid him in making decisions and coordinating the work of the federal government.

Historical background

The **cabinet** is an advice-giving group selected by the president, membership of which is determined by both tradition and presidential discretion. The traditional members are the heads of the executive departments. Originally there were just three — State, War and the Treasury. Now, there are 15. The president also has the discretion to award cabinet rank to other administration officials. In January 2012, President Obama announced that he was elevating the administrator of the Small Business Administration, Karen Mills, to cabinet status. By doing this, the President was signalling the importance he placed on small businesses in promoting economic recovery in America.

The cabinet is not mentioned in the Constitution. The Founding Fathers created a *singular* executive — no councils or cabinets. However, the Constitution does state in Article II that the president:

> may require the opinion in writing of the principal officer in each of the executive departments upon any subject relating to the duties of their respective offices.

Four words or phrases in this brief extract indicate precisely what the president can require from the heads of the executive departments.

- First, the word 'may' is significant. This means that, whatever the Constitution prescribes in this section is voluntary, not obligatory. Constitutions are usually about 'shall', not 'may'.
- Second, the president may require 'opinions' — this is a very low-level word. These are not 'decisions' or even 'recommendations', merely 'opinions'.
- Third, he may require these opinions 'in writing'. No meeting is envisaged.
- Finally, there is the restriction as to what these 'opinions in writing' may be about: not 'upon any subject', but rather 'upon any subject *relating to the duties of their respective offices*'. In other words, the secretary of the treasury will offer opinions only on Treasury matters; the secretary of state only on State Department matters. This is certainly not the recipe for what students of UK politics understand by a 'cabinet meeting'.

Why, then, do presidents have a cabinet? In 1789, President Washington thought it would be helpful to have a meeting with the secretaries of War, the Treasury and State, plus the attorney general. The press called them 'cabinet meetings'. Every president since then has had a cabinet and held cabinet meetings. According to presidential scholar Richard Fenno (1959), the cabinet is 'institutionalised by usage alone'. In other words, it is used because it is used.

It is also important to differentiate between the cabinet as individuals and the cabinet as a group. Failure to see these two different uses of the term can lead to misunderstandings. The answer to the question 'Was President Obama's cabinet important?' is impossible to answer until we have established in which sense the term is being used. As individuals, cabinet members were important: some, like first-term Secretary of State Hillary Clinton and Treasury Secretary Timothy Geithner, were very important. On the other hand, cabinet meetings were hardly ever held, so, as a group, the cabinet was unimportant.

Pools of recruitment

A new president needs to recruit a completely new cabinet. In a presidential system such as in the USA, there is no 'shadow cabinet' waiting to take office. Furthermore, in a 'separated' system, in which members of the legislature cannot at the same time serve in the executive, the president must cast his net more widely for potential cabinet members. There are four major pools of recruitment.

- **Congress.** The president may try to recruit from Congress, but asking serving members of Congress to give up their seats to join the cabinet — where both prestige and job security are often in short supply — is usually a hard sell. It is therefore more likely that presidents will try to recruit retiring or former members of Congress. That said, Donald Trump persuaded three incumbent members of Congress — Senator Jeff Sessions and representatives Tom Price and Ryan Zinke — to join his cabinet in 2017.

- **Serving or former state governors.** These are another pool of cabinet recruitment, and as such people have executive experience, they are usually much better suited to running a large federal bureaucracy than are former legislators. Two former governors joined the Trump cabinet in 2017 — Sonny Perdue of Georgia as secretary of agriculture, and Rick Perry of Texas as secretary of energy.
- **Big city mayors.** City mayors bring executive experience. Obama's second-term cabinet included two former mayors — Anthony Foxx of Charlotte, North Carolina, as secretary of transportation, and Julian Castro of San Antonio, Texas, as secretary of housing and urban development.
- **Academia.** America's top universities are another potential pool of recruitment for the president's cabinet. Steven Chu, appointed by President Obama as secretary of energy in 2009, was professor of physics at the University of California. When he departed in 2013, another physics professor, Ernest Moniz of the Massachusetts Institute of Technology (MIT), replaced him.

What the president is really looking for in cabinet officers is policy specialists. In 2017, Trump appointed a retired Marine Corps General, John Kelly, as secretary of homeland security; a former partner at investment bank Goldman Sachs, Steven Mnuchin, as secretary of the treasury; and a former state attorney general, Jeff Sessions, to head up the Department of Justice — all policy specialists. However, one was left wondering what retired neurosurgeon Ben Carson knew about housing as he was appointed to head up the Department of Housing and Urban Development (HUD).

President Trump's first cabinet meeting, March 2017

All the cabinet appointments are subject to confirmation by a simple majority vote in the Senate (see Chapter 3). It is highly unusual for the Senate to reject the president's nominees. The last time this occurred was in 1989 when the Senate rejected President George H.W. Bush's nomination of John Tower as secretary of defense. However, in February 2017, Vice President Mike Pence had to cast a 51st vote in order to break a 50–50 tie when the Senate voted to confirm Betsy DeVos as secretary of education — the first time this had occurred. Fifty Republicans had voted yes, but two had joined the 46 Democrats and two independents in voting no — hence the tie. A week later, Trump's nominee to be secretary of labor, Andrew Puzder, withdrew his name from consideration after it became clear that he lacked the necessary votes to be confirmed.

A balanced cabinet

Presidents like to have a balanced cabinet — balanced in terms of gender, race, region, age and political ideology.

- **Gender.** This is now an important factor in appointing cabinet members. Gone are the days when Richard Nixon and Ronald Reagan could appoint all-male cabinets. In 2001, George W. Bush appointed three women as heads of executive departments. For Obama in 2009, that number increased to four, but the total was back to just two for the incoming Trump cabinet in 2017.
- **Race.** Race is an equally important factor in cabinet appointments. Once Lyndon Johnson had appointed the first African-American to the cabinet in 1966, there were expectations that the president's cabinet would no longer be all white. In 2001, Bush's incoming cabinet included five members who were from ethnic minorities, at the time the most ethnically diverse cabinet ever appointed. Furthermore, Bush filled top-tier departments with people from ethnic minorities — Colin Powell as secretary of state in the first term and Condoleezza Rice in the second term. Barack Obama's 2009 cabinet included six members of ethnic minorities, such as Eric Holder at the department of justice. But Trump's 2017 cabinet had the 'white male' look about it with just three heads of departments being members of ethnic minorities — African-American Ben Carson at HUD, Asian-American Elaine Chao at Transportation and Hispanic Alexander Acosta at Labor.

Table 4.4 President Donald Trump's cabinet, January 2017

Post	Cabinet officer
Secretary of State	Rex Tillerson
Secretary of Defense	General James Mattis
Secretary of the Treasury	Steven Mnuchin
Attorney General (Department of Justice)	Jeff Sessions
Secretary of Agriculture	Sonny Perdue
Secretary of the Interior	Ryan Zinke
Secretary of Commerce	Wilbur Ross
Secretary of Labor	Alexander Acosta
Secretary of Health and Human Services	Tom Price
Secretary of Housing and Urban Development	Ben Carson
Secretary of Transportation	Elaine Chao
Secretary of Energy	Rick Perry
Secretary of Education	Betsy DeVos
Secretary of Veterans' Affairs	David Shulkin
Secretary of Homeland Security	General John Kelly

- **Region.** By appointing cabinet members from different regions of the country, presidents can reinforce a picture that they intend to govern for the whole country, not just segments of it where their support was strongest. That said, the president's home state and region tend to fare well in cabinet appointments.

- **Age.** As a rule of thumb, the average age of the cabinet usually reflects the age of the president. The youngest ever cabinet was appointed by the youngest elected president — John F. Kennedy. Their average age was just 47. However, this rule was broken when George W. Bush appointed one of the oldest cabinets in modern times. Its average age was 58. The average age of Obama's first cabinet was also surprisingly old — at just over 55. But neither Bush nor Obama could match the 'senior' look of the first Trump cabinet with an average age of 63. Indeed, only four members were under 60 upon taking office, with three in their 70s — Jeff Sessions (70), Sonny Perdue (70) and Wilbur Ross (79). At least it matched Trump — the oldest person to be first elected president.

- **Ideology.** Finally, whether it is a Democratic or Republican administration, the president will want to have the different ideological wings of their party represented: liberal Democrats, conservative Democrats and New Democrats; conservative Republicans, moderate Republicans and Tea Party Republicans. It is also not unusual for a president to pick someone from the other party. In his second term, Democrat President Obama appointed former Republican senator Chuck Hagel as his secretary of defense. In 2017, President Trump appointed one of his predecessor's number twos at the Department of Veterans' Affairs, David Shulkin, to be its new boss.

Cabinet meetings

The frequency of cabinet meetings varies from one president to another. During his first year in office, Ronald Reagan held 36 cabinet meetings, while in his first year Bill Clinton held only six. In some administrations there is a trend to hold fewer cabinet meetings the longer the president remains in office. Reagan's 36 meetings in his first year became 21 in the second year and just 12 in each of the third and fourth years. In eight years, George W. Bush held 49 cabinet meetings, an average of just over six meetings a year. But unlike with his immediate predecessors there was no wild fluctuation in the number of meetings per year. He never held more than nine in any year (2001) and never fewer than four (2007) – see Table 4.5.

This was exactly what Bush had in mind when he arrived in Washington at the start of his first administration in January 2001. Just a month into his presidency, I interviewed Bush's secretary to the cabinet, Albert Hawkins, in his West Wing office. Hawkins told me that President Bush envisaged full cabinet meetings being held 'once every couple of months'. And an average of six meetings a year is just about on the nail. Hawkins explained that cabinet meetings would be used 'to brief cabinet members on big picture items'.

Barack Obama held 16 cabinet meetings in his first term, and just 12 in his second term. This is far fewer than even George W. Bush (see Table 4.5) and more in line with the frequency of cabinet meetings under Bill Clinton. But presidents use — or do not use — cabinet meetings in very different ways. Like George W. Bush, Obama tended to schedule meetings just before or immediately after notable political events such as the State of the Union Address or the midterm elections and used them as an opportunity for him to deliver a team talk to his cabinet on big ticket items.

Table 4.5 Number of cabinet meetings held per year by George W. Bush and Barack Obama

Year	President	Number of cabinet meetings	Year	President	Number of cabinet meetings
2001	George W. Bush	9	2009	Barack Obama	5
2002		5	2010		4
2003		8	2011		4
2004		6	2012		3
2005		5	2013		4
2006		6	2014		3
2007		4	2015		3
2008		6	2016		2
Average meetings per year		**6**	**Average meetings per year**		**3.5**

Who attends cabinet meetings and what does the scene look like? All the heads of the executive departments (see Table 4.4), the vice president and all other administration officials granted cabinet rank are expected to attend. The cabinet room contains a huge mahogany table which tapers to both ends, allowing the president — seated in the middle of one side — to see all the participants. All regular attendees are assigned places around the table according to the seniority of the department which they head up. Opposite the president sits the vice president. To the president's right and left are, respectively, the secretary of state and secretary of defense. To the vice president's right and left are, respectively, the secretary of the treasury and the attorney general. Other attendees — mostly senior members of the White House staff — sit around the room, looking in towards the cabinet table.

Meetings of the president with the full cabinet tend to get a bad press. Zbigniew Brzezinski, who served in the cabinet of President Carter, commented that:

> Carter cabinet meetings were almost useless. The discussions were desultory. There was no coherent theme to them, and after a while they were held less and less frequently.

Part of the trouble is that so many of the people sitting round the table are policy specialists. They have little or nothing to contribute to discussions in other policy areas. As Reagan's labor secretary Bill Brock put it:

> The problem with the cabinet is that it has become too large. We keep adding new departments, so there are too many issues that come up where people have neither jurisdiction nor competence.

Since Brock sat in the cabinet, two more departments have been created — Veterans' Affairs (1989) and Homeland Security (2002).

However, formal meetings held in most organisations are probably described by at least some of the participants in deprecating terms. It does not necessarily mean that such meetings should not be held or that they perform no useful functions. The same is true of the president's cabinet, for the cabinet meeting performs many useful functions, both from the president's perspective and from that of the cabinet officers.

The functions of cabinet meetings for the president

Cabinet meetings can potentially perform several functions from the president's perspective.

Table 4.6 Policy items discussed at selected Obama cabinet meetings

Date	Policy items discussed
2013	
12 September	Syria
30 September	Partial shutdown of the federal government
2014	
1 July	Economy, jobs
7 November	Unemployment, bureaucratic efficiency, Ebola
2015	
3 February	Budget, policy agenda for 2015
15 October	Domestic response to Ebola
2016	
1 July	Use of executive orders, promoting a customer-friendly government

- **Team spirit.** The ability of cabinet meetings to engender team spirit is especially important at the beginning of an administration. Presidents do not have a shadow cabinet waiting to come into office. Many of the president's cabinet officers will be complete strangers to him. Cabinet meetings can help to weld them into *his* team to move forward *his* agenda. Once this has been achieved — probably within the first year — this function ceases. This may partly explain why cabinet meetings decline in number from that point in most administrations.

- **Collegiality.** It is important for presidents to appear collegial and consultative, especially since President Nixon. The Nixon administration was notorious for its lack of openness. A political novel written of the era was famously titled *Washington: Behind Closed Doors*. Cartoonists drew Nixon's Oval Office with guards outside dressed in Prussian-style military uniforms, holding 'no entry' signs. Cabinet meetings with a media photo opportunity either before or after the meeting are a good way for the president to send reassuring signals that he is running an open administration. To this extent, cabinet meetings can be a public relations exercise and an opportunity for the president to make some comments that will receive coverage in the media.

- **Exchanging information.** Cabinet meetings provide opportunities for both information giving and information gathering. The president can make statements at a cabinet meeting knowing that every member has heard them, and he can go round the table asking cabinet officers what is going on in their departments. President Carter's cabinet meetings usually took the form of the president going clockwise — the next time, anticlockwise — round the cabinet table, asking each member to give a brief report on current departmental issues and activity. Cabinet meetings can be an efficient method by which the president keeps in touch with what is going on in the vast federal bureaucracy.

- **Policy debate.** Some presidents have liked to use cabinet meetings as a forum in which to debate policy. Reagan's defense secretary, Frank Carlucci, remembered that 'cabinet meetings were often vigorous, such as the one on the pros and cons of building the Russian oil pipeline — it was quite a shouting match'. Michael Jackson, a senior member of President George H.W. Bush's Office of Cabinet Affairs who attended meetings as an observer, stated:

    > At the meeting prior to the Malta summit [with Soviet president Gorbachev in December 1989], the President engaged the cabinet in a very significant discussion of foreign policy. It allowed the President to broaden his consultations.

- **Presenting 'big picture items'.** At cabinet meetings the president can present so-called big picture items that affect all cabinet officers: the budget; up-coming elections; a major legislative initiative or foreign trip. For example, President Obama used his cabinet meeting on 30 September 2013 to discuss the likely implications of the upcoming partial shutdown of the federal government.

- **Monitoring Congress.** Some presidents have used cabinet meetings to check up on legislation going through Congress in which they have a particular interest. Willard Wirtz, labor secretary to President Johnson, stated:

    > If the Congress was in session, and you knew there was a cabinet meeting coming up in a day or two, you tried to make sure that there was some progress to report to the President. He knew the system so well. He could often embarrass you. Johnson would often pressurise you into making sure things moved quicker.

    President George W. Bush used his 24 September 2002 cabinet meeting to push for congressional action on three key issues: authorisation for military action against Iraq; the passage of the Homeland Security Bill; and the budget. On 3 February 2015 President Obama used a cabinet meeting to discuss his policy agenda in Congress for that year.

- **Prompting action.** Presidents can use cabinet meetings to goad cabinet members into action. By July 2014, Secretary of Defense Chuck Hagel had — it appeared to President Obama — been dragging his feet over the release of prisoners from Guantánamo Bay. After the cabinet meeting on 1 July Obama confronted Hagel, seated in the chair next to him around the table. 'I don't think you're moving fast enough, Chuck,' said Obama. The President then instructed White House chief of staff Denis McDonough to 'get together with [Hagel] and fix this'.

- **Personal contact.** Finally, cabinet meetings provide an opportunity for the president to see cabinet members whom he would not otherwise be likely to see. Whereas the 'first-tier' cabinet officers — such as the secretary of state and the secretary of defense — are likely to have fairly frequent meetings with the president, this will not be the case for such 'second-tier' cabinet officers as the secretary of veterans' affairs and the secretary of agriculture. Again, whereas the Treasury Department is only half a block from the White House, other departments are situated in far-flung parts of downtown Washington. There is no obvious reason for the president to see many cabinet officers except at a cabinet meeting. The president might even forget who is in the cabinet. HUD Secretary Sam Pierce never lived down the story of when President Reagan spotted him one day at a White House reception for visiting city mayors and mistook Pierce for a visitor: 'How are you, Mr Mayor?' asked the President of his housing secretary. 'How are things in your city?'

The functions of cabinet meetings for cabinet officers

There are good reasons for cabinet officers, too, to see cabinet meetings as potentially useful occasions, despite their frequent critiques of them:

- **Getting to know each other.** Cabinet meetings provide initial get-to-know-you opportunities. Not only will the president not know many of the cabinet officers; they will often not know each other.
- **Resolving disputes.** Cabinet meetings can be used to resolve interdepartmental disputes. Ford's secretary to the cabinet, James Connor, remembers a cabinet meeting in which a dispute about affirmative action for African-Americans was aired. 'It was one hell of a show,' stated Connor.
- **Speaking to cabinet colleagues.** Meetings in many organisations are often as useful for what goes on before and after them as for what occurs during them. The same can be true for the president's cabinet meetings. They can prove a useful opportunity to speak with other cabinet officers, and as there are precious few other opportunities to run into one's cabinet colleagues — unlike in a parliamentary system — these can be valuable occasions.
- **Speaking to the president.** It may even be possible to catch the president after the meeting, should he linger in the cabinet room. However, such situations can present danger for a president who agrees too readily to what may appear to be an innocent, off-the-cuff request from a cabinet officer. George W. Bush's secretary to the cabinet explained how he would be 'hovering [around the President] at the end of a meeting, not exactly eavesdropping, but at a respectful distance' to ensure that no cabinet officer took advantage of the President in such an unscheduled moment.
- **Increased status for cabinet officers.** Finally, attendance at cabinet meetings gives cabinet officers increased standing back at their departments. They have just heard the president. They know what he wants, today, as opposed to what others might *think* he wanted, yesterday. President George H.W. Bush's agriculture secretary, Clayton Yeutter, summed up a number of these functions this way:

> [Cabinet meetings] were useful for being informative. You got an insight on the top stories. It was for some just the thrill to have a meeting with the President. The 'second tier' cabinet officers don't get to see him that often. They would go back to their departments and be able to say: 'I just came from a cabinet meeting.' They would then hold their own staff meetings and the stories would be passed out to sub-cabinet people and so to the rest of the department. They were evangelistic.

An assessment of the cabinet

How important, then, is the president's cabinet? Individually, its members are very important — they all run large departments and spend large budgets. Some are more important than others. But as Robert Shrum wrote in late 2008: 'No one in a cabinet outshines the president.' Collectively, there are five structural reasons why the president's cabinet can never be of prime importance.

- First, the Constitution grants 'all executive power' to the president. Cabinet officers have no executive power vested in them directly.
- Second, there is no doctrine of collective responsibility. The president is not 'first among equals'. He is simply 'first'. As Professor Anthony King put it: 'He doesn't sum up at the end of the meeting; he *is* the meeting.'
- Third, cabinet officers are not the president's political rivals. The cabinet is not seen as a stepping stone to the presidency, as Hillary Clinton belatedly discovered in 2016. The last person to step from the cabinet directly to the presidency was Herbert Hoover in 1929. Hoover had served as commerce secretary to presidents Warren Harding and Calvin Coolidge.
- Fourth, the members of the president's cabinet have loyalties other than to the president. Charles Dawes (vice president 1925–29) once remarked that members of the cabinet are 'a president's natural enemies'! They also do not work in the White House. Some of them may see the president rarely.

  It was for this reason that during his second term, George W. Bush required all cabinet members to spend several hours a week working at the White House compound — not in the West Wing itself, but in an office suite set up for them in the Eisenhower Executive Office Building just next door to the White House. 'It allows us to work on a much more regular basis with the Cabinet in helping to manage issues,' commented Claude Allen, Bush's domestic policy adviser. Although this rule applied to all 15 executive department heads, the heads of the Defense, State, Homeland Security and Justice departments were required at the White House so often that they rarely used the new cabinet suite, according to Erin Healy, a Bush staffer. Another White House official said that this new policy had caused 'some consternation' among some of the cabinet officers, but they were defending the new practice, at least in public. 'Having an office and time to work at the White House is a great way to build an effective and cohesive team,' said labor secretary Elaine Chao. But according to Professor Paul Light, the whole idea is 'shocking' and merely 'confirms how little the domestic cabinet officers have to do with making policy'.'
- One more significant limit to the cabinet's importance is the existence, since 1939, of the Executive Office of the President (EXOP). In the EXOP, the cabinet has something of a rival, and a rival with a number of key advantages.

Debate

Is the president's cabinet important?

Yes
- It contains some of the most important people in the executive branch (e.g. secretary of state, secretary of defense).
- All the heads of the 15 executive departments are automatically members.
- The president always chairs the meetings.
- Cabinet meetings can fulfil a number of important functions, both for the president and for cabinet officers.
- Some presidents hold frequent meetings (e.g. Reagan).

No
- Article II of the Constitution vests 'all executive power' in the president.
- There is no doctrine of collective responsibility.
- The members are neither the president's equals nor his political rivals.
- The president often views members of his cabinet with some suspicion because of their divided loyalties.
- EXOP is the main source of advice-giving for the president.

The Executive Office of the President

Key term

Executive Office of the President The umbrella term for the top staff agencies in the White House that assist the president in carrying out the major responsibilities of office.

The **Executive Office of the President** (EXOP, or EOP) is an umbrella term for an organisation that consists of the top presidential staff agencies that provide help, advice, coordination and administrative support for the president.

In 1939, the Brownlow Committee reported to President Franklin Roosevelt (FDR) that 'the president needs help'. Why did presidents from the mid-twentieth century 'need help' in running the federal government?

■ There had been a huge increase in the size and scale of the federal government, caused mainly by the westward expansion and industrialisation of the nineteenth century. In 1789, there were just three executive departments of the federal government — State, War and the Treasury. By 1939, a further five had been added: Interior (1849), Justice (1870), Agriculture (1889), Commerce and Labor (both 1903).

The White House and (to the left) the West Wing

■ When the great depression hit the USA in the late 1920s, the states looked to the federal government for help. FDR responded to this with his 'New Deal' programme — a whole raft of federal government schemes to promote employment, agriculture, industrial expansion and a huge building programme of schools, roads, hydroelectric schemes and the like.

■ The USA was about to become a major player on the stage of world politics. This added considerably to the president's role as commander-in-chief. The presidents of the second half of the last century had to spend much of their time dealing with the consequences of the Cold War — in southeast Asia, eastern Europe and Central America.

> ## Box 4.1
>
> ### Executive Office of the President, 2017
>
> At the beginning of President Trump's administration, the Executive Office of the President (EXOP) was made up of 12 offices:
>
> - Council of Economic Advisers
> - Council on Environmental Quality
> - Executive Residence
> - National Security Council
> - Office of Administration
> - Office of Management and Budget
> - Office of National Drug Control Policy
> - Office of Science and Technology Policy
> - Office of the United States Trade Representative
> - Office of the Vice President
> - President's Intelligence Advisory Board
> - White House Office — subdivided into a further 36 offices, including:
>   — Domestic Policy Council
>   — Office of Cabinet Affairs
>   — Office of the Chief of Staff
>   — Office of Communications
>   — Office of Legislative Affairs
>
> Source: www.whitehouse.gov/administration/eop

As a result, presidents found more demands made on them. Overload became a real danger. So EXOP was established to help the president cope with these increased demands. Through the second half of the twentieth century, EXOP grew to include around a dozen offices, the most important being the White House Office, the National Security Council and the Office of Management and Budget. By 2009, the Executive Office of President Obama included 15 offices, but President Obama had reduced this number to just 11 by the end of his first term (see Box 4.1). Altogether, EXOP came to number over 2,000 staff. The most important EXOP personnel, including the key presidential advisers, work in the West Wing of the White House, which is where the Oval Office is located.

The White House Office

The **White House Office** includes the president's most trusted and closest aides and advisers. Although the White House Office is only one of the dozen or so offices which make up the Executive Office of the President, it is itself made up of over 30 different offices, such as the Office of Cabinet Affairs and the Office of Legislative Affairs. In charge of running the White House Office is the White House chief of staff. Their principal function is to provide advice and administrative support for the president on a daily basis. Whether in the White House, travelling within the United States or out of the country, these people are never far from the president.

Specifically, the White House Office is responsible for a host of duties. It acts as liaison between the White House and the vast federal bureaucracy. At the beginning of the George W. Bush administration, the secretary to the cabinet — himself a White House Office member — explained that if a cabinet officer wanted to talk one-to-one with the President, then that cabinet officer would first talk either with himself or with chief of staff Andrew Card. Those who work in the White House Office act as liaison between the White House and Congress, too. The Office of Legislative Affairs is a branch of the White House Office with that sole responsibility. The staff member designated as head of congressional liaison is the person who arranges for members of Congress to meet with the president. Anyone whose job description includes deciding who has a meeting in the Oval Office with the president of the United States is a potentially important person.

Obama's personal secretary, Katie Johnson, collecting documents after a morning briefing. Her office was next to the President's

Even telephone calls to the president are screened by the White House Office to decide who should and who should not be put through to the president. The same goes for paperwork. President Eisenhower was known to read only those documents that included the letters 'OK. SA' on them — indicating that his chief of staff, Sherman Adams, had 'okayed' them. Senior members of the White House Office are responsible for drawing up the president's daily schedule, for the day-to-day running of the White House and for personnel management. They ensure that decisions are arrived at in an orderly fashion — that all relevant options, pros and cons have been presented to the president for him to make his decision. They deal with crisis management and act as 'lightning conductors', taking the blame when things go wrong.

In order to fulfil these important functions, members of the White House Office are meant to act as 'honest brokers', not as policy-makers. They are meant not to be always in the media spotlight, but to have something of what the Brownlow Report called 'a passion for anonymity'. If senior members of the White House Office are thought to be pursuing their own rather than the president's agenda, this can lead to trouble. In President George H.W. Bush's administration, Chief of Staff John Sununu was thought by many to be pursuing his own conservative policy agenda rather than what the President wanted. Sununu's access to the President put him at a significant advantage over other policy players, who came to resent Sununu's role. Bush eventually had to fire him.

The White House chief of staff

There's a scene in the television series *The West Wing* where the President is just about to leave the White House for Capitol Hill to deliver his State of the Union Address and the 'designated survivor' — the cabinet officer who does not attend the event, so that he or she survives any terrorist attack on the Capitol while the entire administration is there — comes to visit. President Josiah ('Jed') Bartlet (Martin Sheen) asks Secretary of Agriculture Roger Tribbey (Harry Groener) some questions just in case Tribbey should become president. 'You got a best friend?' asks Bartlet. 'Yes, Sir,' replies Tribbey. 'Is he smarter than you?' 'Yes, Sir,' replies Tribbey with a wry smile. 'Would you trust him with your life?' There's a slight pause before Tribbey replies once more, 'Yes, Sir.' 'That's your chief of staff,' responds the President.

The role of the White House chief of staff is the most crucial job of all within the White House staff and the appointment of the chief of staff is probably the most important that a president makes in terms of the executive branch — hence the truth of the anecdote above. Some, like Sherman Adams (Eisenhower), Don Regan (Reagan) and John Sununu (Bush), became too obtrusive and too powerful — almost a kind of 'deputy president'. A joke which used to circulate during Republican Dwight Eisenhower's presidency imagined two Democrats talking to each other. 'Wouldn't it be terrible,' says one Democrat, 'if Eisenhower died and Vice President Nixon became president.' Replied the other Democrat, 'Not as bad as if Chief of Staff Sherman Adams died and Eisenhower became president!' But other chiefs of staff, such as Thomas 'Mack' McLarty (Clinton), were simply overwhelmed by the job because of their lack of Washington experience.

The best model for chief of staff is someone who always seeks the president's best interests rather than his own, and who protects the president from political harm. President Ford's chief of staff, Dick Cheney, once remarked of his relationship with Ford: 'He takes the credit; I take the blame.' Jack Watson, who served as chief of staff to President Carter, described his job as being like that of a 'javelin catcher' — protecting the president from incoming missiles that could hurt him. Watson continued:

> The chief of staff's role is to see that all the relevant people have a full and fair opportunity to present their views to the president. To act as an honest broker means that I view my role as a fulcrum rather than being a weight on one end. I must ensure that the president hears conflicting views, and not seek to make the judgement for him.

In a May 1993 *Washington Post* article on the role of the White House chief of staff, Lloyd Grove stated:

> It is the hottest seat in town and its occupant is the orchestrator of presidential paper flow, the 'honest broker' of ideas and opinions, the fearsome disciplinarian of wayward staffers, the president's trusted adviser and sounding board, the White House's apologist and occasionally, when necessary, the president's fall guy.

Those who have received high marks for their chief of staff role include Leon Panetta (Clinton: 1994–97), Andrew Card (George W. Bush: 2001–06) and Rahm Emanuel (Barack Obama 2009–10). It was Andrew Card who was famously seen whispering into President George W. Bush's ear on the morning of 11 September 2001, as the President sat in front of an elementary school class in Sarasota, Florida. Card was informing the President of the second plane hitting the World Trade Center in New York. 'America is under attack,' he told the President. Scott McClellan, who served as President George W. Bush's press secretary (2003–06), comments in his recent book, *What Happened* (2008), about Andrew Card:

> He was a tireless public servant who brought years of experience to his position as chief of staff. His sphere of influence was built on both his position and his closeness to the President. His role was to serve as an honest broker among the staff inside the White House, and help make sure all views were heard.

Andrew Card informs President Bush of the second plane hitting the World Trade Center, 11 September 2001

Whereas President Obama was served by four different chiefs of staff during his first term, Denis McDonough served throughout the second term. One of McDonough's strengths was his experience on Capitol Hill as a congressional staffer. He served three years (1996–99) as a staff member to the House Foreign Affairs Committee before crossing to the Senate to serve on the staff first as a senior foreign policy adviser to Senator Tom Daschle and then as legislative director to Senator Ken Salazar — both Democrats. Then, in 2007, he joined the staff of Senator Obama's Washington office as chief foreign policy adviser. These 12 years on Capitol Hill gave him a helpful insight into the workings and personnel of Congress. As liaison with Congress is an important role of a White House chief of staff, McDonough was well prepared for his role of running the Obama White House. He particularly made a priority of reaching out to Republican senators, and one of their number — Bob Corker of Tennessee — went so far as to say that McDonough was 'like a breath of fresh air'.

On the down side, McDonough was known in the White House as something of a 'control freak'. He would spend hours on tasks that previous chiefs of staff would have delegated to those lower down the chain of command. He would, for example, spend huge amounts of time deciding exactly when the President would be assigned to make phone calls, or who was to be on the passenger list of Air Force One. He also very tightly controlled who got access to the President — and some thought the control was too tight, depriving Obama of a much-needed range of views. But ultimately, it is the president who largely decides how he wants the White House organised and run. Staff are there essentially to carry out presidential instructions.

There was early criticism of President Trump's first chief of staff, Reince Priebus who came to the post having served as chairman of the Republican National Committee. As the Trump administration staggered from one self-inflicted crisis to another in its first weeks, close Trump confidante Christopher Ruddy was briefing the press about the Chief of Staff.

> It's my view that Reince is the problem. I think on paper Reince looks good as the chief of staff — and Donald trusted him — but it's pretty clear the guy is in way over his head. He's not knowledgeable of how federal agencies work, how the communications operations work.

That was just day 24 of the Trump administration. The omens were not good.

President Trump in the Oval Office with chief of staff Reince Priebus

The Office of Management and Budget

Richard Nixon created the Office of Management and Budget (OMB) in 1970 when he revamped what was previously called the Bureau of the Budget. The OMB has three principal functions: first, to advise the president on the allocation of federal funds in the annual budget; second, to oversee the spending of all federal departments and agencies; third to act as a kind of clearing house for all legislative and regulatory initiatives coming from the executive branch. The last function means that all proposed legislation and regulations coming from the executive branch must go through the OMB so that they can be analysed both for their budgetary implications and for their compatibility with the president's overall policy programme.

The OMB director

The Office of Management and Budget is headed by the OMB director — just about the only EXOP post that requires Senate confirmation. The job of OMB director is both to run the Office and to give advice and speak on behalf of the president on budgetary matters. Some have performed the job with distinction and thereby the president has received the credit. Bill Clinton benefited hugely from the efficient work of his first OMB director, Leon Panetta. Panetta had served in Congress, rising to chair the House Budget Committee. He was widely credited with getting Clinton's first budget through Congress in 1993 — by the narrowest of margins. 'Clinton could not have had a better salesman,' one media commentator said in praise of Panetta.

But others have been less competent and have thereby caused problems and embarrassments. It was, for example, OMB Director Richard Darman who persuaded the first President Bush to break his 'no new taxes' pledge. Bush had made the pledge during his 1988 election campaign, turning it into a famous catchphrase: 'Read my lips: no new taxes.' Yet just two years later, Darman persuaded Bush to break the pledge in order to get his 1990 budget through a Democrat-controlled Congress. It proved to be akin to political suicide and cost the President dearly in his re-election campaign in 1992.

Under President Obama, the OMB initially struggled to make its mark due mainly to a high turnover in the top job. Obama got through six directors — either full or acting — during his first six years, as directors were recruited for other administration jobs. But Shaun Donovan then brought stability for Obama's last two-and-a-half years, moving from the department of housing and urban development to become OMB director in July 2014.

The budget process

The OMB has a staff of some 500 people, almost all career civil servants, many of high professional skill and substantial experience in the budget process. Like other offices within the Executive Office, its staff are meant to operate in a non-partisan way. The scope and importance of their work can be gauged by a brief overview of the budget process as it affects the executive branch.

The budget process takes roughly two years from formulation to enactment. Thus the budget for the fiscal year 2016 began in April 2014. The formulation of the budget begins in the executive branch with a set of structured discussions and negotiations between the president, the OMB and the executive departments. At this point, it is the responsibility of the OMB to present the president with an analysis of the state of the economy and projections for economic performance in the coming year. Once the president has laid out his budget guidelines, the OMB formulates guidelines for the departments, which then respond with their suggested budgetary requirements for the coming year. The OMB analyses their suggestions and advises the president on how to respond.

After further feedback from the president via the OMB, the departments then submit their formal budget proposals. The OMB reviews these requests, holds hearings on each request and makes recommendations to the president, who then sets each department's budget allocation. The OMB informs them of the president's decisions. This part of the process concludes with the OMB preparing the president's budget message to Congress, the deadline for which is the first Monday in February, around ten months into the process. Congress then, officially, has until the end of June to complete the legislative part of the process, ready for the budget to come into effect on 1 October, but the process usually overruns.

The National Security Council

The National Security Council (NSC) was established in 1947 to help the president coordinate foreign, security and defence policy. Headed by the national security adviser (NSA), the NSC began life as an in-house think-tank for the president. The NSC would coordinate information coming to the White House from the State Department, the Defense Department, the Central Intelligence Agency (CIA), the Joint Chiefs of Staff and American ambassadors around the world. It would liaise with the relevant congressional committees, too. Like the White House Staff, the NSC was designed to operate as an 'honest broker', a 'facilitator', presenting carefully argued options for presidential decision making.

President Nixon changed the way the NSC worked. Distrustful of the State Department, which he saw as too liberal and establishment-orientated, Nixon decided to run foreign policy from the White House. He appointed Henry Kissinger as his national security adviser to act as a roving foreign policy-maker, largely cutting out the State Department's traditional role. But this enhanced and politicised role for the NSC caused grave problems for subsequent presidents.

Subsequently, Bill Clinton, George W. Bush and Barack Obama returned the NSC to its 'honest broker' role. For Bill Clinton, Sandy Berger played the role of behind-the-scenes coordinator. Writing in *The New Republic* in April 1998, Jacob Heilbrunn described Berger as 'the chief coordinator and adviser to the President; the glue that holds the foreign policy team together'.

Table 4.7 lists the national security advisers from 2001 onwards. For George W. Bush, Condoleezza Rice played an important but facilitating role during his first term. Bob Woodward (2003) said of Rice:

> She saw her job as twofold: first to coordinate what Defense, State, the CIA and other departments and agencies were doing by making sure the President's orders were carried out; and second, to act as counsellor — to give her private assessment to the President, certainly when he asked, perhaps if he didn't. In other words she was the President's trouble-shooter.

Jean Edward Smith (2016) tells of Rice defining her job as 'Bush's enabler and enforcer, a translator of his instincts and intuition into policy'. But as Smith comments: 'That was not what Bush needed, but it appears to have been what he wanted.'

When Condoleezza Rice was moved to be secretary of state in Bush's second term, Rice's number two, Stephen Hadley, took over as national security adviser. But Hadley was more deferential to the President. And that, coupled with Bush's

Table 4.7 National security advisers, 2001–17

National Security Adviser	President	Time in office
Condoleezza Rice	George W. Bush	2001–05
Stephen Hadley	George W. Bush	2005–09
James Jones	Barack Obama	2009–10
Tom Donilon	Barack Obama	2010–13
Susan Rice	Barack Obama	2013–17
Michael Flynn	Donald Trump	2017
Herbert (H.R.) McMaster	Donald Trump	2017–

National Security Adviser Stephen Hadley and Secretary of State Condoleezza Rice confer in the Oval Office, May 2007

'no doubt' approach, led to some problems during Bush's second term. Bob Woodward (2008) commented of the relationship between Bush and Hadley:

> A president so certain, so action-orientated, so hero-worshipped by his national security adviser, almost couldn't be halted. The administration lacked a process to examine consequences, alternatives and motives. There was no system to slow down the process so that the right questions were asked and answered, or alternative courses of action seriously considered. The national security adviser has to be a negotiator and an arbiter, someone who tries to consider every angle to a problem. But Hadley had become the lawyer for the president's foreign policy, his unwavering advocate and a cheerleader for his greatness.

During the Obama first term, there was no doubt at all that the lead voices in foreign policy were those of the President and Secretary of State Hillary Clinton. With such a big name at the State Department, the NSC stayed in the background, performing its traditional coordinating role. During these first four years, Obama was served by two national security advisers — General James Jones followed by Tom Donilon, who had earlier served as Jones's deputy. Both men fitted the 'honest broker' style of working and both had the 'passion for anonymity' which is meant to characterise those who work in the Executive Office of the President. Bob Woodward (2010) reported Jones's views on his number two and his eventual successor:

> Jones praised [Donilon's] substantive and organizational skills, and told Donilon that he was indispensable to the President and the whole NSC staff. But Donilon had made three mistakes. First, he had never gone to Afghanistan or Iraq or really left his office for a serious field trip. Second, he frequently spoke with absolute declarations about places he'd never been, leaders he'd never met, or colleagues he worked with. Third, he had too little feel for the people who worked day and night on the NSC staff, their salaries, their maternity leaves, their promotions, their family troubles, all the things a manager of people has to be tuned into.

In 2015, Donilon was replaced by the more politically minded Susan Rice. Rice had always coveted the post of secretary of state and had hoped to succeed

Hillary Clinton at the state department in 2013, but had to withdraw from consideration after she became embroiled in the Benghazi affair — when the US Ambassador to Libya was killed in an attack on the American diplomatic mission in Benghazi. But the two jobs — secretary of state and national security adviser — are two very different roles, and those likely to perform well in one are unlikely to be able to perform well in the other. Rice, an African-American, came in for some criticism when she made a speech in Florida in May 2016 in which she said that the nation's national security workforce was 'too white, too male and too Yale' — the latter referring to the elite university in Connecticut — and seemed to suggest that this posed a national security threat to the nation. This is not the kind of political controversy that a White House honest broker should be entering, and certainly not in public.

President Trump's first action regarding the NSC was to remove the chairman of the joint chiefs of staff and the director of national intelligence from permanent status. They would attend meetings only when summoned. In their place, Trump placed his chief strategist Steve Bannon as a permanent NSC member. This seemed to signal Trump's intention to use the NSC as a political — rather than a coordinating — forum. But this arrangement lasted less than three months as Bannon was removed from the NSC in early April. Trump also set a record for having the shortest-serving national security adviser when Michael Flynn resigned from the post after just 24 days. His resignation followed accusations that he had misled the Vice President over a phone call Flynn had made to the Russian ambassador in Washington during the closing days of the Obama administration.

EXOP–cabinet rivalries

Presidents must guard against the development of unhealthy rivalries and distrust between those who work in the EXOP, on the one hand, and the heads of the executive departments — the cabinet — on the other. Such rivalries and distrust can inflict serious wounds on a presidency, as presidents Richard Nixon and Jimmy Carter discovered.

There is a danger that those who work in the White House may come to regard cabinet officers as distant and disloyal. Similarly, cabinet officers may come to regard those who work in the White House as too close and too loyal to the president.

Physical distance

Some of these feelings are born of natural circumstances. Cabinet officers are physically distant from the White House. The office of the secretary of state, for example, is on the seventh floor of the State Department building in Foggy Bottom — an area of Washington about seven blocks west of the White House, making it a good 10 minutes away from the Oval Office. The secretary of defense is even further away. The Pentagon — the department's headquarters — is over the other side of the Potomac river, 15–20 minutes away. In comparison, the national security adviser's office is a 30-second walk from the Oval Office.

It is hardly surprising that the secretaries of state and defense seem — and feel — a bit distant. Those who work in the EXOP have the key advantage of proximity. Daniel Patrick Moynihan, who served in the White House under President Nixon, commented: 'Never underestimate the power of proximity.' Former secretary of defense Donald Rumsfeld refers to this in his comments about national security adviser Condoleezza Rice, with whom he worked in the Bush administration (see Box 4.2).

Divided loyalties

It is understandable to some extent that cabinet officers sometimes appear disloyal. Although they are appointed by the president and serve only at his pleasure, they have other loyalties. They have a loyalty to Congress, whose votes decide their departmental budgets and whose committees can call them to account in person. They have a loyalty to their own departmental bureaucracy and to interest groups with which their department has close links. On the other hand, those who work in the EXOP have only one loyalty — to the president. They are *All the President's Men* — the title of a 1970s book (and a film starring Robert Redford and Dustin Hoffman) about the Nixon White House and the Watergate affair.

In his recent book on the presidency of George W. Bush, Jean Edward Smith (2016) comments that 'Bush relied on the White House staff rather than his cabinet' and that this was particularly true in foreign policy. In 2001 he told Russian president Vladimir Putin, 'Contact [Condoleezza] Rice if there is a problem' — not Colin Powell or the State Department. In this way, cabinet members can quickly feel like the outsiders that they are.

Policy 'czars'

The first term of the Obama administration, like pretty much all its predecessors, experienced its tensions between members of the cabinet and those who worked in the White House as part of EXOP. Obama's extensive use of White House policy 'czars' signalled that policy making was going to take place at the White House and not in the 15 executive departments scattered around downtown Washington.

The term 'czar' has no generally agreed definition in American politics. It tends to be used — especially by journalists — to refer to members of the administration who seem to be obviously in charge of a particular policy area. In Obama's first term, for instance, Carol Browner was portrayed as the energy and climate czar; Lawrence Summers was seen as the economic czar; Nancy-Ann DeParle as the health czar. It all sounds well structured and clear, but as James Pfiffner (2011) points out, there are problems:

The real problem with White House czars (and sometimes even the national security adviser) is that they confuse the chain of command and leave open the question of who is in charge of administration policy. Czars are often frustrated because they lack the authority to carry out their responsibilities. That is, they do not control budgets or appointments, and they cannot order cabinet officers to do their bidding. The other problem with czars is that cabinet officers often resent the dilution of their policy-advising authority. So the biggest problem is who is in charge of a given policy area. Who has the lead in developing policy alternatives for the president's consideration?

Obama's cabinet resented not only the White House czars but also the treatment they received from Chief of Staff Emanuel, who they felt treated them as 'minions' rather than as major administration officials. Emanuel insisted all cabinet officers had to send him weekly reports of what they were doing in their department. The reports would be returned with Emanuel's comments and instructions scribbled on them.

The president's relations with Congress

The power to persuade

The late Professor Richard Neustadt famously remarked that 'the president's power is the power to persuade'. An example will show how important, and also how limited, this can be. On 31 August 2011, President Obama was getting ready to use his persuasive powers. Frustrated by the slow recovery in the nation's economy, he wanted to go on the record to show his support for a major new stimulus package currently before Congress, the American Jobs Act. So the President announced that he would deliver a primetime televised speech to a joint session of Congress.

As is customary on such occasions, the President sent a letter to the Speaker of the House of Representatives asking if he would schedule the address for the early evening of 7 September. Before the President could persuade others, he had to persuade the Republican Speaker, John Boehner. The Speaker said no. 'It is my recommendation,' replied Speaker Boehner to the President, 'that your address be held on the following evening, when we can ensure there will be no parliamentary or logistical impediments that might detract from your remarks.'

President Obama speaks with John Boehner in the Oval Office

To understand this rebuff to the President, one needs to know two further pieces of information. First, 7 September was the evening on which the Republican presidential candidates for 2012 had scheduled a televised debate at the Reagan Presidential Library in California. The President had hoped to upstage it, but the Speaker was having none of it. Second, 8 September was the evening of the opening game of the NFL American football season.

No Speaker of the House had ever before refused a presidential request to address a joint session of Congress. But this Speaker refused to be persuaded, despite much back-and-forth between the Speaker's office and the White House. In the end, the President spoke on the 8th. The president's power is, indeed, the power to persuade — except when he can't!

Why persuasion?

But why does a president need to resort to persuasion? What's wrong with all those powers he has? The problem is that almost every power that the president possesses is checked by Congress. The president, therefore, needs Congress's agreement. He needs his persuasion to succeed. However, in a system of 'separated institutions sharing powers' this is by no means easy.

Party links may not help much. The president and the majority of Congress may well be of different parties, as shown in Table 4.8. Indeed, from 1993 to 2018, the president and both houses of Congress will have been controlled by the same party for only 10½ of those 26 years. Even when the two branches are controlled by the same party, there is no guarantee of success — witness the difficulties experienced by Bill Clinton in his failed attempt to pass healthcare reform in 1993–94. As Richard Neustadt (1990) stated: 'What the Constitution separates, the political parties do not combine.'

Table 4.8 Party control of the presidency and Congress, 1993–2018

Years	Presidency	House	Senate
1993–94	**Democrat (Bill Clinton)**	**Democrat**	**Democrat**
1995–96	Democrat	Republican	Republican
1997–98	Democrat	Republican	Republican
1999–2000	Democrat	Republican	Republican
January–May 2001	**Republican (George W. Bush)**	**Republican**	**Republican**
June 2001–02	Republican	Republican	Democrat
2003–04	**Republican**	**Republican**	**Republican**
2005–06	**Republican**	**Republican**	**Republican**
2007–08	Republican	Democrat	Democrat
2009–10	**Democrat (Barack Obama)**	**Democrat**	**Democrat**
2011–12	Democrat	Republican	Democrat
2013–14	Democrat	Republican	Democrat
2015–16	Democrat	Republican	Republican
2017–18	**Republican (Donald Trump)**	**Republican**	**Republican**

Bold type indicates those years in which both houses of Congress were controlled by the president's party.

The president can do very little without the agreement of Congress. There is an intricate system of checks and balances devised by the Founding Fathers, who wanted it to be difficult for the president to get his way in Congress.

As Nelson Polsby (1976) put it: 'Conflict and cooperation between Congress and the president are not merely the result of whim or wilfulness at one end or the other of Pennsylvania Avenue.' Professor S.E. Finer (1970) has likened the president and Congress to 'two halves of a bank note, each useless without the other'. However, the Founding Fathers' desire for cooperation and compromise between these two branches of government — 'ambition must counteract ambition', as James Madison put it — often leads to inaction and gridlock.

There is a famous story of President Truman sitting at his Oval Office desk in December 1952, contemplating what it would be like for his successor coming into office in just a few weeks' time. His successor was to be Dwight Eisenhower — a former army general, affectionately known as 'Ike'. Truman was contemplating how strange it would be for the general-turned-president.

> He'll sit here and he'll say, 'Do this! Do that!' And nothing will happen. Poor Ike, it won't be a bit like the army. He'll find it very frustrating.

General Dwight Eisenhower, president, 1953-61

It would be 'not a bit like the army' because in the army Eisenhower could get what he wanted by issuing commands. As president, Eisenhower would learn that little happens as a result of command; most happens as a result of persuasion. Truman knew that. Earlier in his presidency he had remarked:

> I sit here all day trying to persuade people to do the things they ought to have the sense to do without my persuading them. That's all the powers of the president amount to.

When it comes to persuasion, there are essentially two methods: the president can use other people to persuade on his behalf; or he can get involved himself through the use of 'perks' that he can offer.

Presidential persuasion through people

The president, if he is to be a successful persuader, must work through a number of other people. He cannot — nor should he — try to do it all himself. There are four groups of people he can use.

- **The vice president.** All of the last seven vice presidents — covering more than 40 years from Walter Mondale to Mike Pence — have been former members of Congress. Barack Obama's vice president, Joe Biden, had served in the Senate for 36 years — longer than any other vice president. With this background, Biden quickly became the lead-man of the Obama administration in Congress and his role was critical for the President on such big-ticket issues as the economic stimulus package, the middle-class taskforce, tax relief and negotiations to end the debt ceiling crisis in 2011. In his time in Congress, Biden had campaigned for many Democratic congressmen and senators who almost owed their political life to him. Certainly when Democrats in Congress had a problem with which they wanted help from the White House, they tended to talk with Biden rather than Obama, as they felt Biden would understand their situation better. It also helps that as president of the Senate, the vice president has a foothold in Congress. He has an office there, where he can meet with members of both houses.

- **Members of the Office of Legislative Affairs.** These are members of the White House Office who work as full-time lobbyists for the president on Capitol Hill. They meet with members of Congress as well as with senior members of their staff. The congressional liaison staff are usually organised in such a way that some work on the House side and others on the Senate side, hoping to build up good relationships with people whom they will get to know well.

- **Cabinet officers.** The cabinet officers can be deployed by the White House to talk with members of Congress in their own policy areas. George W. Bush used Education Secretary Rod Paige to sell his education reform package to Congress in 2001. The following year, Secretary of State Colin Powell was dispatched to Congress to help persuade members to support authorisation of the use of US troops against Iraq.

- **Party leadership in Congress.** Finally, the president can work through the party leadership in Congress — the House Speaker; the majority and minority leaders of both houses; the party whips; the committee chairs and ranking minority members. It helps, of course, if the president and the majority party leadership are of the same party — an asset that Obama experienced for only two years in the House during his two terms and for six years in the Senate. President George W. Bush was known to have a somewhat frosty relationship with the Democrat Speaker of the House, Nancy Pelosi, during the last two years of his administration. Personality plays a part here too. A gregarious president like Ronald Reagan or Bill Clinton can more easily develop good relations with members of Congress than a more private and solitary president such as Barack Obama. Contrasting Obama and Biden in their interaction with people, Chuck Todd (2014) had this to say:

> Walk into the Oval Office with your family and the President will be very courteous, give you a warm handshake...Walk into the vice president's residence and get ready for a lot of touching...man hugs, and kisses for the women. It's just in his DNA — just as much as being less huggy and kissy is in Obama's.

President Ronald Reagan (centre) shares a joke with House Speaker Thomas O'Neill (second from left), 1986

Presidential persuasion through perks

Any of these people, however, may report back to the president that, in order to secure the vote of a particular member of Congress, the president himself needs to get involved by utilising a range of 'perks' which he has at his disposal. As David Mervin (1993) stated:

> The president must bargain, he must make deals, he must negotiate with those with whom he shares power. Bargaining skill is therefore indispensable in a president.

The president may, for example, make a personal phone call to certain members of Congress. In an important budget vote in the House in August 1993, President Clinton phoned Democrat House member Marjorie Margolies-Mezvinsky in a hallway just off the chamber of the House of Representatives. She cast the crucial 218th vote to ensure passage of his budget by 218 votes to 216.

When receiving a personal phone call from the president, it is important not to do what Republican congresswoman Ileana Ros-Lehtinen of Florida did when she received a call from President-elect Barack Obama in December 2008. Thinking the call was a hoax, she replied: 'You know, you're a better impersonator than that guy who does Obama on *Saturday Night Live*.' When Obama persevered, asking how he could convince her that he really was the President-elect, Mrs Ros-Lehtinen merely replied: 'Yeah, sure, have a great day' and hung up!

The president might offer help with legislation that benefits that member's state or district. He might offer to look more favourably on a judicial or executive branch appointment of interest to the member. The president might invite members of Congress for an Oval Office meeting — either individually or in a small group. He might even go to Capitol Hill to meet with a selected group of members of Congress there. If a member whose support is sought is of the president's party, the president might offer to campaign for them in the next congressional elections. A popular president can use this perk to great effect. If all else fails, the president might go on national television to appeal over the heads of Congress directly to the people. This is what President Johnson called 'putting Congress's feet to the fire'.

Obama's healthcare reform bill (2010)

In the run-up to the passage of the Patient Protection and Affordable Care Act in 2010 — popularly known as Obamacare — President Obama made a number of attempts to persuade members of Congress to support the legislation. During a two-month period between 27 January and 20 March, the President:

- delivered the State of the Union Address to Congress (27 January)
- addressed the Republican House Issues Conference in Baltimore (29 January)
- took part in a televised session with Senate Democrats in Washington DC (3 February)
- addressed the Democratic National Committee winter meeting in Washington DC (6 February)
- hosted a bipartisan healthcare reform meeting at Blair House, Washington DC (25 February)
- met with 11 House Democrats at the White House (4 March)
- met with the New Democratic Coalition Leadership in the Oval Office (4 March)
- met with Senator Charles Schumer (D-New York) in the Oval Office (4 March)
- addressed the House Democratic Caucus on Capitol Hill (20 March)

This was on top of addressing numerous Town Hall meetings around the country, including those in Tampa, Florida (28 January), Nashua, New Hampshire (2 February), St Louis, Missouri (10 March) and Strongsville, Ohio (15 March).

Box 4.3 lists the ways in which President Obama sought to persuade Congress to support his healthcare reforms. However, persuasion needs to be a two-way street. If members of Congress get the idea that the only time they hear from the president — either directly or indirectly — is when he wants them to cast a difficult vote for him, cooperation will soon dry up. Small courtesies from the White House can pay off. An invitation to a bill-signing ceremony, dinner with the president at the White House, a trip on Air Force One — all these small perks can help to make the wheels of cooperation turn more smoothly.

The results of presidential persuasion

David Mervin (1993) described the US president as 'bargainer-in-chief'. Presidents bargain for a purpose: that their legislation is passed, their appointments are confirmed, their budgets are agreed to, their vetoes are sustained and their treaties are ratified. As Mark Peterson (2000) stated: 'Leaders are those who make things happen that otherwise would not come about.' The president's success rate is measured each year in what is called the presidential support score. This annual statistic measures how often the president won in recorded votes in the House and Senate on which he took a clear position, expressed as a percentage of the whole.

Table 4.9, which shows the presidential support score between 1993 and 2015, reveals some interesting information. Presidential support tends to decline during a presidential term. Having one's party control both houses of Congress usually results in a high support score. Loss of control of Congress means a dip in the president's support score: witness Clinton in 1995, George W. Bush in 2007 and Barack Obama in 2011.

The score is a useful guide to presidential success, but it does have certain limitations. First, the score does not measure the importance of votes. The president might win trivial votes while losing important ones or vice versa. Second, presidents can avoid low scores by simply not taking positions on votes they expect to lose. There has been a significant decline in recent years in the number of votes on which presidents have declared a position. In 1978, President Carter announced a position on 306 votes; and in 2011,

Table 4.9 Presidential support scores, 1993–2015

Year	President	Support score (%)	Unified/divided government?
1993	**Bill Clinton**	86.4	Unified
1994		86.4	Unified
1995		36.2	Divided
1996		55.1	Divided
1997		53.6	Divided
1998		50.6	Divided
1999		37.8	Divided
2000		55.0	Divided
2001	**George W. Bush**	87.0	Unified/divided
2002		87.8	Divided
2003		78.7	Unified
2004		72.6	Unified
2005		78.0	Unified
2006		81.0	Unified
2007		38.0	Divided
2008		48.0	Divided
2009	**Barack Obama**	96.7	Unified
2010		85.8	Unified
2011		57.1	Divided
2012		53.6	Divided
2013		56.7	Divided
2014		68.7	Divided
2015		45.7	Divided

Source: Bipartisan Policy Center

Debate

Is the president's power still the power to persuade?

Yes

- The president has no formal disciplinary hold over members of Congress.
- Party discipline in Congress, though tighter than it used to be, cannot guarantee votes for the president.
- The president may be faced with one or both houses of Congress controlled by the other party.
- The president is dependent upon members of Congress for legislation, confirmation of appointments and treaty ratification.
- The president's 'direct authority' has limited use.
- The president can offer his support for things members of Congress regard as important.

No

- In an era of partisanship, few (if any) members of Congress from the opposition party are open to presidential persuasion, especially on big-ticket items.
- Partisanship also makes persuasion a less useful tool for the president trying to persuade voters to support him and then pressurise recalcitrant members of Congress to do likewise.
- Presidents nowadays tend to have low approval ratings (and high disapproval ratings) and therefore their persuasion is much less effective.
- Second-term presidents have always found their persuasive power to be very limited.

President Obama announced a position on just 184 votes, and that was out of nearly 1,200 recorded votes held in Congress that year — over 900 in the House and over 200 in the Senate. Third, the score does not count bills that fail to come to a vote on the floor in either house. President Clinton's high score in

1994 took no account of the failure of his Healthcare Reform Bill even to reach the floor of either house, yet this was his flagship policy.

It is worth keeping in mind that changes in Congress — and more widely in the US political system — make the president's job of trying to build support for his legislation more difficult than was the case in the 1950s or 1960s. There are three possible reasons to consider.

- Members of Congress are now more aware of constituents' wishes — through the effects of such factors as C-SPAN and e-mail — and therefore are perhaps less willing merely to go along with what the president wants.

- Changes in the methods of selecting presidential candidates have resulted in Washington outsiders becoming president — Governors Carter, Reagan, Bill Clinton, George W. Bush and most notably Donald Trump. They know much less about the workings of Congress than did presidents who had worked in Congress — Truman, Kennedy, Johnson, Nixon and Ford — and do not have the personal ties to members of Congress that presidents such as Truman and Johnson enjoyed. Even Obama had served less than four years in Congress before being elected president.

- The third reason is the most significant. Not only is it less likely these days that the president and a majority of both houses of Congress will be of the same party, but increased levels of partisanship have made it much more difficult for a president to gain the support of members of the opposition party in Congress. Take the final passage votes on three landmark bills passed by Congress during the Obama era: the Economic Stimulus Package (2009) received no Republican votes in the House and just three in the Senate; the Dodd–Frank Wall Street Reform Act (2010) received the votes of just six Republicans — three in each house; and the Patient Protection and Affordable Care Act (2010) received no Republican votes at all. That said, the era of bipartisan cooperation is not completely over. The Every Student Succeeds Act (2015) — a reauthorisation of George W. Bush's No Child Left Behind Act — received the support of 12 Republicans in the Senate and 64 in the House.

Direct authority

Frustrated by the checks imposed upon them as well as the partisan gridlock of Washington, presidents resort to the use of what we might call direct authority — actions that require no congressional approval and yet can achieve some of the political goals that presidents seek. We shall consider four types of direct authority that presidents may use: executive orders, signing statements, recess appointments and executive agreements.

Executive orders

Executive orders have the effect of law and they depend on some grant of authority in the Constitution. But they are what we would call an 'extra-constitutional power' — a power outside of the Constitution. They do not require congressional approval. They are often drafted in the departments and agencies of the federal government and sometimes in the OMB. In either case, the OMB has developed the role of 'executive order clearance' — screening them to ensure that they fit with the president's policy interests and with existing law.

Although the public's awareness of executive orders has increased in the last few years, they are by no means a new phenomenon. Franklin Roosevelt (1933–45) issued over 3,000 of them in just over 12 years. In 1961, President

Kennedy introduced the term 'affirmative action' to federal policy through Executive Order 10925, requiring federal contractors to take 'affirmative action' to ensure equal treatment of employees and job applicants 'without regard to their race, creed, colour, or national origin'.

However, just as executive orders are easy for a president to issue, they are equally easy for a successor to revoke. For example, in 1984, President Reagan signed an executive order that prohibited family planning clinics that received federal funds from informing their clients about abortion options. However, within days of taking office in 1993, Bill Clinton revoked the order. Then, on 22 January 2001 — his second full day in office — George W. Bush reinstated the Reagan order. But on 22 February 2009, it was revoked again by Barack Obama.

Executive orders under Obama

As a candidate in 2008, Obama had been deeply sceptical of executive power, but having been frustrated by Congress for a number of years, he soon got a taste for executive orders which allowed him to get things done that Congress refused to go along with. One policy area in which the Obama administration used executive orders to advance its goals was gay rights. People with HIV were no longer barred from entering the country; federal housing rules were changed to stop discrimination according to sexual orientation; health insurance companies were prevented from discriminating against gay people; married same-sex couples could now take family and medical leave; and the Internal Revenue Service treated same-sex married couples no differently from other married couples.

By the autumn of 2011, after a stand-off between the President and Congress led to a partial government shutdown, the President expressed his disdain for 'an increasingly dysfunctional Congress,' and pledged that 'where they won't act, I will'. Regular planning sessions began to be held in the West Wing, drawing up lists of policy goals that the administration might be able to achieve without Congress. In his State of the Union Address in January 2014, the President declared that 'whenever I can take steps without legislation to expand opportunities for more American families, that's what I'm going to do'. He announced executive orders to increase the federal minimum wage to $10.10 an hour and restrict greenhouse gas emissions.

Although executive orders circumvent the checks by Congress, they may still be declared unconstitutional by the courts. In November 2014 President Obama issued an executive order — the Deferred Action for Parents of Americans and Lawful Permanent Residents (DAPA) — to allow certain illegal immigrants to be granted 'deferred action status'. This meant that, although not granted full citizenship, they would be subject to an indefinite delay in their deportation from the United States. In December of the same year, Texas along with 25 other states, all with Republican governors, challenged the President's action in federal court, calling it 'one of the largest changes in immigration policy in our nation's history', and claiming that the President could not carry out such a programme without Congress's approval.

In November 2015, the federal appeals court found that President Obama did not have such powers, and that his action was unconstitutional as it breached the clause of Article II of the Constitution that requires the president to 'take care that the laws be faithfully executed'. The Justice Department announced that it was asking the Supreme Court to review this decision. Its 4–4 tied decision in 2016 left in place the federal appeals court decision blocking the plan. Walter Dellinger, a Clinton administration lawyer, commented: 'Seldom have the hopes of so many been crushed by so few words.' The hopes of the President were among them.

Executive orders under Trump

When President Donald Trump arrived in the Oval Office in January 2017, his first week in office seemed to have him signing one executive order after another, giving the appearance, at least, that he believed that this was mostly what being president amounted to. For example, on learning at a meeting with business leaders on his first full working day that the nation's pipelines are not necessarily made with US steel, on the Tuesday the President signed an executive order requiring them to be made with solely American-made materials — but without seeming to realise that this contravened World Trade Organisation rules. Rena Steinzor of the University of Maryland's law school commented:

> President Trump needs to go back to civics class because although he can direct his employees to do various things, he cannot repeal laws through his executive orders because he needs congressional consent — and the executive orders themselves say that...He can't just sit there and show people pieces of paper with his overly emphatic signature and say, 'I have changed the world,' because that's not how we do it.

Trump signed 12 executive orders in his first week, including those to withdraw the United States from the Trans-Pacific Partnership (although the Senate had never ratified it anyway) and a freeze on federal government hiring (though there were exceptions).

But the executive order that really caught the headlines — and prompted nationwide and worldwide protests — was the one issued at the end of his first week in office placing a four-month ban on refugees and a three-month ban on citizens from seven predominantly Muslim countries including Iran, Iraq and Syria. Three days later, Trump fired Acting Attorney General Sally Yates after she ordered staff at the Department of Justice not to defend the order in court. The federal courts then placed a temporary restraining order on the President's order.

New Yorkers protest against President Trump's 'Muslim travel ban', 27 January 2017

Signing statements

Presidents have also expanded their use of direct authority through the use of signing statements. Signing statements date back as far as President James Monroe (1817–25). Presidents who used them most were Jimmy Carter, George H.W. Bush and Bill Clinton. George W. Bush and Barack Obama actually issued fewer signing statements, just as they became more widely talked about and controversial. Earlier presidents had issued signing statements more often to add a commentary or some celebratory note to the bill they were signing. But George W. Bush's signing statement increasingly challenged the constitutionality of some part of the bill he was signing into law. Table 4.10 shows that 81% of Bush's signing statements raised some constitutional question compared with just 19% of Bill Clinton's.

Table 4.10 Presidential signing statements, 1977–2016

President	Signing statements	Raising constitutional questions	As percentage of total
Jimmy Carter	225	23	10.2
Ronald Reagan	249	51	20.5
George H.W. Bush	228	67	29.4
Bill Clinton	381	72	18.9
George W. Bush	160	130	81.2
Barack Obama	41	21	51.2

This has opened up a debate about whether or not these statements are legitimate. At the heart of this debate is this question: Is it proper for a president to sign a bill into law but at the same time to state that they will not enforce part of it because they believe it violates the Constitution or other federal laws? Critics of signing statements claim that this is an overuse of presidential power; that the correct and constitutional course of action would be for the president either to veto the bill, or to await a ruling on the law's constitutionality from the Supreme Court. By using statements, presidents seem to be adding a fourth option to the three options presented to them in the Constitution upon receiving a bill passed by Congress — veto, pocket veto, or sign. By using this fourth option, presidents appear to be signing only part of the bill into law. This, in strict terms, would be what is called a line-item veto, a power granted to the president by Congress in 1996, but declared unconstitutional by the Supreme Court two years later (see Chapter 3).

What is agreed is that signing statements add significantly to the president's power over legislation. It may also be one of those powers that become much more attractive when one is on the inside of the White House rather than on the outside. While in the Senate, Obama had criticised Bush for using them 'to accumulate more power to the presidency' and to 'make laws as he's going along'. But Obama had been in the Oval Office for less than two months when he circulated a memorandum to the heads of the executive departments commending the practice. Box 4.4 shows two signing statements from the Obama administration — the first of a congratulatory nature, the second of a constitutional nature.

Naturally, members of Congress are upset by the practice. To them, a signing statement often blocks the enforcement of a law that Congress has duly passed and they regard them as the equivalent of an unconstitutional line-item veto. While the Supreme Court has allowed signing statements to clarify unclear legislation, it has never given a clear ruling on the constitutional standing of such documents. Signing statements are therefore a good example of what one scholar has called the 'invitation to struggle' that the Constitution has created between the president and Congress.

Box 4.4

Two Obama signing statements

On the HIV Organ Policy Equity Act, 21 November 2013

Earlier today I signed into law the HIV Organ Policy Equity (HOPE) Act, a bipartisan piece of legislation that allows scientists to carry out research into organ donations from one person with HIV to another. For decades, these organ transplants have been illegal. It was even illegal to study whether they could be safe and effective. But as our understanding of HIV and effective treatments have grown, that policy has become outdated. The potential for successful organ transplants between people living with HIV has become more of a possibility. The HOPE Act lifts the research ban, and in time, it could lead to life-saving organ donations for people living with HIV while ensuring the safety of the organ transplant process and strengthening the national supply of organs for all who need them. Improving care for people living with HIV is critical to fighting the epidemic, and it's a key goal of my National HIV/AIDS Strategy. The HOPE Act marks an important step in the right direction, and I thank Congress for their action.

On the Act concerning participation of Taiwan in the International Civil Aviation Organization, 12 July 2013

Today I have signed into law an Act concerning participation of Taiwan in the International Civil Aviation Organization... I note that sections 1(b) and 1(c) of the Act contain impermissibly mandatory language purporting to direct the Secretary of State to undertake certain diplomatic initiatives and to report to Congress on the progress of those initiatives. Consistent with longstanding constitutional principle, my Administration will interpret and implement these sections in a manner that does not interfere with my constitutional authority to conduct diplomacy and to protect the confidentiality of diplomatic communications.

Activity

- Go to website of the American Presidency Project at www.presidency.ucsb.edu.
- Click on 'Data'.
- In the 'Document Archive' on the left, click on 'Signing Statements'.
- In the 'Year' window, select the most recent year and click 'Display'.
- From the data displayed, find numbers and examples of the most recent signing statements.

Key term

Recess appointment A temporary appointment of a federal official made by the president to fill a vacancy while the Senate is in recess.

Recess appointments

Under the appointments clause of the Constitution (Article II, Section 2, Paragraph 2), the president and the Senate share the power to fill high-level politically appointed positions in the federal government. But the **recess appointments** clause (Paragraph 3) also empowers the president unilaterally to make a temporary appointment to such a position if it is vacant and the Senate is in recess, and thereby unable to confirm the appointment. Such an appointment — referred to as a recess appointment — expires at the end of the following session of the Senate.

One can see why the framers included such a provision in the Constitution as for the first century and more the Senate was on average in session for less than half the year. Like executive orders, recess appointments flourished in the new era of partisanship in Washington (see Table 4.11). Presidents began to see them as a way

Table 4.11 Recess appointments, 1993–2016

President	1st year	2nd year	3rd year	4th year	5th year	6th year	7th year	8th year	Total
Bill Clinton	0	3	1	31	9	11	11	73	139
George W. Bush	1	22	38	45	21	40	4	0	171
Barack Obama	0	28	0	4	0	0	0	0	32

Source: Congressional Research Service

round Senate intransigence. Getting wise to this, the Senate began to hold so-called 'pro forma sessions' (often with just one senator present) every few days during recesses, thereby trying to stop the president from making recess appointments.

The matter came to a head between 2012 and 2014. In January 2012, during the Christmas–New Year 'recess', President Obama had made three recess appointments to the National Labor Relations Board (NLRB). The following month the NLRB ruled against the Noel Canning Corporation, a soft-drinks company, in a labour dispute. But the Noel Group appealed the ruling, claiming that as a majority of the NLRB members were recess appointees when the Senate had not been in recess at all, the Board's ruling had no legal standing. In the case of *National Labor Relations Board v Noel Canning* (2014), the Supreme Court ruled that the President had exceeded his powers in making the recess appointments to the NRLB. It was a stunning rebuke to the President, the more so as it was a unanimous decision of the Court. President Obama made no further recess appointments during the last four years of his presidency.

Executive agreements

Executive agreements are yet another type of direct authority that presidents can use. An **executive agreement** is an agreement reached between the president and a foreign nation on matters that do not require formal treaties. The first recorded executive agreement was signed by President James Monroe in 1817. For the next one hundred years, numbers remained small, picking up somewhat in the early twentieth century under President Theodore Roosevelt (1901–09) and swelling to a crescendo under Franklin Roosevelt (1933–45). Subsequent presidents have signed an average of some 200 executive agreements per year, with a peak of over 300 per year reached under Jimmy Carter, Ronald Reagan, and George W. Bush's second term. They cover such matters as basing American troops on foreign soil and resolving claims made by citizens of one country against the government of another. They could be concerned with regulating international trade or anti-terrorism policies.

Commentators and academics have generally contended that presidents use executive agreements, rather than treaties, as political devices to circumvent the Senate because executive agreements, unlike treaties, do not require Senate ratification. So the use of executive agreements is especially useful for the president when the Senate is controlled by the other party. But there can be a price to pay for the president because senators jealously guard their powers in foreign policy. When President Bill Clinton cut a deal with North Korea in 1994 by signing an executive agreement rather than a treaty, a number of Republican senators — including John McCain of Arizona — went ballistic, saying that a deal of that magnitude ought to have been brought before Congress. In the same year, Bill Clinton secured the North American Free Trade Agreement (NAFTA) by an executive agreement. Here is yet another example of the Constitution inviting a struggle for power between the president and Congress.

Key term

Executive agreement
An agreement reached between the president and a foreign nation on matters that do not require a formal treaty.

Most casual observers of the American presidency think that it's 'the most powerful office in the world'. But the reality of the presidency is that, in itself, it is not a powerful office. The Founding Fathers never intended it to be powerful. In 1960, as we have already seen, Richard Neustadt spoke of the president's principal power as 'the power to persuade'. Four decades later, he wrote this:

> Weakness is still what I see — weakness in the sense of a great gap between what is expected of a man (or, some day, a woman) and assured capacity to carry through.

Indeed, given the plethora of potential obstacles that stand in their way, it is sometimes remarkable that presidents accomplish anything at all of any significance, especially in domestic policy. Furthermore, in today's era of partisanship in Washington, where members of the opposition will rarely vote with the president — especially on controversial, big-ticket issues — one might question the usefulness of any persuasive skills the president may have. After all, if there are few people who are persuadable, where is the virtue of persuasion?

But the presidency did not burst, full-grown, onto the political stage. It has evolved significantly since the time of George Washington. Presidential scholars have used various terms to signal this evolution. The 'modern presidency' and the 'institutionalised presidency' both had their birth in the administration of Franklin Roosevelt (FDR). It was during FDR's presidency that the role of the federal government expanded significantly, EXOP was established and the USA took on its full-time world leadership role. The pendulum swung in the direction of presidential power and away from congressional authority. Congress seemed to become more subservient to the president. This trend continued with FDR's Democratic successors — Truman, Kennedy and Johnson — as well as with Republican Richard Nixon, who succeeded them.

The imperial presidency

Critics of this presidential assertiveness soon materialised. The one whose criticism received the widest recognition was Professor Arthur Schlesinger. In 1973 he published *The Imperial Presidency* and the term became a catchphrase for critics of the growth of presidential power. According to Schlesinger's thesis, 'the imperial presidency was essentially the creation of foreign policy'. He traced its origins to the Japanese attack on Pearl Harbor in December 1941 — a crisis that allowed FDR to break free from Congress's conventional ties on the executive.

To see how quickly presidential power had increased, there is no need to look further back than 1950. When North Korea invaded South Korea that year, President Truman immediately sent US troops to South Korea without any congressional authorisation, and Congress raised barely a murmur. In 1958, President Eisenhower sent 14,000 US troops to Lebanon. Again, there was no congressional authorisation. In 1961, President Kennedy launched the disastrous attack on the Bay of Pigs in Cuba without congressional authorisation. Congress played no role at all in the Cuban missile crisis the following year. In 1964, Congress signed a virtual blank cheque — the Tonkin Gulf Resolution — to allow President Johnson to take 'all necessary measures' to sort out the problems in Vietnam. In 1970, President Nixon bombed Cambodia without even the knowledge, let alone the authorisation, of Congress.

Key term

Imperial presidency A presidency characterised by the misuse of presidential powers, especially excessive secrecy — especially in foreign policy — and high-handedness in dealing with Congress.

New York Post cartoon, May 1973, on the damage being done to the presidency by the Watergate affair

The imperial presidency might have been the creation of foreign policy, but it soon spread to the conduct of domestic policy. President Nixon's policies to clamp down on the anti-Vietnam War protests smacked to some of excessive use of power. Even the way he organised and conducted business in the White House looked to some more like an emperor's court than a presidential office. The Watergate affair, which broke in 1972 and forced Nixon to resign in August 1974, added fuel to the fire. Watergate was about illegal bugging and break-ins, the payment of hush money, secrecy, impoundment of congressional funds and obstruction of justice — all at the very highest levels of the Nixon administration.

Was the 'imperial presidency' a reality or merely something conjured up by Nixon's critics? David Mervin (1990), one of a number of presidential scholars who are sceptical of the Schlesinger thesis, wrote:

> In the wake of Watergate and other scandals, the pejorative connotations of the imperial presidency gained added weight, but the concept was always something of a cliché. The word 'imperial' summons up images of the president as an emperor, a supreme sovereign authority, a master of all he surveys. Roosevelt, at the beginning of the 1930s and at the height of World War II, may have briefly approached such a position of pre-eminence, but none of his successors has come even close to such a situation.

Indeed, one could argue that Nixon's forced resignation was proof that the imperial presidency did *not* exist. In his resignation statement, Nixon said he was resigning because 'I no longer have a strong enough political base in the Congress.' Nixon resigned, forced out by Congress. In his own memoirs, Nixon (1978) stated that he believed that:

> The 'imperial presidency' was a straw man created by defensive congressmen and disillusioned liberals who in the days of FDR and John Kennedy had idolised the ideal of a strong presidency. Now that they had a strong president who was a Republican — and Richard Nixon at that — they were having second thoughts.

In 1986, even Schlesinger recanted his thesis to some extent.

The imperilled presidency

Congress's reaction to the 'imperial presidency' was re-assertiveness. It passed a number of pieces of presidency-curbing legislation, especially in the field of foreign policy. The Case Act (1972) forced presidents to inform Congress of all executive agreements made with foreign states. The War Powers Act (1973) attempted to limit presidents' use of troops unless Congress declared war or gave 'specific statutory authorisation'. Thus, presidents Ford and Carter — the immediate post-Watergate presidents — found their hands much more tied in what became known as the era of the **imperilled presidency**. In 1975, President Ford found he was impotent when the North Vietnamese communists finally overran the South Vietnamese capital, Saigon, including the US embassy compound in the city. Ford complained of congressional meddling in presidential powers. In an article for *Time* magazine four years later, Ford wrote:

Key term

Imperilled presidency A term coined by President Gerald Ford to refer to a presidency characterised by ineffectiveness and weakness, resulting from congressional over-assertiveness.

153

Some people used to complain about what they called an 'imperial presidency'. But now the pendulum has swung too far in the opposite direction. We have not an imperial presidency but an imperilled presidency. Under today's rules, which include some misguided 'reforms', the presidency does not operate effectively. That is a very serious development, and it is harmful to our overall national interests.

The post-imperial presidency

Reagan's eight years in the White House meant that the 'imperilled presidency' thesis had to be rewritten. In contrast to the 'failed', one-term presidents Ford and Carter, Reagan launched an ambitious legislative programme at home, restored America's damaged self-confidence abroad and was re-elected by a landslide in 1984. At home the economy boomed — though so did the federal budget deficit. It was 'morning again in America', according to Reagan's 1984 television commercials. Abroad, Reagan called the Soviet Union 'the evil empire'. In 1987, Reagan even went to Berlin's Brandenburg Gate and declared: 'Mr Gorbachev, open this gate! Mr Gorbachev, tear down this wall!' His call did not have instant effect, but the Berlin Wall eventually fell. The Soviet Union collapsed. The USA was the world's only superpower. Presidential power was back.

President Reagan at Berlin's Brandenburg Gate, June 1987

George H.W. Bush's presidency, successful in foreign policy, fell because of the economic recession at home in the early 1990s and Americans' growing concerns about the ballooning federal budget deficit. Enter Bill Clinton, under whose stewardship the economy boomed. Clinton's contribution to the presidency, however, was to repeat Nixon's sin, besmirching its aura and compromising its integrity. Monica Lewinsky was not Watergate. Clinton survived his impeachment trial in the Senate and became the first Democrat president to serve two terms since FDR. But the tawdry affair, the lying, the attempts at concealment, the hair-splitting legalisms all served to diminish the office of the presidency. Political commentator Elizabeth Drew (1999) wrote:

> The presidency must have a certain aura of majesty and mystique. Clinton's lack of dignity, not to mention his sexual recklessness, was an assault on the office itself.

It also harmed his ability to work effectively.

George W. Bush came to the presidency pledged to be 'a uniter and not a divider'. But the circumstances surrounding his election in 2000 — he lost the popular vote, and won the Electoral College vote only after a controversial ruling by the Supreme Court about the counting of votes in Florida — made him a divisive president from the start. Following the events of 9/11, Bush briefly took on the role of 'unifier-in-chief' as he brought the nation together in the 12 months or so following the attacks on the nation. But once he had committed troops to Iraq, Bush quickly returned to being a divisive figure with an unpopular war, encroachments on civil liberties and enhancements of presidential power. Add to that mix perceived incompetence over the federal government's response to Hurricane Katrina, a collapsing economy and a ballooning federal budget deficit, and Bush's revival of what some regarded as an imperial presidency quickly reverted to the more usual talk of a lame-duck presidency.

Barack Obama took office in 2009 at a time of deep economic crisis at home and a world facing threats from a far-reaching terrorist network. In his first two years, while enjoying Democratic majorities in both houses of Congress, Obama used his power and persuasive skills to refashion the nation's national security policy, pass a massive economic stimulus bill through Congress, enact a federal 'bailout' for the banking and car manufacturing industries, reform the regulation of Wall Street, and dramatically expand the role of the federal government in the provision of healthcare. In all this, the President worked with Congress, moulding and channelling public opinion through televised news conferences, town hall meetings, formal speeches and private meetings with recalcitrant members of Congress.

But once the House (2010) and then the Senate (2014) fell to Republican control, the President found himself severely limited in what he could achieve, and resorted to the use of executive orders, recess appointments and the unilateral use of military force abroad, such as when he ordered air strikes in Libya without prior congressional approval, sparking off a renewed debate over the limits of presidential power, and accusations of a renewal of the imperial presidency.

But according to David Mervin (1993), the imperial presidency 'was always something of a cliché' as it 'summons up images of the president as an emperor, a supreme sovereign authority, a master of all he surveys', which is clearly not an accurate description of the American presidency. Sam Tannenhaus (2002) put it this way:

> The imperial presidency is not a useful idea. It is an epithet, dredged up whenever a president combines strength with imagination. Presidents are, in sum, leaders not rulers — which means, of course, they are not imperial at all.

What we can say is that presidential power is limited — the Founding Fathers intended it to be so. All this makes being a successful and effective president exceedingly difficult.

The role and power of the president in foreign policy

If you want to know who controls crisis foreign policy making, then think of two iconic photographs from the past two decades. The first dates from 11 September 2001, and appeared a few pages back. It is of White House Chief of Staff Andrew Card whispering to President George W. Bush the news of the second plane having hit the World Trade Center in New York that morning. The second dates from 1 May 2011 and shows President Obama — along with other senior members of his administration — in the White House Situation Room watching the events unfold in Abbottabad, Pakistan, which would culminate in the killing of Osama bin Laden. The expressions on each face tell

President Obama with senior administration officials watching a video link of the capture of Osama bin Laden — White House Situation Room, 1 May 2011

the story of the drama. Such photographs tell us quite clearly that, when it comes to conducting foreign policy in a time of crisis, it is the president — not Congress — who is in charge.

The lines of authority are less clear, however, when it comes to non-crisis foreign policy making and the Constitution does not exactly help. In the words of Professor Edward Corwin, the Constitution is 'an invitation to struggle for the privilege of directing American foreign policy'. It gives powers over foreign policy to both branches of government and a number of the constitutional provisions are somewhat vague.

The Constitution and control of foreign policy

As we saw in the section on the powers of the president, the Constitution granted the president two specific powers relating to foreign policy — to act as commander-in-chief of the armed forces and to negotiate treaties. As we also saw, both of these powers are subject to significant powers vested in Congress. The president's commander-in-chief power is checked by Congress's powers to declare war and to control the purse strings. However, the effectiveness of these checks is open to question. Congress has not declared war since 1941 and its power of the purse has often proved to be of questionable use once a president has already committed troops abroad, as was the case once President George W. Bush had sent troops to Iraq.

The Constitution also grants the president the power to make appointments to the executive branch, some of which have foreign policy implications, such as secretary of state, secretary of defense, secretary of homeland security, director of the Central Intelligence Agency, chairman of the joint chiefs of staff, and national security adviser. There are also all the ambassadors whom the president appoints — both those to nation states and those to international organisations such as the United Nations, the European Union and NATO. Indeed, it is by appointing an ambassador to a country that the United States formally recognises the government of that country as being legitimate. All of these appointments, with the exception of the national security adviser, are subject to Senate confirmation.

Setting the tone

The president has the ability to set the tone of foreign policy. The president performs this role mainly through set-piece speeches, notably the inaugural address or the State of the Union Address. President Kennedy, in his noteworthy inaugural address in 1961, promised that America would 'pay any price, bear any burden, meet any hardship, support any friend, oppose any foe in order to ensure the survival and success of liberty'. This was the tone of foreign policy during those decades of the Cold War, exemplified by American involvement in the wars in south-east Asia.

The Bush Doctrine

Following the 9/11 attack on the United States, George W. Bush set the tone of foreign policy when talking about an 'axis of evil' in his 2002 State of the Union Address. The events that America had just lived through and the perceived threats that it faced allowed the President to formulate and announce a new foreign policy doctrine — the Bush Doctrine. This grand strategy was formally unveiled in September 2002 and would have implications for America's relations with every country and international organisation.

The Bush Doctrine was based on two fundamental claims — the virtue of American primacy and the nation's right to wage pre-emptive war against perceived threats. The 'virtue of American primacy' was grounded in the idea that by defeating communism and fascism, the USA had left the world with 'a single sustainable model for national success — freedom, democracy and free enterprise'. America would not impose this model on unwilling nations but would seek to 'shape a balance of power that favours human freedom'. The right to wage pre-emptive war would allow America to strike first against enemies determined to inflict imminent harm on the United States. According to Steven Hook and John Spanier (2013), the Bush administration believed that the rise of terrorist groups such as al Qaeda and the nations which either harboured or sponsored them 'changed the calculus of world politics to such an extent that conventional instruments of coercive foreign policy no longer applied'. The only thing that would work, President Bush had concluded, was America taking the offensive rather than playing defensive.

Obama's 'soft power'

In his inaugural address on 20 January 2009, Barack Obama clearly set a different tone:

> Recall that earlier generations faced down fascism and communism not just with missiles and tanks, but with sturdy alliances and enduring convictions. They understood that our power alone cannot protect us, nor does it entitle us to do as we please. Instead, they knew that our power grows through its prudent use. Our security emanates from the justice of our cause; the force of our example; the tempering qualities of humility and restraint.

To this end, Obama announced that America would return to a reliance on 'soft power' — what he described as 'the ability to get what you want by attraction rather than coercion'. He announced that his administration would revive diplomacy as a core instrument of foreign policy. 'We will extend a hand if you are willing to unclench your fist,' said Obama in his inaugural address. To what extent the administration's foreign policy lived up to those expectations is debateable. The promised closure of the Guantánamo Bay detention camp never materialised. The largest offensive by coalition forces in Afghanistan was launched in 2010, and in 2011 Obama signed a four-year extension of the USA PATRIOT Act and significantly increased the use of Drone attacks. There were estimated to have been some 300 such attacks during Obama's first term compared with fewer than 50 during Bush's second term. But 2011 saw the last American troops withdraw from Iraq and a date of December 2016 was eventually set for withdrawal from Afghanistan.

Congress and foreign policy

But, as we have already seen in Chapter 3, Congress has powers relating to foreign policy too: to declare war, to agree to budgets, and to investigate, as well as the Senate's powers to confirm appointments and to ratify treaties. Fearing that its power had been usurped by an increasingly imperial presidency, Congress passed a series of laws in the 1970s to try to reassert its foreign policy authority. Most notable was the War Powers Act, passed over President Nixon's veto in 1973. But even this has proved to be largely ineffective and Congress has seen itself being relegated merely to authorising the use of troops abroad, as it did in October 2002 before President Bush's incursion into Iraq. As Gene Healy (2008) commented in his study of the US presidency:

When it comes to matters of war and peace, Congress now occupies a position roughly analogous to that of a student council in university governance. It may be important for the administration to show pro forma respect and deference to it — but there can no longer be any doubt about where the real authority resides.

Even when the Democrats reclaimed control of both houses of Congress in January 2007, they made very little headway in enhancing their real influence in foreign policy against the wishes of the Republican Bush administration. 'Now Congress must use its main power, the power of the purse, to put an end to our involvement in this disastrous war,' thundered Democrat senator Russell Feingold on the Senate floor in 2007. But when the Democratic majority tried to do just that, Bush vetoed the bill and the Democrats did not have the votes to override the veto.

Congress possesses a great deal of expertise in its foreign policy-related committees — the Senate's Armed Services Committee and Foreign Relations Committee, and the House of Representatives' Armed Services Committee and Foreign Affairs Committee. In the autumn of 2007, these committees were the scenes of congressional investigation into the conduct of the war in Iraq as members of Congress debated the reports authored by Ryan Crocker, the US ambassador to Iraq, and General David Petraeus, commander of the multinational force in Iraq, and questioned the authors in face-to-face hearings. But Congress's ability to change the direction of policy was negligible. As former president Gerald Ford put it: 'Our forefathers knew you could not have 535 commanders-in-chief and secretaries of state. It just wouldn't work.'

Limitations on presidential power

Writing in 2000, Professor James Pfiffner, a noted scholar on the presidency, remarked that 'the presidency is not a powerful office'. Another presidential scholar, Thomas Cronin put it like this: 'Opportunities to check power abound; opportunities to exercise power are limited.' Here we bring together the many checks that limit the power of the president.

Congress

The checks and balances that Congress has on the president are highly significant. As we saw in both Chapters 2 and 3, Congress may:
- amend, delay or reject the president's legislative proposals
- override the president's veto
- amend his budgetary requests through the power of the purse
- check his commander-in-chief power, through the power of the purse as well as through the power to declare war
- refuse to ratify treaties negotiated by the president (Senate only)
- reject nominations made by the president (Senate only)
- investigate the president's actions and policies
- impeach and try the president with possible removal from office if found guilty

Supreme Court

As we shall see in Chapter 5, the Supreme Court can check the president's power too. Recent examples include:
- declaring President Nixon's actions in refusing to release the so-called White House tapes to be unconstitutional (1974)
- declaring President Clinton's claim of immunity from prosecution by Paula Jones to be unconstitutional (1997)

159

- declaring the military commissions set up by President George W. Bush to try Guantánamo Bay detainees to be unconstitutional (2006)
- declaring President Obama's use of recess appointments to be unconstitutional (2014)
- declaring President Obama's use of an executive order to implement his immigration reform programme to be unconstitutional (2016)

We also saw early on in the Trump administration the district and appeal courts of the federal system weighing in on the President's 'travel ban' executive order. As a result, the executive order was declared inoperative by the courts.

Other checks

The president is also subject to checks from interest groups that will mobilise public opinion for or against him or his policies. President Obama experienced this when the National Rifle Association mobilised public opinion to oppose his gun control proposals following a number of mass shootings. The media also has a role to play in checking the president. Presidents today live in the 24/7 news cycle. As a result, what the media report and say can profoundly influence what presidents can do.

The federal bureaucracy is another potential check. The president is only one person in an executive branch made up of 15 executive departments and some 60 federal agencies, boards and commissions employing around 3 million civil servants. And as many federal government programmes are implemented by the states, state governments — and especially state governors — are another potential check. Witness the opposition President Obama experienced in the states' implementation of his healthcare reforms.

Factors that affect presidential success

There are a number of important variables that affect presidential success. We shall consider five of the most important factors.

Electoral mandate

The larger the president's electoral mandate at the last election, the greater is the president's chance of success. Thus Ronald Reagan was potentially in a much stronger position during his second term — following his re-election in 1984 with 59% of the vote and victory in 49 states — than was Bill Clinton at the start of his first term, having been elected with only 43% of the vote. And George W. Bush was in a very politically weak position in January 2001, having lost the popular vote to his opponent Al Gore.

It is also worth noting that in the present era of hyper-partisanship, presidents are less likely to be able to sweep the board in an electoral landslide like Lyndon Johnson did in 1964, Richard Nixon did in 1972, and Ronald Reagan did in 1984. No president has been elected with more than 55% of the vote since Reagan's landslide in 1984. And as Donald Trump took office in January 2017, he would have to cope with not only falling well short of gaining 50% of the popular vote, but even getting just short of 3 million votes fewer than his rival Hillary Clinton. For all Trump's bluster about his 'Electoral College landslide', his electoral mandate in numerical terms was weak.

Public approval

Elections measure popularity in a snapshot on Election Day, but what about during the months and years between elections? It is then that the president's public approval rating will be important and will affect his ability to get things done. In the immediate aftermath of the 9/11 attacks in 2001, Bush's approval rating reached 90%. But during his last three years in office, his approval rating rarely went above 40%, reaching a low of just 25% in 2008. Clearly a president with a high approval rating has more political clout than one with a low approval rating. Indeed, it was Bill Clinton's high approval ratings during 1999 that probably saved him from conviction in the Senate during his impeachment trial that year. Democrat senators were reluctant to remove from office a president of their own party who was still popular with the electorate.

In the current era of partisanship, there has been a notable widening of the gap in the way Americans view their president according to party. This landscape of the partisan presidency is shown in Figure 4.1, which traces the average support for presidents from Eisenhower to Obama both from their own party and from the other party. Marmite, the famous British yeast extract spread, advertises with the line: 'Marmite: you love it or you hate it.' In this sense the presidencies of Bill Clinton, George W. Bush, Barack Obama, and doubtless Donald Trump have brought us into the era of 'the Marmite presidency' — as far as the individual is concerned, you either love him or you hate him.

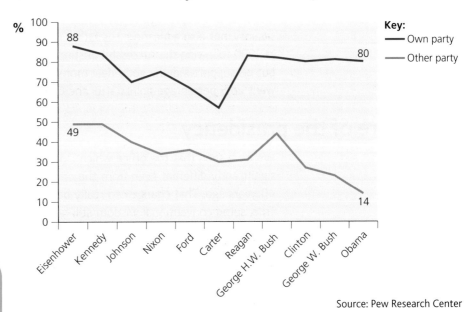

Source: Pew Research Center

Figure 4.1 Partisan gap in presidential approval, 1953–2016

Activity

- Go to the Gallup polling organisation website at **www.gallup.com**.
- Click on 'Presidential Job Approval Center'.
- At the bottom of the page, click on 'Trends A-Z'.
- Click on 'Presidential Approval Ratings — Gallup Historical Statistics and Trends'.
- Using these data, try to discover similar patterns in presidential approval ratings over presidents' first/second terms and try to account for significant changes in these ratings.

First/second term

Presidents usually find it easier to gain success during their first term — especially during the first two years — than during the latter stages of their second term. This is one of the unintended consequences of the Twenty-Second Amendment limiting the president to two terms. In their second terms, presidents quickly become lame ducks. The average first-year presidential support score for presidents from Reagan to Obama is 83%, while the average last-year score is around 48%.

This is related to the previous point concerning public approval. George W. Bush's approval rating averaged 62% during his first term but just 37% during his second. Barack Obama's highest approval rating during his presidency was 67%, recorded during his first week in office in 2009. His low point was 40%, just after his second midterm elections in 2014. This is why presidents always try to pull off their top policy priorities early in their first term.

Unified/divided government

A president will usually find it much easier to be successful with Congress if both houses are controlled by his party — what we call **unified government** — and much more difficult if there is divided government, with the opposition party controlling one or both houses of Congress. Back in Table 4.9 (page 145) we can see how presidents achieve significantly higher levels of support in Congress under unified government than under divided government. For presidents Bill Clinton to Barack Obama, the average presidential support score for years of unified government was 83% while the average score for years of divided government was just 53%.

Crises

After the attacks of 11 September 2001, President Bush's approval soared in what is known as a 'rally effect' — or, more fully, a 'rally-round-the-flag effect' — a phenomenon that often occurs during times of crisis when Americans tend to rally around the commander-in-chief. On 7 September, Bush's approval rating was 51%; two weeks later it was 90%. Bush's approval ratings stayed above 80% for six months, and above 70% for a further four months. During this time Bush was able to win passage of key pieces of legislation, not only concerning national security, but also education. His father experienced a similar surge of support back in 1990 following the successful ousting of Iraq's Saddam Hussein from Kuwait, but his support faded a good deal more quickly. Bill Clinton's approval ratings went up 5 percentage points after the Oklahoma City bombing in April 1995.

The future of the presidency

We have seen that the office which Donald Trump inherited in 2017 is significantly different even from the one which Ronald Reagan inherited nearly 40 years ago. That change can really be summed up in one word — partisanship. True, some conventional wisdom still holds, but the landscape has changed. So what does the future hold for the presidency in an era of partisanship?

To answer this, we need to pose one further question. Will presidents conclude that persuasion and compromise are things of the past? As George C. Edwards (2009) has suggested, might presidents in the context of polarised politics conclude that they can no longer govern by adopting an inclusive approach to policy making, that there is little potential for persuasion, and the only way to govern is on the basis of a '50% plus 1' majority?

This is what we have seen with both Bush and Obama — that rather than seeking compromise with their opponents by bringing them into an inclusive coalition and supporting legislation broadly acceptable to the electorate, they sought, as Edwards put it, 'to defeat the opposition, creating winners and losers in a zero-sum game'. If so, then presidential elections will be no more than an effort to mobilise one's own party base rather than convince undecided and swing voters of the merits of one's vision for the country — which is really what we saw in 2016.

Comparing the US president and the UK prime minister

Structural differences in the executive

The structural differences between the executive branches of the United States and the UK are wide ranging. The presidency as an office is a product of revolution — of the War of Independence, and the constitutional convention that followed some years later. There is no doubt that George Washington was the first president and that Donald Trump is therefore the forty-fifth. In the United States, all executive power is vested in the president. The president is elected by the people, through the Electoral College, for a maximum of eight years. Once in office, the president gains the title of party leader, but that means little in practice. The president is entirely separate from the legislature and often has never been a member of it. The president's cabinet is no more than an optional advisory group and has no decision-making powers.

In the UK, the office of prime minister is the product of evolution over many centuries. The title of prime minister is generally regarded to have been first accorded, posthumously, to Sir Robert Walpole who was First Lord of the Treasury between 1721 and 1742. But the office he held was so unlike that of the modern-day prime minister as to be almost unrecognisable. In Britain, executive power is divided between the monarch, and the prime minister and cabinet. The prime minister is not directly elected to the office and there is no limit on the length of time he or she may serve. The prime minister gains that office only by being the leader of the largest party in the House of Commons and is the *de facto* leader of that house. The prime minister and cabinet together form a plural executive with the prime minister described as 'first among equals'.

The contrasts are stark. Even the architecture speaks of difference. In Washington DC, the White House may not be on the grand scale of Buckingham Palace, but it is certainly more imposing than 10 Downing Street, and the White House Residence — where the president and their family live and entertain visiting dignitaries — is certainly far more spacious than the third floor flat in Number 10, which is so cramped that recent prime ministers have occupied a slightly more spacious flat next door at Number 11. And when it comes to office space, the president has the Oval Office, the West Wing and the 566-room Eisenhower Executive Office Building, compared with the very limited space prime ministers have for themselves and their staff. Indeed, the prime minister is usually pictured working in the cabinet room — a room that speaks as much about collegiality as the Oval Office does about individuality.

The Eisenhower Executive Office Building stands to the west of the White House

Roles and powers

Earlier in this chapter we identified 11 formal powers of the president. Of those 11, only four can be said also to be performed by the British prime minister — propose legislation, submit the annual budget, act as chief executive and nominate executive branch officials (see Table 4.12). But even these shared powers are not identical and here once again we are seeing the effect of the structural differences between the two systems.

Table 4.12 US president and UK prime minister: comparing roles and powers

US president	UK prime minister
Elected as president	Elected as party leader
Chief executive and head of state	Head of government only
Legislation: initiating and veto powers	Draws up government's legislative programme with cabinet
Appoints cabinet but subject to Senate confirmation	Appoints cabinet (no confirmation)
Commander-in-chief of the Armed Forces, but only Congress can declare war	Can use royal prerogative to declare war and deploy troops abroad but recently more subject to parliamentary approval
Has vice president	May appoint deputy prime minister
Has (large) Executive Office of the President	Has (small) Number 10 staff and Cabinet Office
Has a variety of means to pursue policy unilaterally: executive orders, signing statements, etc.	More likely to pursue policy collectively, through either cabinet or cabinet committees
Limited to two full terms in office	No term limits

- When the president proposes legislation to Congress in the State of the Union Address, it is really no more than a wish list. But at least it is the president's own speech. The British prime minister gets to write the speech but it is delivered by the monarch in what today is called the Queen's Speech. But it's a lot more than a wish list. It is the government's 'to do' list for the coming year — a list of near certainties. Clearly the two offices are affected by the separation of powers structure in the United States and the fusion of powers structure in the United Kingdom.
- Both the president and prime minister may submit their annual budgets to their respective legislatures. But in the United States this marks only the beginning of many months of bargaining during which the president may be defeated on many items. In the UK, the budget submitted is to all intents and purposes the budget that will be passed.
- Both the president and the prime minister fulfil the role of chief executive — though the president does so as part of a singular executive, while the prime minister is, in theory at least, part of a collective executive. Again, structural differences mean differences of political outcome.
- Both also get to appoint numerous executive branch officials, but unlike the president, the prime minister does not require anyone to confirm those appointments before they take effect.

The British prime minister lacks some significant powers that the American president enjoys, and most of them are performed by the monarch:

- The president can sign and veto legislation. In Britain that is the power of the monarch, though a monarch has not refused to sign a bill passed by Parliament since 1707 — 80 years before the US Constitution was conceived.

- The president appoints all federal judges, but in Britain the power to appoint judges was given in 2006 to the independent Judicial Appointments Commission.
- The president has the power of pardon — a power reserved to the monarch in Britain.

Theresa May and Queen Elizabeth II on the day that May became British Prime Minister, 13 July 2016

- Most importantly, the president is not only chief executive (head of government) but also **head of state**. In Britain the two roles are separated with the monarch fulfilling the head of state role.

However, the prime minister enjoys certain roles and powers of their own:
- Prime ministers play an important role in Parliament and none more so than in answering questions at their weekly half-hour Question Time. A prime minister's ability to 'stand and deliver' at Prime Minister's Question Time is vital to their survival. Presidents face no such ordeal.
- Prime ministers also make occasional statements to Parliament, appear before the Commons' Liaison Committee and occasionally lead in significant parliamentary debates. Again, the American president plays none of the equivalent roles.
- The prime minister's patronage also extends beyond executive branch appointments to such posts as the chairmanship of the BBC and Church of England bishops and archbishops, and recommending life peerages.

Accountability and relations with the legislature

The relations of the US president and UK prime minister with their respective legislatures are compared in Table 4.13. As we already know, the most significant difference is structural: the US president is not and cannot be a member of Congress whereas the British prime minister must be a serving member of Parliament. Indeed, anyone elected president who is currently a member of Congress must resign their seat — as Barack Obama did after the 2008 election.

The president has no formal links with Congress. Indeed, his party may be in the minority in one or both houses. But the president's continuance in office does not rely on him winning votes in Congress. There are no votes of confidence that could abruptly bring his administration to an end and precipitate new elections. Even were the president to be impeached, found guilty and removed from office, the vice president would step up and take over. The president lacks both the sticks and carrots that the British prime minister enjoys in controlling the legislature. The sticks of party discipline are wholly ineffective; the carrots of appointments to his administration are almost always unwanted.

Furthermore, Congress possesses some significant checks on the president's powers. It can:

- amend, block or reject the bills and budgets he proposes
- override the presidential veto
- reject appointments to the executive and the judiciary (Senate)
- reject treaties (Senate)

It also possesses powers to hold the president accountable through investigation and impeachment of any executive branch official, including the president.

Table 4.13 US president and UK prime minister: comparing relations with legislature

US president's relations with Congress	UK prime minister's relations with Parliament
State of the Union Address	Queen's Speech
Dependent on Senate for confirmation of numerous appointments	Makes numerous appointments without need for legislature to consent
Possibility of divided government	May not have majority in House of Lords
Budget may be significantly amended or defeated in Congress	Budget subject to parliamentary scrutiny
No executive branch members in Congress	Executive branch members in both houses, and dominate House of Commons
Not subject to personal questioning by members of Congress	Prime Minister's Question Time
Gets agreement in Congress mostly by persuasion and bargaining	Gets agreement in Parliament mostly by party discipline and reliance on the payroll vote in the House of Commons
President individually subject to impeachment (House) and trial (Senate)	Prime minister and government collectively subject to vote of no confidence

On the other hand, the prime minister is the leader of the largest party in the House of Commons. Prime ministers' survival depends on both their maintaining their leadership position and their party maintaining its majority status. Not only is the prime minister a member of Parliament, but so are the other members of their administration.

For its part, Parliament has certain methods of scrutinising and checking the actions of the executive. It can hold the prime minister and government to account through: Question Time; select committees; policy debates; early day motions; and votes of no confidence. The effectiveness of these methods of scrutiny and accountability can, however, be questioned. In the battle between the executive and legislature, the prime minister holds most of the trump cards. The prime minister has wide-ranging powers of patronage and the expertise of the civil service.

Cabinets

In their respective cabinets we see more structural differences between the two systems, which give rise to different political outcomes (see Table 4.14). The president's cabinet — and even that term is significant — exists as part of a singular executive. All executive power is vested in the president, none in the cabinet, which is why its members are correctly referred to as cabinet *officers* or *secretaries*, not cabinet *ministers*. They are excluded from the legislature and many have no obvious party political affiliation. Neither does the president have an entirely free hand in appointing cabinet officers, as they must be approved by a majority vote in the Senate.

Cabinet officers will not have served together as part of a shadow cabinet before taking office. Indeed, they may be complete strangers both to each other and even to the president. They are not the president's equals and have no elective base. Politically, they are not the president's political rivals. Much of this is dictated by the doctrine of the separation of powers. The structure determines the function. As a result, the president's cabinet functions merely as a somewhat distant advice-giving body with little collective significance in most administrations.

Table 4.14 US president and UK prime minister: comparing cabinets

US cabinet	UK cabinet
Serving members of the legislature barred from serving	Membership exclusive to members of Parliament
Presidential appointments subject to Senate confirmation	No formal limits on cabinet appointments
President decides frequency and regularity of meetings	Prime minister obliged to maintain frequency and regularity of meetings
Cabinet members are subordinate to the president who is in no way 'first among equals'; cabinet does not make decisions — the president does	Cabinet is a collective decision-making body
Cabinet members are mostly recruited for their policy specialisation: rarely do they move to a different department	Cabinet members are usually policy generalists: hence cabinet reshuffles
Cabinet members are often strangers to the president; no shadow cabinet	Cabinet made up of long-serving parliamentary colleagues and former shadow cabinet members
Cabinet meetings are often the only time some cabinet members see the president	Prime minister sees cabinet colleagues regularly in Parliament
No doctrine of collective responsibility	Collective responsibility usually applies

But the cabinet in Whitehall — and one really cannot call it the *prime minister's* cabinet — exists as part of a plural executive with the prime minister as 'first among *equals*'. The members are *ministers* because they have real administrative power vested in them. Like the prime minister, most are members of the House of Commons and their elective base is the same as that of the prime minister — elected by a constituency. The prime minister need gain no political approval for the cabinet appointments he or she makes. Far from being strangers, the prime minister and cabinet are likely to have served together both in Parliament and possibly in a shadow cabinet for some years before taking their seats around the cabinet table in Number 10. Some will even be regarded as the prime minister's potential political rivals. When Prime Minister David Cameron faltered in 2016, his Home Secretary Theresa May succeeded him.

The stark structural differences between the two systems mean that the cabinet in Whitehall is an entirely different beast from its namesake in Washington. Indeed, one could say that all they have in common is the name. True, many decisions in Whitehall will be made by the prime minister and a few close advisers, or in cabinet committee. But no prime minister could ignore the collective will of the cabinet the way an American president can, and hope to survive in office for very long.

Presidential and prime ministerial government

In both systems, allegations have arisen in recent decades concerning what some see as the unjustifiable increase in the power of the chief executive — it is argued that individuality has increased at the expense of collegiality, and that the executive branch has increased in power at the expense of the legislature. These are by no means new ideas. As we saw earlier, the concept of the imperial presidency dates from the early 1970s, and in Britain Lord Hailsham popularised the phrase 'the elective dictatorship' in 1976.

The concepts of 'presidential government' and 'prime ministerial government' both contain some truth, but they have tended to be presented in an overly one-sided manner by their most ardent supporters. Talk of the imperial presidency in America soon gave way to talk of the 'imperilled presidency'. And the idea of the British prime minister as an elective dictator seemed less convincing following the demise of Margaret Thatcher in 1990, and also of David Cameron in 2016. Likewise, talk of a 'golden age of the legislature' — whether in Washington or Westminster — may actually be slightly fanciful.

Furthermore, our understanding of the structures of government in the United Kingdom should make us cautious of describing the office of the prime minister as having been 'presidentialised'. In terms of what they can get done in the legislature, British prime ministers have always been in a much stronger position than American presidents. On the other hand, to call prime ministers 'presidential' in terms of their staff and support has always been very wide of the mark. The office occupied and run by Tony Blair, Gordon Brown, David Cameron and Theresa May looks nothing like the Executive Office of the President in Washington under George W. Bush, Barack Obama or Donald Trump. The offices remain different, mainly because the structures in which they operate are so different.

References

Cronin, T.E. and Genovese, M.A., *The Paradoxes of the American Presidency*, Oxford University Press, 1998.

Drew, E., *The Corruption of American Politics*, Birch Lane Press, 1999.

Edwards, G.C., *The Strategic President: Persuasion and Opportunity in Presidential Leadership*, Princeton University Press, 2009.

Fenno, R.F., *The President's Cabinet*, Harvard University Press, 1959.

Finer, S.E., *Comparative Government*, Penguin, 1970.

Healy, G., *The Cult of the Presidency*, Cato Institute, 2008.

Hook, S. and Spanier, J., *American Foreign Policy Since World War II*, CQ Press, 2013.

McClellan, S., *What Happened Inside the Bush White House and Washington's Culture of Deception*, Public Affairs, 2008.

Mervin, D., *Ronald Reagan and the American Presidency*, Longman, 1990.

Mervin, D., *The President of the United States*, Harvester-Wheatsheaf, 1993.

Neustadt, R.E., *Presidential Power and the Modern Presidents: The Politics of Leadership from Roosevelt to Reagan*, Free Press, 1990.

Nixon, R.M., *RN: The Memoirs of Richard Nixon*, Sidgwick and Jackson, 1978.

Peterson, M.A., 'Presidential power and the potential for leadership', in R.Y. Shapiro *et al.* (eds), *Presidential Power: Forging the Presidency for the 21st Century*, Columbia University Press, 2000.

Pfiffner, J., *The Modern Presidency*, Bedford-St Martin's, 2000.

Pfiffner, J., 'Organising the Obama White House', in J.A. Thurber (ed.), *Obama in Office*, Paradigm Publishers, 2011.

Polsby, N.W., *Congress and the Presidency*, Prentice-Hall, 1976.

Schlesinger, A.M., *The Cycles of American History*, Houghton-Mifflin, 1986.

Shrum, R., 'The Hillary Test', *The Week*, 2 December 2008.

Smith, J.E., *Bush*, Simon and Schuster, 2016.

Tannenhaus, S., 'Imperial? No, Presidential. Bush is no "Caesar"', *Wall Street Journal*, 27 December 2002.

Todd, C., *The Stranger: Barack Obama in the White House*, Little, Brown and Company, 2014.

Woodward, B., *Bush at War*, Simon and Schuster, 2003.

Woodward, B., *The War Within*, Simon and Schuster, 2008.

Woodward, B., *Obama's Wars*, Simon and Schuster, 2010.

Further reading

Ashbee, E., 'Obama's second term: success or failure?' *Politics Review*, Vol. 26, No. 4, April 2017.

Bennett, A.J., 'Obama's first term: promise unfulfilled?' *Politics Review*, Vol. 22, No. 4, April 2013.

Bennett, A.J., 'Are second-term presidents lame ducks?' *Politics Review*, Vol. 25, No. 4, April 2016.

Lemieux, S. and Tarrant R., 'Is Obama too cautious a president?' *Politics Review*, Vol. 24, No. 2, November 2014.

Whiskerd, N., 'The modern president: transformational leader or facilitator?' *Politics Review*, Vol. 23, No. 4, April 2014.

The place to start in studying the presidency online is the White House website at www.whitehouse.gov.

One of the best academic websites on the presidency is the American Presidency Project based at the University of California at Santa Barbara. The web address is www.presidency.ucsb.edu. You will find detailed information there on matters ranging from State of the Union Addresses to presidential vetoes.

Individual departments and agencies all have their own websites and if it is statistics you are after then try https://fedstats.sites.usa.gov.

Exam focus

Edexcel

Section A (Comparative)

1 Examine the ways in which the US and UK cabinets are different. (12)

2 Examine the differences in the bureaucratic support for the US president and the UK prime minister. (12)

Section B (Comparative)

In your answer you must consider the relevance of at least one comparative theory.

1 Analyse the different relationships between the US president and the UK prime minister and their respective legislatures. (12)

2 Analyse the differences between presidential government and prime ministerial government. (12)

Section C (USA)

In your answer you must consider the stated view and the alternative to this view in a balanced way.

1 Evaluate the extent to which there is an 'imperial presidency' in the USA. (30)

2 Evaluate the extent to which the president controls foreign policy. (30)

3 Evaluate the extent to which 'the president's power is the power to persuade'. (30)

4 Evaluate the extent to which the president can get his way in Congress. (30)

AQA

Section A (USA)

1 Explain and analyse three ways in which the president can influence foreign policy. (9)

2 Explain and analyse three ways in which the president may use his cabinet. (9)

Section A (Comparative)

1 Explain and analyse three ways in which structural theory could be used to study cabinet appointments in the USA and the UK. (9)

2 Explain and analyse three ways in which structural theory could be used to study the US president's and the UK prime minister's relationships with their respective parties. (9)

Section B (USA)

Is the imperial presidency still alive?

The idea of an 'imperial presidency' was popularised following the administrations of Franklin Roosevelt, Lyndon Johnson and especially Richard Nixon. Many believed that the presidency was characterised by unchecked power, excessive secrecy and even illegality. The checks and balances of the Constitution were no longer doing their job. This was especially thought to be the case in foreign policy where the president's commander-in-chief role gave him the power to take unilateral initiatives in the use of troops abroad. Congress was left floundering in his wake with a now redundant power to declare war, and the ineffective power of the purse.

But then came Gerald Ford and Jimmy Carter who seemed impotent in the face of congressional re-assertiveness. It was also pointed out that Johnson was forced to step aside in 1968 and Nixon to resign in 1974 — so maybe the presidency was not so powerful after all. Then with Clinton, Bush and Obama, the presidency looked weaker in an era of hyper-partisanship in which supporters of the other party seemed entirely uninterested in offering cooperation or compromise, and where presidential persuasion tended to fall on deaf ears.

Analyse, evaluate and compare the arguments in the above passage for and against the view that the US presidency is 'imperial'. *(25)*

Section C (Comparative)

In your answer you should draw on material from across the whole range of your course of study in Politics.

1 'The constitutional power of the US president exceeds that of the UK prime minister.' Analyse and evaluate this statement. *(25)*

2 'It is much harder for a US president to get their way in Congress than for a UK prime minister to get their way in Parliament.' Analyse and evaluate this statement. *(25)*

3 'Cabinets in both the US and UK systems of government are little more than talking shops.' Analyse and evaluate this statement. *(25)*

Chapter 5

The Supreme Court and civil rights

The Supreme Court

> **Learning outcomes**
>
> Key questions answered in this section:
> - What is the structure of the federal courts?
> - What is the membership of the Supreme Court?
> - What is the judicial philosophy of the justices?
> - How does the appointment and confirmation process work?
> - What is the power of judicial review?
> - What is judicial activism?
> - How has the Supreme Court interpreted the Bill of Rights?
> - How has the Supreme Court influenced public policy?
> - How has the Supreme Court checked congressional power?
> - How has the Supreme Court checked presidential power?
> - What do these decisions tell us about the Supreme Court?
> - What are the principal similarities and differences between the US and UK Supreme Courts?

Introduction

In 1997, the Texas state legislature passed a law requiring the University of Texas to admit all high school seniors (18-year-olds) who were in the top 10% of their high school classes. But after a few years the university discovered that its admissions were still slanted towards white students, so it modified its admissions policy. The university would still admit all Texas top 10% students who applied, but for the remainder of in-state applicants they would consider race as an admissions factor, favouring those of minority race.

In 2008, 18-year-old Texan Abigail Fisher applied for admission to the University of Texas, but not being a top 10% student her admission was not automatic and she was rejected. Ms Fisher filed a lawsuit against the university, claiming that she had been denied entry on the basis of her race — she is white — as students of minority races with lower academic scores had been admitted. Fisher claimed that her equal protection rights under the Fourteenth Amendment had therefore been violated. And so it was that eventually the United States Supreme Court had to decide whether or not the Equal Protection Clause of the Fourteenth Amendment permitted consideration of race in undergraduate admissions decisions. (You will need to read on in the chapter to discover what the Court eventually decided.)

But here is a classic example of how the Supreme Court plays a critical role in making decisions in highly controversial areas of American life by virtue of its power to act as umpire of the Constitution. And it further illustrates the Court's role as one of the protectors of the civil rights and liberties of ordinary Americans. It is these two areas — the Supreme Court and civil rights — that we address in this chapter.

One summer's afternoon in July 2003 while at my cottage in Suffolk, I was enjoying Sunday lunch at The Swan Hotel in Lavenham's picturesque high street. I noticed four well-dressed and quite elderly gentlemen enter the dining room, who were then seated at a table just across from me. I had noted their American accents, but as I looked at them more closely I did a double-take. 'Surely not!' I thought. I summoned over the Maître d' and asked if he knew anything about these four diners. He told me that all he knew was that they were American judges who had arrived for the day from Cambridge, and asked why I wanted to know. 'Because,' came my reply, 'one of them is probably the second most powerful man in America!' He looked startled and somewhat puzzled. So I had to explain that one of the foursome was none other than William H. Rehnquist, the Chief Justice of the United States. And as we shall see in this chapter, it is not too much of a stretch so to describe the chief justice.

Structure of the federal courts

The United States Supreme Court sits at the top of the federal judiciary. According to the original Constitution, the Supreme Court was to be the only federal court. Article III, Section 1, begins:

> The judicial power of the United States shall be vested in one supreme Court and in such inferior Courts as the Congress may from time to time ordain and establish.

By passing the Judiciary Act of 1789, Congress immediately set up a system of lower federal courts. Below the Supreme Court are 13 Courts of

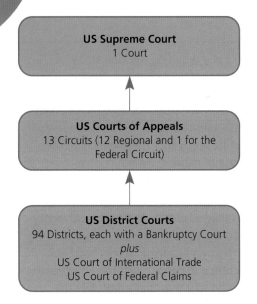

US Supreme Court
1 Court

US Courts of Appeals
13 Circuits (12 Regional and 1 for the Federal Circuit)

US District Courts
94 Districts, each with a Bankruptcy Court
plus
US Court of International Trade
US Court of Federal Claims

Figure 5.1 The structure of the federal courts

Appeals, known as Circuit Courts, and below those are the 94 trial courts known as District Courts (see Figure 5.1). The vast majority of federal cases begin in the District Courts. Once the case has been decided there, it may be appealed to one of the Circuit Courts and from there to the United States Supreme Court. Cases may also arrive at the United States Supreme Court from the state Supreme Courts, if questions involving the federal government are raised. The United States Supreme Court hears only those cases that it wishes to hear. There is no automatic right to have one's case heard before the United States Supreme Court. It hears only those cases that it believes are of major constitutional significance.

Membership of the Supreme Court

Today there are nine members of the Supreme Court — one chief justice and eight associate justices. The number is fixed by Congress and has remained unchanged since 1869. They are appointed by the president and must be confirmed by a simple majority vote in the Senate. Once appointed and confirmed, they hold office for life — 'during good behaviour', as Article III, Section 1 of the Constitution puts it. This means that members of the Court can be removed only through the impeachment process. The House must impeach a justice by a simple majority and the Senate must then try that justice. If found guilty by the Senate by a two-thirds majority, the justice is removed from office. However, no Supreme Court justice has ever been impeached, although Associate Justice Abe Fortas resigned from the Supreme Court in 1968 rather than face impeachment. Thus, barring impeachment, justices leave the Court only as a consequence of voluntary retirement or death.

A visit to the United States Supreme Court is a memorable experience. Until 2010, one could enter up the marble steps from First Street, through the imposing bronze doors and straight into the Alabama marble hallway which leads to the court chamber. (Today one is forced to enter round the side — for security reasons.) When the Court is in session, the justices sit along a bench at the front of the chamber in high-back chairs with a backdrop of a plush red curtain (see photograph on page 50). Sitting in the middle of the nine justices is the chief justice. Although his powers are in most respects the same as those of his colleagues, the chief justice has the opportunity to set the tone of the Court.

The current chief justice, John Roberts, is only the sixteenth person to hold the office in nearly 230 years. His predecessors include a number of illustrious names, such as John Marshall (1801–35), Roger Taney (1836–64), William Howard Taft (1921–30) and Charles Evans Hughes (1930–41), but students need to be familiar only with Chief Justice Roberts and his three immediate predecessors — Earl Warren (1953–69), Warren Earl Burger (1969–86) and William Rehnquist (1986–2005). Commentators often use the name of the chief justice to denote an era in the Court's history. Thus, we talk of the 'Rehnquist Court' and now the 'Roberts Court'. The membership of the Supreme Court in January 2017 is set out in Table 5.1.

Table 5.1 Supreme Court membership, 2017

Justice	Date appointed	President appointing
Chief Justice		
John Roberts	2005	George W. Bush (R)
Associate Justices		
Anthony Kennedy	1988	Ronald Reagan (R)
Clarence Thomas	1991	George H.W. Bush (R)
Ruth Bader Ginsburg	1993	Bill Clinton (D)
Stephen Breyer	1994	Bill Clinton (D)
Samuel Alito	2006	George W. Bush (R)
Sonia Sotomayor	2009	Barack Obama (D)
Elena Kagan	2010	Barack Obama (D)
Neil Gorsuch	2017	Donald Trump (R)

The US Supreme Court justices, 2017

Philosophy of the justices

It is often suggested that presidents wish to appoint justices who share their judicial philosophy. From a philosophical perspective, justices can be classified as 'conservatives' or 'liberals'. Another classification used is that of **strict constructionists** and **loose constructionists**.

Strict constructionist judges are usually conservative in outlook. In their decisions they tend to interpret the Constitution in a strict or literal fashion — they look at the original intent of the Founding Fathers and hence are

Key terms

Strict constructionist A Supreme Court justice who interprets the Constitution strictly or literally, and tends to stress the retention of power by individual states.

Loose constructionist A Supreme Court justice who interprets the Constitution less literally, and tends to stress the broad grants of power to the federal government.

Originalist A Supreme Court justice who interprets the Constitution in line with the meaning or intent of the framers at the time of enactment.

Living constitution The Constitution considered as a dynamic, living document, interpretation of which should take account of the views of contemporary society.

sometimes referred to as **originalists**. They often favour states' rights over the power of the federal government, and they tend to be appointed by Republican presidents. Chief Justice John Roberts and associate justices Clarence Thomas, Samuel Alito and Neil Gorsuch fall into this category. Strict constructionist judges focus on *the text* of the Constitution. For them, the language is supreme and the Court's job is to derive and apply rules from the words chosen by those who framed the Constitution. In their view, constitutional principles are fixed, not evolving. The late Justice Antonin Scalia, a noted originalist in his day, once declared:

> The Constitution that I interpret and apply is not living but dead. Our first responsibility is not to make sense of the law — our first responsibility is to follow the text of the law.

In an interview on the CBS News programme *60 Minutes*, Justice Scalia put it this way:

> You think there ought to be a right to abortion? No problem. The Constitution says nothing about it. Create it the way most rights are created in a democratic society. Pass a law. A Constitution is not meant to facilitate change. It is meant to impede change, to make change difficult.

Loose constructionist judges, on the other hand, are usually liberal in outlook. Their decisions tend to interpret the Constitution in a loose fashion — reading elements into the document that they think the framers of the Constitution would approve. They see the document as a **living constitution**. They tend to favour the power of the federal government over states' rights, and they are usually appointed by Democratic presidents. At the time of writing, associate justices Ruth Bader Ginsburg, Stephen Breyer, Sonia Sotomayor and Elena Kagan fell into this category — the first two appointed by President Clinton, the last two by President Obama.

Neil Gorsuch (left) is sworn in as an associate justice of the Supreme Court by Associate Justice Anthony Kennedy (right), April 2017

In contrast to a strict constructionist, a loose constructionist such as Justice Breyer would say that he looks at *the context* of the Constitution. The language of the text is only the starting point of an inquiry in which a law's purpose and a decision's likely consequence are the more important elements. He saw Scalia's approach as 'too legalistic' and one that 'placed too much weight upon language, history, tradition and precedent alone'.

The case of capital punishment

The debate between originalists and those who believe in a living constitution can be well illustrated with reference to the issue of capital punishment. As we shall see later, one of the issues that the Supreme Court has had to address in recent decades is whether the death penalty is constitutional or whether it contravenes the ban on 'cruel and unusual punishments' in the Eighth Amendment. To an originalist it is clearly constitutional for two reasons:

- Capital punishment was widely accepted when the Eighth Amendment was written (1791) and therefore the death penalty was not in the minds of the framers when they wrote these words. Originalists base their constitutional interpretation on original intent.
- The Fifth Amendment, which was written at the same time, actually refers to 'capital crime'.

Box 5.1

Problems of terminology

Sometimes Supreme Court justices are classified using *ideological* labels of 'conservative' or 'liberal'. In this chapter, we prefer to talk of judicial *philosophy* rather than of ideology. A judicial philosophy means a theory about *how* justices go about deciding the big policy issues that come before them, whereas an ideology would refer to *what* one would like the justices to decide.

So, for example, to refer to someone as a 'conservative' justice could mean a number of things. It could mean a justice who:

- has a strong belief in the principle of *stare decisis* (see page 188) and a respect for precedent, *or*
- has a narrow view of the Constitution — especially the Bill of Rights — somewhat akin to originalism, *or*
- uses their power to advance a conservative political agenda

For clarity, and to ensure that we distinguish clearly between judges and politicians, we therefore prefer where possible to avoid such ideological labels. Hence we tend to focus on strict/loose constructionists and originalism/living constitution, as these classifications focus on the *how* of judicial decision making rather than the *what*.

However, when discussing the decisions that the justices make, we will also use the terms 'liberal' and 'conservative' in the sense that these decisions fit into a general political ideology.

But those who believe in a living constitution might well argue that the death penalty is unconstitutional because, as Justice William Brennan — who was on the Court between 1956 and 1990 — stated, it violates 'the sparkling vision of the supremacy of human dignity of every individual' that guided those who wrote the original text. To an originalist, the only way to get rid of the death penalty would be by legislation. To someone who believes in the Constitution as a living and evolving document, judicial interpretation can — and should — achieve similar ends.

The appointment and confirmation process

There are five stages in the appointment process of Supreme Court justices, as listed in Box 5.2.

> **Box 5.2**
>
> ### The appointment process of Supreme Court justices
>
> 1 A vacancy occurs through voluntary retirement, death or impeachment.
> 2 The president instigates a search for possible nominees and interviews short-listed candidates.
> 3 The president announces his nominee.
> 4 The Senate Judiciary Committee holds a confirmation hearing on the nominee, and makes a recommendatory vote.
> 5 The nomination is debated and voted on in the full Senate. A simple majority vote is required for confirmation.

The vacancy

First, the president must wait for a vacancy to occur. There have been 119 vacancies to fill on the Supreme Court since 1789 — which is around one every two years. Thus, a president might expect to make two such appointments in a four-year term, and three or four appointments in two terms. Bill Clinton, George W. Bush and Barack Obama put only two justices on the Court during each of their eight years (see Table 5.2). However, some presidents are not even as fortunate as that. Carter made none at all in his four years. No vacancies occurred on the Court for just short of 11 years between August 1994 and July 2005 — the longest period without a vacancy since the Court remained unchanged for 12 years between 1812 and 1824.

Table 5.2 Supreme Court appointments by presidency, 1981–2017

President/party	Years in office	Number of Supreme Court nominations
Ronald Reagan (R)	1981–89	3
George H.W. Bush (R)	1989–93	2
Bill Clinton (D)	1993–2001	2
George W. Bush (R)	2001–09	2
Barack Obama (D)	2009–17	3*
Donald Trump (R)	2017–	1

*The Senate took no action on Obama's third nomination (2016).

Second, because of the life tenure that the justices enjoy and the great importance of the Supreme Court, presidents regard Supreme Court appointments as the most important of their presidency. Most other appointments that presidents make last only for as long as the president remains in office. Cabinet officers, for example, are lucky to serve more than two or three years, and all of them will almost certainly leave office the moment the president departs. The same goes for most other appointees — ambassadors, agency heads and Executive Office personnel. But Supreme Court justices will, politically speaking, almost certainly outlive the president.

Indeed, they may even outlive him physically. President Nixon left office in 1974 and died in 1994, but Justice William Rehnquist, whom Nixon appointed to the Supreme Court in January 1972, served until his death in September 2005 — a period of nearly 34 years. Rehnquist thus served on the Supreme Court for 11 years after Nixon's own death. In this sense, the Supreme Court can often appear to be something of an echo chamber, through which the voices and views of earlier decades can still be heard to speak. In 2017, Reagan appointee Anthony Kennedy was still on the Court, almost 30 years after Reagan left office.

The search and pools of recruitment

Once a vacancy has occurred, the president commissions a search for suitable candidates. Of course, if a vacancy has been anticipated, this search might have been going on surreptitiously for some time. The president seeks advice from different sources. First, he asks his political advisers — senior White House aides and top officials in the Justice Department — for possible nominees. In addition, he might hear some names being mentioned by key members of Congress of his own party — possibly from members of the influential Senate Judiciary Committee, who have a more formal role to play later in the process. Second, the president — especially Democrats — might seek advice from professional groups such as the American Bar Association (ABA). Third, the president might turn to personal friends and confidants.

The most likely pool of recruitment for Supreme Court justices is the federal Courts of Appeals (see Table 5.3) — the courts one tier below the Supreme Court and the courts that will usually have heard cases before they arrive at the Supreme Court. This has become an increasing trend in the last three decades. Of the current Court membership, all but one of the justices were recruited from the federal Courts of Appeals, Elena Kagan being the exception.

Table 5.3 Most common posts held by Supreme Court nominees at their time of nomination, 1789–2017

Post held at time of nomination	Most recent example	Number of nominees holding that post
Federal judge	Neil Gorsuch (2017)	34
Practising attorney	Lewis Powell (1971)	22
State court judge	Sandra Day O'Connor (1981)	18
Cabinet member	Arthur Goldberg (1962)	14
Senator	Harold Burton (1945)	7
Solicitor General	Elena Kagan (2010)	3
State governor	Earl Warren (1953)	3

Alternatively, the president might look to the state courts. When President Reagan had his first opportunity to fill a vacancy on the Supreme Court back in 1981, he nominated Sandra Day O'Connor, who was then a judge on the Arizona state Court of Appeals. David Souter, nominated by President Bush in 1990, had been on a federal Court of Appeals for only three months. Before that he was a member of the New Hampshire state Supreme Court.

Another possible pool of recruitment is the Department of Justice. In 2010, when President Obama nominated Elena Kagan to the Supreme Court, she was serving as Solicitor General at the Department of Justice.

The announcement

Once a shortlist has been drawn up, FBI background checks are conducted on all the possible nominees and the president personally interviews two or three finalists. Having decided on the nominee, the president makes the formal announcement (hopefully before the identity of the nominee is leaked to the press). The public announcement is a major political event attended by the nominee, members of his or her family, key members of Congress and the executive branch, as well as members of the press.

Table 5.4 ABA ratings and Senate votes on selected Supreme Court nominees

Nominee	Year	ABA rating	Senate Judiciary Committee vote	Senate vote
Robert Bork	1987	Well qualified	5–9	42–58
Clarence Thomas	1991	Qualified	7–7	52–48
Ruth Bader Ginsburg	1993	Well qualified	18–0	96–3
John Roberts	2005	Well qualified	13–5	78–22
Elena Kagan	2010	Well qualified	13–6	63–37
Neil Gorsuch	2017	Well qualified	11–9	54–45

There then follows a part of the appointment process that is entirely unofficial but has become accepted by tradition: this is the rating by the ABA Standing Committee on the Federal Judiciary (see Table 5.4). Nominees are given one of three ratings: 'well qualified'; 'qualified'; 'not qualified'. As this is a nomination to the USA's highest court, a 'well qualified' rating would be expected. Not to gain that rating would be a significant problem. The only recent Supreme Court nominee to be given a rating other than 'well qualified' was Clarence Thomas, who, when nominated by George H.W. Bush in 1991, was awarded a rating of 'qualified' by the majority of the ABA committee, but a minority submitted a 'not qualified' rating.

The confirmation process

The focus moves to Capitol Hill for the confirmation process. The nominee first has to appear before the Senate Judiciary Committee. Hearings are held at which the witnesses include not only the nominee but also supporters, and maybe critics, of the nominee. Witnesses might be individuals with close knowledge of the nominee or representatives of interest groups who support or oppose the nomination.

If the process goes badly for the nominee, they might be tempted to withdraw. Alternatively, the president might be tempted to call a halt to the nomination to save further embarrassment and a possible defeat on the Senate floor. In October 2005 Bush nominee Harriet Miers withdrew after conservative Republican senators were unconvinced as to her ideological credentials. What was extraordinary about Miers' withdrawal was that it came as a result of hostility from members of the President's own party.

Once the hearings have concluded, the committee votes on whether or not to recommend further action. This is therefore only a recommendatory, not a decisive, vote. However, the committee vote is a clear pointer to the likely outcome when the full Senate makes the final decision. If the Senate Judiciary Committee votes unanimously or overwhelmingly in favour of a nominee, the nomination is nearly certain to be confirmed. If, however, the committee vote is close or is lost, defeat on the floor is a near certainty. The 1987 defeat of the nomination of Robert

Bork in the Judiciary Committee was a prelude to his defeat on the Senate floor (see Table 5.4). When the committee voted 7–7 on the nomination of Clarence Thomas, it was clear that he was in for a fight on the Senate floor. The Senate did eventually confirm Thomas, but only by a margin of four votes. However, Ruth Bader Ginsburg (1993) followed her unanimous approval by the committee with a 96–3 vote on the Senate floor. A simple majority is required for confirmation.

The Senate has rejected 12 nominations since 1789 (see Figure 5.2), the most recent example being the rejection in 1987 of Reagan nominee Robert Bork by 42 votes to 58. Bork's critics regarded him as being both too conservative and too closely associated with former president Richard Nixon. Bork had played a role in the Watergate affair when, at the orders of President Nixon, he had fired the independent prosecutor, Archibald Cox, who was investigating the Watergate cover-up. A further ten nominations have been withdrawn by the president, the latest being George W. Bush's withdrawal of the Harriet Miers nomination in 2005. The Senate took no action on five nominees — the latest being on Obama's nomination of Merrick Garland in 2016.

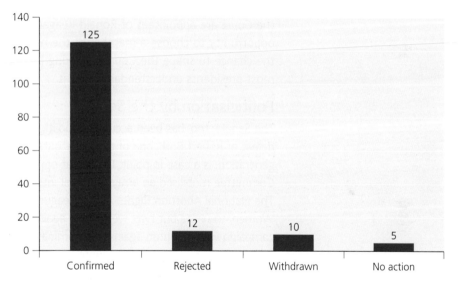

Figure 5.2 Result of Supreme Court nominations, 1789–2017

What is wrong with the process?

Most modern-day criticism of the appointment and confirmation process centres on accusations of politicisation — by the president, by the Senate and by the media that cover the process (see Box 5.3 on page 183).

Politicisation by the president

Although presidents always deny any political consideration in the appointment process, it seems nonetheless to underlie the choosing of Supreme Court justices. Presidents are tempted to choose a justice whose political and judicial philosophy reflects their own. Republican presidents want to pick a justice who is conservative and takes a strict and literal view of the Constitution. Democrat presidents, on the other hand, want to choose a justice who is liberal and takes a looser, adaptive view of the Constitution. There is always the danger that presidents use a 'litmus test' on Court nominees, often scrutinising their previous judgements on controversial cases, such as those regarding affirmative action, capital punishment or abortion.

When President Bush announced his nomination of David Souter to the Supreme Court in 1990, the first question he was asked by the press after he had delivered his introductory statement was: 'Did you ask Judge Souter his views on abortion?' Bush said that he had not, stating: 'It would have been inappropriate to ask him his views on specific issues.' Then, for good measure, the President added:

> What I am certain of is that he will interpret the Constitution and not legislate from the federal bench...You might think the whole nomination had to do with abortion...I have too much respect for the Supreme Court than to look at one specific issue.

On this occasion, however, the President might indeed have been right to deny any political considerations in his choice. Justice Souter, in almost two decades on the Supreme Court, made decisions which would find little favour with President Bush in particular or conservative Republicans in general. He proved to be one of the most consistently *liberal* members of the Court.

Most presidents pick politically, and it is no coincidence that the two Clinton appointees on the Court deliver opinions that are consistently of a liberal position. It is no coincidence either that the most conservative members of the Court are appointees of Ronald Reagan and George W. Bush. Given the opportunity to choose a member of the nation's highest court and thereby have the chance to shape the Court's thinking for the next 15–20 years or more, most presidents understandably take it.

Politicisation by the Senate

The Senate, too, has been accused of politicising the confirmation process. The defeat of Robert Bork, one of the most outstanding jurists and scholars of his generation, is a case in point. Democrat opponents on the Senate Judiciary Committee mobilised an array of liberal interest groups against Bork's nomination. The National Abortion Rights Action League and the National Organization for Women, to name but two, weighed in against Bork. Even a television advertising campaign was mounted against his nomination, costing in the region of $15 million. Conservative groups mounted a counter-attack, but to little avail.

A similar situation arose when President Bush nominated another conservative, Clarence Thomas, in 1991. In this case, the Senate could justifiably have questioned Thomas's nomination on his lacklustre qualifications. It chose instead to concentrate on his conservative philosophy and the allegations of sexual harassment brought against him by a black female work colleague. Thomas was unimpressed by the confirmation process, issuing a forthright denunciation of the Senate's work:

> This is a circus. It's a national disgrace. From my standpoint as a black American, it is a high-tech lynching for uppity blacks who in any way think for themselves... No job is worth what I've been through — no job. No horror in my life has been so debilitating. Confirm me if you want. Don't confirm me if you have been so led. But let this process end. Let me and my family regain our lives.

When the process ended and the Senate finally voted on Thomas's nomination, the vote was almost entirely along party lines. Only 11 Democrats — mostly southern conservatives — voted in favour, and only two Republicans voted against. This does little to rebut the allegation that Thomas's nomination was considered in a partisan fashion by both sides.

In 2006, the *Washington Post* reported that over a three-month period of the nomination debate concerning Samuel Alito, 'hundreds of advocacy groups on both sides of the battle aggressively competed to shape public opinion, spending more than $2 million in advertising and blanketing the country with millions of e-mails'. As was also seen in the Alito nomination, senators from the president's party tend to use the occasion to throw soft questions at the nominee, not really trying to probe them for answers that might reveal whether or not they are suitably qualified for the job. This means that, provided a president has party control of the Senate, he can just about get anyone he wants confirmed by the Senate. That is not a recipe for effective checks and balances.

Meanwhile, senators from the opposition party tend to look for opportunities to attack and embarrass the nominee. They are often more interested in scandal, innuendo and gossip than in competence. This happened in the Clarence Thomas hearings in 1991 and, to a lesser extent, in the Alito hearings in 2006. A few years ago, Calvin Mackenzie published a book with the title *Innocent Until Nominated: The Breakdown of the Presidential Appointments Process* (2001). His conclusion was that the confirmation process is characterised by 'invasive scrutiny' and 'cruel and punishing publicity' for the nominee, which discourages qualified people from being prepared to be nominated for high office and thereby 'hinders the president's ability to govern'. A former solicitor general, Theodore Olson, claimed in 2007 that the Senate had abandoned its role of 'advise and consent' for a policy of 'search and destroy'.

Box 5.3

Criticisms of the appointment and confirmation processes

- Presidents have tended to politicise the nominations by attempting to choose justices who share their political views and judicial philosophy.
- Senate has tended to politicise the confirmation process by focusing more on litmus test issues such as abortion than on qualifications and suitability for the job.
- Members of the Senate Judiciary Committee from the president's party tend to ask soft questions of the nominee.
- Members of the Senate Judiciary Committee from the opposition party attempt through their questions to attack or embarrass the nominee rather than elicit relevant information. 'Advise and consent' has been replaced by 'search and destroy.'
- Justices are now frequently confirmed by party-line votes.
- The media conduct a 'feeding frenzy' often connected with matters of little relevance to the nominee's judicial qualifications.

Justices are now frequently confirmed on party-line votes, another indicator of a politicised process. In January 2006 an editorial in the *Washington Post* — a left-of-centre newspaper — described Samuel Alito as 'superbly qualified'. An editorial was headed simply 'Confirm Samuel Alito'. The editorial stated:

> Supreme Court nominations have never been free of politics, but neither has their history generally been one of party-line votes or of ideology as the determining factor. To go down that road is to believe that there is a Democrat law and a Republican law, which is repugnant to the ideal of the rule of law. No president should be denied the prerogative of putting a person as qualified as Judge Alito on the Supreme Court.

Yet not a single Democrat in the Senate Judiciary Committee voted to recommend Alito's confirmation, and on the Senate floor only four Democrats voted to confirm him.

Then in 2016, the Republican-controlled Senate refused even to consider Judge Merrick Garland — President Obama's nominee to fill the vacancy following the death of Justice Antonin Scalia. The refusal to consider Garland as a nominee for the Supreme Court was unprecedented.

Politicisation by the media

The media came out of the Thomas hearings with little credit. Their 'feeding frenzy' on the allegations made against Thomas was liberally interspersed with sexual details that bordered on the prurient. Rather than have an informed debate about judicial philosophy and qualification, much of the media chose to compete for who could come up with the most lurid allegations and the most tasteless details. Thomas's use of the word 'lynching' was intended to have racist overtones. According to Edward Lazarus (1999):

> The Thomas affair powerfully reinforced the idea that Supreme Court confirmations were not occasions for seriously evaluating the nominee's legal thinking and qualifications but rather election campaigns for political control of the Court, to be waged by any means necessary.

Clarence Thomas during the Senate confirmation hearings, 1991

With the Court so finely balanced between conservatives and liberals — witness the large number of 5–4 decisions in recent years — it is unlikely that either the president or the Senate of either party is going to give up on trying to get its own way.

Why are Supreme Court nominations so important?

There are five reasons why the president's nominations to the Supreme Court are so important:

- Appointments to the Supreme Court occur infrequently. Whereas appointments to the cabinet, for example, can come up two or three times a year — and there is a whole new set at the beginning of each new administration — appointments to the Supreme Court come up on average only once every two years, and sometimes there can be a long period with no vacancies at all, as between 1994 and 2005.
- These appointments are for life. When George W. Bush nominated Condoleezza Rice to be secretary of state in 2005, everyone knew that the longest she would remain in office would be four years — until the end of Bush's second term. But when later that year Bush nominated the 50-year-old John Roberts to the Supreme Court, it was clear that Roberts was going to be on the Court for much longer than four years — possibly 20 or even 30 years and more.

- There are only nine members of the Supreme Court, so in appointing a new justice a president is replacing one-ninth of the Court's membership. A member of the House of Representatives is one of 435, a senator is one of 100 — you need respectively 217 and 50 other people to agree with you to get something done. But as a member of the Supreme Court you are one of nine — with four others you are a majority. If the Supreme Court had, say, 50 members then replacing just one of them would not be a big deal. But replacing one of nine is.

The last two reasons why Supreme Court appointments are important concern what we are about to study — the power of the Court.

- Supreme Court appointments are so important because of the Court's power of judicial review. As we will see, this is an extraordinarily important and significant power.
- Finally, the nominations to the Court are important because, through its power of judicial review, the Court can profoundly affect the lives of ordinary Americans as the Court makes decisions in such areas as abortion, affirmative action, gun control and freedom of speech.

It is to the power of judicial review and its effects on American society that we now turn.

The power of judicial review

Key terms

Judicial review The power of the Supreme Court to declare Acts of Congress, actions of the executive, or Acts or actions of state governments, unconstitutional.

Civil rights Positive acts of government designed to protect persons against arbitrary or discriminatory treatment by government or individuals.

Civil liberties Those liberties, mostly spelt out in the Constitution, that guarantee the protection of persons, expression and property from arbitrary interference by government.

Judicial review is the power of the Supreme Court to declare Acts of Congress, or actions of the executive — or Acts or actions of state governments — unconstitutional, and thereby null and void. The power is not mentioned in the Constitution; it might be said that the Supreme Court 'found' the power for itself in the 1803 case of *Marbury* v *Madison*. This was the first time that the Supreme Court declared an act of Congress unconstitutional. In 1810, in the case of *Fletcher* v *Peck,* the Supreme Court first declared a state law unconstitutional.

By using its power of judicial review the Court can, in effect, update the meaning of the words of the Constitution, most of which was written over two centuries ago. Hence, as we have seen, the Court decides what the phrase in the Eighth Amendment (written in 1791) forbidding 'cruel and unusual punishments' means today. Likewise, it decides whether the First Amendment right of 'freedom of speech' applies to the internet, for example. As former Chief Justice Charles Evans Hughes once remarked: 'We are under a Constitution, but the Constitution is what the judges say it is.'

Using its power of judicial review, the Supreme Court has involved itself in a host of political issues, not least in acting as a guarantor of fundamental **civil rights and liberties**. It is this that helps give the Court its political importance, because many of the issues dealt with by the Court are the key political issues of the day — matters over which political parties disagree and elections are fought. For example, political commentator Mark Shields has been quoted as saying that America's two major parties are 'separated [only] by the issue of abortion'. Which branch of government decides women's rights concerning abortion? The answer is the Supreme Court. In addition, the Supreme Court has handed down landmark decisions in recent years on such politically contentious issues as the rights of racial minorities, capital punishment, gun control and freedom of speech.

The political importance of the Court is demonstrated in the case of *George W. Bush* v *Albert Gore Jr* (2000). Five weeks after the presidential election, on 11 December 2000, the Supreme Court ruled that the manual recount scheme devised

185

by the Florida state Supreme Court was unconstitutional because it violated the **equal protection clause** of the Constitution's Fourteenth Amendment. In the same decision, the Court also ruled that because of the time constraints, 'it is evident that any recount seeking to meet the December 12 [deadline] will be unconstitutional'. The Court was seen by some to be handing the election to George W. Bush.

The power of judicial review not only gives the Court political importance, but is also said to turn it into a quasi-legislative body. This is because the decisions that the Court hands down have almost the effect of a law having been passed by Congress. So, for example, when in its 1973 decision in *Roe* v *Wade* the Court stated that women have a constitutional right to choose an abortion, the effect was comparable to an abortion rights law having been passed by Congress. In this sense, the Court has been described as 'a third house of the legislature'.

Judicial activism and judicial restraint

In a genuine democracy, the people rule themselves through elected officials who make decisions on their behalf. We sometimes call this deliberative democracy. Within such a democracy, the judiciary obviously plays an important role in deciding how the laws and the Constitution apply in specific cases. But controversy arises if the judiciary — which is unelected and therefore largely unaccountable — overturns the actions of directly elected officials in either the legislature or the executive. This brings us to the debate concerning judicial activism which is as old as the Constitution itself.

Judicial activism

The Founding Fathers were determined to try to keep the judiciary politically independent — free from political pressure — so that judges could decide cases on their legal merit and with no regard to political favour. That was why federal judges were given life tenure and Congress was prohibited from reducing judicial salaries. But whenever the Supreme Court made controversial and what some regarded as political decisions, accusations regarding **judicial activism** would reappear. It happened in 1803 when the Court first declared a federal law unconstitutional (see Table 5.5). More recently the Court has faced similar accusations as a result of its decisions in three cases:

- *Brown* v *Board of Education of Topeka* (1954), which outlawed racial segregation in public (i.e. state-run) schools
- *Roe* v *Wade* (1973), which declared a woman's right to an abortion to be a constitutionally protected right
- *Bush* v *Gore* (2000), which effectively awarded the presidency to George W. Bush

An activist Court is said to be one which sees itself as leading the way in the reform of American society. Thus the Court under Chief Justice Earl Warren was said to be activist in the 1950s and 1960s in trying to move society along in the areas of black civil rights and the rights of arrested persons.

Judicial activism also sees the Court as an equal partner with the legislative and executive branches of government. Professor Lino Graglia has defined judicial activism as 'the practice by judges of disallowing policy choices by other governmental officials or institutions that the Constitution does not clearly prohibit'. In other words, activist judges are not inclined to be deferential to the other branches of government. In this sense, according to T.R. van Geel (2008), judicial activism can be understood as a judicial attitude which says: 'I'm in charge, and I will seek to be a player equal to the other branches in shaping policy.'

Supporters of Al Gore and George W. Bush demonstrate in front of the Supreme Court building, 11 December 2000

Table 5.5 Federal laws declared unconstitutional by the Supreme Court, 1790–2016

Years	Federal laws	Years	Federal laws
1790–99	0	1910–19	6
1800–09	1	1920–29	15
1810–19	0	1930–39	13
1820–29	0	1940–49	2
1830–39	0	1950–59	5
1840–49	0	1960–69	16
1850–59	1	1970–79	20
1860–69	4	1980–89	16
1870–79	7	1990–99	23
1880–89	4	2000–09	18
1890–99	5	2010–16	11
1900–09	9		

Academics, politicians and judges continue to disagree about how activist the courts should be. There is also an added complication that the term 'judicial activism' is often used pejoratively about any decision to which a particular group or individual is opposed or with which they disagree. In this sense 'activist' judges are simply judges who make, in the view of the person speaking, the wrong decision. Critics of an activist Court might say that the justices are 'legislating from the bench' or that America now has an 'imperial judiciary'. As Kermit Roosevelt comments in his scholarly book, *The Myth of Judicial Activism* (2006): 'perceptions of appropriate judicial behaviour are invariably affected by ideology'. In other words, people will all too often label as 'judicial activism' those decisions of the Supreme Court of which they disapprove. Roosevelt concludes:

People call the Court activist because they disagree with its decisions. But the kind of people who use the word 'activist' are generally disagreeing on political grounds; the decisions they see as illegitimate are the ones whose results they do not like.

So should we be concerned by judicial activism? We must keep in mind that it is the job of the Court to limit the political branches of government if they step outside their constitutional powers. This means that the judiciary will have to declare laws passed by elected officials unconstitutional as well as put a stop to unconstitutional actions taken by the president. This is what they are supposed to do. The concern is that the courts might appear to be leading the way in public policy making. However, judges know that if their decisions stray too far or for too long outside the mainstream of public opinion, then they will be forced to moderate their decisions or lose their only true method of enforcement — the acceptance of their decisions as legitimate by the populace.

Judicial restraint

But there is a view that judges should wherever possible be deferential to both elected institutions and legal precedent. This allows us to explain two other terms with which we need to be familiar — judicial restraint and *stare decisis*.

Judicial restraint describes the Court when it is more inclined to accept the views and actions of elected officials. A court exercising judicial restraint would also tend wherever possible to defer to what has gone before, more inclined to leave things as they are. The Court exhibiting 'judicial restraint' puts a good deal of importance, therefore, on what is called *stare decisis* — best translated from the Latin as 'to stand by that which is decided'. Under this principle, once a matter has been decided in a case, it forms a precedent that should not be overturned except under pressing and changed circumstances.

Under the principle of judicial restraint, we shall see that having, for example, announced a woman's right to abortion in *Roe* v *Wade*, the Court has been willing to see limits put on that right but not to overturn the 1973 decision completely. Judicial restraint also sees the Court as somewhat deferential to the legislative and executive branches of government, as they — unlike the judiciary — are directly accountable to the voters. The Court following the approach of judicial restraint is therefore less likely to declare acts of Congress, or the state legislatures, unconstitutional. For this reason, some writers prefer the term 'judicial deference' to 'judicial restraint' as the opposite of 'judicial activism'.

US Government and Politics for A-level

Key terms

Judicial restraint An approach to judicial decision making which holds that judges should defer to the legislative and executive branches, and to precedent established in previous Court decisions.
Stare decisis A legal principle that judges should look to past precedents as a guide wherever possible (literally, 'let the decision stand').

Distinguish between

Judicial activism and judicial restraint

Judicial activism occurs when:
- judges are seen to lead the way in matters of public policy
- judges tend not to defer to the actions of elected officials
- the courts frequently strike down Acts of Congress as well as state laws
- the courts frequently declare actions of the executive branch unconstitutional
- the courts are in effect 'making' rather than 'interpreting' the law

Judicial restraint occurs when:
- judges tend to defer to elected institutions and officials in matters of public policy
- judges are reluctant to strike down Acts of Congress or state laws
- judges rarely declare actions of the executive branch unconstitutional
- the courts refrain from 'legislating from the bench'
- the courts tend to rely on precedent from previous decisions

The Supreme Court and the Bill of Rights

As discussed in Chapter 2, when the Constitution's framers wanted to better protect the fundamental rights and liberties of American citizens, they added the Bill of Rights — the first ten amendments — to the Constitution. But what do these words, written over 200 years ago, mean today? It is the Supreme Court that answers that question. Here we consider four sets of rights — those concerning freedom of religion, freedom of speech, guns and capital punishment. So, as we study some of the recent landmark decisions of the Supreme Court (see Table 5.6), we need to be aware of the ways in which such decisions:

- enable the Court to interpret the Constitution
- turn the Court into a political institution
- give the Court a quasi-legislative power
- protect civil rights and liberties in the USA today

First Amendment: freedom of religion

The First Amendment begins with this statement:

> Congress shall make no law respecting an establishment of religion, or prohibiting the free exercise thereof.

It is a right that is grounded in the wish of the eighteenth-century framers of the Constitution to preserve a level of religious freedom within the United States which had been noticeably lacking in those countries from which many of their forebears had come. However, these opening 16 words of the First Amendment contain something of a conundrum: how to ensure that there is no established religion while preserving citizens' rights to practise their religion freely. It has posed a seemingly insuperable problem for the Court in its attempts to protect religious freedoms. Critics of the Court — these days mainly evangelical Christians — believe that the Court has been too attentive to the first half of this opening phrase while ignoring the second half.

For a long time, the Supreme Court declined to enter this particular area of civil liberties. But from the 1960s through to the 1990s, the Court handed down a number of judgements that ruled that overtly Christian practices in America's state-run schools — things such as prayer or Bible reading — were unconstitutional as, in the view of a majority of the Court, they constituted 'an establishment of religion'.

Table 5.6 Recent landmark Bill of Rights decisions

Amendment	Decisions
First Amendment: Freedom of religion	*Zelman* v *Simmons-Harris* (2002) *Town of Greece* v *Galloway* (2014) *Burwell* v *Hobby Lobby Stores Inc.* (2014)
First Amendment: Freedom of speech	*McConnell* v *Federal Election Commission* (2004) *Citizens United* v *Federal Election Commission* (2010) *McCutcheon* v *Federal Election Commission* (2014)
Second Amendment: Right to bear arms	*District of Columbia* v *Heller* (2008) *McDonald* v *City of Chicago* (2010)
Eighth Amendment: Death penalty	*Ring* v *Arizona* (2002) *Roper* v *Simmons* (2005) *Baze* v *Rees* (2008) *Glossip* v *Gross* (2015) *Atkins* v *Virginia* (2002) *Hall* v *Florida* (2014)

In what some saw as a change of emphasis, in *Zelman* v *Simmons-Harris*, the Court upheld a programme in Ohio giving financial aid to parents to allow them to send their children to religious or private schools. In a 5–4 decision, the Court upheld the so-called 'school voucher' programme being run in the state of Ohio, and so appeared to breach the wall of separation between Church and state. In this case, the four liberal members of the Court — justices John Paul Stevens, David Souter, Ruth Bader Ginsburg and Stephen Breyer — all dissented.

The programme was supported by the Bush administration, the Republican Party and ideological conservatives. They saw the voucher programme as the best way to help poor people whose children would otherwise have to attend failing inner-city schools. The opponents were the Democratic Party, the teachers' unions and ideological liberals. They saw the programme as a threat to the state-run school system.

The case was of particular interest because it involved not only issues of religious freedom but also issues of race, as most of the children involved in the voucher programme were African-Americans. Under the programme in Cleveland, Ohio, the parents of some 3,700 children had been given vouchers worth up to $2,250 to send them to private schools rather than the free, state-run, local school. Of these 3,700, around 96% had opted to send their children to private religious schools.

In December 2000, the Federal Court of Appeals had declared that the programme had the 'impermissible effect of promoting sectarian schools' and thereby violated the First Amendment's prohibition against 'the establishment of religion'. The majority of the Supreme Court disagreed. The majority opinion authored by Justice Thomas was most striking. Justice Thomas is the Court's only African-American and he often credits his own rise from poverty to the rigorous education that he received in a Roman Catholic school in Savannah, Georgia. He wrote:

> The promise of public school education has failed poor inner-city blacks. If society cannot end racial discrimination, at least it can arm minorities with the education to defend themselves from some of discrimination's effects.

The Chief Justice, William Rehnquist, wrote in this case for the majority, too, stating that the key issue was not that almost all of the students who used vouchers went to religious schools, but rather that the vouchers were just one part of an array of alternatives to the state-run schools. Rehnquist concluded:

> The question is whether Ohio is coercing parents into sending their children to religious schools, and that question must be answered evaluating all options Ohio provides Cleveland school children, only one of which is to obtain a [voucher] and then choose a religious school.

In other words, it didn't matter that 96% of these children with vouchers happened to enrol in religious schools. That was a choice made by their parents, not the government. The dissenting minority were unimpressed by this logic, calling the decision a 'potentially tragic' mistake that could 'force citizens to subsidise faiths they do not share even as it corrupts religion by making it dependent on government'.

In *Town of Greece* v *Galloway*, the Supreme Court ruled (5–4) that legislative bodies such as town and city councils could begin their meetings with prayer, even if those prayers clearly favoured one particular religion. The Court ruled that such prayers did not violate the First Amendment ban on 'an establishment of religion'. 'Ceremonial prayer is but a recognition that, since this Nation was founded and until the present day, many Americans deem that their existence must be understood by precepts far beyond the authority of government,' wrote Justice Anthony Kennedy for the Court's conservative majority.

In *Burwell* v *Hobby Lobby Stores Inc.* the Court ruled (5–4) that a provision of the Affordable Care Act (2010), popularly known as 'Obamacare', violated the Religious Freedom Restoration Act (RFRA) of 1993. As the Court had already declared the RFRA to be constitutional in a decision back in 2006, it was Obamacare that took a hit. The Affordable Care Act's requirement that family-owned corporations pay for health insurance coverage for contraception violated the RFRA.

Hobby Lobby, the company at the centre of the case, is a chain of arts and crafts stores run on Christian principles. The proprietors of Hobby Lobby had claimed that certain methods of contraception included in the health insurance coverage were against their religious principles. As in the landmark campaign finance ruling in 2010 of *Citizens United* v *FEC* (see below), the Court's majority stated that as corporations are 'people', they have the same constitutional rights as individual Americans. Justice Samuel Alito, writing for the majority, emphasised the limited scope of this decision, stating that only certain family-run corporations would be covered by the ruling. But Justice Ruth Bader Ginsburg in her dissent attacked the majority for what she saw as a radical overhaul of corporate rights. 'The Court's expansive notion of corporate personhood invites for-profit entities to seek religion-based exemptions from regulations they deem offensive to their faiths,' she wrote.

The decision was a clear rebuff to the Obama administration. Not only did it strike down part of the President's flagship reform legislation, but it clearly went against the administration's stance favouring women's rights. Josh Earnest, the White House press secretary, stated that the Court's decision 'jeopardises the health of women employed' by Hobby Lobby, adding that 'women should be able to make personal health care decisions for themselves, rather than their bosses deciding for them'. But Lori Windham, the lawyer for Hobby Lobby, stated that 'the Supreme Court recognised that Americans do not lose their religious freedom when they run a family business'.

First Amendment: freedom of speech

The First Amendment talks about more than just freedom of religion. It goes on to state:

> Congress shall make no law...abridging the freedom of speech, or of the press.

Here again, the Supreme Court has played an important role in protecting these fundamental rights. In *Buckley* v *Valeo* (1976) the Court declared unconstitutional part of the Federal Election Campaign Act (1974) that limited expenditure by presidential candidates. The Court claimed that such limits infringed the 'freedom of speech' provision of the First Amendment.

The Court made another important judgement on freedom of speech as it affects political campaigning in its 2004 decision in *McConnell* v *Federal Election Commission*. In this decision, the Supreme Court upheld the provisions of the Bipartisan Campaign Reform Act (BCRA), commonly known as the McCain–Feingold Act after its two Senate sponsors — Republican John McCain and Democrat Russell Feingold. In upholding the statute, the Court rejected the argument of its opponents that in banning soft money the law stifled free speech and was therefore contrary to the provisions of the First Amendment.

In *Citizens United* v *Federal Election Commission* (2010), the Court ruled that when it comes to rights of political speech, business corporations and labour unions have the same rights as individuals, a decision which overturned federal laws and Court decisions going back to 1947.

Artist's sketch of the courtroom during *Citizens United* v *Federal Election Commission*

But what exactly constitutes 'speech' and what would it mean for it to be 'abridged'? In *McCutcheon* v *Federal Election Commission* (2014), the Court struck down a 1970s limit on the total amount of money wealthy donors can contribute to candidates and political committees. 'There is no right more basic in our democracy than the right to participate in electing our political leaders,' wrote Chief Justice John Roberts for the majority.

> We have made clear that Congress may not regulate contributions simply to reduce the amount of money in politics, or to restrict the political participation of some in order to enhance the relative influence of others.

Roberts was joined by Anthony Kennedy and his fellow conservative justices Antonin Scalia, Samuel Alito and Clarence Thomas, although Thomas thought the majority should have gone further and struck down all contribution limits.

Second Amendment: gun control

In 2008, the Supreme Court — for the first time in its history — ruled in a case relating to the meaning of the Second Amendment. In *District of Columbia* v *Heller*, the Court declared unconstitutional a law passed by the District of Columbia in 1976 banning the ownership of handguns and requiring that shotguns and rifles be kept unloaded and either disassembled or with the trigger locked.

> We hold that the District's ban on handgun possession in the home violates the Second Amendment, as does its prohibition against rendering any lawful firearm in the home operable for the purpose of immediate self-defence

wrote Justice Antonin Scalia for the five-member majority, in which he was joined by Chief Justice Roberts, and associate justices Kennedy, Thomas and Alito.

At issue was the meaning which the framers of the Constitution intended in writing the Second Amendment, which reads:

> A well regulated Militia, being necessary to the security of a free State, the right of the people to keep and bear Arms, shall not be infringed.

There have come to be two interpretations of this amendment. Some interpret it as guaranteeing a *collective* right to own guns related only to the formation of state militias. This is the view taken by most liberals, Democrats and supporters of gun control legislation such as the Brady Center to Prevent Gun Violence. But others interpret the amendment as guaranteeing an *individual* right to own guns. They argue that just as all the other rights and liberties — of religion, free speech and the like — contained within the Bill of Rights are individual, not collective, so is this right. This is the view taken by most conservatives, Republicans and groups opposing most gun control legislation such as the National Rifle Association.

Up until this point, federal courts had never specifically decided whether the rights bestowed in the Second Amendment were collective or individual. But in this case, the majority of the Court took the view that the 'the right to keep and bear arms' protected by the Second Amendment is, indeed, an individual right and thus declared the District's handgun ban unconstitutional. For the dissenting minority, Justice Stevens called the decision 'a strained and unpersuasive reading' of the text.

In a follow-up case, *McDonald* v *City of Chicago* (2010), the Court declared that the Second Amendment gives to Americans a fundamental right to bear arms and that the due process clause of the Fourteenth Amendment means that this right cannot be infringed by state or local governments.

The Eighth Amendment: the death penalty

First, some background. Currently 19 of the 50 states, plus the District of Columbia, do not use the death penalty. These are almost all in the northern tier of states, plus the Northeast, the Mid-Atlantic, as well as Alaska and Hawaii. Six states have abolished the death penalty in the last ten years — New Jersey (2007), New Mexico (2009), Illinois (2011), Connecticut (2012), Maryland (2013), and Nebraska (2015). At the other end of the scale, five states dominate the death penalty league table with Texas clearly in the lead (see Table 5.7).

Table 5.7 Executions by state, 1976–2016 (states with 20 or more executions)

State	Total	2015	2016
Texas	538	13	7
Oklahoma	112	1	0
Virginia	111	1	0
Florida	92	3	1
Missouri	87	6	1
Georgia	69	5	9
Alabama	58	0	2
Ohio	53	0	0
North Carolina	43	0	0
South Carolina	43	0	0
Arizona	37	0	0
Louisiana	28	0	0
Arkansas	27	0	0
Mississippi	21	0	0
Indiana	20	0	0

Source: www.deathpenaltyinfo.org

The Supreme Court has over the past two decades made a number of decisions regarding the right guaranteed by the Eighth Amendment against 'cruel and unusual punishments'. In *Ring* v *Arizona* (2002) the Court declared (7–2) that death sentences imposed by judges, rather than by juries, were unconstitutional because they infringed the Sixth Amendment right to trial by jury.

In *Roper* v *Simmons* (2005) the Court decided (5–4) that it is unconstitutional to sentence anyone to death for a crime he or she committed when younger than 18. In the 2008 case of *Baze* v *Rees,* the Court decided that lethal injection — the method used by the federal government and 35 states to execute criminals — did not constitute a 'cruel and unusual punishment' and therefore did not violate the Eighth Amendment.' The Court reiterated this decision in 2015, in the case of *Glossip* v *Gross*. Of the 1,413 people executed in the United States since the death penalty was reinstated in 1976, 1,238 (88%) have been by lethal injection. This is why the Court's decisions about lethal injection are so important. For if the Court were to declare this form of execution unconstitutional, it could be the death knell for the death penalty in the United States.

In 2002, in *Atkins* v *Virginia*, the Court stated that the execution of mentally retarded criminals infringed the Eighth Amendment, but it did not state what constituted mental retardation. States had therefore passed laws to fix the IQ scores below which a criminal would fall into this category.

In *Hall* v *Florida* (2014), the Court ruled unconstitutional state laws that drew such a rigid numerical line. In Florida, an inmate who scored above 70 on an IQ test could be executed while one scoring 70 or below could not. The case involved Freddie Hall, a 68-year-old who has lived half his life on Florida's death row for raping and killing a 21-year-old pregnant girl in 1978. Hall argued through his lawyer that Florida's rigid IQ score line was arbitrary and therefore breached his constitutional rights under the Eighth Amendment. Hall had taken several IQ tests, gaining a range of scores from 71 to 80.

The Supreme Court and public policy

As well as interpreting the Bill of Rights, the Supreme Court decides cases affecting matters of public policy that are in the forefront of American political debate. Here we consider two such policy areas — abortion and so-called marriage equality. These are issues that have featured in recent election campaigns with the two major parties taking differing views.

Abortion

Supreme Court decisions concerning a woman's right to choose an abortion have dominated the argument about rights and liberties in America for over 30 years.

Roe v *Wade*

In 1973 the Court announced in *Roe* v *Wade* that the Fourteenth Amendment right of 'liberty' included 'freedom of personal choice in matters of marriage and family life' and that this right 'necessarily includes the right of a woman to decide whether or not to terminate her pregnancy'. The case centred upon Norma McCorvey — identified in the case only by the alias of 'Jane Roe' — who had been denied an abortion by the state law of Texas. (Henry Wade was a Dallas County district attorney.)

Anti-abortion protesters in front of the US Supreme Court on the anniversary of the *Roe* v *Wade* decision

The *Roe* v *Wade* decision was one of the most politically important decisions of the twentieth century. It came at a time when the issue of women's rights was gaining importance and support in the USA. It took on political significance as the 'pro-choice' lobby (those who supported the decision) became closely associated with the Democratic Party, while the 'pro-life' lobby (those who opposed the decision) became closely associated with the Republicans. It was a 7–2 decision by the Court in which the recently appointed William Rehnquist — later to be appointed chief justice — was one of the two dissenters.

Gonzales v *Carhart*

Another landmark decision on abortion rights was handed down in *Gonzales* v *Carhart* (2007). In a 5–4 decision, the Court upheld the Partial-Birth Abortion Ban Act of 2003. By this time, O'Connor had retired to be replaced by Alito, and the effect was dramatic. On this occasion, Anthony Kennedy wrote the majority opinion, joined by Chief Justice Roberts and associate justices Antonin Scalia, Clarence Thomas and Samuel Alito. Here was another instance of the Court chipping away at the right of a woman to have an abortion.

First, though, we need some background on this decision. Most abortions — probably well over 90% — are performed within the first three months of pregnancy. The procedure ends with the doctor vacuuming out the embryonic tissue. This procedure would be unaffected by this decision. However, if the abortion occurs much later in the pregnancy then some form of surgical operation is required. The woman will be placed under anaesthetic, her cervix dilated and the foetus removed in pieces.

Some doctors use a different procedure for these 'late-term' abortions, to reduce risks to the woman of bleeding, infection and permanent injury. This other procedure involves partly delivering the foetus and then crushing its skull to make removal easier. Opponents say this amounts to infanticide, as the foetus could be viable (able to survive outside the uterus) at the time. It is this procedure that Congress voted to ban in the so-called Partial-Birth Abortion Ban Act of 2003.

195

Writing for the majority in upholding the legislation, Justice Kennedy announced that 'the government may use its voice and its regulatory authority to show respect for the life within the woman'. He continued:

> While we find no reliable data to measure the phenomenon, it seems unexceptional to conclude some women come to regret their choice to abort the infant life they once created and sustained.

For the minority, Ruth Bader Ginsburg stated that the majority opinion of the Court in this case

> cannot be understood as anything other than an effort to chip away at a right declared again and again in this court — and with increasing comprehension of its centrality to women's lives.

She accused the majority of being paternalistic in its attitude towards women. Ginsburg stated:

> The solution the Court approves is not to require doctors to inform women adequately of the different procedures they might choose and the risk each entails. Instead the Court shields women by denying them any choice in the matter.

This was a most significant decision for three reasons:

- For the first time in its history, the Court declared that a specific abortion procedure could be banned and made no exception for the health of the woman, although it did provide an exception if the life of the woman was threatened. This decision was therefore seen by Democrats and liberal activist groups as a serious in-road into abortion rights.
- The decision had a potential political significance in terms of the party political debate on abortion. Conservative interest groups, such as Concerned Women for America, the Eagle Forum and the National Right to Life Committee, were jubilant at the Court's decision. Whereas such groups used to see their goal as getting the Court to overturn *Roe* v *Wade*, now they take a much more incremental approach — the 'chipping away' of which Justice Ginsburg spoke in her dissenting opinion.
- The decision showed again the significance of the change in membership of the Court, with the more conservative Samuel Alito having replaced the more centrist Sandra O'Connor. Back in 2000, in *Stenberg* v *Carhart*, the Court had struck down a Nebraska state law prohibiting the same late-term procedure. But in that case, O'Connor had sided with the Court's four liberal justices — Stevens, Souter, Breyer and Ginsburg — to author a majority opinion which, while recognising the procedure could be 'gruesome', nonetheless decided that it was sometimes necessary.

Whole Woman's Health v *Hellerstedt*

This case concerned two parts of a Texas state law that imposed strict requirements on abortion providers in the state, signed into law in July 2013 by the then governor Rick Perry. One restriction required all abortion clinics in the state to meet the standards of what Americans call an ambulatory surgical centre — a medical facility that offers procedures that are too complicated for a doctor's surgery, but do not require in-patient, overnight care. Another restriction required doctors performing abortions to have direct access to in-patient facilities at a nearby hospital.

In his majority decision in *Whole Woman's Health v Hellerstedt* (2016), Justice Breyer concluded that 'neither of these provisions offers medical benefits sufficient to justify the burdens upon access [to abortion services] that each imposes'. He continued:

> Each places a substantial obstacle in the path of women seek an abortion, each constitutes an undue burden on abortion access, and each violates the Constitution.

Breyer was joined by justices Kennedy, Ginsburg, Sotomayor and Kagan. Chief Justice Roberts, along with justices Thomas and Alito, dissented. But it was Justice Kennedy's vote that was the critical one. Had Kennedy voted the other way, resulting in a 4–4 tie, the decision of the appeal court that had taken the contrary view and upheld the Texas law would have prevailed. At the time, the Supreme Court had only eight members following the death of Justice Antonin Scalia earlier in the year.

David Cohen, a law professor at Drexel University in Philadelphia, described Kennedy's vote in this case as 'a puzzle', adding that 'he may have been swayed by the burdens placed on women having to drive hundreds of miles to have an abortion, or by the lack of medical evidence justifying the restrictions — or both'. Or, of course, Justice Kennedy may not be able to see a potential majority that he doesn't want to join.

President Obama was pleased with the Court's decision, tweeting:

> Pleased to see the Supreme Court reaffirm every woman has a constitutional right to make her own reproductive choices.

But Texas Attorney General Ken Paxton ridiculed the Supreme Court for its decision, commenting that 'the Court is becoming a default medical board for the nation, with no deference being given to state law'. As a result of the law, the number of abortion clinics in Texas had dropped from 41 to 20. Critics of the law claimed that, had the Supreme Court decision gone the other way, the number could have been halved again.

'Marriage equality'

The first significant decision on what has become known as marriage equality was in the case of *United States v Windsor* (2013), in which the Court declared (5–4) the Defense of Marriage Act (1996) unconstitutional because it denied federal benefits to married same-sex couples that were available to other married couples. But this decision opened the door for a much more wide-ranging and significant ruling two years later.

In *Obergefell v Hodges*, the Court ruled (5–4) that state bans to prohibit same-sex marriage were a violation of the Fourteenth Amendment, which forbids states from denying the equal protection of the laws to any person within their jurisdiction, and were therefore unconstitutional. The case was brought by James Obergefell, who had married John Arthur in Maryland in 2013. But their state of residence, Ohio, would not recognise the marriage. Arthur was terminally ill, and when Obergefell asked to be named as the surviving spouse on the death certificate, the state authorities in Ohio refused. Obergefell then filed in federal court, claiming an infringement of the Fourteenth Amendment by the state's ban on same-sex marriage.

Jim Obergefell (centre), the plaintiff in the *Obergefell v Hodges* case

Here was a case which clearly illustrated the difference between strict and loose constructionists on the Court. In the view of the four conservative dissenting justices, this was an issue that should have been left to the states to decide. 'This Supreme Court is not a legislature,' wrote Chief Justice Roberts for the minority:

> Whether same-sex marriage is a good idea should be of no concern to us. Under the Constitution, judges have power to say what the law is, not what it should be. The people who ratified the Constitution authorised the courts to exercise 'neither force nor will but merely judgement'

— a quotation from Alexander Hamilton. It was a classic statement of a strict constructionist position.

But the majority took the loose constructionist position. To them, the 'life, liberty and property' rights of the Fourteenth Amendment 'extend to certain personal choices central to individual dignity and autonomy, including intimate choices that define personal identity and beliefs'. This is a clear example of the loose constructionist's 'reading things into' the words of the Constitution. The word 'dignity' appeared nine times in Justice Kennedy's majority opinion, yet it never appears in the Constitution itself. It is also a clear example of the power of judicial review being used to turn the Court into a quasi-legislative body — in effect making rather than merely interpreting law. Justice Scalia was scathing about the majority and then ended in sarcasm.

> They have discovered in the Fourteenth Amendment a 'fundamental right' overlooked by every person alive at the time of [the amendment's] ratification and almost everyone else in the time since. Those justices know that limiting marriage to one man and one woman is contrary to reason: they know that an institution as old as government itself, and accepted by every nation in history until 15 years ago, cannot possibly be supported by anything other than ignorance and bigotry.

What was startling about this case was that the view held by President Obama just seven years earlier when he first campaigned for the office — that marriage was a God-ordained institution between one man and one woman — had now been declared illegal as a basis of law in all 50 states. Such is the power of the United States Supreme Court.

The Supreme Court and congressional power

Not only does the Court rule on the rights and liberties guaranteed in the various amendments to the Constitution, but it also from time to time rules on the powers of the other two branches of government — Congress and the presidency — and their powers as laid out in Articles I and II of the Constitution, as well as the relationship between the federal government and the states. The particularly relevant parts of the Constitution regarding the powers of Congress are to be found in Article I, Section 8, and especially in what are referred to as 'the commerce clause' and 'the necessary and proper clause' which occur in that section.

As well as granting very specific powers to Congress — to coin money, to raise and support armies, to declare war, and such like — this section of Article I also grants to Congress the power 'to regulate Commerce...among the several states' and 'to make all Laws which shall be necessary and proper for carrying into Execution the foregoing Powers'. Congress has used such vague clauses as a means of expanding its powers over many decades, and especially since the 1930s, and it has fallen to the Supreme Court from time to time to decide whether or not Congress has exceeded its powers under these provisions.

Healthcare reform

The most recent judgement of the Court in relation to Congress's power under the commerce clause came in the landmark decision on President Obama's healthcare reform — the Affordable Care Act — in June 2012, in the case of *National Federation of Independent Business* v *Sebelius*. In this decision the Court, by 5 votes to 4, upheld most of the provisions on the Affordable Care Act, with Chief Justice Roberts joining the Court's liberal foursome — justices Ginsburg, Breyer, Sotomayor and Kagan.

But the significance of the decision was not so much in the upholding of the Act as in the reasoning of the Chief Justice in writing the majority opinion. Democrats in Congress and the Obama administration had consistently argued that the provisions of the Act were constitutional because of the powers granted to Congress by the commerce clause (see Chapter 2). Congress, they claimed, could write into the Act the so-called 'individual mandate' requiring every American to get health insurance or pay a 'penalty'. Therefore although this decision was on the surface about the constitutional standing of the Affordable Care Act, much more significantly it was about the power of Congress and the relationship between the federal government and the states within a federal system of government.

Chief Justice Roberts set the scene right at the start of his majority opinion:

> In our federal system, the National Government possesses only limited powers: the States and the people retain the remainder. Nearly two centuries ago, Chief Justice Marshall observed that 'the question respecting the extent of the powers actually granted' to the Federal Government 'is perpetually arising, and will probably continue to arise, as long as our system shall exist'. In this case we must again determine whether the Constitution grants Congress powers it now asserts, but which many States and individuals believe it does not possess.

The Chief Justice then rehearsed the arguments put forward by the Act's supporters for an expansive view of the Constitution's commerce clause before declaring in two epoch-making words, 'We disagree.' Roberts argued that the

Act was not 'regulating' commerce but the lack of it. Americans were to be penalised for not buying health insurance. This is how Roberts argued the case in his majority opinion:

> The power to *regulate* commerce presupposes the existence of commercial activity to be regulated...The individual mandate, however, does not regulate existing commercial activity. It instead compels individuals to *become* active in commerce by purchasing a product on the grounds that their failure to do so affects interstate commerce...The Framers [of the Constitution] knew the difference between doing something and doing nothing. They gave Congress the power to *regulate* commerce, not to *compel* it. Ignoring that distinction would undermine the principle that the Federal Government is a government of limited and enumerated powers. The individual mandate thus cannot be sustained under Congress's power to 'regulate commerce'.

Indeed, Roberts argued, if the Court allowed Congress to claim the commerce clause power to force people to buy health insurance, Congress might also think that the clause gave it the power to force people to buy cars or broccoli. But rather than declare the individual mandate unconstitutional, the Chief Justice then went on to say that it was constitutional because it was not a 'penalty' but a 'tax' and therefore allowable by the constitutional power granted to Congress in Article I, Section 8, to 'lay and collect taxes'. It was a remarkable piece of judicial conjuring.

Immigration

In another landmark decision in 2012, *United States* v *Arizona*, the Court struck down three provisions of an Arizona immigration law because they encroached on areas of congressional authority to regulate immigration. Thus the Court can both protect as well as limit the powers of Congress, thereby keeping a balance between the powers of the federal government and those of the individual states.

The Supreme Court and presidential power

Not only does the power of judicial review give the Supreme Court the power to declare Acts of Congress unconstitutional, but it also includes the power to declare actions of any member of the executive branch unconstitutional, including the president. In some landmark decisions over the past 15 years, the Court has done just that and in doing so has shown itself to be a check on presidential power.

Bush and Guantánamo Bay detainees

In 2004, in the case of *Rasul* v *Bush*, the Supreme Court struck down some important parts of the Bush administration's legal policy regarding its 'war on terror' in general and the detainees at Guantánamo Bay in particular. In its decision (6–3) the Court ruled that the foreign detainees — including some British citizens — held at the US base in Guantánamo Bay on the island of Cuba did have access to the United States federal courts to challenge their detention.

While agreeing that it was within President Bush's powers to order the detention of members of al Qaeda or the Taliban as 'enemy combatants', the Court rejected the administration's view that the detainees were outside the jurisdiction of the federal courts. 'We have long since made it clear that a state of war is not a blank cheque for the president,' stated Justice Sandra O'Connor for the majority. The three dissenting votes in this case were cast by conservatives Rehnquist, Scalia and Thomas.

In the case of *Hamdan* v *Rumsfeld*, the Court declared unconstitutional the military commissions set up by President George W. Bush to try people held at Guantánamo Bay. This was a 5–3 decision. Chief Justice Roberts did not participate because he had served on the three-judge Appeal Court panel whose decision to uphold commissions was being reviewed in this case. If Roberts had participated, one can reasonably assume this would have been a 5–4 decision.

The majority opinion was written by Justice Stevens, joined by Breyer, Souter, Ginsburg and Kennedy. Scalia, Thomas and Alito dissented. This will go down as another landmark decision of the Supreme Court as it put a significant limit on the commander-in-chief power of the president, even in time of war. The Court seemed to be clipping the wings of a president who had employed not only military commissions that were struck down by this ruling, but also warrantless wiretapping. Thus, the broad assertion of presidential power — which was a hallmark of the George W. Bush administration — was questioned by the Court.

Camp Delta, Guantánamo Bay, Cuba

The Supreme Court handed down yet another rebuff to the Bush administration on the Guantánamo Bay detainees in 2008 in the case of *Boumediene* v *Bush*. In a 5–4 decision, with Justice Kennedy siding with the liberal members of the Court — Stevens, Souter, Ginsburg and Breyer — the Court held that the procedures set up by the Bush administration and Congress following the *Hamdan* decision in 2006 were inadequate to ensure that the detainees received their day in court. 'The laws and the Constitution are designed to survive, and remain in force, in extraordinary times,' wrote Justice Kennedy for the majority. 'Liberty and security can be reconciled.' Writing for the minority, Justice Scalia called the decision 'a self-invited incursion into military affairs'. Chief Justice Roberts in a separate dissent defended the procedures set up beforehand as 'the most generous set of procedural protections ever afforded to aliens detained by this country as enemy combatants'.

Obama and recess appointments

Article II Section 2 of the Constitution states that 'the President shall have Power to fill up vacancies that may happen during the Recess of the Senate'. But this begs the question as to what constitutes a Senate recess.

In *National Labor Relations Board* v *Noel Canning*, the Court ruled (9–0) that President Obama lacked the constitutional authority to make high-level executive branch appointments at a time when the Senate was technically available to give its advice and consent.

The case arose from a labour dispute involving a soft-drinks company, the Noel Canning Corporation of Yakima in Washington State, which bottles much of Pepsi's output in the western United States. The National Labor Relations Board (NLRB) ruled against the company in a labour dispute, saying that it had engaged in an unfair labour practice by refusing to enter into a collective bargaining agreement. But the Noel Group appealed, arguing that the NLRB had been powerless to make its ruling because a majority of its members had been appointed by President Obama during a 20-day period when the Senate was convening every three days for so-called pro forma sessions without conducting business. The President, who viewed such pro forma sessions as a tactic to keep the Senate open so that he could not make recess appointments, made the appointments anyway. Since three of the Board's five members had in the Noel Group's view not been properly appointed, the company argued that the NLRB's ruling was void.

In a unanimous judgement, the Court found the President to have exceeded his powers in making the three NLRB appointments back in 2012. It was a stunning rebuke for the President, a decision as highly significant as it was unusual. Even his own two appointees to the Court — Sonia Sotomayor and Elena Kagan — found against him.

Obama and immigration reform

Congress having failed to deliver any meaningful immigration reform legislation, in November 2014 President Obama issued an executive order — the Deferred Action for Parents of Americans and Lawful Permanent Residents (DAPA) — to allow certain illegal immigrants to be granted 'deferred action status'. This means that, although not granted full citizenship, they would be subject to an indefinite delay in their deportation from the United States. To be eligible for DAPA, a person must:

- have lived in the United States without interruption since 1 January 2010
- be physically present in the United States when applying
- have a child who is a US citizen or lawful permanent resident
- be free from any criminal conviction
- not pose a threat to national security

This would have allowed some 5 million unauthorised immigrants who were parents of lawful residents to remain legally in the country.

In December of the same year, Texas along with 25 other states, all with Republican governors, challenged the President's action in federal court, calling it 'one of the largest changes in immigration policy in our nation's history', and claiming the President could not carry out such a programme without Congress's approval. In November 2015, the federal appeals court found that President Obama did not have such powers, and that his action was unconstitutional as it breached the clause of Article II of the Constitution that requires the president to 'take care that the laws be faithfully executed'. The Justice Department announced it was asking the Supreme Court to review this decision.

The 4–4 tied decision left in place the federal appeals court decision blocking the plan. The Supreme Court's judgement in *United States* v *Texas* (2016) amounted to just nine words: 'The judgement is affirmed by an equally divided court.' But such brevity masks the enormity of the decision. Walter Dellinger, a

Clinton administration lawyer, commented: 'Seldom have the hopes of so many been crushed by so few words.' The President was distraught, stating:

> Today's decision is frustrating to those who seek to grow our economy and bring rationality to our immigration system. It is heartbreaking for the millions of immigrants who have made their lives here.

But Texas attorney general Ken Paxton was delighted with the outcome, stating:

> Today's decision keeps in place what we have maintained from the start: one person, even a president, cannot unilaterally change the law. This is a major setback to President Obama's attempts to expand executive power, and a victory for those who believe in the separation of powers and the rule of law.

The brief judgement did not disclose how the justices voted, but they undoubtedly split along ideological lines with the conservatives (Roberts, Thomas and Alito) plus Kennedy on one side, and the liberals (Ginsburg, Breyer, Sotomayor and Kagan) on the other. The President's side had optimistically hoped that Chief Justice Roberts might join his four more liberal colleagues and save the programme, as he had done over Obamacare. Robert Barnes, writing in the *Washington Post*, described President Obama as having 'suffered the biggest legal defeat of his administration'.

What do these decisions show about the Supreme Court?

Let us return briefly to the four points of analysis which we mentioned before studying these landmark decisions.

The Court's power of judicial review enables it to interpret the Constitution

We have seen in these decisions a number of clauses of the Constitution which have been interpreted by the Court. In the death penalty cases, the Court was saying what the phrase 'cruel and unusual punishments' in the Eighth Amendment — written in 1791 — means today. In the abortion cases, it was what the word 'liberty' in the Fourteenth Amendment — written in 1865 — means today. The Court has also tried to say what the First Amendment phrase forbidding 'an establishment of religion' — another 1791 addition — means in today's America. Or what does the right to 'freedom of speech' granted by the First Amendment mean for campaign finance regulation? What does the Second Amendment right to 'keep and bear arms' mean in the twenty-first century? In countless decisions, the Court is, *in effect*, amending the Constitution — not formally by changing the words, but interpretatively, by changing the meaning of those words. Indeed, this is one of the reasons why it is unnecessary to keep passing formal amendments to the Constitution.

The Court's power of judicial review turns it into a political institution

Because the Supreme Court is making decisions in policy areas that are politically contentious and about which the two major parties fundamentally disagree — affirmative action, the death penalty, abortion, school prayers and gun control, to give but five examples — the Court is to some extent turned into a political institution. The Democrats, as a general rule, favour affirmative action, abortion rights for women and gun control, but oppose the death penalty and school prayers. Republicans, as a general rule, oppose affirmative action, abortion rights for women and gun control, but support the death penalty and school prayers. And debate about these policies is the very stuff of American elections, at the national as well as the state level. Any institution which makes decisions in these kinds of areas is bound to be seen as something of a political institution.

Is the Supreme Court a political institution?

Yes

- Appointed by a politician (the president)
- Confirmed by politicians (the Senate), often on party-line votes
- Makes decisions on issues that feature in elections (e.g. abortion, immigration, gun control) and over which the two main parties disagree
- Some of its decisions have a quasi-legislative effect: it is as if a new law has been passed
- Some people have described it as 'a third house of the legislature'

No

- Its members are judges, not politicians
- The Court is independent — not subject to political pressure
- Justices do not involve themselves in party politics, elections, campaigning, endorsing candidates
- Makes decisions based upon legal and constitutional argument, not political ideology

The Court's power of judicial review gives it a quasi-legislative power

This is quite simply because many of the Court's decisions have almost the same effect as if a piece of legislation had been passed. In the UK, policy matters such as abortion rights, the death penalty and gun control, for example, are decided by Parliament. In the USA, they are settled largely by the Supreme Court. The quasi-legislative power of the Court is seen particularly in decisions which are authored by loose constructionist judges — those who read things into the wording of the Constitution, who, in the view of their critics, 'legislate from the bench'. A clear example of this was seen in the *Obergefell* v *Hodges* decision.

The Court's power of judicial review enables it to protect civil rights and liberties in today's America

It is in the Constitution that most of the fundamental rights and liberties enjoyed by Americans are found. All three branches of the federal government have a role to play in protecting and guaranteeing these freedoms. But the Court's power of judicial review does give this institution an especially important role in protecting those rights and liberties. It also gives the Court the power to say exactly what they mean in today's America. It allows, for example, the Court to interpret the right of free speech in the age of the internet and Twitter. It has allowed the Court to extend the rights of racial minorities and women as society's understanding of those rights has evolved. It has even allowed the Court to lead where both Congress and the president have been either unable or unwilling to move.

But it would be misleading to suggest that the Court has always carried out this role effectively. After all, it was the Supreme Court that for almost a century after the Civil War kept African-Americans in segregated schools. And in recent years, many women would see the Court as having nibbled away at the rights regarding abortion choice that the Court had given them in 1973.

On the other side of this issue, others would see the Court as failing to protect the rights of the unborn child. So how one views the degree of effectiveness with which the Court has protected Americans' rights may depend on one's position on any particular right or liberty. One person's equality is another person's discrimination.

Debate

Does the Supreme Court have too much power?

Yes
- The Court gave itself the power of judicial review.
- It has declared more Acts of Congress unconstitutional as the decades have passed.
- It has made decisions that are out of line with the majority of public opinion.
- It is an unelected body.
- It is a largely unaccountable body.
- It has abused its power to bring about significant policy change (e.g. abortion, same-sex marriage).
- Yes — when justices believe in a living constitution.

No
- It is checked by Congress, which may initiate constitutional amendments effectively to override Court decisions.
- Congress has the power of impeachment.
- It has no initiative power.
- It is dependent upon the rule of law and other branches of government to enforce its decisions.
- Public opinion is a restraining force on the Court's power.
- It is checked by the words of the Constitution: where it is precise and not open to interpretation by the Court.

Comparing the US and UK Supreme Courts

Origins

The very different ways in which these two supreme courts came into existence tell us a lot about the structural differences of the two governmental systems as well as the cultural differences between the United States and the United Kingdom. The US Supreme Court had its origins in the writing of the Constitution back in the late eighteenth century when the framers wrote into the original document in 1787 in Article III:

> The judicial power of the United States, shall be vested in one Supreme Court, and in such inferior Courts as the Congress may from time to time ordain and establish.

Thus the only federal court created by the Constitution was the United States Supreme Court, although by the Judiciary Act of 1789 Congress did create federal trial and appeal courts. But the US Supreme Court is as old as the nation and the esteem in which it is held reflects its relative antiquity.

True, the US Supreme Court did not at first have its own building and was initially somewhat itinerant. It met first in February 1790 at the Merchants' Exchange Building in New York, before moving to Philadelphia and then to Washington, where for more than a century it occupied various rooms in the United States Capitol. Only in 1935 did the Court move into its own purpose-built building on Capitol Hill. But although it lodged within the Capitol between 1800 and 1935, there was never any doubt that the Supreme Court was structurally and politically entirely separate from Congress. The Founding Fathers' belief in the doctrine of 'separated institutions' was strictly adhered to and reflected a cultural distrust of 'fused powers' that still typified government structures in Britain.

Chamber of the UK Supreme Court

The origins of the UK Supreme Court could hardly be more different. Far from being one of the nation's oldest institutions, it is indeed its newest, coming into existence as a result of an Act of Parliament in October 2009. By this time, the US Supreme Court was already in its 220th year, which considering the relative ages of the two nations is somewhat remarkable. Thus 1 October 2009 was a defining moment in the constitutional history of the United Kingdom as the Supreme Court replaced the Appellate Committee of the House of Lords as the nation's highest court.

At the same time, the UK's highest court also did what the US Supreme Court had done three-quarters of a century earlier — move out of the legislative building to its own quarters, though these were not purpose-built. Thus, finally, the UK's highest court structurally and politically separated itself from the nation's legislature, thereby emphasising the independence of its judges and increasing the transparency between Parliament and the courts. The Supreme Court was established in the former Middlesex Guildhall in Parliament Square. Indeed, some have even suggested that the new political architecture of Parliament Square is symbolic of the new separation of powers in Britain, with the square's four sides occupied by the Palace of Westminster (the legislature), the Treasury (the executive), the Supreme Court (the judiciary) and Westminster Abbey (the established church).

Appointments, membership and tenure

Here too, there are more differences than similarities. The nine members of the United States Supreme Court are nominated by the president, confirmed by the Senate and serve for life 'during good behaviour'. There is no mandatory retirement age. Indeed, in January 2017, two of the justices (Ruth Bader Ginsburg and Anthony Kennedy) were over 80 and another (Stephen Breyer) was less than two years off his 80th birthday. Justice Antonin Scalia was less than a month away from his 80th birthday when he died in February 2016. Three of the nine-member Court are women. One justice (Clarence Thomas) is an African-American; another (Sonia Sotomayor) is Hispanic. Given the politicisation of the appointment process, we might detect the opportunity for self-interested presidents to nominate and self-interested senators to confirm justices who share their particular judicial philosophy.

The membership of the US and UK Supreme Courts

US Supreme Court
- 9 justices
- Appointed by the president with the consent of the Senate
- All justices hear all cases (unless recused)
- Justices have life tenure
- Presided over by the Chief Justice of the United States
- Justices may be removed only by impeachment (House) and trial (Senate)

UK Supreme Court
- 12 justices
- Vacancies filled by a Selection Commission who recommend a candidate to the Lord Chancellor
- Between 5 and 11 justices hear cases
- Justices must retire at 70 if appointed to a judicial office after 31 March 1995; otherwise at 75
- Presided over by the President of the Supreme Court
- Justices may be removed by petition to the monarch from both houses of Parliament

By contrast, the 12 members of the UK Supreme Court are nominated by an independent body — the Judicial Appointments Commission. They must retire at age 70, thus Lord Toulson who was appointed to the Court in April 2013 had to retire in September 2016 having served less than four years. At the time of writing, of the 20 judges who have served on the Court, there has been only one woman — Lady Hale appointed in June 2013. There have been none from ethnic minorities. But then by 2016 only 25% of judges in England and Wales were women and just 5% were from ethnic minorities. In comparison, in the United States federal courts just over one-third are women and around 14% are from ethnic minorities.

As for removal from office, members of the US Supreme Court can be removed only by impeachment by the House followed by trial and conviction by the Senate. The only Supreme Court justice to be impeached was Samuel Chase, who was impeached by the House in March 1804 but acquitted by the Senate in March 1805. A judge of the UK Supreme Court could be removed by the monarch following an address by both houses of Parliament.

Powers

The one significant power of the US Supreme Court is judicial review. But this was not explicitly granted by the Constitution. Rather it was, as it were, 'found' in the Constitution by the justices themselves in the landmark decision of *Marbury* v *Madison* in 1803 when for the first time the Court declared a federal law to be unconstitutional and thereby null and void. This power was extended in the same way to state laws in *Fletcher* v *Peck* in 1810. It is this power that has given the Court its stature among the three branches of the federal government.

This is all a far cry from when Alexander Hamilton wrote in 1788 that the judiciary would be 'the least dangerous branch' because it has 'no influence over either the sword or the purse', referring to war and the budget. Continued Hamilton: 'It may truly be said to have neither force nor will, but merely judgement.' But as we have seen in this chapter, the Court has had a fundamental effect on a whole range of policies and issues that are at the very centre of everyday life in America. Hence it has come be described as 'the third house of the legislature'.

When we consider the powers and influence of the UK Supreme Court we have, at the time of writing, less than a decade of evidence. How different the US Supreme Court would have looked in 1799. The UK Supreme Court is the final domestic court of appeal and, like its US namesake, is becoming an important political actor. According to its website, its powers include 'hearing appeals on arguable points of law of the greatest public importance for the whole of the United

Kingdom in civil cases, and for England, Wales and Northern Ireland in criminal cases'. Additionally, it hears cases on devolution matters under the Scotland Act (1998), the Northern Ireland Act (1998) and the Government of Wales Act (2006).

Also on its website, in its 'Frequently Asked Questions' section, the question 'Can the UK Supreme Court overrule the UK Parliament?' is answered with an emphatic 'no'. As Philip Norton (2014) has written:

> Under the doctrine of parliamentary sovereignty, the judiciary lacks the intrinsic power to strike down an Act of Parliament as being contrary to the provisions of the constitution or any other superior body of law.

But that does not mean that the Supreme Court is powerless when it comes to decisions concerning laws passed by Parliament, as the courts can interpret the *meaning* of parliamentary law. And that's where clarity gives way to ambiguity, for what exactly amounts to 'interpreting the meaning' of a law? The Court's website recognises this grey area by adding to the answer quoted above:

> It is not the Court's role to formulate public policy, but to interpret law and develop it where necessary through well-established processes and methods of reasoning.

A power that both these supreme courts to some extent share is power over the actions of the executive branch. The US Supreme Court can declare actions to be unconstitutional, and the UK Supreme Court can declare actions to be *ultra vires* — that is, beyond the powers granted by Act of Parliament. This is what is meant by 'judicial review' in the UK and it is in this area of declaring the action of ministers to be *ultra vires* that the debate concerning 'judicial activism' is conducted. So whereas in the USA judicial activism centres on the Supreme Court's tendency to declare Acts of Congress unconstitutional, in the UK it centres on the Court's tendency to declare the actions of ministers *ultra vires*. These differences are the consequence of structural differences in the way the two political systems are set up and the processes within them.

Distinguish between

The powers and roles of the US and UK Supreme Courts

US Supreme Court
- Final court of appeal for federal cases and also hears cases on appeal from state supreme courts
- Rules on the constitutionality of federal and state laws
- Rules on the constitutionality of actions of the federal and state executives
- Rules on the meaning of the Constitution

UK Supreme Court
- Final court of appeal for all UK civil cases and for criminal cases in England, Wales and Northern Ireland
- Cannot overrule or strike down the laws passed by the UK Parliament — can interpret the laws passed by Parliament
- Rules on whether or not actions taken by ministers are *ultra vires*

There is one further structural difference in terms of powers we need to notice. Whereas in the United States the Supreme Court is in all matters of rights and liberties the supreme authority, in the United Kingdom the Supreme Court can be subject to a higher authority — namely the European Court of Human Rights in Strasbourg. It is the duty of the UK Supreme Court to interpret all existing legislation so that it is compatible with the European Convention on Human Rights (ECHR), so far as this is possible to do. Furthermore, in giving effect to rights contained in the ECHR, the UK Supreme Court must take into account any related decision made by the Court in Strasbourg. Even though the ECHR is a separate entity from the European Union, the British prime minister Theresa May announced in late 2016 her intention to campaign for Britain to leave the ECHR but in the 2017 general election this plan was dropped.

Independence

It is vitally important in a democracy that individual judges as well as the judiciary as a whole are independent of all external pressures. Such pressure could come from:

- the executive
- the legislature
- pressure groups
- the media
- other judges, especially senior judges

Judicial independence is protected in a number of ways:

- Judges have immunity from prosecution for any acts they carry out in performance of their judicial function.
- They also have immunity from lawsuits of defamation for what they say about parties or witnesses while hearing cases.
- The salaries of judges cannot be reduced.

By judicial independence we mean, according to Heywood (2002), 'the constitutional principle that there should be a strict separation between the judiciary and other branches of government'. In an episode of the 1980s BBC political comedy *Yes, Prime Minister*, Prime Minister Jim Hacker is incensed by a leak to the press about some derogatory remarks made about him in the forthcoming memoirs of his predecessor. Hacker is discussing the matter in the cabinet room at Number 10 with the Cabinet Secretary, Sir Humphrey Appleby.

Prime Minister: I want to nail the leak. I want to trace the culprit. And I want a prosecution. And I want a conviction!

Sir Humphrey: We can try and trace the culprit, we can prosecute, but under the present political system there are problems about the government actually guaranteeing a conviction.

Here is a humorous reference to an independent judiciary that 'under the present political system' is not at the beck and call of politicians.

For there to be an independent judiciary there needs to be a distinct body of people who alone exercise judicial authority and who are not subject to undue influence from others within the political and governmental structure. In 1985, the United Nations approved the document *Basic Principles on the Independence of the Judiciary* which laid down four principles (see Box 5.4).

Box 5.4

Extract from the UN's *Basic Principles on the Independence of the Judiciary*, 1985

- The independence of the judiciary shall be guaranteed by the State and enshrined in the Constitution or the law of the country.
- The judiciary shall decide matters before them...without any restrictions, improper influences, inducements, pressures, threats or interferences, direct or indirect, from any quarter or for any reason.
- The judiciary shall have jurisdiction over all issues of a judicial nature.
- There shall not be any inappropriate or unwarranted interference with the judicial process, nor shall judicial decisions by the courts be subject to revision.

Source: Reproduced from David O'Dell, 'Judicial independence and judicial neutrality', *Politics Review*, Vol. 23, No. 4, April 2014

Judicial independence in the USA

Judicial independence was something that was much debated by the Founding Fathers and discussed in *The Federalist Papers*. By giving federal judges life tenure and prohibiting Congress from reducing their salaries, the framers were showing a determination to insulate judges from political pressure. And the debate over judicial independence has resurfaced again and again throughout the republic's history, most notably following the Supreme Court's decision in *Bush* v *Gore* (2000) which effectively handed that year's presidential election to Republican George W. Bush. The prominent American civil rights lawyer Alan Dershowitz (2001) wrote of the Court's decision to halt the recount of votes in Florida that a number of the justices were 'so determined to ensure a Republican victory that they engineered a short-term resolution locking in that victory at the risk of considerable long-term costs to the credibility of the Supreme Court'. In his dissenting opinion, Justice John Paul Stevens stated:

> Although we may never know with complete certainty the identity of the winner of this year's presidential election, the identity of the loser is perfectly clear. It is the nation's confidence in the judge guarding the rule of law.

That said, there are probably more examples of justices of the United States Supreme Court exhibiting their judicial independence than of decisions that bring such independence into question. So, for example, when in 1974, the Supreme Court in *United States* v *Nixon* decided unanimously against President Nixon in a case concerning Nixon's claim of executive privilege in withholding material demanded both by the courts and by Congress, Nixon appointees Warren Burger, Harry Blackmun and Lewis Powell joined the decision. Much the same thing occurred in 1997 in *Clinton* v *Jones* when President Clinton's two appointees Ruth Bader Ginsburg and Stephen Breyer joined a unanimous decision rejecting Bill Clinton's claim of immunity from prosecution while president.

We also saw issues concerning judicial independence being raised in the opening weeks of the Trump presidency when the lower federal courts declared the President's executive order relating to limitations on entry into the United States from seven mainly Muslim countries to be unconstitutional. The President criticised the decision as 'outrageous', described the federal judge who made the initial decision as a 'so-called judge' and claimed that the decision 'will be overturned'.

Judicial independence in the UK

In the United Kingdom, the independence of the judiciary, though well established in the culture and practice of the nation, was for many centuries obscured by the structure of the upper echelons of the courts — most notably that the Law Lords sat in the upper house of the legislature and that the nation's highest court was, in essence, a committee of that chamber. Further, there was a confusing structural overlap in the post of Lord Chancellor, who was head of the judiciary, the presiding officer of the House of Lords, and a member of the cabinet. Such structures did not spell out judicial independence.

It was only with the passage of the Constitutional Reform Act of 2005 that this structural arrangement was changed with the transfer of the Lord

Chancellor's judicial role to the Lord Chief Justice and the role of presiding officer of the Lords to the Lord Speaker. But, as Philip Norton (2014) has pointed out, the structures are still somewhat confused. The post of Lord Chancellor doubles as the Secretary of State for Justice, responsible for the efficient functioning and independence of the courts. Furthermore, there are other members of the executive who at the same time hold judicial appointments — notably the Attorney General and the Solicitor General, in which roles they serve as legal advisers to the government but also lead for the Crown in major prosecutions.

Independence in the face of executive criticism

In both the UK and the USA, by virtue of the cases they hear and the decisions they are obliged to make, judges are inevitably drawn into the public debate on matters of great national importance, be it in the court room or when chairing public inquiries into particular disasters or scandal. And in both systems, members of the executive branch will often step in with criticism of judicial decisions. When the US Supreme Court in *Texas* v *Johnson* (1989) declared a Texas state law forbidding the desecration of the US flag to be unconstitutional, President George H.W. Bush described the decision as 'wrong, dead wrong'.

In his 2010 State of the Union Address, President Barack Obama aimed a broadside at the Court's judgement in *Citizens United* v *Federal Election Commission*:

> Last week, the Supreme Court reversed a century of law that I believe will open the floodgates for special interests — including foreign corporations — to spend without limit in our elections.

Justice Samuel Alito, one of six justices in the audience, was caught by the television cameras shaking his head and mouthing the words 'not true'. Two months later, in a question-and-answer session with law students at the University of Alabama, Chief Justice John Roberts was asked whether it was right for the President to 'chide' the Court for its decision at the State of the Union. In what appeared to be a carefully crafted answer, Roberts began his reply:

> First of all, anybody can criticise the Supreme Court without any qualm. Some people, I think, have an obligation to criticise what we do, given their office, if they think we've done something wrong. So I have no problems with that.

But then Roberts addressed the issue of the forum in which the incident had occurred — the sight of all the Democrat members of Congress jumping to their feet to applaud the President's criticism of the Court's decision:

> On the other hand, there is the issue of the setting, the circumstances and the decorum. The image of having the members of one branch of government standing up, literally surrounding the Supreme Court, cheering and hollering, while the Court — according to the requirements of protocol — has to sit there expressionless, I think is very troubling.

Supreme Court justices attending what is nowadays little more than a political pep rally seems somewhat incongruous with an independent judiciary.

British newspapers the day after the High Court ruling on Article 50, November 2016

The British judiciary has also come in for sharp criticism from members of the executive. In 2013, the then home secretary, Theresa May, criticised the judiciary over what she saw as the courts ignoring rules passed by Parliament aimed at deporting more foreign criminals. She accused the judges of 'subverting' British democracy, making British streets more dangerous and 'ignoring Parliament's wishes'. She continued:

> Unfortunately, some judges evidently do not regard a debate in Parliament on new immigration rules, followed by the unanimous adoption of those rules, as evidence that Parliament actually wants to see those rules implemented. It is essential to democracy that the elected representatives of the people make the laws that govern this country — and not the judges.

In response, Lord Neuberger, the president of the Supreme Court, called Mrs May's criticism 'inappropriate, unhelpful and wrong' and stated that it risked 'destabilising' the delicate balance between Parliament and the judiciary. 'For a minister to attack a judge, I think is wrong,' Lord Neuberger added.

A similar scenario was played out in 2016–17 when the Supreme Court ruled on the role that Parliament should play in the triggering of Article 50 in order to begin the British government's exit from the European Union following the 2016 Referendum vote. Indeed, when the High Court had ruled in November 2016 that only Parliament, and not ministers, could trigger Article 50, the *Daily Mail* denounced the 'out of touch' judges as 'enemies of the people' who had 'declared war on democracy'. But judicial independence is a cornerstone of liberal democracy or, as the eighteenth-century French lawyer and political philosopher Montesquieu put it: 'There is no liberty if the power of judging is not separated from the legislative and executive powers.'

Civil rights

> ## Learning outcomes
>
> Key questions answered in this section:
> - What is affirmative action and what are its pros and cons?
> - How have voting rights been advanced in the USA?
> - What has been done to improve the representation of racial minorities?
> - What significant steps have been taken in immigration reform?
> - What are the principal similarities and differences between the protection of rights in the USA and the UK?

This is not the place to set out the history of the civil rights movement in America, though you might have studied that as part of your History course. Painting with a very broad brush, suffice it to say that in the 150 years or so from the end of the Civil War (1865) to the beginning of the twenty-first century, many different methods had been used to try to bring practical equality to racial minorities in the United States — constitutional amendment, legislation, decisions of the Supreme Court, presidential leadership and what one might call citizen action, as well as the role played by interest groups and political parties (see Table 5.8).

Table 5.8 Examples of advancements in the civil rights of racial minorities in America

Method	Example	Year
Constitutional amendment	Twenty-Fourth Amendment: Voting rights not be denied for non-payment of poll tax	1964
Legislation	Voting Rights Act: Ended literacy and other tests as requirements for voter registration	1965
Decision of the Supreme Court	*Brown* v *Board of Education of Topeka*: Declared segregated schools to be unconstitutional	1954
Presidential leadership	President Eisenhower: Sent federal troops to Little Rock, Arkansas, to integrate local high school	1957
	President Kennedy: Created Equal Employment Opportunity Commission	1961
Citizen action	Montgomery, Alabama, bus boycott	1955
	Freedom riders	1961
	March for Jobs and Freedom	1963

Affirmative action

The twentieth century saw an ongoing argument between what has been called 'equality of opportunity' on the one hand and 'equality of results' on the other. From the middle of the century, many civil rights advocates came to believe that minority rights and representation could not be guaranteed solely by 'giving' rights to people — 'equality of opportunity'. This would merely give the *theory* of rights and equality. If people wanted to see the *practice* of rights and equality, they had to work towards 'equality of

Busing The mandated movement of school children between racially homogeneous neighbourhoods — white suburbs and black inner cities — to create racially mixed schools.

Quotas A programme by which a certain percentage (quota) of places in, e.g., higher education or employment, is reserved for people from previously disadvantaged minorities.

Affirmative action A programme giving members of a previously disadvantaged minority group a head start in, e.g., higher education or employment.

results'. The only way to overcome racial *disadvantage* was by introducing racial *advantage* through such policies as busing, quotas and affirmative action. But the most important, and the most enduring, was that of affirmative action.

Given how disadvantaged African-Americans had been during the 100 years after the Civil War, many Democrat politicians began to believe that the government needed to discriminate positively in favour of African-Americans in such areas as housing, education and employment, in what became known as affirmative action programmes.

This takes us back to the 'equality of results' versus the 'equality of opportunity' debate. Many civil rights organisations had become convinced, and Democrat politicians had tended to agree, that the burdens of racism could be overcome only by taking race into account in designing suitable remedies. Groups which had been disadvantaged were now to be advantaged (what in Britain is often referred to as 'positive discrimination'). Rights in themselves would not deliver changes to society; benefits had to be added. Affirmative action in education meant busing and racial quotas. Affirmative action in employment meant preferential hiring practices for minority groups. And affirmative action was meant to lead to diversity and multiculturalism — the view that the school, the college, the firm, the workplace should reflect the racial diversity of the nation. This is 'equality of results'.

Busing students from the suburbs of Charlotte, North Carolina, 1973

But what is affirmative action to some is merely reverse discrimination to others. More conservative groups, and many Republican politicians, came to believe that affirmative action programmes were both patronising to minorities and unfair to majorities. They believed that the Constitution and both federal and state laws should be 'colour blind'. Children of minority families should certainly be given equal opportunity to attend the school of their choice, but using busing or quotas to achieve an artificial racial balance was, in their view, wrong. In employment, by all means open up all jobs for all applicants regardless of race, but numerical targets, goals and quotas were off-limits. This is 'equality of opportunity'. As we shall see, it would be largely up to the Supreme Court to umpire between these two views of American society.

The Supreme Court and affirmative action

In *Gratz* v *Bollinger* (2003) the Court ruled (6–3) that the University of Michigan's affirmative action-based admissions programme for its undergraduate students was unconstitutional because it was too 'mechanistic'. All black, Hispanic and American-Indian applicants were automatically awarded 20 of the 150 points required for admission. But in *Grutter* v *Bollinger* (2003), the Court ruled (5–4) that the University Law School's admissions programme was constitutional because it used a more 'individualised' approach in considering the racial profile of its applicants.

The net effect of these two rulings was to permit universities to continue to use race as a 'plus factor' in evaluating applicants, provided they took sufficient care to evaluate each applicant's ability individually. A majority of the Court also signed up to the idea that affirmative action programmes should not be seen as a permanent fixture of US society, urging universities to prepare for the time when it should no longer be necessary. The Court suggested that this might occur within the next 25 years. It was 25 years previously in *Regents of the University of California* v *Bakke* (1978) that the Supreme Court ruled out racial quotas in university admissions programmes but left the door open to race being considered in admissions procedures.

Writing for the majority in *Grutter* v *Bollinger*, Justice Sandra Day O'Connor stated:

> Effective participation by members of all racial and ethnic groups in the civic life of our nation is essential if the dream of one nation, indivisible, is to be realised. Moreover, universities, and in particular law schools, represent the training ground for a large number of our nation's leaders. In order to cultivate a set of leaders with legitimacy in the eyes of the citizenry, it is necessary that the path to leadership be visibly open to talented and qualified individuals of every race and ethnicity.

In his dissenting opinion, Chief Justice Rehnquist denounced the law school admissions plan as a 'sham' and a 'naked effort to achieve racial balancing', seeing it as 'a carefully managed programme designed to ensure proportionate representation of applicants from selected minority groups'. Justice Clarence Thomas, the only black member of the Court, reverted to his typically colourful language in denouncing racial diversity programmes as 'the faddish slogan of the cognoscenti' that do 'nothing for those too poor or uneducated to participate in elite higher education'.

In another pair of related cases in 2007 — *Parents Involved in Community Schools Inc.* v *Seattle School District* and *Meredith* v *Jefferson County (Kentucky) Board of Education* — the Court declared it unconstitutional to assign students to public schools solely for the purpose of achieving racial balance. Both school systems centred upon racial quotas of white and minority representation in schools that would not otherwise be achieved because of racially segregated housing

Rally against the ban on affirmative action, Lansing, Michigan, 2006

patterns in Seattle, Washington, and Louisville, Kentucky. Both sides of the Court in the 5–4 ruling saw themselves as protecting the equal protection rights announced in the landmark 1954 *Brown* decision. Writing for the majority, Chief Justice Roberts stated that:

> Before *Brown*, school children were told where they could and could not go to school based on the colour of their skin. The school districts in these cases have not carried the heavy burden of demonstrating that we should allow this once again — even for different reasons. The way to stop discrimination on the basis of race is to stop discriminating on the basis of race.

The Chief Justice also made it clear that he and his conservative colleagues on the Court had a concern that allocating students to schools on the basis of racial quotas violates the equal protection clause of the Fourteenth Amendment. 'Simply because the school districts may seek a worthy goal does not mean that they are free to discriminate on the basis of race to achieve it,' Roberts declared. Justice Clarence Thomas wrote waspishly that what the dissenting minority would really like to do would be to 'constitutionalise today's faddish social theories', adding that 'if our history has taught us anything, it has taught us to beware of elites bearing racial theories'.

Here we return to the story that we mentioned right at the start of this chapter. Abigail Fisher, a young woman from Texas, applied to the University of Texas but was rejected. Fisher, who is white, then filed a lawsuit arguing that she had been a victim of racial discrimination because minority race students with less impressive qualifications than hers had been accepted. In *Fisher* v *University of Texas* (2013) the Court ruled that the university's use of race in its admission policy must be subjected to a stricter scrutiny because it involved possible discrimination. The federal appeal court was therefore instructed to rehear the case using the stricter scrutiny.

In July 2014, the appeal court reheard the case and again found in favour of the University of Texas. Ms Fisher again appealed the decision to the Supreme Court, where the case was heard again in 2016. The expectation was that a majority of the Supreme Court would strike down the appeal court's ruling and uphold Ms Fisher's claim of racial discrimination, thereby delivering a severe blow to this affirmative action programme. But the Court did no such thing. In a 4–3 ruling — Justice Kagan took no part having already been involved while serving as Solicitor General before joining the Court, and Justice Scalia's seat remained vacant — the Court upheld the appeal court ruling, thereby also upholding the university's affirmative action programme. Here's what Justice Kennedy, joined by liberal justices Ruth Bader Ginsburg, Stephen Breyer and Sonia Sotomayor, had to say:

> A university is in large part defined by those 'intangible qualities which are incapable of objective measurement but which make for greatness'. Considerable deference is owed to a university in defining those intangible characteristics, like student body diversity, that are central to its identity and educational mission. But still it remains an enduring challenge to our Nation's education system to reconcile the pursuit of diversity with the constitutional promise of equal treatment and dignity.

In his dissenting opinion, Justice Alito — joined by John Roberts and Clarence Thomas — called this 'affirmative action gone berserk based on offensive and unsupported stereotypes'. He went on:

The majority's uncritical deference to the University of Texas's self-serving claims blatantly contradicts our decision in the prior judgement of this very case. Something very strange has happened since our prior decision.

According to Justice Alito:

Even though the University of Texas has never produced any coherent explanation for its asserted need to discriminate on the basis of race, and even though the University of Texas's position relies on a series of unsupported and noxious racial assumptions, the majority concludes that the university has met its heavy burden. This conclusion is remarkable — and remarkably wrong.

Reaction to the decision was varied. President Obama led the praise of the Court's ruling, saying that the Court had 'upheld the basic notion that [racial] diversity is an important value in our society and that this country should provide a high-quality education for all our young people, regardless of their background'. Of course, the irony is that Ms Fisher would agree with that, and here lies the great conundrum of affirmative action — that ending racial discrimination is brought about by what some see as racial discrimination. Laurence Tribe, a law professor at Harvard, surpassed even the President's eulogy by claiming that 'no decision since *Brown* v *Board of Education* in 1954 has been as important as *Fisher* will prove to be in the long history of racial inclusion and educational diversity'.

As for affirmative action, the debate continues, not only in the courts, but also in the other two branches of government and in academia.

Advantages and disadvantages

Arguments for affirmative action

- Such programmes lead to greater levels of diversity, which would not have been achieved by just leaving things as they were.
- Affirmative action is justified on the basis that it rights previous wrongs. The previously disadvantaged are now advantaged.
- It opens up areas of education and employment which minorities otherwise would not have considered.
- In education, a diverse student body creates not only a better learning environment but also one in which ethnic and racial tolerance is promoted.
- It is the most meaningful and effective means thus far devised by government for delivering the promise of equal opportunity.
- It works. For example, between 1960 and 1995, the percentage of black people aged 25–29 who graduated from university rose from 5% to 15%. As President Clinton remarked in 1995, 'affirmative action has been good for America'.

Arguments against affirmative action

- Advantage or preference for one group leads inevitably to disadvantage for another group. This is the issue of reverse discrimination which the Supreme Court was first asked to address in the *Bakke* case in 1978. As California State Assemblyman Bernie Richter puts it: 'When you deny someone who has earned it and give it to someone else who has not earned it...you create anger and resentment.'
- It can lead minorities to be admitted to courses or given jobs with which they are ill-equipped to cope. In a study of American law schools in the November 2004 *Stanford Law Review*, Richard Sander found that putting black students into classes with white students who had higher SAT scores and college grades resulted in 'close to half of black students ending up in the bottom tenth of their classes'.
- Affirmative action can be condescending to minorities by implying that they need a helping hand in order to succeed, thereby demeaning their achievement.
- It perpetuates a society based on colour and race, thereby encouraging prejudice.
- Affirmative action is no more than a quota system under another name.
- It focuses on groups rather than individuals. As David McKay (2005) succinctly explains:

  'Affirmative action is inherently problematic because it involves a clash between the liberal notion of what the individual is worth and the collective interests of a group or race.'

Has affirmative action been a success?

Richard Kahlenberg (2008), writing in *The Atlantic* two days after the 2008 presidential election, wrote:

> This election was a stunning triumph for the notion of colour-blindness: don't discriminate against people of colour — or in favour of them. The election of America's first black president was a moving and long overdue affirmation of the civil rights movement's enduring struggle for equal treatment. The candidate never asked Americans to vote for him because he was black.

On Election Day 2008, the president of the Children's Defense Fund, Marian Wright Edelman, wrote:

> This morning, as I stood in line to vote, I was moved by the realisation that finally this is the day on which my fellow Americans are willing to do what Martin Luther King envisioned: vote for a president based on the content of his character rather than the colour of his skin.

In order to judge whether or not affirmative action has been a success, we must first establish what it was meant to achieve. Back in 1978, Justice Harry Blackmun suggested that the legitimacy of affirmative action programmes was to be measured by how fast they moved society towards a time when they would no longer be needed and a society in which race no longer mattered. This was the line of argument which Justice Sandra Day O'Connor took up in her opinion in the *Grutter* decision in 2003 when she announced the 25-year 'limit' to affirmative action programmes. So how successful have affirmative action programmes been by this measure? There is evidence on both sides.

Some politicians and philosophers, however, think that affirmative action is bound to fail by this measure because a programme that is based on race is unlikely to move society to a point where race no longer counts. In the view of philosopher Carl Cohen (1995), 'the moral issue [about affirmative action] comes in the classic form: "important objectives appear to require impermissible means"'. In other words, often the only way we can achieve something is by means which are not allowed. Asks Cohen: 'Might we not wink at the Constitution this once and allow [affirmative action programmes] to do their good work?' In other words, can't we just overlook any constitutional defects in such programmes because they achieve so much that is good and worthwhile? But Cohen, along with a majority opinion on the Supreme Court, has said 'no'. 'In the distribution of benefits under the laws, all racial classifications are invidious.' This was Justice Clarence Thomas's conclusion in a 1995 decision when he stated:

> I believe that there is a moral and constitutional equivalence between laws designed to subjugate a race and those that distribute benefits on the basis of race in order to foster some notion of equality. Government cannot make us equal.

Affirmative action and public opinion

Trying to assess public opinion towards affirmative action is not easy. It depends very much on what question one asks. When asked 'In order to overcome past discrimination, do you favour or oppose affirmative action programmes?' 63% said they were in favour with only 29% opposed. Likewise, when pollsters asked: 'Do you think affirmative action programmes designed to increase the number of black and minority students on college campuses are a good or a bad thing?' 60% said they were a good thing and just 30% thought they were bad.

But in both these questions, a specific purpose of the programme was stated — 'to overcome past discrimination' and 'to increase the number of black and minority students on college campuses'. When one asks about 'fairness', the answers are quite different. To the question, 'Do you think affirmative action programmes designed to increase the number of black and minority students on college campuses are fair or unfair?' while 47% thought they were fair, 42% thought them unfair. 'A good thing' they may be, but in the minds of many, that does not stop them from being 'unfair'.

If the idea of a group getting 'preferential treatment' is suggested, then the figures change dramatically. In answer to the question, 'Do you think that we should make every possible effort to improve the position of blacks and other minorities, even if it means giving them preferential treatment?' only 24% agreed and 72% disagreed.

But maybe the most surprising finding of the poll evidence on affirmative action concerns the effect such programmes are perceived to have had. Among the white population, just 2% tell pollsters that they have been 'helped' by such a programme and only 13% say they have been 'hurt', leaving 84% saying they were not affected at all. But African-Americans — the group one might expect to have been most affected by affirmative action programmes — were similarly detached. A mere 4% said they had been 'helped' by such a programme while 8% said they had been 'hurt', and 87% said that as far as they were concerned the programmes had no effect at all.

What to do with affirmative action?

Put simply, there would seem to be four alternatives as to what to do with affirmative action programmes: abolish them, gradually phase them out, reform them, or keep them as they are. These various options tend to equate with the political ideology of those who support them.

Conservatives — found mostly in the Republican Party — tend to favour the abolition of affirmative action programmes. They would argue that society is not about 'equality' but 'equality of opportunity'. They would further suggest that an unequal society has the benefit of providing incentives — to better oneself. Offering 'quotas' is, in their view, a disincentive to hard work and self-improvement. Furthermore, conservatives would point to certain minorities within the USA, such as immigrants from Southeast Asia, who have succeeded without the benefit of affirmative action programmes. Against those who argue that affirmative action is necessary to make up for past discrimination, they would argue that today's issues of inequality are not about past discrimination but are rooted in the lifestyle choices — such as those concerned with drugs, alcohol and parenting — that people make for themselves today. Finally, as we have already seen, conservatives argue that affirmative action is based on a false premise — the same false premise upon which the discredited policy of segregation was based: racism. As Chief Justice Roberts put it in 2007 (*Parents Involved v Seattle School District*), 'the way to stop discrimination on the basis of race is to stop discrimination on the basis of race'.

Others of a more moderate persuasion would agree with some of the above but would be more impressed by all that affirmative action programmes have achieved. Their argument would be very much in agreement with that of then Associate Justice Sandra Day O'Connor in the *Grutter* decision in 2003 that if affirmative action has achieved all that its supporters claim for it, there must surely come a time when these programmes become unnecessary. Justice O'Connor therefore stated that 'we expect that 25 years from now, the use of racial preferences will no longer be necessary'. In other words, there is an argument for phasing out such programmes.

A third argument is that expressed by President Clinton's 'mend it, don't end it' catchphrase, suggesting that such programmes will need tweaking as their effect is more widely felt, and that reform, rather than abolition, is what is called for.

But liberals — found mostly in the Democratic Party — would see affirmative action as something that needs to continue and has much left still to do. For example, they would point out that both African-Americans and Hispanics are under-represented in terms of bachelor degree awards at American universities. Liberals would therefore argue that the vision of an equal society is still a vision of the future.

Debate

Has affirmative action been good for America?

Yes

- It has helped reverse decades (and more) of discrimination and righted numerous wrongs.
- It has given the black American community hope — and education, jobs and housing.
- There is increasing evidence of minority students at top universities.
- It has helped to promote community diversity.
- It has helped promote equality of opportunity and equality of outcome.

No

- It has divided the black community rather than empowered it.
- Like the racism it sought to end, it is itself a programme based on race.
- It has led to some resentments and inequalities for the majority community.
- It lowers aspirations by offering racial preferences.
- It puts minority students into academic places where they then struggle to compete and succeed.

Source: based on Debate article by Katie Shapiro and Kay Moxon in *Politics Review*, Vol. 26, No. 4, April 2017

Voting rights

During his unsuccessful campaign for the Democratic Party's presidential nomination in 1988, black civil rights leader Jesse Jackson marvelled at the progress African-Americans had made in terms of voting rights. 'Hands that picked cotton,' observed Jackson, 'can now pick a president.' And 20 years later, they — along with the majority of American voters — picked the first African-American president. That would have been unlikely to have occurred without Congress passing significant civil rights laws, such as the Voting Rights Act of 1965. Then in 2006, with support from President George W. Bush, Congress re-authorised the Voting Rights Act's key provisions for another 25 years, including the controversial Section 4 which included the preclearance formula used to determine which states and localities must have major changes in their voting laws approved in advance at the federal level.

But in the case of *Shelby County* v *Holder* (2013), the Supreme Court struck down the preclearance formula as unconstitutional. Chief Justice Roberts, writing for the majority, believed that 'our country has changed'. He recalled the Freedom Summer of 1964. He mentioned Bloody Sunday in 1965 when police officers beat the black marchers in Selma, Alabama. Roberts drew attention to the fact that today this town is governed by an African-American mayor. In the majority's view, 'whilst any racial discrimination in voting is too much, Congress must ensure that the legislation it passes to remedy that problem speaks to current conditions'.

The decision had immediate consequences. Within days, Texas announced that a voter identification law that had been blocked would go into immediate effect and that the state's redistricting maps that would no longer need federal government approval. President Obama, whose election was often cited by those who say the Act is no longer needed, said he was 'deeply disappointed' by the Court's decision and called on Congress to draw up a new formula for determining whether or not states' voter laws were racially discriminatory.

Certainly voter turnout among black voters has increased significantly over the past 40 years. Back in 1980, only 50% of eligible black voters went to the polls compared with 61% of white voters. By 2012, 62% of eligible black voters cast their ballot compared with less than 58% of white voters and just 32% of Hispanic voters.

Table 5.9 Estimates of disenfranchised African-Americans with felony convictions, 2016

State	Disenfranchised African-American felons (%)	Disenfranchised adult felons (all races) (%)
Kentucky	26.1	9.1
Virginia	21.9	7.8
Florida	21.3	10.4
Tennessee	21.2	8.3
Wyoming	17.1	5.3
Mississippi	15.9	9.6
Alabama	15.1	7.6
Nevada	11.8	4.0

Source: The Sentencing Project

But there are more worrying developments that disproportionately affect black voters:

- Nine states had introduced a photo ID requirement for all voters in the run-up to the 2016 elections. These included six states — Alabama, Mississippi, South Carolina, Tennessee, Texas and Virginia — with high proportions of black voters.
- By 2016, the Brennan Center for Justice estimated that 6 million Americans had lost their right to vote because of previous criminal convictions — what is referred to as 'felony disenfranchisement'. The Center also estimated that 1 in every 13 voting-age African-Americans had lost their right to vote because of a past conviction, that rate being four times higher than for all other Americans.
- Research conducted by the Sentencing Project showed that felony disenfranchisement among the black community had risen sharply since 1980. In 1980, just two states — Arizona and Iowa — had disenfranchised more than 10% of black voters because of past convictions. But by 2016, eight states had disenfranchised more than 10% of their black voters (see Table 5.9), and four states — Kentucky, Virginia, Florida and Tennessee — had disenfranchised over 20%, with Kentucky topping the list at 26.1%. However, the felony disenfranchisement rate for all adult Kentuckians was just 9%.

Representation

Not only have minorities looked for decisions in government that take their preferences and choices into account, but they have looked for adequate representation in government as well — to paraphrase a Bill Clinton phrase, to have a government that 'looks like America'. So how well are racial minorities represented in the three branches of the federal government?

Minority representation in Congress

When Jesse Jackson first ran for the Democratic Party's presidential nomination in 1984, there were just 21 African-American members of Congress — all in the House of Representatives. But over the next two decades, this number increased quite significantly, mainly due to the creation in some states of majority-minority districts for elections to the House of Representatives. As we saw in Chapter 3, these are electoral districts in which a majority of voters are from a specific racial minority group.

The 115th Congress which began in January 2017 is the most racially diverse on record. The number of African-Americans had increased from 46 to 49 — 46 in the House and 3 in the Senate. There are also a record number of Hispanic members with 34 in the House and 4 in the Senate. The number of Asian members was also at a record high — up from 11 to 15, with 12 in the House and 3 in the Senate.

Minority representation in the executive branch

The presidency

It was in 1972 that Shirley Chisholm became the first major-party African-American candidate for the presidency when she competed in that year's Democratic primaries, winning 152 delegates to the party's national convention. Twelve years later, Jesse Jackson won over 3 million votes in the Democratic primaries, finishing third in the 1984 contest. Jackson became the first African-American to win a major-party presidential primary, winning four state primaries plus the one in the District of Columbia. Jackson ran again in 1988 and did even better, winning 11 contests and finishing second behind the eventual nominee Michael Dukakis.

But it was 20 years before another serious black candidate emerged for the presidency. And even Barack Obama in 2008 started way behind that year's Democratic front-runner, Hillary Clinton. Obama, of course, went on to win not only the nomination but the presidency and was re-elected to a second term four years later. But there are still few members of racial minorities in the usual pools of recruitment for the presidency. And in 2016, of the 22 declared major-party presidential candidates, only one — Ben Carson — was black, and only two others — Bobby Jindal and Marco Rubio — were from ethnic minority groups.

Congresswoman Shirley Chisholm

The cabinet

Six years before Chisholm launched her ground-breaking campaign, President Lyndon Johnson had appointed Robert Weaver as secretary of Housing and Urban Development (HUD). Weaver thus became the first African-American to head a federal executive department and thereby become a member of the president's cabinet. Since Weaver's appointment, 20 other African-Americans have headed an executive department with the most recent being Ben Carson's appointment as HUD secretary in the Trump administration.

The most racially diverse cabinet to date was the one appointed by Barack Obama in January 2009. It included African-American Eric Holder (Justice), two Hispanics — Ken Salazar (Interior) and Hilda Solis (Labor) — as well as two Chinese-Americans — Steven Chu (Energy) and Gary Locke (Commerce) — plus Japanese-American Eric Shinseki (Veterans' Affairs) and Lebanese-American Ray LaHood (Transportation). But if African-Americans thought that the election of 'one of us' to the Oval Office in 2008 would result in a number of black cabinet members, they were to be disappointed. Eric Holder was the only African-American to head up an executive department during Obama's first term — no different from the days of Ronald Reagan when Sam Pierce was the only black among the departmental heads.

By 2017 diversity seemed to be forgotten in Donald Trump's first cabinet. Indeed, it was in danger of reverting to the days of Richard Nixon when someone described the cabinet as a lot of 'grey-haired old men called George'.

Immigration reform

> Give me your tired, your poor, your huddled masses yearning to breathe free, the wretched refuse of your teeming shore. Send these, the homeless, tempest-tossed to me. I lift my lamp beside the golden door.

So reads the inscription on the Statue of Liberty in New York Harbour, a gift from the people of France, and the welcoming sight of immigrants arriving from abroad for almost a century-and-a-half. But immigration is a controversial issue, for while on the one hand it taps into a national characteristic of America as a melting pot of peoples and as a safe harbour for those 'yearning to breathe free', on the other hand it has implications in the areas of fairness, national identity, economic opportunity and — especially since 9/11 — homeland security.

Four sets of figures point towards some of the political issues associated with immigration, both legal and illegal. First, Table 5.10 shows a sharp increase in the percentage of the foreign born in America through the last three decades of the twentieth century, but the rate of increase slowed during the first decade of this century. But second, Figure 5.3 shows that illegal immigration also rose sharply during the 1990s to a peak of 12.2 million in 2007. The figure then fell sharply during 2008 and 2009 to 11.3 million — possibly accounted for by the worsening economic conditions in the United States during these years.

Third, Table 5.11 shows that during 2013, 2014 and 2015, well over half of those apprehended for attempting to enter the United States illegally were from Mexico. Furthermore, if one added those from the Central American nations El Salvador, Guatemala and Honduras — immediately south of Mexico — they would in 2015 constitute 93% of all illegal aliens apprehended. It is hardly surprising therefore that the controversy regarding illegal immigration has focused on trying to secure the 2,000-mile border between the United

Table 5.10 Foreign-born population as a percentage of total population, 1900–2010

Year	Percentage foreign born
1900	13.6
1910	14.7
1920	13.2
1930	11.6
1940	8.8
1950	6.9
1960	5.4
1970	4.7
1980	6.2
1990	7.9
2000	11.1
2010	12.9

States and Mexico. In 2006, Congress authorised the building of 700 miles of fence along part of the border and by 2010 646 miles of it had been erected along with a 'virtual fence' made up of sensors and other control systems. But this controversy came to a head during the 2016 presidential campaign with Donald Trump's promise to 'build a wall' along the entire border and make the Mexican government pay for it.

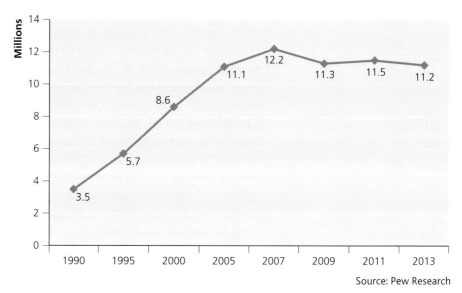

Source: Pew Research

Figure 5.3 Estimated unauthorised immigrant population, 1990–2013 (millions)

Table 5.11 Illegal aliens apprehended showing percentage from Mexico, 2013–15

Year	Total illegal aliens apprehended	Total from Mexico	Percentage from Mexico
2013	662,483	424,978	64
2014	679,996	350,177	51
2015	462,388	267,885	58

Source: Department of Homeland Security

Fourth, Figure 5.4 shows a dramatic fall in illegal aliens apprehended during the Obama years. Of course, one can read those figures two ways. It could be that more illegal immigrants are entering the United States undetected. But it could be that would-be illegal immigrants were deterred by the increased number of border patrol agents and the enhanced physical barriers at the border.

George W. Bush had tried during his eight years to get meaningful immigration reform through Congress but failed. In his 2008 campaign, Barack Obama promised he would succeed where Bush had failed. The Development, Relief and Education for Alien Minors (DREAM) Act was reintroduced and passed by the House late in 2010, but met with filibustering in the Senate and was never passed. So, as we have seen, in 2012 Obama decided to act without congressional authorisation and effectively implement certain aspects of immigration reform by executive order.

After more than a decade-and-a-half of the new century, then, meaningful immigration reform had pretty much hit a brick wall. It remained to be seen whether the next president — who had threatened so often to build a wall — could persuade Congress to enact legislation on this policy or on any other relating to race and civil rights in America that would, to quote Martin Luther King, be 'deeply rooted in the American dream'.

Activity

- Go to **www.icivics.org** and click on 'Play'. Then click on 'Supreme Decision' and follow the on-screen instructions. This is a simulation of how Supreme Court justices make decisions about individual rights.
- This website has other interactive games on topics relating to the Supreme Court and rights which you might want to try.

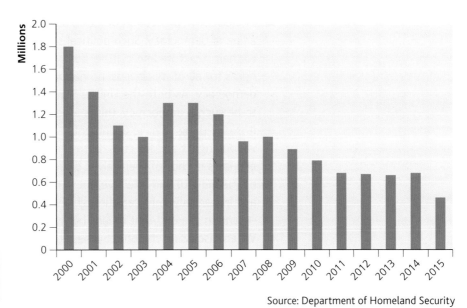

Source: Department of Homeland Security

Figure 5.4 Illegal aliens apprehended, 2000–15 (millions)

Comparing the protection of rights in the USA and UK

In the USA, civil rights appear in written form in the Constitution, most notably in the first ten amendments — known as the Bill of Rights (see Chapter 2) — as well as in later amendments such as the Fifteenth, the Twenty-Fourth and Twenty-Sixth (voting rights), and the Nineteenth (gender). They also appear in laws passed by Congress, such as various Civil Rights Acts, the Voting Rights Act (1965), the Americans with Disabilities Act (1990) and the Lilly Ledbetter Fair Pay Act (2009).

But in the UK, the formal enumeration of rights is quite different. Without a codified constitution (see Chapter 2), people in Britain have relied on what the early-twentieth-century constitutional theorist A.V. Dicey called 'the three pillars of liberty' — Parliament, a culture of liberty and the courts — which between them offered the effective protection of civil rights. Things changed significantly in 1998 when the Labour government of Tony Blair passed the Human Rights Act, which incorporated the European Convention on Human Rights into British law. This added into the formal structure of British law many of those rights we find in the US Constitution — freedom of expression, freedom of religion, the right to a fair trial and the right to life.

The significant difference, however, is that in the UK these rights are not entrenched (see Chapter 2). They are enumerated in what is ordinary legislation, unprotected by special amendment procedures. This was drawn into sharp focus when, following the 2015 general election, the Conservative government announced plans to replace the Human Rights Act with a British Bill of Rights. That could be achieved by simple majorities in both houses of Parliament. In this formal sense, civil rights in the United States enjoy more protection and are consequently more secure than they are in the UK.

Effectiveness of the protection of rights

The effective protection of rights is a role played by all three branches of government, as well as by other parts of the political system, including pressure groups, political parties and the media. But it is undoubtedly legislatures and judiciaries which are in the forefront. However, we need to establish three basic principles at the outset:

- The effective protection of rights and liberties is a defining characteristic of a liberal democracy. Such political systems can vary in many ways according to their structure and culture, but without the effective protection of rights for all of its citizens, no nation state can rightly claim to be a liberal democracy. As both the United States and the United Kingdom would claim to be such a democracy, this is a defining area for both political systems.
- It is one thing to have documents — constitutions or laws — that proclaim various rights and liberties. Both the USA and the UK do. But constitutions and laws do not of themselves offer *effective* protection of those rights. To be meaningful and effective, these rights need to be rigorously, consistently and impartially enforced through the political system, mostly by the courts — and in the end that means by the nation's highest court.
- When discussing the effectiveness of the protection of rights, it is important to keep in mind that balancing rights is rather like balancing scales. As one group's rights are 'protected', a different group may well feel that their rights have been eroded or threatened.

Rights protection in the USA

In the United States, it is possible to find examples of rights not being effectively protected despite the provisions of the Constitution or federal law. The passage of the post-Civil War amendments did not end racial discrimination. And when the Supreme Court established the so-called 'separate but equal' doctrine in its 1896 decision of *Plessy* v *Ferguson*, the Court was clearly not protecting the rights of African-Americans. Neither did the Twenty-Fourth Amendment (1964) immediately end all discrimination against racial minorities in voter registration throughout all the states. Those in the gay and lesbian community would have considered the Defense of Marriage Act (1996) not to be protective of their rights to same-sex marriages. Equally, there were those in the white majority community who regarded affirmative action as unprotective of their rights, especially in education, and those in the evangelical Christian community who regarded the Supreme Court's decision in *Obergefell* v *Hodges* (2015) to be unsupportive of their right to hold an orthodox Christian view of marriage. There are those who regard the protection of a woman's right to choose an abortion as having led to a decrease in the protection of the rights of the unborn child.

Following the attacks on America on 11 September 2001, there was a lively debate concerning the appropriate balance between protecting rights and liberties on the one hand and protecting the nation from terrorist attack on the other. Many Americans felt that Congress's passage of the so-called USA PATRIOT Act tilted the balance too far in terms of national security, thereby endangering the effective protection of individual rights. New rules on the detention of immigrants, new search powers of homes and businesses as well as of telephone, e-mail and financial records, all caused civil rights groups considerable unease. On top of that, the existence of the detention camp at Guantánamo Bay, plus all the other facets of the 'war on terror' during the administration of George W. Bush, caused some to be concerned over the balance of security as against rights.

Equally, in today's America, the rights of those with disabilities, those from racial minorities and those of women — to mention but three groups — are more effectively protected than they were half-a-century ago. This more effective protection has been brought about by the combined action of courts, presidents, legislators (at both federal and state level) and pressure groups.

Rights protection in the UK

In the UK, the effective protection of rights can be achieved by the judiciary in a number of ways:

- the use of judicial review, including ruling that government actions are *ultra vires*
- upholding of the provisions of the Human Rights Act
- declarations regarding common law
- judicial inquiries

Parliament also has a part to play by passing legislation to enable the more effective protection of rights. In past decades, Parliament had passed:

- the Equal Pay Act (1970)
- the Sex Discrimination Act (1975)
- the Race Relations Act (1976)
- the Disability Discrimination Act (1995)
- the Freedom of Information Act (2000)

But in 2010 the Equality Act effectively consolidated all the UK's anti-discriminatory legislation into one law, protecting as it does rights based on gender, disability, race and sexuality.

There was a similar debate in the UK as we saw in the USA regarding the balance between individual rights and national security following the bombings in London in July 2005. Legislation drawn up that year by the Blair government ran into opposition regarding plans to allow police to detain terror suspects for up to 90 days without charge. There was to be a new offence of 'glorifying terrorism' as well as new government powers to curb religious 'hate speech' and religious extremism. But how were such terms to be defined? Where did national security issues trump rights of freedom of religion and freedom of speech?

In both the USA and the UK there is an overriding cultural belief in the principle of the rule of law — an Anglo-American concept that emphasises the supremacy of the law, stresses the protection of individual rights from arbitrary interference from government officials, and reinforces respect for the law and adherence to the courts' enforcements of it.

Table 5.12 US pressure groups in three areas of civil rights

Issue	Pressure groups
Abortion	National Right to Life Committee
	Planned Parenthood
	National Organization for Women
	Center for Reproductive Rights
	National Association for the Repeal of Abortion Laws
	National Abortion Rights Action League
Gun rights	National Rifle Association
	Brady Center to Prevent Gun Violence
Race	American Association for Affirmative Action
	National Association for the Advancement of Colored People
	Black Lives Matter

Role of pressure groups in the protection of rights

Pressure groups and rights in the USA

Pressure groups are studied in detail in Chapter 7. Here we need to be aware that they do play an important role in the protection of rights in both the USA and the UK. In the landmark civil rights decision in 1954, it was the legal defence and education fund of the National Association for the Advancement of Colored People (NAACP) that brought the *Brown v Board of Education of Topeka* to court. Indeed, many of the Supreme Court's most important civil rights cases have involved sponsorship by a pressure group. Earlier in this chapter we came across a number of interest groups engaged in protecting rights by bringing cases to the Supreme Court:

- Citizens United
- National Federation of Independent Business
- Parents Involved in Community Schools

Table 5.12 gives some examples of pressure groups active in three specific areas of civil rights in the USA.

Then there are pressure groups that submit *amicus curiae* briefs to the courts. This is a legal term meaning 'friend of the court', by which groups (or individuals) who are not party to a case can try to influence the court as it reaches its decision. Some may indeed be asked to put their case in person before the court. In landmark decisions regarding such issues as abortion, gun control and affirmative action, interest groups on both sides of the case may be influential in submitting such arguments to the court. And there is evidence that these briefs do influence court deliberations, so pressure groups hire top lawyers to write them. In the two affirmative action cases in 2003 — *Gratz* v *Bollinger* and *Grutter* v *Bollinger* — supporters of the University of Michigan's admissions programmes deluged the Court with such briefs. Indeed, Justice John Paul Stevens said in his opinion that the Court had relied on 'the powerful consensus of the dark green briefs' — the colour of the cover in which such briefs must be submitted to the Court. The *McDonald* v *City of Chicago* case in 2010 attracted 33 *amicus* briefs.

One of the most influential pressure groups in terms of civil rights and the courts is the American Civil Liberties Union (ACLU). Formed out of the Red Scare of supposed communist infiltration of the United States, the ACLU now has some three-quarters of a million members, and a staff of some 200 attorneys and offices throughout the United States. It joined the NAACP in challenging school segregation in the 1950s and was involved in the landmark abortion case of *Roe* v *Wade* in 1973. In 1997 it brought a case against Attorney General Reno (*ACLU* v *Reno*) that resulted in the Supreme Court striking down the 1996 Communications Decency Act because of its broad banning of 'indecent' material on the internet. This is just one example of the ACLU defending rights which many — possible a majority of — Americans will think are indefensible. The ACLU has been widely criticised for defending the rights of such groups as the American Nazis, the Ku Klux Klan and the Nation of Islam. But according to the ACLU:

> We do not defend them because we agree with them; rather, we defend their right to free expression and free assembly. Once the government has the power to violate one person's rights, it can use that power against everyone. We work to stop the erosion of civil liberties before it's too late.

And since 9/11, the ACLU has, according to its website, been 'working vigorously to oppose policies that sacrifice fundamental freedoms in the name of national security'.

Pressure groups and rights in the UK

Given the increase in the UK courts' use of judicial review over the past three decades, UK pressure groups have been encouraged to focus their campaigning on the courts, and not just on Parliament and relevant government departments. So, for example, the Countryside Alliance has been highly influential in challenging the ban on fox hunting with dogs in the courts.

We also have examples in the UK where the effective protection of the rights of one group leads to concerns over the infringements of rights of another group, with a resulting clash of pressure group lobbying of the courts. Take the Ashers Bakery case in Northern Ireland, in which the Christian owner of a bakery, Colin McArthur, was prosecuted under the Equality Act (Sexual Orientation) Regulations (NI) of 2006 for refusing to produce a cake for Gareth Lee bearing the slogan 'Support Gay Marriage'. McArthur claimed that his firm could not produce the cake as to do so would be contrary to his religious beliefs and therefore in good conscience he declined the order. References were also made during this case to various sections in the European Convention on Human Rights.

So whose rights were to be protected — those who support gay marriage, or those who hold genuine, sincere and orthodox Christian beliefs? McArthur's case was taken up by the Christian Institute, whose Legal Defence Fund fights civil rights cases where Christians are being prosecuted concerning matters relating to the practice of their faith. Mr Lee's case was supported by many gay rights groups as well as those supporting same-sex marriage. When the courts found against Mr McArthur, the prominent gay rights campaigner Peter Tatchell came out in support of Mr McArthur's rights. Writing in the *Independent*, Tatchell explained what to some might have been his surprising opposition to the Court's ruling in this case:

> This verdict is a defeat for freedom of expression. It seems that the judges have decided that businesses cannot lawfully refuse a customer's request to propagate a message, even if it is sexist, xenophobic or anti-gay and even if the business owners have a conscientious objection to it. Although I strongly disagree with Ashers' opposition to marriage equality, in a free society neither they nor anyone else should be compelled to facilitate a political idea they oppose. Discrimination against LGBT people is wrong and is rightly unlawful. But in a democratic society, people should be able to discriminate against ideas they disagree with.

The role of pressure groups in protecting rights in both the USA and the UK is clearly fraught with some significant contradictions.

Playing a similar role to that performed by the ACLU in the USA is the UK civil rights group Liberty. It was formed in the 1930s as the National Council for Civil Liberties. It campaigned for the rights of women, for the rights of protestors during the anti-Vietnam War protests of the late 1960s and early 1970s, and for civil rights during the troubles in Northern Ireland, and it was an early supporter of gay rights. But it is in the last two decades, and especially following the anti-terrorist legislation being passed by Parliament in 2005, that Liberty has come to play a prominent role in defending civil rights and liberties in the UK courts. Today it campaigns on issues such as the use of torture and extradition, as well as the rights of asylum seekers, refugee children and members of the UK armed forces. It is also prominent in campaigning against the issue of modern slavery.

References

Cohen, C., *Naked Racial Preference*, Madison Books, 1995.

Dershowitz, A.M., *Supreme Injustice: How the High Court Hijacked Election 2000*, Oxford University Press, 2001.

Heywood, A., *Politics* (2nd edition), Palgrave, 2002.

Jones, B. and Norton, P., *Politics UK* (8th edition), Routledge, 2014.

Kahlenberg, R., 'What's next for affirmative action?', *The Atlantic*, 6 November 2008.

Lazarus, E., *Closed Chambers: The Rise, Fall and Future of the Modern Supreme Court*, Penguin, 1999.

Mackenzie, G.C., *Innocent Until Nominated: The Breakdown of the Presidential Appointments Process*, Brookings, 2001.

McKay, D., *American Society Today*, Blackwell, 2005.

Roosevelt, K., *The Myth of Judicial Activism*, Yale University Press, 2006.

van Geel, T.R., *Understanding Supreme Court Opinions*, Pearson, 2008.

Further reading

Billingsley, K. and Bennett, A.J., 'Does the Supreme Court have too much power?' *Politics Review*, Vol. 22, No. 4, April 2013.

Singh, R., 'The US Supreme Court: a political, not a judicial, institution?' *Politics Review*, Vol. 24, No. 3, February 2015.

Singh, R., 'The US Supreme: an effective protector of civil rights and liberties?' *Politics Review*, Vol. 26, No. 2, November 2016.

Each edition of my *US Government and Politics: Annual Update* has a chapter reviewing the previous year's key decisions by the Supreme Court.

The place to start for electronic sources on the US Supreme Court is the Court's own website at www.supremecourt.gov. Click on 'About the Court' on the home page. But for material on the decisions it is better to go to www.scotusblog.com which is written in much less technical language. Click on 'Plain English' for more simple explanations of Court procedure, terminology and cases. The 'Statistics' page is also well worth visiting.

You might also want to consult websites relating to some of the specific rights and liberties discussed in this chapter. These might include:

www.aclu.org — American Civil Liberties Union
www.freespeechcoalition.com
www.firstamendmentcenter.org
www.nra.org — National Rifle Association
www.bradycenter.org — Brady Center to Prevent Gun Violence
www.deathpenaltyinfo.org
www.nrlc.org — National Right to Life Committee
www.plannedparenthood.org
www.now.org — National Organization for Women

Exam focus

Edexcel

Section A (Comparative)

1 Examine the ways in which the members of the US and UK Supreme Courts are appointed. (12)

2 Examine the role of pressure groups in the protection of rights in the USA and the UK. (12)

Section B (Comparative)

In your answer you must consider the relevance of at least one comparative theory.

1 Analyse the differences in the powers of the US and UK Supreme Courts. (12)

2 Analyse the effectiveness of the protection of rights in the USA and the UK. (12)

Section C (USA)

In your answer you must consider the stated view and the alternative to this view in a balanced way.

1 Evaluate the extent to which the Supreme Court is a political institution. (30)

2 Evaluate the extent to which the Supreme Court can rightly be described as 'a third house of the legislature'. (30)

3 Evaluate the extent to which minority representation has increased in US government and politics. (30)

4 Evaluate the extent to which affirmative action has been successful. (30)

AQA

Section A (USA)

1 Explain and analyse three ways in which the Supreme Court could be regarded as a political institution. *(9)*

2 Explain and analyse three ways in which affirmative action has been successful. *(9)*

Section A (Comparative)

1 Explain and analyse three ways in which structural theory could be used to study the US and UK Supreme Courts. *(9)*

2 Explain and analyse three ways in which cultural theory could be used to study the protection of rights in the USA and the UK. *(9)*

Section B (USA)

Does the US Supreme Court have too much power?

There is no denying the US Supreme Court is a potentially powerful body, and its power far exceeds that which was envisaged by the Founding Fathers. The Court had not been in existence 15 years when it performed a power grab by awarding itself the power to declare Acts of Congress — and later state laws, too — unconstitutional. Soon it added the power to declare the actions of both federal and state executives to be unconstitutional. With this power of judicial review, the Supreme Court can nullify actions of both the other branches of government — and frequently does. Yet it remains a wholly unelected and unaccountable body with members permitted to serve for two, three, or more decades.

True, the Supreme Court is subject to the checks and balances of the Constitution. It has no initiation power. Congress can nullify its decisions through initiating constitutional amendments — though this rarely occurs. Even public opinion is something of a check on the Court's power. Chief Justice John Roberts has asserted that he and his colleagues are mere 'umpires' and 'servants of the law', and that theirs is a 'limited role'. But the power of the Supreme Court in such public policy areas as abortion, gun control, affirmative action, the death penalty, campaign finance, freedom of speech and religion, and more recently same-sex marriage, gives all the appearance of nine people with far too much power.

Analyse, evaluate and compare the arguments in the above passage for and against the view that the Supreme Court has too much power. *(25)*

Section C (Comparative)

In your answer you should draw on material from across the whole range of your course of study in Politics.

1 The political significance of the US Supreme Court far exceeds that of the UK Supreme Court.' Analyse and evaluate this statement. *(25)*

2 'Citizens' rights are better protected by the judiciary in the USA than in the UK.' Analyse and evaluate this statement. *(25)*

Elections

Introduction

On 30 April 2011, Barack Obama — the forty-fourth president of the United States — gave the final orders for the carrying out of Operation Neptune Spear, an operation led by America's Central Intelligence Agency to capture Osama bin Laden, the perpetrator of the 9/11 attacks just less than ten years before. That same evening, Obama hosted the annual White House correspondents' dinner, at which one of the guests was business and entertainment icon Donald Trump. Both Obama and *Saturday Night Live* comedian Seth Myers set about telling jokes at Trump's expense. 'Donald Trump has been saying he will run for president as a Republican — which is surprising, since I just assumed he was running as a joke,' quipped Myers. But it was no joke. And 5 years, 6 months and 9 days later Donald J. Trump was elected as the forty-fifth president of the United States.

But how could someone with no electoral or political experience, no long-standing ties with either of the two main political parties, who had never served in the military, and who was so reviled and disliked by a majority of Americans — even by many within his own adoptive Republican Party — be elected to the nation's highest office? But then how could a peanut farmer from Georgia (Jimmy Carter), or someone who had starred in a Hollywood movie alongside a chimpanzee named Bonzo (Ronald Reagan), be elected to the same office?

The answer in its shortest and simplest form has to be about the method by which presidential candidates are chosen, and the way in which presidential elections are conducted. And those two issues will be the focus of much of this chapter so that by the end of it, you should be better placed to understand how it was that the candidate who almost everyone believed could never become president, did just that.

Presidential elections

When presidential elections occur

America has fixed-term elections that occur every four years. The first presidential election was held in 1788. Since then, a presidential election has been held every four years, even during wartime. If the president dies in office, there is still no special election. When President John Kennedy was assassinated in November 1963, Vice President Lyndon Johnson automatically became president and completed the remaining months of Kennedy's term. The next presidential election was not until 1964. The fact that these elections occur every four years is laid down in Article II of the Constitution. But federal law goes even further, stating that the election shall be held on the Tuesday after the first Monday in November of every fourth year. In practice, that means that the election occurs between 2 and 8 November.

Presidential elections can best be thought of as occurring in seven distinct stages (see Table 6.1). The first four are concerned with choosing the candidates. The last three are concerned with electing the president.

Requirements for a presidential candidate

What does a person need to become a candidate for the presidency? In answering such a question, consider carefully the word 'need'. There are two possible meanings: first, what is *absolutely essential* — the constitutional

Table 6.1 Presidential elections: a seven-stage process

Stage	Functions	Occurs
1 Invisible primary	<ul><li>Candidates' announcements</li><li>Increasing name recognition</li><li>Fundraising</li><li>Intra-party TV debates</li></ul>	Calendar year before the election
2 Primaries and caucuses	<ul><li>Show popular support for candidates</li><li>Choose delegates to attend national party conventions</li></ul>	January/February to early June
3 Choosing vice presidential candidate(s)	<ul><li>Presidential candidates announce choice of running-mate</li></ul>	Some days/weeks before convention
4 National party conventions	<ul><li>Confirm presidential and vice presidential candidates</li><li>Approve party platform</li><li>Acceptance speech delivered by presidential candidate</li></ul>	Usually July/August (each lasts for four days)
5 General election campaign	<ul><li>Campaign between the candidates of the various parties</li></ul>	September, October, first week of November
6 Election Day	<ul><li>Registered voters go to the polls (although many may have participated in early voting)</li></ul>	Tuesday after the first Monday in November
7 Electoral College voting	<ul><li>Electors vote in their state capitals to choose president and vice president</li></ul>	Monday after the second Wednesday in December

requirements; and second, what is *very helpful* — things without which your candidacy either won't be taken very seriously or won't get very far.

Constitutional requirements

Several constitutional qualifications are necessary in order to be president:

- One must be a natural-born American citizen.
- One must be at least 35 years old. The youngest ever president was Theodore Roosevelt, who was just 42 when he became president following the assassination of President William McKinley in 1901. The youngest ever *elected* president was John Kennedy, who was 43.
- There is a residency qualification of 14 years.

In 1951, the Constitution was amended to limit presidents to two terms in office. The first president to feel the effect of this two-term limit was Dwight Eisenhower in 1960. Subsequently, four more presidents have been term limited: Ronald Reagan, Bill Clinton, George W. Bush and Barack Obama. So a fourth constitutional requirement could be added — not to have already served two terms as president.

Extra-constitutional requirements

In addition to the constitutional requirements, there are a number of other elements which candidates need to stand a chance of making a serious bid for the presidency. They are not mentioned in the Constitution, hence they are 'extra-constitutional' requirements. They fall into seven areas.

Political experience

Conventional wisdom would have told us that probably the most important of these extra-constitutional requirements is political experience. Two groups of politicians have tended to be good pools of recruitment for the presidency: state governors and senators. Of the 22 declared candidates for the Republican and Democratic presidential nominations in 2016, 11 had served as state governor and 8 in the Senate. The other three — Republicans Donald Trump, Ben Carson and Carly Fiorina — had no previous political experience. In 2016, Trump became the first person to be elected president without any experience in either politics or the military.

Of the 19 people who were nominated as presidential candidates from 1968 to 2016, ten had served in the Senate and six had been state governors. Six had also served as vice president — another office that may lead to the presidency. What was noteworthy about the 2016 Republican presidential nomination contest was that candidates with political experience — such as governors John Kasich, Chris Christie, Rick Perry and Jeb Bush, and senators Ted Cruz, Rand Paul and Marco Rubio — were unable to defeat a political novice in Donald Trump.

Table 6.2 Winning and losing candidates in presidential elections, 1980–2016

Year	Winning candidate	Losing candidate
1980	Ronald Reagan (R)	Jimmy Carter (D)
1984	Ronald Reagan (R)	Walter Mondale (D)
1988	George H.W. Bush (R)	Michael Dukakis (D)
1992	Bill Clinton (D)	George H.W. Bush (R)
1996	Bill Clinton (D)	Bob Dole (R)
2000	George W. Bush (R)	Al Gore (D)
2004	George W. Bush (R)	John Kerry (D)
2008	Barack Obama (D)	John McCain (R)
2012	Barack Obama (D)	Mitt Romney (R)
2016	Donald Trump (R)	Hillary Clinton (D)

Major party endorsement

If someone is serious about becoming president, it is vital to be chosen as the candidate for one of the two major parties (see Table 6.2). Even Eisenhower in 1952 had to become a Republican. The political endeavours of George Wallace (1968), John Anderson (1980), Ross Perot (1992 and 1996), Pat Buchanan (2000) and Gary Johnson (2016) show that third-party or independent candidacies do not lead to the White House.

Personal characteristics

One has traditionally begun this discussion by pointing out that all presidential candidates for major parties have been white males. No longer. A remarkable fact of the 2008 Democratic presidential nomination race was that it came down to a choice between a white woman (Hillary Clinton) and a black man (Barack Obama). Given the pools of recruitment — the vice presidency, state governors and US senators — it is hardly surprising that, until 2008, major-party presidential candidates had all been white males. In 2016, Hillary Clinton became the first female major-party presidential candidate. And one reason why the domination by white males is unlikely to end any time soon is that the pools of recruitment are still dominated by men.

It is an advantage to be married. There has been only one bachelor president — James Buchanan, elected in 1856. It used to be said that scandal involving marital infidelity could rule out a possible candidate. But in 1992 Bill Clinton managed to secure the Democratic Party's nomination despite allegations surrounding Gennifer Flowers, which surfaced early in the campaign. Three of the Republicans' last eight presidential candidates — Ronald Reagan,

John McCain and Donald Trump — had all divorced and remarried, in Trump's case twice.

Ability to raise large sums of money

The ability to raise money is crucial to a successful bid for the presidency. Campaigns are so expensive that very few candidates can afford to finance their own campaigns. Only billionaire candidates such as Ross Perot (1992) and Steve Forbes (1996 and 2000) have been able to finance their campaigns from their own pockets. Candidates need to raise large sums of money even before the primaries and caucuses begin, which means raising money in the year before the election itself. According to the Open Secrets website (www.opensecrets.org), Hillary Clinton raised just over $700 million during her unsuccessful White House bid in 2016.

Effective organisation

During the candidate selection process, the major parties cannot endorse specific candidates. A candidate is running to *become* the Republican or Democratic presidential candidate, so candidates cannot use the party's organisational structure, either nationally or in each state. They must therefore create their own organisation. This is time consuming, expensive and demanding. But candidates who fail to put together an effective organisation will stumble badly during the campaign.

Oratorical skills and being telegenic

In the media age, the abilities to speak well and look good on television are crucial. It would be interesting to see whether candidates such as Abraham Lincoln — lampooned for his long, gangling physique — or wheelchair-bound Franklin Roosevelt could have made it to the White House in the television age. 'I'm no good at television,' Democratic candidate Walter Mondale complained in 1984. Republican Senator Phil Gramm went even further in 1996, declaring: 'I'm too ugly to be president.' Donald Trump's mastery of the media was an important factor in his successful campaign in 2016, as it had been for Barack Obama eight years earlier.

Sound and relevant policies

There is a danger that presidential elections are portrayed as all style and no substance. Style is important, but voters will soon detect a candidate whose campaign turns out to be a 'policy-free zone'. A candidate must have policies that are both practical and relevant. Trump was something of an exception here in 2016, for although his campaign clearly focused on policy areas that appealed to key groups of voters, such as jobs and immigration reform, Trump's campaign rhetoric was noticeably thin on policy detail and tended to consist mostly of his much-repeated promise to 'make America great again'.

The invisible primary

Unlike many democracies, in which the political parties choose candidates themselves, in the USA the candidates are chosen by ordinary voters. Although presidential elections are held in every fourth year, the manoeuvring in preparation for the elections begins months, if not years, beforehand. Because these events take place before the official first stage — the primaries — and because there is very little to see, this stage is often referred to as the **invisible primary**. The term was originally the title of a book by White House journalist

Key term

Invisible primary The period between candidates declaring an intention to run for the presidency and the first primaries and caucuses.

Arthur T. Hadley published in 1976. The invisible primary is said to be critically important for a candidate to gain name recognition and money, and to put together the necessary organisation. There is a high correlation between who is leading in the polls at the end of the invisible primary and who actually wins the presidential nomination.

The invisible primary is played out mainly in the media. A candidate will hope to be 'mentioned' as a possible serious presidential candidate in such newspapers as *The Washington Post* and *The New York Times*, or there might be a positive article in *Time* magazine. There might be offers of an in-depth interview on such serious political television programmes as *Face the Nation* (CBS), *News Hour* (PBS) or one of CNN's political talk shows, such as *State of the Union with Jake Tapper*, or *The Situation Room with Wolf Blitzer*.

Candidate announcements

Then there are the candidates' formal announcements of their entering the presidential race. The first major Republican candidate to announce his candidacy for the 2016 presidential race was Senator Ted Cruz of Texas, who made his announcement on 23 March 2015 — over ten months before the Iowa caucuses. By the end of July 2015, there were 17 declared Republican candidates. On the Democratic side, Hillary Clinton announced her intention to run on 12 April 2015. In the next three months, four other Democrats joined the race.

Support for a candidate at this stage is demonstrated principally by opinion polls. Some of these polls, reported regularly by the press, may be based on a certain state while others are regional. From time to time, some polling organisations may conduct a nationwide poll. They may run head-to-head match-ups to see how candidates of one party might fare against fancied contenders from the other party. During 2015, polling organisations published frequent head-to-head match-ups between the presumptive Democratic Party nominee Hillary Clinton and possible Republican candidates such as Jeb Bush, Marco Rubio, Ted Cruz and Donald Trump.

Televised party debates

Not all the 'invisible' primary is invisible. Some relatively formal events do occur. Between 6 August 2015 and voting beginning in February 2016, there were seven televised debates between the would-be Republican candidates. This was a significant decrease on the 16 such debates held during 2011. It was in the tenth of those 2011 debates that Governor Rick Perry of Texas had a much-publicised memory loss when he could not recall the three federal executive departments he would close down if elected president. Governor Perry began his answer: 'Commerce, Education and the...uh, um, what's the third one there, let's see.' After almost a minute of trying to recall the third — which was later revealed as the Department of Energy — Perry ended his halting response with the word 'Oops!' to much audience amusement. Just over two months later, Perry ended his 2012 presidential bid, having finished sixth in the New Hampshire primary with less than 1% of the vote.

In the 2015–16 invisible primary, there were so many Republican candidates that the sponsoring media outlets couldn't even fit them all on the same platform. To get around the problem, they started to run two debates. On each designated date there was a secondary, afternoon debate (referred to as the 'kids' table') for those in the lower half of the national polls, followed by

Republican presidential candidates gather for debate, 16 September 2015

a main, evening primetime debate for the leading candidates. In the end, just six candidates — Jeb Bush, Ben Carson, Ted Cruz, John Kasich, Marco Rubio and Donald Trump — were invited to all seven of the main debates, though Trump chose to boycott the last one. But with the numbers involved, and with Donald Trump mostly involved, these debates turned into a political circus with little if any serious policy debate occurring. As a slightly dejected Ben Carson commented after the debate just four days before voting started:

> This format is not the best format for convincing anybody of anything. We're dealing with sound bites as opposed to being able to explain something in depth. But unfortunately that's characteristic of the society we live in today.

Fundraising

The invisible primary is also the period when money raising has to occur in earnest to accumulate a large enough 'war chest' to be taken seriously. Money brings the ability to campaign and advertise, which brings improved poll ratings, which brings more money. How truly was it said that money is 'the mother's milk of politics'.

Table 6.3 shows the amounts of money raised by the leading Republican candidates during the invisible primary prior to the 2016 primaries. The eventual nominee, Donald Trump, came in fifth, but one needs to be aware that by this stage in the campaign, Trump had donated just short of $18 million of his own money to his campaign which when added to the $25.5 million he had raised put him third in the money-raising table. That said, it was clear in this election cycle that fundraising during the invisible primary was no indicator of future electoral success. Ben Carson's near $58 million and Jeb Bush's $33.5 million won them not a single primary. Indeed, Bush failed to make it past the third week of the primaries before ending his campaign.

Table 6.3 Total campaign receipts for leading Republican candidates from 1 January 2015 to 31 January 2016

Candidate	Total campaign receipts ($m)	Total loans/receipts from the candidate ($m)
Ben Carson	57.9	0.2
Ted Cruz	54.7	0
Marco Rubio	33.7	0
Jeb Bush	33.5	0.4
Donald Trump	25.5	17.8
John Kasich	8.6	0
Chris Christie	8.0	0

Source: Federal Election Commission

On the Democratic side, Hillary Clinton out-raised her nearest challenger Senator Bernie Sanders during the invisible primary, but by a much closer margin than one would have imagined at the start of the race. Up to the end of January 2016, Clinton raised $130 million to Sanders' $96 million. Given Clinton's advantages in name recognition, organisational structure and sheer inevitability, one would have expected her to have out-raised Sanders two- or three-fold.

Front-runners

Over many election cycles, the conventional wisdom has been that it was important to end the invisible primary as the front-runner, according to the opinion polls. Whichever candidate was leading in the polls just before the primaries and caucuses began was usually confirmed as the nominee.

This was not the case in the Democrat race in 2004, in which the early front-runner, Howard Dean of Vermont, crashed in the primaries. And it certainly was not the case for either party in 2008. In the *USA Today*/Gallup poll conducted on 1–2 December 2007, right at the end of the invisible primary, Hillary Clinton held a 15-percentage point lead over Barack Obama. The same poll reported a 10-percentage point lead for Rudy Giuliani over John McCain in the Republican race. Indeed, McCain was in third place, having been overtaken by Mike Huckabee. Yet it was Obama and McCain who went on to win their respective party nominations.

However, in the 2016 cycle, Hillary Clinton and Donald Trump fitted the more conventional pattern of the early front-runner being confirmed as the eventual nominee. By the end of the invisible primary in January 2016, Hillary Clinton enjoyed a 14-point lead over Bernie Sanders, and Donald Trump a 16-point lead over his nearest rival, Ted Cruz. Once again, the so-called invisible primary had shown itself to be the critical stage in discerning who the likely presidential candidates would be — even before a single vote had been cast.

Table 6.4 Republican winners of invisible primary and eventual nominees, 1972–2016 (excluding incumbent presidents)

Year	Republican winner of invisible primary	Republican presidential candidate
1976	Gerald Ford	Gerald Ford
1980	Ronald Reagan	Ronald Reagan
1988	George H.W. Bush	George H.W. Bush
1996	Bob Dole	Bob Dole
2000	George W. Bush	George W. Bush
2008	**Rudy Giuliani**	**John McCain**
2012	Mitt Romney	Mitt Romney
2016	Donald Trump	Donald Trump

Since the reformed nomination process came into being back in 1972, Table 6.4 shows that in seven out of eight cycles the Republican candidate leading in the polls at the end of the invisible primary went on to become the party's presidential nominee, with Rudy Giuliani in 2008 being the only exception. This shows the great significance of the invisible primary for the Republican Party — a party that tends to nominate its front-runner almost without question. But Table 6.5 shows that it is slightly less important for the Democrats, who have failed to nominate the invisible primary front-runner on four out of nine occasions during the same period, including in both the 2004 and 2008 cycles. Indeed, Hillary Clinton holds the unfortunate distinction of being the party's invisible primary front-runner in two cycles — 2008 and 2016 — yet chosen as the nominee only once, and never winning the ultimate prize.

Table 6.5 Democratic winners of invisible primary and eventual nominees, 1972–2016 (excluding incumbent presidents)

Year	Democratic winner of invisible primary	Democratic presidential candidate
1972	**Hubert Humphrey**	**George McGovern**
1976	Jimmy Carter	Jimmy Carter
1984	Walter Mondale	Walter Mondale
1988	**Gary Hart**	**Michael Dukakis**
1992	Bill Clinton	Bill Clinton
2000	Al Gore	Al Gore
2004	**Howard Dean**	**John Kerry**
2008	**Hillary Clinton**	**Barack Obama**
2016	Hillary Clinton	Hillary Clinton

Primaries and caucuses

Here we enter the second stage of the process for electing the president — the primaries and caucuses. A primary is an election to choose a party's candidate for an elective office, in this case the presidency. A few states hold caucuses instead. A caucus is a meeting for the selection of a party's candidate for an elective office.

States that hold caucuses are usually geographically large but thinly populated, such as Iowa, North Dakota and Nevada. In 2016, the Republicans held caucuses in 10 states and the Democrats held them in 14 states. In a caucus, would-be voters must attend a meeting rather than go to a polling station. Turnout is generally lower in caucuses than in primaries and those who do turn out are disproportionately more ideological than primary voters. Hence, caucuses tend to favour more ideological candidates. In 2016, Democratic presidential candidate Bernie Sanders, who was on the liberal wing of his party, had some of his strongest showings in caucus states. For example, he won 68% in the caucuses in Kansas and 82% in Alaska. In all of the caucuses, Sanders averaged 66% of the vote to Clinton's 33%.

Primaries have two specific functions: to show the popularity of presidential candidates; and to choose delegates to go to the national party conventions. They are run under state law, which means that a great number of variations exist. The main rules of thumb are outlined below.

Timing of primaries

States must decide when to hold their primary or caucuses. The national parties usually lay down the earliest and latest possible dates — often mid-January to the beginning of June — but within that period each state can decide its own date. Some states, such as New Hampshire, schedule their contest early and on a day when no other primaries are being held, thereby hoping to give their primary a prominence that it would not otherwise have. Other states deliberately arrange their primaries to coincide with other, often neighbouring, states, thereby creating a regional primary. In 2016, the first Tuesday in March, when 11 states arranged their primaries and caucuses together, was dubbed Super Tuesday. The first Super Tuesday was held back in 1988 as an attempt by a block of southern states to increase their importance in the candidate selection process.

An increasing number of states like to schedule their primary early in election year, believing that the earlier primaries have more influence over candidate selection. This move to early scheduling is called front loading. The number of states holding their primaries or caucuses before the end of March increased from just 11 in 1980 to 42 in 2008, and those 42 states included the eight largest states — California, Texas, New York, Florida, Illinois, Pennsylvania, Ohio and Michigan. California, for example, has moved from early June (1980) to early February (2008); New York moved from mid-April to early February. By 5 February 2008, 55% of the delegates to the Democratic and Republican conventions had already been chosen. But both 2012 and 2016 saw some slippage in front loading with both parties encouraging a more extended, deliberative primary calendar. By the end of March 2016, 32 states had voted, but New York (19 April), Pennsylvania (26 April) and California (7 June) were still to come.

Types of primary

There are a number of different ways of classifying primaries by type. Let us consider two: closed and open primaries; and proportional and winner-take-all primaries.

Closed and open primaries

First, primaries can be divided into closed primaries and open primaries. It is important to understand that any registered voter can vote in a primary. But in some states, when you register, you are asked to declare your party affiliation — whether you consider yourself to be a Democrat or a Republican. In a closed primary, only registered Democrats can vote in the Democrat primary and only registered Republicans can vote in the Republican primary. In an open primary, any registered voter can vote in either primary. You decide on the day of the primary. In some states, even those who describe themselves as independents are allowed to participate.

Open primaries allow what is called *cross-over voting*, which means that Democrat voters can opt to participate in the Republican primary and vice versa. This became an important issue in the Democratic primaries in 2008 when, in open primary states, significant numbers of independents and Republicans opted to vote in the Democratic primary and voted for Senator Barack Obama. In the 2012 Wisconsin Republican open primary, 11% of voters said they were Democrats. While Mitt Romney won the primary overall with 44% of the vote to 37% for Rick Santorum, among Democrats Santorum beat Romney by 20 percentage points. This suggests one of two things: either these were conservative Democrats who genuinely preferred Santorum's policies to

Key terms

Super Tuesday A Tuesday in February or early March when a number of states coincide their presidential primaries and caucuses to try to gain influence.

Front loading The phenomenon by which a state schedules its presidential primaries and caucuses earlier in the nomination cycle in an attempt to increase its importance.

Key terms

Closed primary A primary in which only registered Democrats can vote in the Democratic primary and only registered Republicans can vote in the Republican primary.

Open primary A primary in which any registered voter can vote in either party's primary.

those of either President Obama or Mitt Romney; or they were mischievous Democrats deliberately casting a vote for someone they perceived as an 'easier' opponent for the President in November. Cross-over voting was not an issue in 2016 when both parties had competitive nomination races.

Modified primaries are like closed primaries, in that only registered party voters can vote, but they also allow those who have registered as independents to vote in either party's primary. So, for example, in the New Jersey primary in 2016, registered Republican voters could vote only in the Republican primary, registered Democrats could vote only in the Democratic primary, but independents could vote in either party's primary.

Proportional and winner-take-all primaries

Primaries can also be classified according to how delegates to the national party conventions are won. In most primaries, candidates are awarded delegates in proportion to the votes they get. These are known as **proportional primaries**. Most states set a threshold — a minimum percentage of votes that a candidate must receive to get any of that state's delegates, usually 10 or 15% of the vote. All Democrat and most Republican primaries are now proportional primaries.

However, some Republican primaries are **winner-take-all primaries**, in which whoever gets the most votes wins all that state's delegates. So in winning the Arizona Republican primary in 2016, Donald Trump received all 58 delegates to the party's national convention because it was a winner-take-all contest (see Table 6.6). But in winning the New Hampshire primary — a proportional primary — Trump won just 11 delegates, with the remaining 12 delegates shared among four other candidates (see Table 6.7).

> **Key terms**
>
> **Proportional primaries**
> Presidential primaries in which delegates are awarded to the candidates in proportion to the votes they get.
>
> **Winner-take-all primaries**
> Presidential primaries, permitted only by the Republicans, in which whoever gets the most votes wins all that state's delegates.

Table 6.6 Winner-take-all primary: Arizona Republican primary, 2016

Candidate	Popular vote (%)	Delegates
Donald Trump	45.9	58
Ted Cruz	27.6	0
Marco Rubio	11.6	0
John Kasich	10.6	0
Ben Carson	2.4	0

Table 6.7 Proportional primary: New Hampshire Republican primary, 2016

Candidate	Popular vote (%)	Delegates
Donald Trump	35.2	11
John Kasich	15.7	4
Ted Cruz	11.6	3
Jeb Bush	11.0	3
Marco Rubio	10.5	2
Chris Christie	7.4	0
Carly Fiorina	4.1	0
Ben Carson	2.3	0

Early primaries and caucuses

Iowa

For many decades now, the early primaries and caucuses have come to be regarded as crucial. Iowa traditionally holds the first caucus. But because caucuses usually attract low turnout — the 2012 Republican caucuses in Wyoming attracted just 2,108 voters — this is usually not regarded as being as important as the first primary. However, the 2016 Iowa caucuses proved to be very important in both the Republican and Democratic races. The Republican caucuses in Iowa were won by Ted Cruz with 27% of the vote, just beating Donald Trump (24%) and Marco Rubio (23%). This positioned all three candidates to make a serious bid for the nomination during the first month.

Collecting ballots at the Republican caucus in Sioux City, Iowa, 1 February 2016

In the Democratic race, Hillary Clinton was doubtless mindful of her third-place finish in the Iowa caucuses back in 2008, with victory on that occasion going to the eventual nominee Barack Obama. But in 2016 she just eked out a victory by the slimmest of margins over Senator Bernie Sanders, and this was how much of the race would develop as Clinton and Sanders played cat and mouse across the primary states over the next four months.

For all the hoopla that surrounds the Iowa caucuses, their record in predicting the eventual nominee is mixed. For the Democrats, no candidate has won their presidential nomination without first winning the Iowa caucuses since 1992 when Bill Clinton finished fourth. Al Gore (2000), John Kerry (2004), Barack Obama (2008) and Hillary Clinton (2016) all won in Iowa. But for the Republicans, John McCain (2008), Mitt Romney (2012) and Donald Trump (2016) lost in Iowa, and since 1980 only two Republican Iowa winners out of seven have gone on to become the nominee — Bob Dole (1996) and George W. Bush (2000).

It always used to be said that Iowa — along with New Hampshire, the host to the first primaries — was a small, unrepresentative state. But that is much less true now than used to be the case. In the last six years, Iowa's population has grown at a rate only slightly below the national average, and the state ranked 29th out of 50 in population growth rates between 2010 and 2016. Iowa has become something of a bellwether state in the general election — voting for the winning candidate in six of the last seven elections.

New Hampshire

For many years it was said that a candidate could not win the presidential nomination — or even the White House — without first winning the New Hampshire primary. However, this has been less true in recent elections. Bill Clinton (1992), George W. Bush (2000) and Barack Obama (2008) failed to win their party's New Hampshire primary, though Donald Trump did. But the amount of time the candidates spend in the state and the level of media attention combine to make the New Hampshire primary a critical contest to win.

In five of the last nine election cycles, New Hampshire primary voters have delivered a rebuff to the front-runner of the challenging party (see Table 6.8), including in four consecutive election cycles between 1992 and 2004. However, in the last three cycles, the New Hampshire voters merely confirmed the challenging party's front-runner. In the same nine elections, the New Hampshire primary confirmed the front-runner of the incumbent party on every occasion bar two — 2008 when Republican front-runner Rudy Giuliani lost to John McCain, and 2016 when Democrat front-runner Hillary Clinton lost to Bernie Sanders.

Table 6.8 Performance of the challenging party in the New Hampshire primary, 1984–2016

Year	Challenging party	Front-runner	New Hampshire primary winner
1984	Democratic	**Walter Mondale**	**Gary Hart**
1988	Democratic	Michael Dukakis	Michael Dukakis
1992	Democratic	**Bill Clinton**	**Paul Tsongas**
1996	Republican	**Bob Dole**	**Pat Buchanan**
2000	Republican	**George W. Bush**	**John McCain**
2004	Democratic	**Howard Dean**	**John Kerry**
2008	Democratic	Hillary Clinton	Hillary Clinton
2012	Republican	Mitt Romney	Mitt Romney
2016	Republican	Donald Trump	Donald Trump

What is really important at this early stage is matching expectations. Take 1992, for example. The numerical winners of the Democratic and Republican New Hampshire primaries were, respectively, Senator Paul Tsongas and President George H.W. Bush. But the moral victors were Bill Clinton and Pat Buchanan. Beset by serious allegations of womanising, drug taking and draft dodging in the Vietnam War, Clinton was not expected to do well. So when he came a respectable second with 25% of the vote, Clinton was able to claim that he was 'the comeback kid'. Although Pat Buchanan finished second in the Republican primary, the fact that he managed to gain 37% of the vote against an incumbent president was an impressive performance, and far better than had been expected.

Victory in Iowa or New Hampshire, or simply exceeding expectations as Barack Obama did in Iowa in 2008, brings three big bonuses: media coverage, money and a boost in the opinion polls. Following his Iowa victory in 2008, Barack Obama enjoyed pages of favourable stories in such weeklies as *Time* and *Newsweek*. He was the cover story of *Newsweek* on 14 January. Following his New Hampshire win, John McCain made it on to the front cover of *Time* on 4 February and the front cover of *Newsweek* the following week.

In February 2008, Barack Obama was able to raise over $50 million, at that time an all-time record for one month's fundraising, following his impressive showings in that year's early contests. Obama also saw his poll numbers shoot up in national polling. Whereas in December 2007, the *USA Today*/Gallup poll showed him trailing Hillary Clinton by 15 percentage points, the 4–6 January 2008 poll conducted immediately after his Iowa victory showed him level with Clinton. By the end of February, Obama had a 51–39% lead. Likewise, failing to live up to expectations can be devastating. The day after coming in fourth with just 7% of the vote in the Republican South Carolina primary in 2016, Jeb Bush withdrew from the race.

Incumbent presidents and the primaries

When an incumbent president is running for re-election, as Barack Obama did in 2012, the primaries for the president's party go on with little or no coverage at all. Some states don't even bother with a primary under such circumstances, and so for example in 2012 Virginia, South Carolina, Florida and New York were among the states that dispensed with a Democratic presidential primary. Incumbent presidents are usually re-nominated by their parties without any serious opposition. This was the case for Ronald Reagan in 1984, Bill Clinton in 1996, George W. Bush in 2004 and Barack Obama in 2012.

That said, President Obama was somewhat embarrassed during the 2012 Democratic primaries to receive less than 90% of the primary vote in 14 states, failing even to reach 60% in West Virginia (59%), Arkansas (58%), Kentucky (58%) and Oklahoma (57%). In West Virginia, the President's opponent, Keith Judd, won more than 40% of the vote despite the fact that he was at the time serving a lengthy prison sentence for extortion. Nonetheless, as Table 6.9 shows, President Obama's showing of 92% of the total Democratic primary vote was certainly in line with other incumbent presidents who went on to win in November. Indeed, it was a better performance than President Clinton's in 1996.

Table 6.9 Incumbent presidents' share of the primary vote, 1976–2012

President	Party	Year	Percentage of primary vote	Result of election
Ronald Reagan	Republican	1984	99	Won
George W. Bush	Republican	2004	98	Won
Barack Obama	Democratic	2012	92	Won
Bill Clinton	Democratic	1996	89	Won
George H.W. Bush	Republican	1992	72	Lost
Gerald Ford	Republican	1976	53	Lost
Jimmy Carter	Democratic	1980	51	Lost

But in the elections of 1976, 1980 and 1992, the incumbent president faced significant opposition from within his own party and therefore the primaries and caucuses were hard fought, even in the president's party. In 1976, Republican president Gerald Ford faced a strong challenge from the former governor of California Ronald Reagan. Four years later, President Jimmy Carter faced an equally stiff challenge from Senator Edward Kennedy in the Democratic primaries. Senator Kennedy won 12 state contests including the primaries in New York and California. And in 1992, President George H.W. Bush had to fight off a challenge from the conservative commentator Pat Buchanan in the

Key term

Incumbent A person who currently holds an office — in this case, an elective office. They can benefit from an advantage often called 'the incumbency effect'.

Republican primaries. Although Buchanan did not win any of the primaries and caucuses, his 37% in the New Hampshire primary was a great embarrassment for President Bush, and Buchanan went on to win more than a quarter of the vote in a dozen states.

It is not coincidental that, although all these three presidents saw off their primary challengers, they all went on to lose in the general election. A strong primary challenge for the president makes him damaged goods even before he faces his real opponent in the general election. What is more, criticism made of the president from within his own party in the primaries is often recycled as damaging campaign material by his opponent later in the year. As Robin Toner wrote in *The New York Times* in February 1992 of Buchanan's criticism of President Bush in that year's Republican primaries, 'down the road, Mr Bush will confront a Democratic Party that has now been given a road map of his vulnerabilities' by Mr Buchanan. And that's exactly what happened. As a parody of President Bush's broken pledge not to raise taxes — 'Read my lips: no new taxes' — Buchanan had used the slogan, 'Read our lips: no second term.' Needless to say, this became a favourite with the campaigns of Bill Clinton and Ross Perot in the autumn of 1992. This is why it is so important for an incumbent president to avoid any significant challenge in the primaries.

Voter turnout in primaries

There is no doubt that since the McGovern–Fraser reforms of the nomination process in the late 1960s (see below), participation in presidential primaries has greatly increased. Partly this has been due to the simple fact that more states hold primaries. In 1968, the last nomination cycle under the pre-reform system, just 12 million people participated in the 17 Democratic and 16 Republican presidential primaries, which represented around 11% of the voting-age population. In 2016, around 61 million people participated in the 37 Democratic and Republican primaries, which represented just under 29% of the voting-age population. Figure 6.1 shows the fluctuations that occurred in primary turnout in both parties during the last ten election cycles.

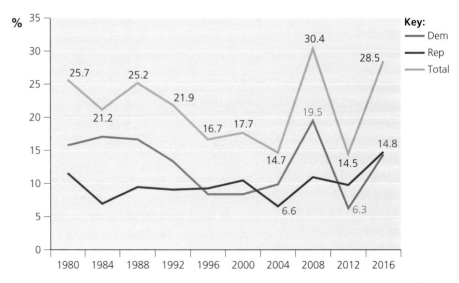

Source: Pew Research Center

Figure 6.1 Votes cast in Democratic and Republican primaries as a percentage of eligible voters in primary states, 1980–2016

Turnout also varies significantly from state to state, even within the same election cycle. So, for example, in 2016, while New Hampshire saw over 52% of eligible voters participate in the presidential primaries, turnout was just 18% in Louisiana. In 2016, 14 states saw over one-third of eligible voters participate in the primaries. The lowest turnouts were as usual in caucus states, with the Kansas caucuses attracting just 5.5% of the state's eligible voters. Even the Iowa caucuses — for all the media hoopla — attracted a turnout of just 15.7%.

Factors affecting turnout in primaries

Turnout is affected by four main factors:

- **Demography.** Turnout varies not just between states but also between demographic groups. Stephen Wayne (2001) found that the better-educated, the higher-income and the older members of the electorate are much more likely to vote in primaries than are younger, less educated and poorer people. In the North Carolina Republican primary in 2016, for example, over half of voters had a college degree, one-third earned more than $100,000 per year, and three-quarters of voters were 45 or older with only 6% being aged 24 or younger. There is also a widely held belief that primary voters are more ideologically extreme in their political beliefs than are general election voters, though the empirical evidence here is mixed. In the same North Carolina Republican primary, 37% described themselves as being 'very conservative'.

- **Type of primary.** Open primaries, which allow any registered voter to vote in either primary, are likely to attract a higher turnout than closed primaries in which only self-identified party supporters can vote. This is especially true when only one party has a competitive race, as was the case in 2012. Of the 11 states which held open primaries in the Republican contest in 2012, ten saw an increase in turnout on 2008 with turnout in Wisconsin up 92% and in Mississippi up 105%. On the other hand, of the 15 states which held closed primaries in the 2012 Republican contest, only two saw an increase in turnout. In Connecticut turnout was down 61% on 2008 and in New York it was down 71%.

Voters queue at a polling station in Fort Worth, Texas, on Super Tuesday 2016

- **How competitive the nomination race is.** This is also shown clearly in Figure 6.1. In 2008 and 2016, when both parties had a competitive nomination race, turnout was very significantly higher than in 2004 and 2012, when only one party had a competitive race and neither John Kerry for the Democrats in 2004 nor Mitt Romney for the Republicans inspired a great deal of voter enthusiasm.
- **Whether the nomination has been decided or not.** Primaries scheduled early in the nomination calendar will be more likely to attract higher turnout than those coming towards the end of the cycle when the identity of the nominee is already known. In 2008, the New York Republican primary was held on 5 February — that year's Super Tuesday — when the race for the Republican nomination was still undecided and a total of 642,894 votes were cast. In 2012, the New York Republican primary was held on 24 April, by which time most of the Republican candidates had dropped out of the race, leaving Mitt Romney as the presumed nominee. Romney won 62% of the vote but the turnout was just 189,599. This again accounts for the higher than usual primary turnout in 2016, with both parties' nomination contests running well into the second half of the primary calendar.

The increased importance of primaries

Nowadays, presidential primaries play an important role in the process of choosing presidential candidates. They really are the only route to becoming the presidential nominee of a major party. However, that was not always the case.

In the 1950s and 1960s, most states did not hold presidential primaries. The parties preferred to control candidate selection through a series of state party conventions. Whereas any registered voter can vote in a primary or caucus, only certain selected party members could participate in these state conventions. Here, in the so-called 'smoke-filled rooms', decisions were made largely by the party bosses — powerful state party leaders such as city mayors. It was they, and not the ordinary voters, who decided who would become the party's presidential candidate. The few primaries that were held were not decisive. In 1968, in neither party did the overall winner of the primaries get his party's presidential nomination (see Table 6.10).

Table 6.10 Presidential primary results, 1968

Candidate	Total popular vote in primaries (%)
Democratic Party	
Senator Eugene McCarthy	38.7
Senator Robert Kennedy	30.6
President Lyndon Johnson	5.1
Vice President Hubert Humphrey*	2.2
Republican Party	
Governor Ronald Reagan	37.9
Former Vice President Richard Nixon*	37.5
Governor Nelson Rockefeller	3.7

*Eventual nominees

This system was deemed undemocratic, elitist, non-participatory and potentially corrupt. It was reformed significantly at the instigation of the Democratic Party following the events at its 1968 national party convention. That convention chose Vice President Humphrey as the party's presidential candidate, despite the fact that he had not entered any primaries at all. The few votes he got were gained by voters writing in his name on the ballot paper — so-called 'write-in' votes.

Following Humphrey's loss to Richard Nixon in the general election that November, the Democrats established the **McGovern–Fraser Commission** to recommend reforms of the presidential nomination process. It was this commission that led to the significant increase in the number of states holding presidential primaries from 1972 onwards. Thus, the nomination process has changed dramatically over the past 40 years.

Strengths of the new nomination process

The new nomination system is certainly an improvement on what went before.

- **Increased participation.** There is an increased level of participation by ordinary voters. In 1968, the last year of the unreformed system, only 11.7 million Americans took part in the nomination process, or 11% of the voting-age population. By 1988, the figure was 35 million, or 21% of the voting-age population. And in 2016, 61 million Americans took part in the nomination process, or just short of 30% of the voting-age population.
- **Increased choice.** There is a significant increase in the choice of candidates. In 1968, there were just five presidential candidates to choose from — three Democrats and two Republicans. In 2016, there were 22 candidates — 17 Republicans and five Democrats.
- **Open to outsiders.** The process is opened up to outsiders — politicians who do not initially have a national reputation, such as Jimmy Carter (1976), Bill Clinton (1992) and Barack Obama (2008). And in 2016, the primaries were the only way Donald Trump could emerge as the presidential candidate — someone with no experience of elective office and who was opposed by most of the hierarchy of his own party.
- **A gruelling race.** The gruelling race through the primaries is seen by many as an appropriately demanding test for a demanding job. In 1992, Senator Paul Tsongas, who had fought back from cancer to run for the presidency, was seen to have a lighter schedule than his rivals. Although many admired Tsongas as a person and liked his policies, they saw in the primaries that he might not have the physical resilience to be president. In 2008, many suggested that Barack Obama was a stronger candidate after his gruelling primary battle with Hillary Clinton than he would have been had he won the nomination without a fight.

Weaknesses of the new nominating process

Writing in *The New York Times* in 2016, Frank Bruni commented on the presidential nominating process: 'American voters are displeased with the candidates they've been given and they're disengaged from the process that winnows the field.' Bruni continued:

> When you treat a campaign as if it were an athletic competition, you turn it into more of a blood sport than it already is. And when you breathlessly promote it the way you would a hit TV show's season finale, it becomes just another piece of theater. Neither approach encourages sober-minded engagement.

> **Key term**
>
> **McGovern–Fraser Commission** The commission established by the Democratic Party following the 1968 presidential election to recommend reforms to the presidential nomination process.

Widespread voter apathy and boredom

As we have already seen, although more people do participate in the nominating process than was the case 50 years ago, the turnout in the presidential primaries various enormously from one election cycle to another. In a year when an incumbent president is running for re-election and therefore only one party has a genuine nomination contest, turnout in the primaries is only around 17%. It was 17.5% in 1996 when President Clinton was running for re-election, and 17.2% in 2004 when George W. Bush was running for re-election. Even when no incumbent president was running in 2000, turnout was still only 19%.

Voters are unrepresentative of the voting-age population

Low turnout would not matter too much if those who did vote were a representative cross-section of the voting-age population — but there is some evidence to suggest that they are not. As we have seen, primary voters tend to be older, better educated, wealthier and maybe more ideological than the voting-age population as a whole. As a result, certain types of candidate — especially more ideological candidates — tend to do better in the nomination process than they should do. In 2012, Ron Paul — a libertarian Republican — won at least 10% of the vote in 40 primaries and caucuses, and in five of those contests his vote exceeded 25%. In the states which held caucuses, Paul's average vote was over 21%, whereas in states which held primaries his average vote was just 12%, showing that issues of unrepresentativeness are magnified in caucus states. The story was the same for Bernie Sanders in the Democratic primaries in 2016.

Voters cast their ballots at a polling station in Los Angeles, November 2016

Process is far too long

In 1960, Senator John Kennedy announced his candidacy for the presidency just 66 days before the first primary. Eight years later, former Vice President Richard Nixon entered the Republican race just 40 days before the New Hampshire primary. Then came the McGovern–Fraser reforms and everything changed. In 1972, the eventual Democratic nominee Senator George McGovern entered the race 414 days before the first primary. And it has been much the same ever since. The first formal candidate announcement for the 2016 nomination race was made by Republican Senator Ted Cruz on 23 March 2015, almost 11 months before voting in the primaries and caucuses began in February 2016.

Process is very expensive

This is something of a circular argument. Candidates need to raise a large amount of money, so they need to start their campaigns early. Campaigns are therefore much longer and much more expensive. With the onset of front loading, there is now little time to raise money once the primaries have started. It has to be done before they begin, so candidates start early. By the end of June 2016, Hillary Clinton had raised $275 million and her Democratic opponent Bernie Sanders had raised $235 million. In the Republican contest, both Donald Trump and Ted Cruz had raised just over $90 million each by that time.

Process is too dominated by the media

In the pre-reform era, decisions about candidates were made by a small group of professional politicians. They were people who knew the candidates. The role for the media was small. But in today's process, the decision-makers — ordinary voters — must rely on the media for information about the candidates. Some think the media ill-suited for this role. The media become the new 'king-makers', the replacements of the latter-day 'party bosses'. Loevy (1995) is critical of this. He writes:

> Our present nominating process has become a televised horse race focusing more on rival media consultants and advertising executives than on competing ideas, programmes, or even the character of the candidates...Popularity polls, slick spot ads and television coverage of the early primaries offer episodes and spectacles and the average citizen is hard pressed to distinguish significance from entertainment.

This has become increasingly the case with the introduction of the intra-party televised debates both before and during the primaries. Indeed, by 2016 it seemed that what happened in these pre-primary debates dictated the way the nomination cycle developed. Candidates' poll ratings seemed to rise and fall almost entirely dependent upon how they had performed in the most recent debate. Furthermore, the debates on the Republican side seemed to be totally devoid of any serious substance as candidates vied with each other to fight in the gutter.

Primaries can easily develop into bitter personal battles

In the 2000 Republican primaries, a McCain television commercial accused George W. Bush of not telling the truth, likening Bush to President Clinton. 'That's about as low as you can get,' shot back an angry Governor Bush. Both nomination battles in 2016 were bedevilled by personal bitterness, most notably on the Republican side where Donald Trump frequently traded insults with his fellow Republicans.

Lack of peer review

Back in the pre-reform era, presidential candidates were selected largely by other professional politicians. This constituted what is known as peer review — the judgement of one's colleagues or equals. They had a good idea of what qualities were required to be a successful president. Nowadays, however, candidates are chosen by ordinary voters, who cannot be expected to know much about presidential qualities, let alone whether this governor or that senator possesses any of them. As a result, primaries tend to test *campaigning* qualities rather than *presidential* qualities. Professors Cronin and Genovese (1998) draw attention to this state of affairs:

> What it takes to become president may not be what is needed to govern the nation. To win a presidential election takes ambition, money, luck and masterful public relations strategies. To govern a democracy requires much more. It requires the formation of a governing coalition and the ability to compromise and bargain. 'People who win primaries may become good presidents, but it ain't necessarily so,' wrote columnist David Broder.

In previous decades, Professor Jeane Kirkpatrick spoke of how professional politicians are 'uniquely qualified' to choose presidential candidates because 'they know the nature of the political job'. Professor Austin Ranney likewise bemoaned the fact that the parties are now 'the prizes, not the judges' in the nomination process. This was clearly the case with the selection of Donald Trump as the Republican candidate in 2016, when his victory in primaries was frequently described as a 'hostile takeover' of the Republican Party by the business tycoon. It is inconceivable that, had Trump been subject to serious peer review by Republican Party politicians, he would have survived as the party's candidate.

Super-delegates

In an effort to bring back some element of peer review into the selection process, the Democrats introduced super-delegates at their 1984 convention. They have had a presence at the Democratic convention ever since. Their role went unnoticed for 20 years, but in 2008 they played a significant role in the nomination of Barack Obama. Neither Obama nor his chief rival, Hillary Clinton, gained the required absolute majority of delegate votes through the primaries and caucuses. Obama was therefore dependent on the votes of super-delegates — Democrat members of Congress, governors and Democratic National Committee members — to give him the 2,210 delegate total required to win the nomination.

There was further controversy in 2016 when super-delegates from states where Bernie Sanders had won the primary nonetheless cast their votes for Hillary Clinton. More than that, many on the more radical wing of the Democratic Party claimed that the whole 2016 primary contest had been rigged by the early and overwhelming support of the super-delegates for Hillary Clinton.

Advantages and disadvantages

Primaries

Advantages
- Increased participation
- Increased choice of candidates
- Process opened up to outsiders
- A gruelling race for a gruelling job

Disadvantages
- Can lead to widespread voter apathy
- Voters are unrepresentative
- Process is too long, too expensive and too dominated by the media
- Can develop into bitter personal battles
- Lack of 'peer review'
- Role of super-delegates (Democrats)

How to improve the nomination process

No one is suggesting that the reforms introduced in the early 1970s have been completely useless, or that there should be a return to the era before the reforms were adopted, with party bosses in smoke-filled rooms, but there are a number of suggested reforms which some think would further improve the nomination process. The reforms are mostly concerned with the timing of primaries and attempts to increase the role of professional politicians without losing the democratic elements of the current system. Possible reforms include a move to regional primaries in which states in one region — the South, the Midwest and so on — would all vote on the same day. Another suggestion is to give greater weight to the votes of elected politicians — members of Congress, state governors and the like — at the party conventions where the presidential nominee is chosen.

David Atkins (2016) has suggested a five-point plan to reform the nomination process:

1 Abolish the caucuses and replace them with primaries, thereby increasing participation levels and making voters more representative of the electorate as a whole.
2 Do away with closed primaries, thereby encouraging voters not allied with one of the two major parties to participate.
3 Rotate the order of primaries to increase geographic and demographic diversity.
4 Tie super-delegate votes to the primary results in their respective states, thereby stopping them from potentially overturning the will of the actual voters.
5 Allow candidates to select their own delegates, thereby preventing the possibility we saw in 2016 when some Trump delegates failed to support the candidate at the convention.

Some might suggest that even much of this is tinkering and leaves a number of criticisms and weaknesses entirely untouched. After their experience in 2016, both parties might have a greater incentive to look long and hard at the nomination process, but whether they can set in motion any meaningful change is another matter.

Choosing the vice presidential candidates

In the past three decades, a new third stage in the election process has opened up — that of choosing the vice presidential candidates. Until 1980, the vice presidential candidate or 'running-mate' was always chosen and announced during the national party convention, the next major stage of the election cycle. Indeed, until 1956 the convention delegates actually chose the running-mate. But for 20 years — from 1960 to 1980 — the presidential candidate himself made the selection and merely announced it during the convention, traditionally on the third day of the proceedings, just before delivering his own acceptance speech.

But then, in 1984, the Democratic presidential candidate Walter Mondale broke with tradition and announced his selection of New York congresswoman Geraldine Ferraro as his running-mate four days before the Democratic convention gathered in San Francisco. From then on, each subsequent Democratic presidential nominee followed suit, announcing their vice presidential candidate ahead of the party's convention. Indeed, in 2004, presidential candidate John Kerry announced his selection of John Edwards almost three weeks before that year's Democratic convention.

It was not until 1996 that the Republicans jumped on the pre-convention announcement bandwagon when presidential candidate Bob Dole announced his choice of Jack Kemp, the former New York congressman and Bush housing secretary, as his running-mate the day before the Republican convention convened in San Diego. Since then, both party nominees have announced their vice presidential candidates ahead of their convention. In 2012, Romney's announcement that he had chosen Congressman Paul Ryan of Wisconsin to be his running-mate came 16 days before their convention gathered in Tampa, Florida. Both running-mates of 2016 — Republican Mike Pence and Democrat Tim Kaine — were publicly announced just three days before their respective national conventions.

Vice presidential candidates, 2016: Tim Kaine (Democrat) and Mike Pence (Republican)

Strategies for choosing vice presidential candidates

Balanced ticket

When choosing the vice presidential candidate, it is often said that a presidential candidate looks for a **balanced ticket**. 'Balance' might be looked for in terms of geographic region, political experience, age and ideology, maybe even gender, race and religion. The best recent example of a balanced ticket was probably in 2008 when Barack Obama chose as his vice presidential running-mate Senator Joe Biden of Delaware. Biden at 65 was a balance to Obama's youthful 47. Biden had served in the Senate for almost 36 years compared with Obama's less than 4 years. Biden also brought significant foreign policy expertise, having served as chairman of the Senate Foreign Relations Committee. Needless to say, there was also a balance of race.

Potential in government

But the balanced ticket strategy is not always the one used in making the choice of running-mate. The presidential candidate may think more long term and choose his running-mate not for what they might bring to the campaign but for what they might bring to the White House. In other words, the focus will be on governing rather than campaigning.

This was clearly the strategy adopted by Governor George W. Bush in 2000 in choosing Dick Cheney. Bush had no Washington experience at all and was generally thought to lack gravitas. His choice of Cheney as his running-mate was made with an eye to what he would need if he won the election and required someone to help him run not only the White House but the whole executive branch of the federal government. Cheney had served as both White House chief of staff to President Ford and secretary of defense to Bush's father. Between these two tours of duty in the executive branch, Cheney had been a member of Congress, rising to become the Republican whip in the House of Representatives — the number-two spot in the House Republican leadership team. Cheney also brought gravitas to the Republican ticket. It was probably this strategy of choosing for governing rather than campaigning that motivated Donald Trump to choose the Governor of Indiana and former congressman Mike Pence in 2016.

Party unity

A third possible strategy in vice presidential selection is to promote party unity, but this strategy is rarely adopted. One way of reuniting the party after the primaries is for the eventual nominee to choose one of his former rivals as his running-mate. This was the strategy adopted by Ronald Reagan in choosing George H.W. Bush in 1980. Bush had been Reagan's principal rival in the Republican primaries, and by choosing him as the number two on the ticket Reagan reunited the party after a somewhat bitter personal battle.

Had Barack Obama adopted this strategy in 2008, he would have chosen Hillary Clinton as his running-mate, and had Donald Trump or Hillary Clinton used it in 2016 they would have chosen, respectively, Ted Cruz and Bernie Sanders. The trouble is, however, that former party rivals are often quite incompatible politically and have often said such harsh things about each other during the primaries that it is somewhat implausible to think they could suddenly become partners on the ticket.

National party conventions

We now move to the fourth stage of the presidential election process — the holding of the national party conventions. The Democrats and Republicans — and some third parties — usually hold a **national party convention** during July, August or possibly early September of election year which usually lasts for three or four days. It is traditional for the challenging party to hold its convention first. In 2016, the Republicans met in Cleveland, Ohio, from 18 to 21 July, while the Democrats met in Philadelphia from 25 to 28 July. This was the earliest date for the Republican convention since 1980, and for the Democrats since 2004.

The venue is decided at least a year in advance by each party's National Committee (see Table 6.11). Conventions are attended by delegates, most of them chosen in the primaries and caucuses. The US — and the world's — media also turn up. Each day of a convention has a theme and a prime-time speaker.

Table 6.11 National party conventions, 1992–2016: venues and candidates

Year	Republican Party		Democratic Party	
	Venue	Candidate	Venue	Candidate
1992	Houston	George H.W. Bush	New York	Bill Clinton
1996	San Diego	Bob Dole	Chicago	Bill Clinton
2000	Philadelphia	George W. Bush	Los Angeles	Al Gore
2004	New York	George W. Bush	Boston	John Kerry
2008	Minneapolis	John McCain	Denver	Barack Obama
2012	Tampa	Mitt Romney	Charlotte	Barack Obama
2016	Cleveland	Donald Trump	Philadelphia	Hillary Clinton

Formal functions

The national party conventions were traditionally said to perform three formal functions.

Choosing the party's presidential candidate

In theory, the conventions choose the party's presidential candidate in a roll-call vote, in which each state's delegates announce which candidate they wish to vote for. In the pre-reform days, delegates came to the convention and made up their minds in the convention hall, but these days the vast majority of delegates arrive at the convention as 'committed delegates' — committed, that is, to vote for a particular candidate in the first ballot if that candidate is still in the race. As the number of committed delegates is known beforehand — because it is decided in each state primary or caucus — the result of the convention ballot to choose the presidential candidate is, these days, a foregone conclusion.

To win the presidential nomination, a candidate must receive an absolute majority of the delegate votes. For example, at the Republican convention in 2016, there were 2,472 delegates so Donald Trump required 1,237 votes to win his presidential nomination, while at that year's Democratic convention there were 4,763 delegates, meaning that Hillary Clinton needed 2,382 to win.

It would be more accurate to say that the convention confirms — rather than chooses — the party's presidential candidate. Not since the Republican convention of 1976 has the choice of the presidential candidate really been in any doubt at the opening of either party's convention. In that year, President Gerald Ford defeated the former Governor of California, Ronald Reagan, by 1,187 votes to 1,070 votes. Had 60 delegates switched from Ford to Reagan, Reagan would have won.

If no candidate gains an absolute majority on the first ballot, balloting continues until one candidate does in what is called a brokered convention. During these ballots, delegates become free agents, no longer committed to vote for a certain candidate. Furthermore, new candidates could enter at this stage. In the 16 elections between 1892 and 1952 there were eight occasions when either one or both parties required more than one ballot to choose their presidential candidate. In the next 16 elections — between 1956 and 2016 — there were no such occasions. Hardly surprising, therefore, that this function is now performed by the primaries, not the conventions, thus diminishing the importance of modern-day conventions. There was a moment during the 2016 Republican nomination contest when the media started to talk up the possibility of a brokered convention but once the candidacies of Marco Rubio, Ted Cruz and John Kasich fizzled out, Trump was left as the unassailable nominee, easily gaining victory on the first ballot.

Choosing the party's vice presidential candidate

As we have already seen, the convention's role in choosing the vice presidential candidate has also been lost in the last two decades. The convention is no longer even the forum for the announcement of the running-mate — the last convention at which a running-mate was announced was the Republican convention in 1988. So here is a second significant function which the modern-day convention has now lost.

> **Key term**
>
> **Brokered convention** A national party convention in which no candidate achieves sufficient delegates during the primaries and caucuses to have an absolute majority on the first ballot.

Deciding the party platform

The party platform is a document containing policies that the candidate intends to pursue if elected president (see Table 7.4 on page 301). It is put together by the Platform Committee under the direction of the party's National Committee. The Platform Committee holds hearings around the country during the first six months of the election year. In 2008, the Democrats held more than 1,600 'listening sessions' in communities across all 50 states, in which nearly 30,000 people from all walks of life participated. The Republicans invited visitors to their website to 'share your thoughts, participate in polls, and communicate directly with the policy-makers who will be shaping the party's agenda'.

The National Committee then agrees to the draft platform, which is presented to delegates at the national party convention. There may be debates at the convention on various parts of the platform — known as 'planks'. More recently, however, parties have sought to avoid heated debates on policy issues at their conventions. The media often portray such debates as evidence of a divided party.

In 2016, the most contentious platform debate at the Republican convention was on issues regarding sexuality. The Platform Committee proposed a platform with a 'staunchly conservative' view on homosexuality, same-sex marriage and transgender issues, calling for the Supreme Court ruling in *Obergefell* v *Hodges* (2015), which declared the rights of same-sex couples to be married a constitutional right, to be overturned. When the platform came to the convention floor, it was approved merely on a voice vote with only a few 'nays' audible.

Activity

From which 2016 party platform is each of these extracts taken?
- 'We believe that cooperation is better than conflict, unity is better than division, empowerment is better than resentment, and bridges are better than walls.'
- 'We believe in protecting every American's right to retire with dignity.'
- 'We believe in the Constitution as our founding document.'
- 'We believe we are stronger and safer when America brings the world together and leads with principle and purpose.'
- 'Americans have earned and deserve a strong and healthy economy.'

Meanwhile, the Democratic platform was the focus of an intense struggle between supporters of Hillary Clinton and Bernie Sanders. The 15-member Platform Committee was made up of six Clinton appointees and five Sanders appointees, with the remaining four appointed by the chair of the Democratic National Committee, Debbie Wasserman Schultz. Bernie Sanders' supporters announced that they were largely satisfied with the resulting document which, for example, expressed support for raising the federal minimum wage to $15 per hour and index-linking it to inflation — a top Sanders priority — as well as support for Wall Street reform, another top Sanders issue.

But given how little reference is made to the platform — either during the campaign, or during the administration of the winning candidate — one is left wondering what all the fuss is about. Furthermore, much of what is in party platforms is little more than support for motherhood, the American Dream and apple pie (see the above Activity). But there are significant differences on certain policies. For example, the 2016 Republican platform stated on the issue of abortion and the right to life:

> We assert the sanctity of human life and affirm that the unborn child has a fundamental right to life which cannot be infringed.

The Democratic platform, on the other hand, asserted that:

> We believe unequivocally, like the majority of Americans, that every woman should have access to quality reproductive health care services, including safe and legal abortion — regardless of where she lives, how much money she makes, or how she is insured.

No mistaking the differences there.

Informal functions

Given that all three of the formal functions of the national party conventions are now questionable, it might appear that there is little point in holding them. The importance of the conventions is in their informal, or hidden, functions.

Promoting party unity

This may be the most important function of all. The primaries can turn into bitter personal battles, and it is vital that internal party wounds are healed before the general election campaign begins. Divided parties are rarely winning parties. The convention gives a golden opportunity to heal the wounds.

At the 2016 Democratic convention, it was important that the party portrayed a united front following the sometimes bitter personal rivalry during the primaries between Hillary Clinton and Bernie Sanders. Certainly on the convention's opening day there was little evidence of party unity on display. The day's advertised theme of 'United Together' seemed something of a forlorn hope as Sanders' delegates booed every mention of Hillary Clinton's name, even during the opening Benediction. So when Bernie Sanders himself took to the podium, he had to tread a fine line between speaking for his own supporters and at the same time uniting behind the nominee. He closed his speech with this ringing endorsement:

> I have known Hillary Clinton for 25 years. I remember her as a great first lady who broke precedent in terms of the role that a first lady was supposed to play as she helped lead the fight for universal healthcare. I served with her in the United States Senate and know her as a fierce advocate for the rights of children. Hillary Clinton will make an outstanding president and I am proud to stand with her here tonight.

The Republican convention in 2016 was less successful as a promoter of party unity mainly because of the failure of a number of prominent Republicans to jump aboard the Trump bandwagon. Indeed, even up to the very opening of the convention, some of Trump's diehard opponents were still plotting ways to deny him the nomination. Some leading Republicans, including the party's 2012 presidential nominee Mitt Romney and former president George W. Bush, stayed away completely. As for Trump's former primary opponents, while some were fully supportive, others — such as Governor John Kasich of Ohio, in whose state the convention was being held — stayed away. And when Senator Ted Cruz, Trump's main rival in the primaries, took to the podium, his 20-minute speech failed to include an endorsement of the nominee, closing with a call for people merely to 'vote your conscience' rather than 'vote for Trump'. Trump's supporters were infuriated and booed Cruz off the stage.

Donald Trump and family (left) at the Republican national convention, July 2016

Enthusing the party faithful

In the general election campaign there is a lot of hard work to do. It is vital that the party faithful in all 50 states feel enthusiastic and committed as they head home to fight for their party and candidate during the nine-week campaign. There will be meetings to organise, phone calls to make, literature to distribute and voters to transport to and from the polls, and they will be at the forefront of the organisation. The convention provides an ideal opportunity to enthuse the party faithful through speeches as well as through appearances by the party's past champions and heroes. In 2016, an inspirational speech at the Democratic convention by First Lady Michelle Obama brought the delegates to their feet and clearly enthused the party faithful to return to their states and work for Hillary Clinton's election.

Enthusing the ordinary voters

It is equally important to enthuse the ordinary voters. As they are not present in the convention hall, this must be done through television. There is one golden opportunity to gain the attention of the ordinary voters during the convention and that is when the newly adopted presidential candidate delivers his acceptance speech — traditionally on the convention's final night.

Most voters will have paid little, if any, attention to the primaries. Now that the candidates have been selected and the policies finalised, voters may well tune in and take their first serious look at the party, its candidate and its policies. First impressions can be important, especially if the candidate is running for national office for the first time — as Donald Trump was doing in 2016.

Key term

Acceptance speech The nationally televised speech delivered by a party's presidential candidate in prime time on the final night of the national party convention.

259

Indeed, Trump was only the second person to win the Republican presidential nomination at the first attempt since Senator Barry Goldwater in 1964, the other being George W. Bush in 2000.

What was noteworthy about the two 2016 acceptance speeches was how dramatically different they were in both tone and temper. In his acceptance speech, Donald Trump presented a picture of a violent, threatened, humiliated country which he was going to 'make great again,' reinforced by the repetition of words and phrases which conjured up a dark and bleak picture of America. It played well to the party faithful in the hall, but one wondered at the time how appealing it was to more independent-minded voters watching on television. By contrast, Hillary Clinton's acceptance speech chorused a much more optimistic refrain of a nation that was 'stronger together', safe and self-confident.

Post-convention 'bounce'

Opinion polls register the immediate effect of the conventions, with instant polls showing what, if any, increase the candidate has enjoyed as a result of the speech. The increase in a candidate's poll rating as compared with the last pre-convention poll is referred to as 'bounce'. In the elections between 1980 and 2012, the average bounce for the candidate of the challenging party was just over 6 percentage points, and for the incumbent party candidate was 6 percentage points. As Table 6.12 shows, Donald Trump scored well-below-average bounce, registering just 1 percentage point — worse than all but two of the last nine challenging candidates.

Table 6.12 Post–convention 'bounce', 1980–2016

Year	Challenging party candidate	Bounce	Incumbent party candidate	Bounce
1980	Ronald Reagan (R)	+8	Jimmy Carter (D)	+10
1984	Walter Mondale (D)	+9	Ronald Reagan (R)	+4
1988	Michael Dukakis (D)	+7	George H.W. Bush (R)	+6
1992	Bill Clinton (D)	+16	George H.W. Bush (R)	+5
1996	Bob Dole (R)	+3	Bill Clinton (D)	+5
2000	George W. Bush (R)	+8	Al Gore (D)	+8
2004	John Kerry (D)	−1	George W. Bush (R)	+2
2008	Barack Obama (D)	+4	John McCain (R)	+6
2012	Mitt Romney (R)	−1	Barack Obama (D)	+3
2016	Donald Trump (R)	+1	Hillary Clinton (D)	+4.5

However, the importance of post-convention bounce can be exaggerated. In an analysis of the impact of political conventions since 1960, Professor Larry Sabato of the University of Virginia concluded that post-convention polls signal the eventual outcome of the election only about half the time. 'You could flip a coin and be about as predictive,' says Sabato. 'It's really surprising how quickly convention memories fade.' And 2016 was another case in point: Hillary Clinton undoubtedly won the battle of the conventions, yet went on to lose the election.

But it would be wrong to write off the national party conventions as useless: they still perform important functions. Not only are they a time for celebrating a glorious past, but they can also be important in identifying the rising stars of the future. In 2004, a little-known state senator from Illinois wowed the Democratic

Are national party conventions still important?

Yes

- The only time the national parties meet together
- Opportunity to promote party unity
- Opportunity to enthuse party members and activists
- Introduce presidential and vice presidential candidates
- Delivery of presidential candidate's acceptance speech
- Can lead to significant 'bounce' in the polls
- Many voters don't tune in to the campaign until the conventions start
- A significant number of voters make their decision about who to support during the conventions

No

- Presidential candidate now decided during the primaries, not at the convention
- Vice presidential candidate now announced before, instead of during, the convention
- Party platform mostly agreed before, rather than during, the convention
- Television coverage much reduced
- More balloons and hoopla than serious policies

convention with his impressive keynote address. His name was Barack Obama, and just four years later he returned to the convention as its presidential nominee.

National party conventions can still be of importance because millions of Americans who have shunned the campaign the whole year will often tune in for the key moments of the conventions. 'That's what makes the convention critically important,' stated Professor Cal Jillson in an interview with *National Journal* in August 2012. He went on: 'Even though the junkies have been riveted for a year, a good half of the public is just about to start paying attention.' As election scholar Stephen Wayne (2001) put it, the conventions 'may have become less newsworthy, but they are still important'.

The general election campaign

Now we come to the fifth of the seven stages in the process for electing the president. The previous four have all been concerned with candidate selection and confirmation. Up to this point the contest has been an *intra-party* contest. Now it becomes an *inter-party* contest as the presidential nominees of the two major parties and their respective running-mates slug it out during the nine-week campaign between the beginning of September and first week of November. The campaign centres around two major issues — campaign finance and the role of the televised debates.

Campaign finance

Mark Hanna, the wealthy late-nineteenth-century Republican political operative, once famously remarked that 'There are two things that are important in politics: the first thing is money, and I can't remember what the second one is.' Certainly Richard Nixon's re-election campaign in 1972 was run on this principle. The vast majority of the money that poured into his campaign funds came from so-called 'fat cats' — wealthy folk who donated huge sums of money. But when the campaign was discovered to have been mired in corruption, Congress set about changing the law on campaign finance.

Changing the rules

The Federal Election Campaign Act of 1974, a direct result of the Watergate scandal which brought down President Nixon, made a number of significant changes by limiting contributions that individuals, unions and corporations could give, hoping thereby to reduce candidates' reliance on a few, very wealthy donors and equalise the amount of money spent by both the major parties. The objectives of these reforms were praiseworthy and they were partly successful. But the law was found to have too many loopholes and was weakened by both the Supreme Court and Congress.

- In 1976, in *Buckley* v *Valeo*, the Supreme Court ruled that limitations on what individuals or political action committees could spend either supporting or opposing a candidate infringed First Amendment rights and were therefore unconstitutional.
- In 1979, Congress further weakened the law by allowing parties to raise money for such aspects as voter registration and get-out-the-vote drives as well as 'party-building' activities. This so-called soft money would soon be regarded by most observers as out of control, leading to the need for further reform.

Matching funds

Between 1976 and 2008, presidential campaigns were funded largely through what were known as matching funds — federal money administered by the newly formed Federal Election Commission (FEC) and given to presidential candidates who met certain criteria and agreed to certain limitations. In the 1976 presidential election, the FEC paid out over $72 million in matching funds, and that had risen to nearly $240 million by 2000. But then in 2008, Democrat nominee Barack Obama opted out of matching funds, which left him free from the fundraising and spending limitations imposed by the FEC, and as a result he was able to significantly outspend his Republican opponent John McCain, who took the $84 million in matching funds for his general election campaign. This was thought to be critical to Obama's win in November and set the pattern for subsequent election cycles.

In 2012, neither President Obama nor Governor Mitt Romney took matching funds — the first time that both major-party candidates had opted out of public financing for the whole election cycle. In 2014, President Obama signed legislation to end the public financing of the parties' national conventions. As a consequence of all of this, by 2016 the FEC's total payouts amounted to only just over $1 million. Only one major-party candidate — Democrat Martin O'Malley — signed up for matching funds, plus Green Party candidate Jill Stein. It would appear that the days of public funding of presidential campaigns are finished.

Bipartisan Campaign Reform Act (2002)

Further reform eventually came in 2002, mainly through the endeavours of two senators, Republican John McCain and Democrat Russell Feingold. This was the Bipartisan Campaign Reform Act, commonly called the McCain–Feingold law (see Box 6.1). The 2004 election saw the appearance of so-called '527 groups', named after the section of the US tax code under which they operate. '527s' such as America Coming Together and Swift Boat Veterans for Truth raised and spent millions of dollars, most of it donated by a few super-rich and largely unknown people.

PACs and Super PACs

Because of the limits on contributions to candidates and political parties, new organisations came to be formed that made independent expenditures on their own. These were known as political action committees (PACs) and spent

Key term

Soft money Money donated to political parties instead of candidates to avoid campaign finance limitations. Parties are allowed to spend the money on certain campaigning activities.

Key term

Political action committee A political committee that raises limited amounts of money and spends these contributions for the express purpose of electing or defeating candidates.

Bipartisan Campaign Reform Act (2002)

- National party committees were banned from raising or spending 'soft money'.
- Labour unions and corporations were forbidden from directly funding issue advertisements.
- The Act prohibited the use of union and corporate money to broadcast advertisements that mention a federal candidate within 60 days of a general election or 30 days of a primary.
- It increased individual limits on contributions to individual candidates or candidate committees to $2,300 (2007/08) — to be increased for inflation in each odd-numbered year (see Table 6.13).
- Contributions from foreign nationals were banned.
- The 'Stand By Your Ad' provision resulted in all campaign ads including a verbal endorsement by the candidate.

Key term

Super PAC A political committee that makes independent expenditures, but does not make contributions to candidates.

money for the express purpose of electing or defeating specific candidates. They either gave money to candidates they supported, or spent money against candidates whom they opposed. Most PACs represent business, labour groups, ideological groups, or single-issue groups.

Then, the landmark Supreme Court decision in *Citizens United* v *Federal Election Commission* (2010) granted corporate and labour organisations the same rights of political free speech as individuals, thereby giving such groups the right of unlimited independent political expenditure. This decision — plus another by the United States Court of Appeal, *Speechnow.org* v *Federal Election Commission* (2010) — led to the setting up of independent expenditure-only committees (IEOCs). Given the awkwardness of the acronym, they were soon dubbed **Super PACs**. These are political committees that may solicit and accept unlimited contributions from individuals, corporations, labour organisations or other political committees. They spend money to achieve their desired objectives but they are forbidden from making any direct contributions to federal candidates or parties — hence they are 'expenditure only'.

These Super PACs played a significant role in fundraising and spending in the 2012 presidential election. Their role received mixed reviews. Supporters see Super PACs as a positive consequence of deregulation that provides an important outlet for political speech, advocating independent calls for the election or defeat of specified candidates. Opponents, however, contend that they are yet another outlet for unlimited money in electoral politics that, while legally independent, are merely functional extensions of one or more campaigns.

Fundraising in 2016

Three Super PACs dominated the scene during the 2016 presidential election cycle. Priorities USA Action raised over $192 million on behalf of Hillary Clinton's campaign, which represented over 90% of all outside group money raised on behalf of her campaign. There were two Super PACs that raised big money in support of Donald Trump: Rebuilding America Now ($22.6 million) and Our Principles PAC ($19 million).

A new type of group known as Hybrid PACs (or Carey Committees) also played a significant role for the first time. Correct the Record, a Carey Committee in support of Hillary Clinton, raised nearly $10 million, and Great America PAC, a Carey Committee in support of Donald Trump, raised over $28 million.

Table 6.13 Individual contribution limit for 2015–16 federal election cycle

Recipients	Individual contribution limit
Candidate Committee	$2,700 per election
Political Action Committee (PAC)	$5,000 per year
State/District/Local Party Committee	$10,000 per year (combined)
National Party Committee	$33,400 per year

Source: Federal Election Commission

Table 6.14 Total cost of presidential elections, 2000–16 (real and inflation adjusted)

Year	Total cost of election	
	Real dollars	Inflation-adjusted dollars
2000	1,413,116,384	1,981,207,952
2004	1,910,230,862	2,441,408,000
2008	2,799,728,146	3,319,447,791
2012	2,621,415,792	2,756,541,454
2016	2,386,733,696	2,386,733,696

Source: Center for Responsive Politics

Figures 6.2 and 6.3 show the different ways Clinton and Trump went about their fundraising in 2016. Whereas 71% of Clinton's money came from individual donations, Trump raised less than half of his money from individuals. But among their individual donation receipts, Clinton raised almost three-quarters from big donors whereas Trump raised almost two-thirds from small donors. Table 6.14 shows that when adjusted for inflation, the 2016 election was estimated to be less expensive than the two previous election cycles.

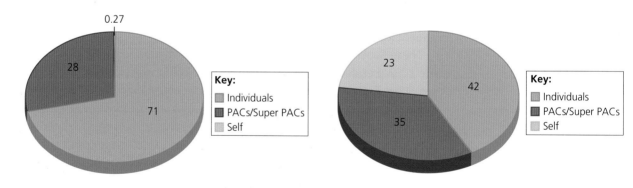

Source: Center for Responsive Politics

Figure 6.2 Sources of campaign receipts: Hillary Clinton, 2016 (%)

Source: Center for Responsive Politics

Figure 6.3 Sources of campaign receipts: Donald Trump, 2016 (%)

Where the money goes

So what do the candidates spend their money on? The summary answer is organisation, campaigning and media.

- **Organisation.** Organisation means staff, and in 2016 it was certainly believed that Trump's staff were well paid, certainly at the higher echelons. But organisation also means field offices — offices spread throughout the country, but mainly in swing states where grassroots contact with voters is critical. Here, Clinton always had the upper hand. It was almost as if Trump just did not think it was worth it. By October, at the height of the campaign, Clinton had 489 field offices to Trump's 178. And organisation means the get-out-the-vote (GOTV) operation on Election Day — the candidates' supporters going door to door and working the phones, encouraging those voters most likely to support their candidate to vote. Indeed, the GOTV operation lasts much longer these days with the significant increase in states allowing early voting. In 2016, 34 states would allow no-excuse early voting with only seven states allowing no early voting at all.

- **Campaigning.** Campaigning sees the candidates travelling from state to state, so the costs here are venue hire, travel, hotel accommodation and the like. One could also include the costs of internal polling as candidates try to use polls to target exactly where to spend their valuable campaigning time. When Trump's polls showed some significant movement towards him in Michigan and Wisconsin — states which earlier in the campaign had looked to be safely in Clinton's column — Trump headed for both states for last-minute campaigning. In Michigan, Trump would win by just over 10,000 votes out of nearly 4½ million.

- **Media.** Because Trump had raised far less money than Clinton, he had much less to spend on media throughout the campaign, relying more on free media coverage on television. But in the final weeks of the campaign, both candidates burned through their stockpiles of cash on media coverage. Trump suddenly increased his spending on television and cable ads. What may also have been decisive in these final days was the money Trump spent on social media advertising. This included negative ads targeted at states Clinton was expecting to win, such as Florida and North Carolina as well as 'Blue Wall' states in the rust belt, including Pennsylvania, Ohio and Michigan. In the end, Trump won in all five. By the time Clinton turned back to try to protect her one-time lead in these states, it was too late.

The role of television debates

History and development

Televised presidential debates between the major-party candidates have now become a traditional part of the campaign. Debates have varied in number and format since they were first used, but a pattern has now developed: three 90-minute debates between the two major parties' presidential candidates and one 90-minute debate between their vice presidential candidates, occurring usually between late September and mid-October.

The first debates were held in 1960, but it was another 16 years before televised debates were held again. In 1987, the non-partisan Commission on Presidential Debates was established, and it has sponsored and organised all the debates since 1988. Over the years, different debate formats have evolved. Initially, the candidates, standing behind podiums some distance from each other, were asked questions by one moderator. This developed into a panel of up to three members of the press who asked questions. A non-participatory audience had been introduced in 1976.

The first televised presidential debate, between John F. Kennedy and Richard Nixon, September 1960

Then, in 1992, what has become known as the Town Hall style of debate was tried for the second of the three debates. The candidates do not stand behind podiums but are seated on bar stools, facing an audience of undecided voters who put questions directly to the candidates. This format has been used for one of the three debates in each election cycle since 1992. The 2000 debates saw another new format — the roundtable discussion in which the candidates talked *with* each other rather than *at* each other or an audience, but this format was not used in the Trump–Clinton debates of 2016.

The only time a third-party candidate was allowed to participate was in 1992, when independent candidate Ross Perot took part in the three presidential debates and his running-mate, James Stockdale, joined the vice presidential debate. In 1980, President Carter refused to show up at a debate to which third-party candidate John Anderson had been invited, so there was one debate between the two challengers — John Anderson and Republican candidate Ronald Reagan. Carter showed up only for the debate to which just Reagan and he had been invited.

How important are they?

But for all the brouhaha surrounding the debates, do they actually make a difference in the campaign? True, they are the time when many Americans will give the candidates their closest attention, and they give the candidates one of their rare opportunities to talk unfiltered to the electorate. But there is only one clear example of a debate having any significant effect on the final result: the debate between Carter and Reagan in 1980, described in Box 6.2.

Box 6.2

Carter versus Reagan, 1980

In 1980 President Jimmy Carter and Governor Ronald Reagan met for their only head-to-head less than a week before Election Day. At the end of the debate, each candidate was given three minutes to make a closing statement. President Carter went first and made remarks that were well meaning but eminently forgettable. Then Governor Reagan closed:

> Next Tuesday all of you will go to the polls, will stand there in the polling place and make a decision. I think when you make that decision, it might be well if you ask yourself, are you better off than you were four years ago? Is it easier for you to buy things in the stores than it was four years ago? Is America as respected throughout the world as it was? Do you feel that our security is as safe, that we're as strong as we were four years ago?

Reagan had cleverly posed a series of questions to which he knew the majority of voters would answer in the negative. And with Election Day less than a week away, he managed to shape the way voters would make up their minds in these vital last days of the campaign. Support for President Carter fell away badly following the debate and on Election Day he won only six states, plus the District of Columbia, for a total of just 49 Electoral College votes.

In 2012, the first debate between President Barack Obama and Governor Mitt Romney temporarily turned the polls in favour of Romney. Up to this point in the campaign, the President had a comfortable and seemingly enduring lead in the polls. But then came the first debate. Romney was animated, coherent and quite aggressive. He seemed to be genuinely enjoying the moment and even looked presidential. The President looked thoroughly disengaged, bored and flat. He let many of Romney's claims go unchallenged and looked as if he was enduring rather than enjoying the occasion. Indeed, Joe Klein writing in his *Time* magazine column stated that this was 'one of the most inept performances by a president' in a televised debate.

The polls after the debate were of one mind: Romney was the overwhelming winner. The Gallup Poll found that of those who watched the debate, 72% thought that Romney had won with only 20% making Obama the winner. This 52 percentage-point margin was the largest in TV debate history. Within a week of the debate Romney was leading both the Gallup seven-day tracking poll and the poll-of-polls published by the Real Clear Politics website. This was the first time Romney had led in both. But Romney's poll advantage was short-lived, and President Obama swept to a comfortable victory on Election Day.

The importance of presidential debates was further brought into question in the 2016 debates between Donald Trump and Hillary Clinton (see Box 6.3). Most presidential debates, then, are not 'game-changing' events. Indeed, the vast majority of the over 60 hours of presidential and vice presidential debates broadcast between 1960 and 2016 passed into political obscurity within minutes of the debate's conclusion.

Donald Trump and Hillary Clinton meet in their second presidential debate, October 2016

Box 6.3

Trump versus Clinton, 2016

With the expectation of some volatile and dramatic exchanges, viewership of the presidential debates between Hillary Clinton and Donald Trump in 2016 reached record numbers. The 84 million who watched the first debate on television beat the previous record — the 80.6 million who watched the Carter–Reagan debate in 1980. But the difficulty in comparing those kinds of figures is twofold:

- The voting-age population has increased significantly in those nearly four decades.
- In 2016 there were many other media platforms on which to watch the debate, with an estimated 8 million watching on Facebook and 2 million on YouTube.

In terms of performance, by all impartial measures, Clinton out-performed Trump in all three debates — most dramatically in the first one. But for all that, Clinton's poll numbers moved only marginally and she still lost the election. When voters were asked in exit polls whether or not the debates were important to their vote, of the 64% who said they were important, Clinton bested Trump by only 4 percentage points: 50 to 46. That a candidate could perform so poorly in the debates yet come out the winner on Election Day should make future candidates question the debates' much-vaunted importance.

Debate rules of thumb

Four rules of thumb are worth noting about presidential debates, two of which were illustrated in the debates of 2016.

- **Style is often more important than substance.** What you say is not as important as how you say it and how you look. In the first Gore–Bush debate in 2000, Gore appeared overly made-up. He interrupted Bush frequently and, while Bush was answering, made audible sighs and rolled his eyes. Within days, Gore was being ridiculed on *Saturday Night Live* as a 'smarty pants'. Just after the start of the second — Town Hall style — debate, Gore strode across the stage to stand right next to Bush while the latter was still speaking. Bush merely gave him a quizzical glance. In the 2016 debates, Trump was widely panned for his abrasive tone, bordering on the plain rude. In the first debate, he repeatedly shouted into his microphone as Hillary Clinton was speaking, telling her she was 'wrong', 'no you're wrong,' 'you're wrong' (see Box 6.4). When in the second debate Hillary Clinton responded to a Trump answer by saying, 'It's just awfully good that someone with the temperament of Donald Trump is not in charge of the law of our country,' Trump immediately blurted out — 'Because you'd be in jail.' And in response to Clinton's proposal in the third debate about her proposed Social Security Trust Fund, Trump leant into his microphone and called out, 'Such a nasty woman!'

- **Verbal gaffes can be costly.** When, in 1976, President Ford mistakenly claimed that Poland was not under the control of the Soviet Union, it was an expensive error. When, in 1980, President Carter tried to personalise an answer by mentioning how he and his 10-year-old daughter Amy had talked about nuclear weapons, the cartoonists had a field day at Carter's expense. In 2000, Gore was caught out in the first debate, making some exaggerated claims to which the Bush campaign immediately drew attention after the debate. Perhaps the worst gaffe for Trump in 2016 was towards the close of the third debate when he repeatedly refused to say that he would respect the result whether he won or lost, ending the lengthy exchange with moderator Chris Wallace of Fox News with the retort: 'What I'm saying is that I will tell you at the time. I'll keep you in suspense. Okay?' But unlike gaffes by previous candidates, Trump's apparent gaffes seemed not to worry his supporters one jot. Indeed, they may have even enhanced his standing among them — another piece of evidence that he was not just 'another professional politician'.

- **Good sound bites are helpful.** Many voters do not watch the full debate but they do see the sound bite that the television networks clip out for their breakfast shows the next morning. In 1996 when debating Senator Dole, President Clinton was asked whether he thought 73-year-old Bob Dole was too old to be president. His answer provided a perfect sound bite: 'I don't think Senator Dole is too old to be president. It's the age of his ideas that I question.' In the final debate in 2008, John McCain got a good sound bite at Barack Obama's expense when Obama kept on trying to link McCain to the unpopular President George W. Bush. 'Senator, I am *not* President Bush,' commented John McCain. 'If you wanted to run against President Bush you should have run four years ago.' In the final debate in 2012, President Obama accused Governor Romney of favouring 'the foreign policy of the 1980s, the social policy of the 1950s, and the economic policy of the 1920s'.

Box 6.4

Extracts from the first presidential debate, 26 September 2016

CLINTON: You even suggested that you would try to negotiate down the national debt of the United States.

TRUMP: Wrong.

HOLT: Stop and Frisk was ruled unconstitutional in New York because it largely singled out black and Hispanic young men.

TRUMP: No, you're wrong.

CLINTON: Well, it's also fair to say, if we're going to talk about mayors, that under the current mayor [of New York City] crime has continued to drop, including murders. So there is —

TRUMP: You're wrong.

CLINTON: Well, I hope the fact checkers are turning up the volume and really working hard. Donald supported the invasion of Iraq.

TRUMP: Wrong.

CLINTON: That is absolutely proved over and over again.

TRUMP: Wrong.

CLINTON: He even said, you know, if there were nuclear war in East Asia well, you know, that's fine, have a good time folks.

TRUMP: Wrong.

- **Debates are potentially more difficult for incumbents than for challengers.** Incumbents have a record to defend and they have words spoken four years earlier that can be thrown back at them this time around. But not only do incumbents have a record to defend, they also nearly always go into the debates as the perceived front-runner, hence expectations of them are higher. We saw that this was a problem for President Obama in 2012. Also, the debate format itself is a great leveller. That the challenger appears on the same platform as the president of the United States and has equal air time brings the president down to the level of an ordinary politician. Furthermore, presidents often go into the debates somewhat rusty in their debate technique. Between June 2011 and February 2012, Governor Romney participated in 19 debates with his fellow Republican presidential candidates. In contrast, the last time President Obama had appeared in a televised debate was October 2008.

All the evidence suggests that debates often do more to confirm what the voters already feel about the candidates than to change many voters' minds. They might also help to convert passive supporters — those who will not turn out and vote on Election Day — into active voters.

The October surprise

The term October surprise has been used in American politics for some 40 years (see Box 6.5). Its first manifestation was during the closing stages of the 1972 presidential election between President Nixon and his Democratic challenger George McGovern. On 26 October — just 12 days before Election Day — Nixon's national security adviser Henry Kissinger announced that 'we believe that peace is at hand' in Vietnam. This completely pulled the rug from under McGovern's anti-war campaign and he went on to lose in 49 states.

Box 6.5

Previous 'October surprises'

1972 White House announcement of 'peace is at hand' in Vietnam. Advantage: President Nixon; disadvantage: George McGovern.

1980 President Carter's announcement of possible imminent release of 52 American hostages held in Iran for almost one year – but the news quickly turned out to be inaccurate. Advantage: Ronald Reagan; disadvantage: President Carter.

1992 Indictment of former secretary of defense Caspar Weinberger, a close colleague of George Bush during the Reagan administration, on matters relating to the Iran–Contra affair. Advantage: Bill Clinton; disadvantage: President Bush.

2000 Press disclosure that George W. Bush had paid a $150 fine for a drink-driving incident in 1976. Advantage: Al Gore; disadvantage: George W. Bush.

2012 Hurricane Sandy wreaked havoc in the mid-Atlantic and the Northeast — especially in New York and New York — on 29–30 October, causing a storm surge that resulted in serious flooding in New York City. Altogether, 24 states were affected by the hurricane and there were 71 deaths in nine states, including 49 in New York and 10 in New Jersey. This all occurred just one week before Election Day. Advantage: President Obama; disadvantage: Mitt Romney.

On 28 October 2016, just 11 days before Election Day, FBI Director Comey sent a letter to certain members of Congress stating that he was reopening his investigation into Hillary Clinton's State Department e-mails — an investigation which he had announced was closed in early July — because of possible new information that 'appeared to be pertinent' to the investigation. This saga revolved around the fact that Hillary Clinton had used a private e-mail server while secretary of state (2009–13) and that classified material had been passed through this server. The news of the reopened investigation was greeted with glee by the Trump team and with gloom by Hillary Clinton, who demanded that Comey, in effect, put up or shut up. Even President Obama did not sound too impressed with his FBI chief. 'We don't operate on innuendo,' said Obama in clear rebuke to Comey. 'We operate based on concrete decisions.'

And then just nine days after the first letter, there was a second Comey letter to Congress stating that nothing significant had been found after all and 'therefore we have not changed our conclusions that we expressed in July with respect to Secretary Clinton'. The whole episode reeked of ineptitude and bungling. But it did allow Donald Trump another round of allegations about 'crooked Hillary'. Certainly Clinton felt that this 'October surprise' had halted her chance to erode Trump's support in key swing states during the final week of the campaign.

Election Day

Finally, almost 18 months after the first candidacy announcement, through the invisible primary, the Iowa caucuses, the New Hampshire primary, Super Tuesday, the securing of the nomination, the choosing of running-mates, the national conventions and a nine-week campaign, Election Day arrives — the Tuesday after the first Monday in November when eligible voters may go to the polls to choose between the candidates.

But many Americans will have voted before Election Day with 34 states now permitting some form of early voting. This makes the last days of the campaign less significant than they used to be, as by these final days of the campaign around one-third of the voters who will vote will have already done so. In 2016 it was estimated that around 47 million voters took advantage of early voting procedures. This was a significant increase on the estimated 32 million early voters in 2012. Hence by the time the infamous Comey letter hit the headlines, a significant proportion of people had already voted.

Voter turnout has been a topic of some debate in recent elections. After peaking at a high of 67% of the voting-age population in the 1960 election, voter turnout dropped in each of the next five presidential elections to 54.7% in 1980. After some small increases, turnout fell to just 51.4% in 1996. The next three elections all registered increases in turnout, reaching 62.3% by 2008. But by 2016, the figure was back to around 54%.

The result of a presidential election is decided principally in the swing states. A large number of states will almost always vote for the Democratic candidate — Massachusetts, New York, California and Illinois, for example. Other states are nowadays solidly Republican — Texas, Kentucky, Kansas and South Carolina, for example. But there are a number of swing states, such as Ohio, Florida and Virginia, which will vote for the Democratic candidate in one election and then the Republican in another. Ohio has now voted for the winner in the last 14 presidential elections, stretching all the way back to 1964.

The incumbency factor

Eight of the last 11 presidential elections have featured an incumbent president seeking another term. One of those was 1976 when Gerald Ford stood for re-election, but Ford had arrived in the Oval Office through appointment rather than election. (He had been appointed vice president in 1973 when Vice President Spiro Agnew resigned; he was then appointed president in 1974 when President Richard Nixon resigned.) Ford lost narrowly to Jimmy Carter. Of the remaining seven re-election bids, five were successful and only two unsuccessful. This suggests that the power of incumbency is strong.

Putting this in a wider perspective, since 1796, 31 presidents have run for re-election. Of these, 22 (71%) of them have won and only 9 have lost. Trying to defeat an incumbent president is difficult, unless he fails to have the undivided support of his own party. The only three modern-day presidents to be defeated for re-election — Gerald Ford (1976), Jimmy Carter (1980) and George H.W. Bush (1992) — were all defeated having already faced significant opposition in the primaries earlier in the year. Gerald Ford was challenged in the primaries by Governor Ronald Reagan, Jimmy Carter by Senator Edward Kennedy, and George H.W. Bush by conservative commentator Pat Buchanan. All three presidents were damaged goods by the time they faced their general election opponent. In contrast, most incumbent presidents — such as Bill Clinton (1996), George W. Bush (2004) and Barack Obama (2012) — can conserve their time, energy and money during the primaries while the candidates of the challenging party wear themselves out and expend vast sums of money just winning the nomination.

It is also significant that all three presidents who lost their re-election bids had presided over generally failing economies in the United States. Carter added further to his problems with a foreign policy debacle when 52 Americans were held hostage in Iran for the final year of his presidency.

Thus Americans' default position tends to be to re-elect incumbent presidents and candidates from the challenging party know they usually face an uphill battle. This produces a knock-on effect of discouraging better-known and maybe stronger candidates from throwing their hats into the ring when an incumbent is standing for the other party. Weaker candidates with less chance of winning attract less money — and so the whole thing becomes something of a self-fulfilling prophecy.

Finally, it is worth noting that only twice since the American Civil War has a president who has completed two full terms been followed by a president of the same party by election — in 1877 when Republican Ulysses Grant (1869–77) was followed by Republican Rutherford Hayes, and in 1989 when Republican Ronald Reagan (1981–89) was followed by Republican George H.W. Bush. Hillary Clinton should have known she was battling the odds in 2016!

> ### Activity
>
> - Go to the website www.americanhistoryusa.com/campaign-trail.
> - Now follow the on-screen instructions to simulate the 2016 presidential election.

The Electoral College

Key term

Electoral College The institution established by the Founding Fathers to indirectly elect the president and vice president. The Electors cast their ballots in their state capitals.

However, the president is not elected by the popular vote but through the **Electoral College**. This is the final stage of the process. In the vast majority of elections, the candidate who wins the popular vote also wins in the Electoral College. But in 2016, though Hillary Clinton won the popular vote by almost 3 million votes, Donald Trump won in the Electoral College (see Table 6.15); hence he rather than Hillary Clinton became president. But more of that anon. First of all we need to understand how the Electoral College system works.

Table 6.15 Result of the 2016 presidential election

Candidate	Popular vote	Popular vote percentage	Electoral College votes
Donald Trump	62,984,825	46.1	304
Hillary Clinton	65,853,516	48.2	227

How it works

In the Electoral College, each state is awarded a certain number of Electoral College votes. This number is equal to that state's representation in Congress — the number of Senators (2 for every state) plus the number of Representatives. Thus in 2012, California had 55 (2 + 53) while Wyoming had just 3 (2 + 1). There are 538 Electoral College votes. To win the presidency, a candidate must win an absolute majority, which is 270.

The popular votes for each candidate are counted in each state. In all but two states, whichever candidate wins the most popular votes receives all the Electoral College votes of that state — the so-called 'winner-take-all' rule. This 'rule', however, is not in the Constitution. It is purely a convention that developed during the nineteenth century in most states. The exceptions are Maine and Nebraska.

The Electoral College never meets together. Its members — called Electors — meet in their respective state capitals on the Monday after the second Wednesday in December. They then send their results to the vice president of the United States in Washington DC. The vice president formally counts the Electoral College votes and announces the result to a joint session of Congress in early January. Thus, on 6 January 2001, Vice President Al Gore had the dubious privilege of announcing his own defeat at the hands of Governor George W. Bush of Texas by 271 Electoral College votes to 266.

What if no candidate wins an absolute majority of Electoral College votes? This could happen either if a 269–269 split occurred between two candidates, or if more than two candidates won Electoral College votes. The former situation almost occurred in 2000. The latter situation might have occurred in 1968 when third-party candidate George Wallace won five states with 45 Electoral College votes. Under such circumstances:

- The president would be elected by the House of Representatives from the three presidential candidates with the most Electoral College votes. Each state would have one vote. The winner would require an absolute majority — 26 of the 50 votes. Balloting would continue until one candidate emerged as the winner.
- The vice president would be elected by the Senate from the two vice presidential candidates with the most Electoral College votes. Each senator would have a vote. The winner would require an absolute majority — 51 of the 100 votes. Again, balloting would continue until this occurred.

Only twice has the Electoral College failed to come up with a winner and the election been thrown to Congress — in 1800 and 1824.

Strengths of the Electoral College

It is not difficult to come up with criticisms of the Electoral College, but the Founding Fathers invented the system because of some presumed strengths, two of which are still of some relevance today.

It preserves the voice of the small-population states

The small-population states, as in 1787, still worry that, were the Electoral College to be abolished, the votes of their inhabitants would become almost worthless, swept aside by the size of such states as California, Texas, New York and Florida. If this was a concern in 1787, it should be even more of a concern now. In the first presidential election, held in 1788, of the 13 states that took part, the smallest had 3 Electoral College votes while the largest — Virginia — had 12: that is, four times as many. But by 2016, California had 55 Electoral College votes — more than 18 times as many as states such as Wyoming and Alaska with just 3.

It tends to promote a two-horse race

This is important in an election for the president, who is both chief executive and head of state — a symbol of national unity. In such a two-horse race, the winner will therefore tend to receive more than 50% of the popular vote, a definite aid to uniting the nation. In 26 of the 39 elections held between 1864 and 2016 — that is, two-thirds — the winner gained more than 50% of the popular vote. But four of the 13 elections in which this did not occur were 1992, 1996, 2000 and 2016. In other words, in only three of the last seven elections has the president won with more than half the votes.

Weaknesses of the Electoral College

Many critics see the Electoral College as beset with problems and potential malfunctions. Here are five criticisms made of it.

Small states are over-represented

This has already been touched upon in the discussion of strengths, but what some perceive as a strength, others see as a weakness. By 2016, California had 55 Electoral College votes representing its 39.2 million inhabitants. Wyoming had 3 votes representing its just over half-a-million inhabitants. Thus California receives one Electoral College vote for every 713,000 people. Wyoming receives one Electoral College vote for every 195,000 people (see Figure 6.4).

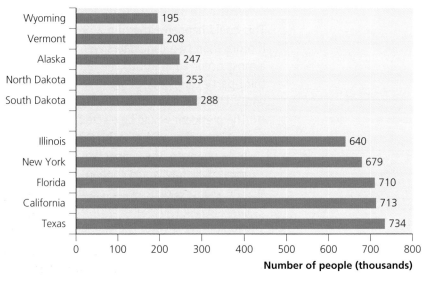

Figure 6.4 Number of people per Electoral College vote: five smallest and five largest states (thousands)

Winner-take-all system distorts the result

In 1996, Bill Clinton won only 49% of the popular vote, yet he won just over 70% of the Electoral College votes (see Figure 6.5). In these seven elections between 1992 and 2016, the Electoral College could be said to have seriously distorted the result on five occasions. What is more, on two occasions — in 2000 and 2016 — the candidate who won the popular vote lost the Electoral College vote. In 2000, Democrat Al Gore won 48.4% of the popular vote to George W. Bush's 48%. But in the Electoral College, Bush came out the winner by 271 votes to 266. In 2016, Democrat Hillary Clinton beat Republican Donald Trump by 48.2% to 46.1% — winning nearly 3 million more votes than Trump. But Trump still managed a comfortable win in the Electoral College. The fact that Clinton, with 3 million more votes, would fall over 70 votes behind Trump in the Electoral College was regarded by many as a scandal. This problem had occurred twice before in the nation's history — in 1876 and 1888.

Unfair to national third parties

In 1980, Congressman John Anderson, running as an independent, won 6.6% of the popular vote. In 1992, another independent candidate, Ross Perot, won 18.9% of the popular vote. In 1996, as the Reform Party candidate, Perot won 8.5% of the popular vote. In 2000, Green Party candidate Ralph Nader won over 3 million votes. But none of these candidates won a single Electoral College vote. Take Perot in 1992: in only one state — Mississippi — did he fail to gain at least 10% of the popular vote, yet in only one state — Maine — did he succeed in getting over 30% of the popular vote. Regional third-party candidates fare better. In 1968, American Independent Party candidate George Wallace won 13.5% of the popular vote — considerably less than Perot's 1992 figure — yet, because his support was concentrated in the Deep South, he managed to win five states with 45 Electoral College votes.

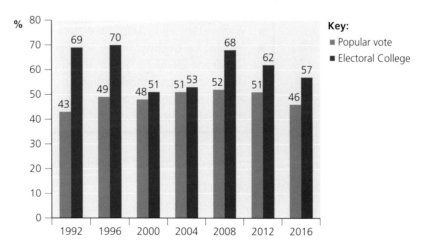

Figure 6.5 Distortion of victory by the Electoral College, 1992–2016

Key term

Rogue (or faithless) Elector
An Elector in the Electoral College who casts their ballot for a candidate other than the one who won the popular vote in their state.

'Rogue' Electors

Many states have state laws requiring Electors to cast their ballots for the state-wide popular vote winner, but others do not, leaving open the possibility that so-called rogue or faithless Electors will cast their ballots some other way. Seven of the 13 presidential elections since 1968 have seen this occur. But on six of those occasions, there was only one Elector who voted for a candidate other than the one for which they should have voted.

In 2016, however, there were multiple rogue Electoral College votes. Indeed, there could have been more as three Clinton Electors in Colorado were dismissed and replaced when they refused to vote for the designated candidate. As it was, five Clinton Electors and two Trump Electors did not vote for their designated candidates. As a result, former secretary of state Colin Powell picked up three votes with one each going to Ohio governor John Kasich, the former Republican congressman and perennial presidential candidate Ron Paul, Senator Bernie Sanders, and the Native American activist from South Dakota Faith Spotted Eagle. As a result, the final tally in the Electoral College was 304 votes for Trump to 227 votes for Clinton — rather than 306–232.

President and vice president of different parties

At the beginning of the Republic, when political parties in the way they are understood today did not truly exist, it did not matter if the president and vice president were of different parties, as a result of the system used in the case of Electoral College deadlock. In 2000, however, it was certainly possible that the House of Representatives could have chosen Republican George W. Bush as president and the Senate could have chosen Democrat Joseph Lieberman as vice president.

Advantages and disadvantages

The Electoral College

Advantages

- Preserves the voice of the small-population states
- Usually promotes a two-horse race with the winner receiving more than 50% of the popular vote

Disadvantages

- Small-population states are over-represented
- Winner-take-all system can distort the result
- Possible for the loser of the popular vote to win in the Electoral College (2000 and 2016)
- Unfair to national third parties
- 'Rogue' or 'faithless' Electors
- Potential problem if Electoral College deadlocked

Possible reforms of the Electoral College

Direct election

When in 2016 the Electoral College — for the second time in just five elections — handed the keys of the White House to the candidate who lost the popular vote, there were renewed calls for the institution to be scrapped altogether. 'Time to End the Electoral College' was the headline of the editorial in *The New York Times* on 19 December 2016, the day when the Electors cast their ballots for Trump and Clinton. 'Americans would prefer to elect the president by direct popular vote, not filtered through the antiquated mechanism of the Electoral College,' stated the paper's editorial board. They reminded their readers that when *The Washington Post* commissioned a national poll on the matter in 2007, 72% supported a popular vote election with only 23% opposed.

But the direct election plan has problems of its own. With the need to gain an absolute majority gone, there would clearly be a multiplicity of candidates making it possible — indeed, even likely — that the president would be elected with well below 50% of the vote, possibly less than 40%. Is this what Americans want for their president? The only way round that would be to have a runoff election between the top two candidates, but do Americans want to add yet another stage to this already seemingly interminable process?

There is a practical problem too. Only a constitutional amendment could bring about this particular reform. With the small-population states wedded to the current system, the requirement of a two-thirds majority in both houses of Congress, and equal representation of large- and small-population states in the Senate, success is highly unlikely.

Congressional district system

The most widely advocated reform would be for the other 48 states to adopt the system used in Maine and Nebraska, which involves awarding one Electoral College vote to a candidate for each congressional district (the constituencies used to elect members of the House of Representatives) that they win and two electoral votes to the candidate who is the state-wide winner. In 2008, Nebraska did split its five Electoral College votes. Although John McCain won the state, Barack Obama won the presidential vote in the second congressional district, thus winning one Electoral College vote, while McCain won the other four — one each for winning the other districts, and two for winning the state-wide vote. Then in 2016, Maine split its four Electoral College votes. Hillary Clinton won the state by 48% to 45, but Donald Trump won the presidential vote in the second congressional district by 52% to 41, thereby winning one Electoral College vote with Clinton winning the other three.

Table 6.16 Winner-take-all system and congressional district systems compared, 1992–2016

Year	Candidates	Winner-take-all system	Congressional district system
1992	Bill Clinton (D)	370	322
	George H.W. Bush (R)	168	216
	Ross Perot (I)	0	0
1996	Bill Clinton (D)	379	345
	Bob Dole (R)	159	193
	Ross Perot (Reform)	0	0
2000	George W. Bush (R)	271	288
	Al Gore (D)	267	250
2004	George W. Bush (R)	286	317
	John Kerry (D)	252	221
2008	Barack Obama (D)	365	301
	John McCain (R)	173	237
2012	Barack Obama (D)	332	264
	Mitt Romney (D)	206	274
2016	Donald Trump (R)	306	290
	Hillary Clinton (D)	232	248

But, as Table 6.16 shows, this reform would lead to the results being only marginally different in most of the last seven elections. Indeed, in 2000 the congressional district system would have produced a *less* proportionate result, with Gore losing in the Electoral College by 38 votes rather than by 4. Neither would it have helped Ross Perot in either 1992 or 1996. In 2004 it would have exaggerated Bush's winning margin significantly. But the biggest problem thrown up by this data is that, had the congressional district system been used in 2012, Mitt Romney would have won the election despite having lost to President Obama by 5 million votes. This is because Obama was winning fewer districts but by huge margins, while Romney won more districts but by small margins. So, for example, in Ohio — where Obama beat Romney by 51% to 48 — Romney won 12 of the state's congressional districts to Obama's 4. Similarly, in Pennsylvania where Obama won state-wide by 52% to 46, Romney won 13 districts to Obama's 5. It seems highly improbable that America would swap one flawed system for another.

Proportional system

Another possible reform would be to allocate Electoral College votes in each state proportional to the popular vote in that state. There would then be a more equable allocation of Electoral College votes. This would render the Electors themselves unnecessary, as the result would be determined by a mathematical computation rather than Electors casting ballots. In reality, therefore, this system would also abolish the Electoral College as such. True, such a system would be much fairer to national third parties, but then it would also encourage more voters to vote for such parties, thereby making it more likely that no candidate would gain an absolute majority of Electoral College votes and throwing the election into Congress or, if that provision were eliminated, requiring a run-off election between the top two candidates, as for the direct election system.

So, for all its flaws, there is little or no agreement on how to reform or replace the Electoral College, and no realistic way to accomplish it either.

Thus, after more than a year of candidate declarations, primaries and caucuses, conventions, campaigns, debates, the raising and spending of thousands of millions of dollars, and millions of votes cast, the presidential inauguration is finally held on the west steps of the Capitol at noon on 20 January of the year following the election and another election cycle is complete — only for the next one to start before Americans have hardly caught their breath.

Activity

- Go to Google's homepage.
- Search for 'Electoral College video for students'.
- Click 'Videos'.
- Then select the video from *The Guardian* website (www.theguardian.com).
- Click on the link.
- Then click on the play button to watch a three-minute video on how the Electoral College works.
- As this video was made just before the 2016 election, find out how the swing states in the video voted in 2016.

Congressional elections

Thus far we have studied in detail the race for the presidency. But there are other elections in the United States of which we need to be aware. Both houses of Congress — the House of Representatives and the Senate — are now directly elected. It was not always the case. Until the passage of the Seventeenth Amendment in 1913, the Senate was indirectly elected — senators were appointed by the state legislatures. But from 1914, there have been direct elections to the Senate, as well as to the House of Representatives. Congressional elections are held every two years and on alternate occasions these elections coincide with the presidential election. So, for example, in 2016, there was both a presidential election and congressional elections.

Timing of congressional elections

Members of the House of Representatives serve two-year terms while senators serve six-year terms, but one-third of senators are up for re-election every two years. Thus, in every two-year cycle of congressional elections, the whole of the House of Representatives and one-third of the Senate are up for re-election. These elections, like those for the president, are held on the Tuesday after the first Monday in November. In years divisible by 4 (2012, 2016, etc.), congressional elections coincide with the presidential election. Elections in the years between presidential elections (2014, 2018, etc.) are therefore called **midterm elections**, as they fall midway through the president's four-year term of office.

> **Key term**
>
> **Midterm elections** Elections for the whole of the House of Representatives and one-third of the Senate that occur midway through a president's four-year term.

Constitutional requirements

The Constitution lays down certain requirements regarding age, citizenship and residency for those wishing to be elected to the House and the Senate. To be a member of the House one must be at least 25 years old, have been an American citizen for at least seven years, and be a resident of the state that they represent. To be a senator, one must be at least 30 years old, have been an American citizen for at least nine years, and be a resident of the state that they represent. In terms of residency, many large states have passed a state law requiring House members to be resident in the congressional district that they represent. This is known as the **locality rule**.

> **Key term**
>
> **Locality rule** A state law that requires members of the House of Representatives to be resident in the congressional district they represent.

The nomination process

The first task for someone wishing to gain a seat in Congress is to secure the nomination of one of the two major parties. Third-party candidates very rarely win seats in Congress. Securing the nomination might mean running in a congressional primary. These differ from presidential primaries in that the winner of the congressional primary automatically becomes that party's candidate in the general election. Congressional primaries are held in the months prior to the November election, usually between May and September.

Sometimes even an incumbent senator or representative might be challenged for the nomination in the upcoming election and therefore will have to contest a primary. For incumbent senators, defeat in a primary is highly unusual. In the elections between 1982 and 2016, only eight incumbent senators were defeated in primaries, and one of those was a senator who had been appointed to fill the vacancy of a retired senator and another was a senator who had switched parties. Two others — Democrat Joe Lieberman of Connecticut in 2006 and Republican Lisa Murkowski of Alaska

Republican Lisa Murkowski was re-elected to the Senate in 2010 depsite losing in the primary

in 2010 — managed to get re-elected despite their defeat in the primary, Lieberman as an independent and Murkowski as a write-in candidate. In 2010, Republican senator Bob Bennett of Utah was denied a place on the Republican primary ballot by his state party convention. The only recent senator to be defeated in a primary was Republican Richard Lugar of Indiana in 2012.

During the same 34-year period, 72 incumbent House members were defeated in primaries, including 13 in 2012. But considering that every two years around 400 House members seek re-election, an average of only four or five primary defeats per election cycle is not high. In 2012, of the 13 House incumbents who lost in the primaries, eight were defeated by fellow incumbents in primaries in which two incumbents were running. This often happens in those election cycles which come immediately after the ten-yearly census and the resulting reapportionment of congressional districts in many states. Of the five who lost to challengers in 2012, two were running in districts which had been substantially redrawn to their disadvantage while another had been embroiled in controversy for some time. Republican John Sullivan of Oklahoma suffered the only genuine upset of the 2012 House primaries.

Trends in congressional elections

Because congressional elections coincide in every alternate cycle with the presidential election — people may be voting at the same time for president, senator, representative — it is difficult to separate voting intentions in these elections from the votes that people cast for the presidency. As a consequence, most analysis of congressional elections comes from the midterm elections, in which voters are not casting a presidential ballot. Five trends are discernible when it comes to congressional elections.

The power of incumbency is significant

As Figure 6.6 clearly shows, there is evidence of strong support for incumbents in congressional elections, especially in the House. The early 1990s showed a temporary blip in this trend with the rise — but almost as quick fall — of the term limits movement and a 'throw the bums out' mentality among many voters. But even at this time, although Congress as an institution and members of Congress in general were held in low esteem, voters often thought that their own senator or representative was doing a good job and deserved to be re-elected. It was as if the voters' slogan was: 'Throw the bums out — but my member of Congress isn't a bum!'

But by the turn of the century, high rates of re-election were back. In the nine election cycles between 2000 and 2016, re-election rates in the House ranged from a low of 85.4% in 2010 to a high of 97.8% in 2000, while in the Senate they ranged from a low of 79.3% in 2006 to a high of 96.1% in 2004. Thus most members of Congress leave by voluntary retirement rather

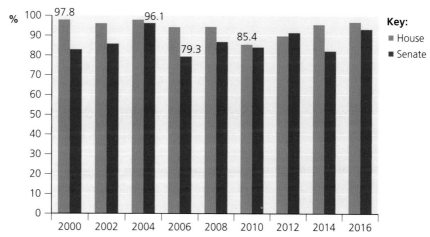

Figure 6.6 House and Senate re-election rates, 2000–16

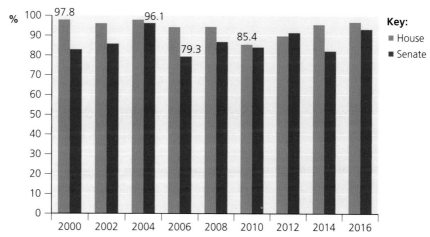

Sources: Center for Responsive Politics, www.opensecrets.org

Figure 6.7 Average raised by congressional candidates: incumbents v challengers, 2016

than by electoral defeat. During this 16-year period, 320 House members and 62 senators left voluntarily — either to seek election to another office or to retire.

The reasons for such high rates of re-election in Congress are mostly linked with the advantages of incumbency:

- As an incumbent, one has the ability to provide constituency services — meaning anything from helping an individual constituent to receive the correct level of service from a federal department or agency, to getting legislation passed that brings federal funds and benefits to the state or district.
- One also has high levels of name recognition in any election compared with a challenger, plus levels of seniority in Congress that brings with it membership — and maybe chairmanship — of prestigious committees and sub-committees, or of ones that are related to constituency interests. To replace an incumbent in Congress means losing the seniority that the member will have gained over their years on Capitol Hill — seniority which may bring significant benefits to the folks back home.
- Most incumbents have a huge advantage in fundraising compared with challengers. Figure 6.7 shows that incumbent Senate candidates raised over seven times as much as their challengers during the 2016 election cycle, and House incumbents out-raised their challengers eight-fold.

The coattails effect is limited

It is sometimes possible to discern a **coattails effect**. A coattails effect occurs when a strong candidate for a party at the top of the ticket — for president, or in midterm elections for state governor — can help other party candidates get elected at the same time. The picture is of these other candidates riding into office clutching the coattails of the presidential or gubernatorial candidate. Few modern-day presidents have enjoyed much in the way of a coattails effect since 1980 when Republican Ronald Reagan helped his party gain 33 seats in the House and a staggering 12 seats in the Senate, when no fewer than nine incumbent Democrat senators were defeated. Bill Clinton, George W. Bush and Barack Obama showed little evidence of presidential coattails.

But in 2016, there was some evidence that Donald Trump's stronger than expected showing in some states had helped some Republican senators gain re-election who had been thought to be facing near certain defeat. Senators Pat Toomey of Pennsylvania, Richard Burr of North Carolina, and most notably

Key term

Coattails effect The effect when an extremely popular candidate at the top of the electoral ticket (e.g. for president or governor) carries candidates for lower offices with him/her into office.

Ron Johnson of Wisconsin all won their races when it was their Democratic opponents who were leading in the polls for most of the campaign, sometimes by large margins. That said, however, of the 21 winning Republican Senate candidates of 2016, 16 won a higher share of the vote in their state than did Donald Trump. So Trump's coattails were fairly short, if they existed at all.

Split-ticket voting is declining

There is evidence of split-ticket voting, which occurs when someone votes for the candidates of different political parties for different offices at the same election. People might vote for a Republican president but a Democrat member of Congress. At the midterm election, they might vote for a Democrat governor but a Republican member of Congress. Because elections in the United States are more candidate- and issue-orientated than simply party-orientated, ticket splitting does not seem odd to American voters. There is some evidence that voters think in terms of divided government — a president of one party but Congress controlled by the other party. In 1996, the Republicans, having virtually admitted that their presidential candidate Bob Dole would lose, appealed to voters in the last days of the campaign to re-elect a Republican-controlled Congress. They did just that.

In presidential election years, evidence of split-ticket voting can be seen in two ways:

- First, it may result in a state supporting a presidential candidate from one party but, at the same election, a senatorial candidate from the other party. In 2004, four states — Arkansas, Colorado, Nevada and North Dakota — voted for Republican George W. Bush in the presidential race, but elected a Democrat to the Senate. In North Dakota, while Bush was beating Democrat John Kerry by 27 percentage points in the presidential race, Democrat Byron Dorgan was being re-elected by a 36 percentage-point margin in the Senate race. Two other states — New Hampshire and Pennsylvania — voted for John Kerry in the presidential race but elected Republicans to the Senate. But just 12 years later, in 2016, when the same Senate seats were being contested in the same states, all 34 states voted the same way in both the presidential and senatorial races. This suggests that as partisanship grows in the electorate, split-ticket voting declines.

- Second, it may result in a congressional district supporting a presidential candidate from one party but, at the same election, a House member from the other party. These are called 'split districts'. As Figure 6.8 shows, the number of split districts has declined hugely over the past three decades, indicating that voters are increasingly voting straight ticket rather than split ticket. In 2016, there were 23 districts that elected a Republican to the House but voted for Hillary Clinton for president, and there were 12 districts that voted for Donald Trump but elected a House Democrat. One of the most exaggerated examples of a split district in 2016 was the seventh district in Minnesota, which gave 62% of its vote for Donald Trump while at the same time electing Democrat congressman Collin Peterson with 53% of the vote.

Related to split-ticket voting is the phenomenon of split Senate state delegations. Back in 1975, 44 states had split Senate delegations — one senator from each party. By 1999, that number had fallen to 30, and by 2017 just 12 states had split Senate delegations. In other words, 38 states have both senators from the same party — another piece of evidence of strictly partisan voting.

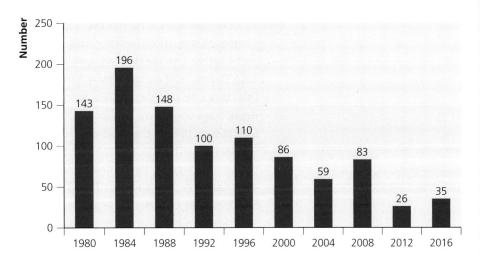

Figure 6.8 Split districts, 1980–2016

There are fewer competitive districts

Time was when around one-quarter of House districts were truly competitive — meaning that they were won by less than 10 percentage points at the previous election. In 1992 there were 111 competitive House districts (Figure 6.9). Gradually over the next decade that number fell, and although there was a rise in competitive districts between 2004 and 2010, the number has again fallen sharply so that by 2016 there were only 31 (or 1 in every 14) seats that were competitive.

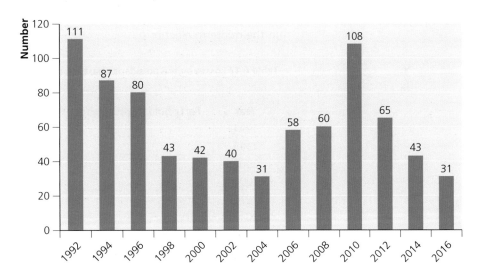

Figure 6.9 Number of House members who won by less than 10 percentage points, 1992–2016

Why is this significant? For two reasons:
- First, it makes it much harder for party control of the House to change hands. In 2016, the Democrats needed to make an overall gain of just 30 seats to win back party control of the House. But of all the seats being contested, only 43 were competitive after the previous election cycle, giving the Democrats very little chance of gaining anything like enough. In the end, the Democrats made an overall gain of just 6 seats, leaving them still 24 seats short of the majority — with only 31 competitive seats to work on in 2018.

- Second, members who represent safe districts — the opposite of competitive districts — are much more likely to vote in line with their own party rather than seek deals with the opposing party. The logic is simple. Take Democratic congressman Sanford Bishop of Georgia, who represents the state's second district. He won 61% of the vote to just 39% for his Republican opponent. It is logical for him to support the Democratic Party line. Meanwhile, in the next-door district is Republican Drew Ferguson — elected with 68% of the vote. It's equally clear which way he will be voting in Congress. By contrast, take Republican Darrell Issa (California 49th District). Issa won just 5,000 more votes (out of over 260,000) than his Democrat opponent. He will need to keep the views of both parties' supporters in mind when he is deciding issues in Congress. But fewer competitive districts equals more partisanship in Congress.

The president's party tends to lose seats in the midterm congressional elections

As we have already observed, the congressional elections which come two years after the presidential election — in 2014 and 2018, for example — are called midterm elections, coming as they do midway through the president's four-year term of office. These midterm elections for the whole of the House and one-third of the Senate display certain characteristics of their own.

There is evidence that the president's party usually loses seats in both houses in midterm elections. In the six midterm elections between 1994 and 2014, the president's party has lost an average of 25 House seats and between four and five Senate seats (see Table 6.17). And this includes 2002, which is the only year in the last 40 years in which the president's party gained seats in both houses in the midterm elections.

Table 6.17 Losses by the president's party in midterm congressional elections, 1994–2014

Year	Party holding presidency	Gains/losses for president's party in:	
		House	Senate
1994	D	−52	−8
1998	D	+5	0
2002	R	+5	+2
2006	R	−30	−6
2010	D	−63	−6
2014	D	−13	−9

The reasons for the president's party to tend to lose seats in the midterms are twofold:
- If a president has had a positive effect for his party in the presidential election two years before, it is likely that his party's House candidates, now devoid of his presence on the ticket, will do less well. The midterms in 2010 are an example of this phenomenon.
- Voters often see the midterm elections as a chance to express their disappointment or disapproval with the president's previous two — or six — years in office. In 2006, voters clearly expressed their disappointment with, among other things, President Bush's failure to successfully conclude the military operation in Iraq.

- Using Wikipedia (https://en.wikipedia.org), search for the page entitled 'Classes of United States Senators'.
- At the bottom of the webpage you will find 'List of current Senators by Class'.
- Class 1 will be up for re-election in 2018; Class 2 in 2020; Class 3 in 2022.
- Find out which senators will be up for re-election in the next cycle of Senate elections.
- Work out the party balance of those senators seeking re-election.
- By clicking the last set of elections for the class in which you are interested (see further up the webpage), find out how close each race was in the previous election.
- Based on these data, how well do you think each party may do in the next set of Senate elections?

Propositions, referendums and recall elections

Key terms

Direct democracy A form of democratic government in which all citizens participate directly and at an equal level in voting, making decisions and passing laws.

Proposition or initiative An electoral device by which citizens of a state can place proposed laws — and in some states, proposed constitutional amendments — on the state ballot.

Next we consider forms of **direct democracy** used by some states but not by the federal government. By direct democracy we mean a system of government in which political decisions are made directly by the people rather than by their elected representatives. Some states practise direct democracy through the use of propositions, referendums and recall elections. We shall consider each in turn, but it is important to remember that we are talking here about *state* governments, not the federal government. The federal government uses none of these forms of direct democracy. In 2016, 162 state-wide ballot measures were certified for the ballot in 35 states. Of these, 76 were put on the ballot by citizens through signature petitions, while the others were placed on the ballot by state legislatures.

Propositions

A **proposition**, more commonly in the USA referred to as an **initiative**, is a process that enables citizens to bypass their state legislature by placing proposed laws and, in some states, constitutional amendments on the ballot. Some examples of propositions voted on in 2016 are listed in Box 6.6.

Box 6.6

Examples of propositions, 2016

Marijuana legalisation:
- Approved: California, Maine, Massachusetts, Nevada
- Defeated: Arizona

Minimum wage increase:
- Approved: Arizona, Colorado, Maine, Washington

Gun laws — background checks for gun purchases:
- Approved: California, Nevada, Washington
- Defeated: Maine

For further details and examples, go to https://ballotpedia.org and under 'State Politics' click on 'Ballot Measures'.

The first state to adopt this form of direct democracy was South Dakota in 1898. Since then, 23 other states have included the proposition or initiative process in their constitutions, the most recent being Mississippi in 1992. That makes a total of 24 states with a proposition process.

There are two types of proposition:

- **Direct.** In the direct process, proposals that qualify go directly on the ballot.
- **Indirect.** In the indirect process, they are submitted to the state legislature, which must decide what further action should follow. Rules regarding this indirect process vary from state to state. In some states, the proposition question goes on the ballot even if the state legislature rejects it, submits a different proposal or takes no action at all. But in other states, the legislature can submit a competing proposal on the ballot along with the original proposal.

When it comes to the rules regarding getting a proposition on to the state ballot paper, no two states are exactly the same. However, there are a few general rules of thumb and the process in most states includes the following steps, by which the proposition must be:

- filed with a designated state official
- reviewed for conformance with state legal requirements
- given a formal title and brief summary for inclusion on the ballot paper
- circulated to gain the required number of signatures from registered voters, usually a percentage of the votes cast for a state-wide office (e.g. US senator, state governor) in a preceding general election
- submitted to state officials for verification of signatures

The number of signatures required to place a proposition on a state ballot varies from state to state. In Alaska, 10% of the total votes cast in the last general election is required. In California it is just 5% of the votes cast for governor in the last election if the proposition is for a new state law, but 10% if the proposition seeks to amend the state constitution. If enough valid signatures are obtained, the question then goes on the ballot or, in states with the indirect process, is sent to the state legislature. Once a proposition is on the state ballot, the general requirement for passage is a majority vote. Of late around a half of all initiatives are approved by voters.

Referendums

A **referendum** is an electoral device, available in all 50 states, by which voters can effectively veto a bill passed by the state legislature. Referendums are in many ways similar to propositions, but the major difference is that rather than citizens taking the initiative, referendums follow from something the state legislators themselves have already done. In some states, the state legislature is required to refer certain measures to the voters for their approval in a referendum. For instance, a number of states require that changes to the state constitution must be approved in a state-wide referendum. In other states, changes in state tax must be approved in this way. In 2012, there were 115 referendums put on the ballot by state legislatures.

But 24 states go further than this and have a provision called a popular referendum. In states such as Alaska, Colorado and New Mexico which have the popular referendum, if the state legislature passes a law that voters do not approve of, they may gather signatures to demand a referendum on the law. Generally, there is a 90-day period after the law is passed during which the petitioning must take place. Once enough signatures have been gathered and verified, the new law appears on the ballot for a popular vote. While the referendum is pending, the law does not take effect. If voters approve the law in the referendum, it takes effect as scheduled. If voters reject the law, it is null and void — a kind of popular veto.

Recall elections

A **recall election** is a procedure which enables voters in a state to remove an elected official from office before their term has expired. Recall elections can be seen as a direct form of impeachment. Impeachment is a legal process whereby politicians can remove one of their own from office. The recall election is a political process whereby ordinary voters can remove a politician from office. Nineteen states currently permit the recall of elected officials by this process.

There have been three recall elections of state governors. In 1921, the voters of North Dakota removed Governor Lynn Frazier by recall election. In 2003, the Democrat governor of California, Gray Davis, was defeated in a recall election by the Republican candidate Arnold Schwarzenegger, who then went on to serve as governor of the state until January 2011. But the most recent and high-profile example was the recall of the Republican governor of Wisconsin Scott Walker in June 2012, in which Governor Walker beat his Democrat opponent, Milwaukee mayor Tom Barrett, by 53% to 46. This recall election was triggered by opposition to Governor Walker's implementation of changes to state employee pension schemes and the limiting of the collective bargaining rights of trade unions within the state.

The recall election is clearly a device which increases democratic accountability, for it makes elected officials directly accountable not only at election time but potentially at any time during their term of office. But some critics see the recall election as demeaning the democratic process by allowing voters to indulge in what one might term 'buyer's regret' — changing one's mind after short-term dissatisfaction. Certainly, were the recall election to be used with any degree of frequency, it could easily destabilise the governing process. Many believe that, short of an elected official committing some crime or impeachable offence, voters should have to live with the consequences of the votes they have cast and not be able to change their minds in midterm. Since 2012, recall efforts have been begun against the governors in Kansas, Oregon, Arizona, Michigan and Alaska, but at the time of writing none has actually come to a vote.

Arnold Schwarzenegger, who served as governor of California from 2003-2011

Comparing US and UK electoral systems

The trouble with comparing elections in the USA and the UK is that one is so often comparing two entirely different things. There is no UK equivalent to a US presidential election. A UK general election is an election for one house of the national legislature, while the US 'general election' every four years sees the election of the president, the whole of the House of Representatives, one-third of the Senate, plus a plethora of state and local officials. The UK has nothing really to compare with the US midterm elections. And that's not all. As we saw in Chapter 1, comparing an election in the United States across 3,000 miles and four time zones — plus Alaska and Hawaii — with an election in the UK, a country the size of Oregon, is a fairly curious comparison. All this means that there are very few meaningful things we can compare regarding the actual conduct of elections in the USA and the UK. But one area that we can compare is the issue of electoral systems.

The United States

It is just about true to say that elections — federal, state and local — in the United States are conducted on a first-past-the-post, single-member district, winner-take-all system. Despite the fact that each state elects two senators, the elections are staggered to occur in different election cycles. If, as sometimes occurs, a special election is required — following the death or resignation of a senator — and that special election coincides with another senate race in the state, two separate elections are held with the winner of each being elected.

As we saw earlier in this chapter, two states — Maine and Nebraska — award their Electoral College votes based on the vote in each congressional district with the two remaining votes going to the state-wide winner. But although this can lead to a split in the electoral vote within the state, this is still really a winner-take-all contest, except the winner in each district is being rewarded.

Then there are the presidential primaries in which the delegates to the party's national convention are awarded on a proportional basis, rather than a winner-take-all basis — all but a few Republican primaries are still winner-take-all. But these are primaries — they are choosing delegates, not electing people to office.

As a result of the progressive movement at the beginning of the twentieth century and in opposition to the party machines of that era, the Proportional Representation League of the United States was formed. But even the League was realistic and pushed for reform of local elections at the city level rather than expecting any change at the state or federal level. A number of cities — mainly in the Northeast — jumped on the proportional representation (PR) bandwagon. But the biggest boost to PR came in 1936 when New York City adopted it for its city elections. Certainly PR had many of the desired effects: a closer correlation between votes won and seats gained; an increase in women and ethnic minority candidates and office holders; greater representation of third parties. But it was the onset of the Cold War and the Red Scare that sounded the death knell of PR, as Communist Party candidates began to win seats on the New York City council, and by the end of the 1950s the experiment had been abruptly halted, never to be repeated.

The electoral system of the United States is certainly the product, therefore, of the culture of the nation, and the vested interests of the state Democratic and Republican parties in, as it were, politically feathering their own nests. Even the perpetuation of the Electoral College system, despite the errant results of 2000 and 2016, is clearly an indication of the power of political elites. Figures 6.5 and 6.6 showed the way the electoral system skews results in the Electoral College.

The key characteristic of electoral systems is the relationship of votes cast to seats gained in elections for legislative chambers. Proportional systems do, as they say, what it says on the tin. They deliver a close correlation between votes won and seats gained. But in elections for the US House of Representatives in which candidates of the two major parties regularly win over 95% of the votes, the correlation of votes to seats has, historically, been quite close even with a winner-take-all system. As the data in Table 6.18 show, in the elections between 2000 and 2010, the difference between the percentage of votes won and seats gained by the winning party averaged out at only 3 or 4 percentage points. Since the reapportionment following the 2010 census, this difference has risen to around 6 percentage points. In 2012, the Republicans won a 33-seat majority in the House despite winning well over 1 million fewer votes than the Democrats.

Table 6.18 Relationship between votes won and seats gained: House of Representatives, 2000–16

Year	Votes (%)		Seats (%)	
	Republican	Democrat	Republican	Democrat
2000	47.6	47.1	50.8	48.7
2002	50.0	45.2	52.6	47.1
2004	49.4	46.8	53.3	46.4
2006	44.3	52.3	46.4	53.6
2008	42.6	53.2	40.9	59.1
2010	51.7	44.9	55.6	44.4
2012	47.6	48.8	53.8	46.2
2014	51.2	45.5	56.8	43.2
2016	49.1	48.0	55.4	44.6

In the Senate, it is difficult to analyse the effect of the electoral system as the elections are staggered over a 6-year cycle with only 33 or 34 states voting in any one cycle. But the fact that Wyoming has two senators to represent its fewer than 600,000 inhabitants, as does California to represent its almost 40 million, has a profound effect on the 'fairness' principle in terms of votes to seats. But the question of the over-representation of the small-population states in Senate is, as we saw in Chapter 2, tied in with the history and culture of the nation as it was being born in the 1780s. And the fact that the folk of Wyoming and Alaska, and of North and South Dakota, have no incentive or intention to make a change in this formula is an example of the rational choice theory of politics in which individuals act in a way that achieves the best outcome for them. Turkeys do not vote for an early Thanksgiving. Furthermore, it shows how the political outcomes are largely determined by the formal structures and processes — in this case, the electoral system — laid out within a political system.

The United Kingdom

Even without elections to the European Parliament following the United Kingdom's exit from the European Union, there will still be five different electoral systems used in the UK:

- first-past-the-post: House of Commons, local elections (England and Wales)
- additional member system: Scottish Parliament, Welsh Assembly, Greater London Assembly
- single transferable vote: Northern Ireland Assembly, local elections (Scotland and Northern Ireland)
- alternative vote: local by-elections (Scotland)
- supplementary vote: London mayoral elections

The fact that five electoral systems are still used in the UK is reflective of the evolving culture of the nation. As devolution grew as an issue in UK politics — in terms of devolved power to Scotland, Wales and Northern Ireland, and to London — electoral systems were adopted that would be more reflective of the cultures of those principalities and cities. For example, the single transferable vote system was adopted to give voice to the different cultural traditions of Northern Ireland, and the additional member system to do the same in Wales and Scotland.

We can see the way the first-past-the-post system operates in electing members to the UK House of Commons as compared to the US House of Representatives. Table 6.19 shows that in the six elections between 1997 and 2017, the correlation between votes and seats for the three main parties was exceedingly poor. In 2001, Labour won over 62% of the seats on a vote of just over 40%, while in 2010 the Liberal Democrats won nearly a quarter of the votes yet won less than 9% of the seats. The position of minor parties was, at times, even worse. In 2015, the Scottish National Party polled 1.4 million votes but won 56 seats, while UKIP polled just under 4 million votes and won just one seat.

Table 6.19 Relationship between votes won and seats gained: House of Commons, 1997–2017

Year	Votes (%)			Seats (%)		
	Con	Lab	Lib Dem	Con	Lab	Lib Dem
1997	30.7	43.2	16.8	25.0	63.4	7.0
2001	31.7	40.7	18.3	25.2	62.7	7.9
2005	32.4	35.2	22.1	30.7	55.1	9.6
2010	36.1	29.0	23.0	47.1	39.7	8.8
2015	36.8	30.4	7.9	50.8	35.7	1.2
2017	42.4	40.0	7.4	48.9	40.3	1.8

So how does the same electoral system produce a House of Representatives with just two parties but a House of Commons with 11? The main reason has to do with the cleavages within the two societies and the nature of the two party systems. In the USA, the two major parties from the 50 states come together to field candidates across the nation for elections to the House of Representatives. For sure, the candidates with the same party label will vary in political ideology — although to a lesser extent than used to be the case — but one Republican Party and one Democratic Party can represent the political interests of a sizable majority of voters. But in the UK, the country — and the parties — are divided along (sub-)national lines. England is the preserve (mainly) of the Conservatives, Labour, the Liberal Democrats and UKIP. The SNP dominates Scotland. Wales divides up among Labour and Plaid Cymru, while Northern Ireland has a party system all of its own. But then, to put it simply, the USA is not made up of four countries. The United Kingdom is. And the electoral system reflects the structure and culture of the nation.

When the UK held a nationwide referendum in 2011 on a proposal to adopt the alternative vote (AV) system for elections to the House of Commons, the result was a very clear 'no' vote — by 68% to 32. The vote was closest in Northern Ireland — 56% (no) to 44% (yes). The Conservative Party came out in opposition to AV, while the Liberal Democrats, Greens, UKIP and the Scottish and Welsh nationalists were strongly in favour. Labour was split and took no official position. Here we see parties lining up

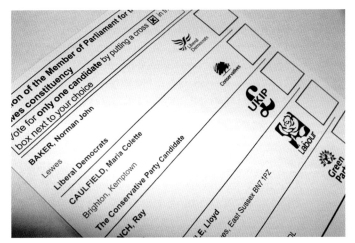

UK general election ballot paper, Lewes, East Sussex (2015)

on a rational choice basis — supporting the system that would be best for them and their supporters.

Electoral systems matter. That is why they are often fought over so strongly. They have an effect on party systems. They clearly affect the make-up of legislatures — especially in terms of political, gender and ethnic representation. They might well affect the way legislators behave when in office. Single-member constituency systems clearly enhance the link between legislators and constituents. But they can also have a knock-on effect on government formation. Often we are asked to judge which system is 'best', but that of course depends on what we want from an electoral system — strong governments, stability, diverse representation, fairness? As Daniele Caramani (2011) concludes:

> There is no denying that electoral systems can make a significant difference to a country's politics. By making a country's system more (or less) proportional, by raising (or lowering) the threshold of representation, by giving voters greater (or less) power to exercise choice among one party's candidates, we know what consequences are likely to follow.

References

Atkins, D., 'How to fix our broken primary system', *Washington Monthly*, April 2016.

Bruni, F., 'No way to elect a president', *The New York Times*, 19 April 2016.

Caramani, D., *Comparative Politics*, Oxford University Press, 2011.

Cronin, T.E. and Genovese, M.A., *The Paradoxes of the American Presidency*, Oxford University Press, 1998.

Loevy, R.D., *The Flawed Path to the Presidency 1992*, State University of New York Press, 1995.

Wayne, S.J., *The Road to the White House*, Bedford-St Martin's Press, 2001.

Further reading

Ashbee, E., 'The 2014 midterm elections: how significant are they?' *Politics Review*, Vol. 24, No. 4, April 2015.

Barrowcliff, C. and Bennett, A.J., 'Are presidential campaigns too long?' *Politics Review*, Vol. 25, No. 2, November 2016.

Bennett, A.J., 'How to fix the presidential nomination process', *US Government and Politics: Annual Update 2015*, Hodder, 2015, pp. 44–50.

Bennett, A.J., 'What can we learn from the 2014 midterm elections?' *US Government and Politics: Annual Update 2015*, Hodder, 2015, pp. 1–16.

Bennett, A.J., 'Where now for televised presidential debates?' *US Government and Politics: Annual Update 2016*, Hodder, 2016, pp. 26–32.

Bennett, A.J., *US Government and Politics: Annual Update 2017* — edition devoted to coverage of the 2016 presidential election, Hodder, 2017.

Clemson, B. and Bennett, A.J., 'Is it now time to abolish the Electoral College?', *Politics Review*, Vol. 27, No. 2, November 2017.

Whiskerd, N. and Bennett, A.J., 'Is the process for nominating presidential candidates hopelessly flawed?' *Politics Review*, Vol. 24, No. 4, April 2015.

Whitton, J., and Endersby, A., 'Should the Electoral College be replaced by a national popular vote?' *Politics Review*, Vol. 23, No. 2, November 2013.

The best places to follow things online regarding presidential and congressional elections are:

www.realclearpolitics.com — an impressive and comprehensive collection of news, articles, polling data and videos with a very good archive

www.thegreenpapers.com — very detailed information on candidates, primaries and general election data. A bit more for the elections geeks among us!

www.electionproject.org — impressive data on turnout in primaries and general elections

www.opensecrets.org — for data on campaign finance, along with...

www.fec.gov — the website of the Federal Election Commission

www.debates.org — the website of the Commission on Presidential Debates

https://ballotpedia.org — for all things electoral; an impressive array of data very well presented

www.270towin.com — Electoral College maps; historical data

www.pollingreport.com

www.cnn.com/politics

www.washingtonpost.com

Exam focus

Edexcel

Note: This Specification does not include a comparison between US and UK elections or electoral systems.

Section C (USA)

In your answer you must consider the stated view and the alternative to this view in a balanced way.

1 Evaluate the extent to which the process of selecting presidential candidates is deeply flawed. (30)

2 Evaluate the extent to which national party conventions still play a meaningful role in presidential elections. (30)

3 Evaluate the extent to which the televised debates between the two major party candidates play a significant role in the presidential campaign. (30)

4 Evaluate the extent to which the Electoral College is an outdated institution. (30)

AQA

Section A (USA)

1 Explain and analyse three ways in which the process for selecting presidential candidates is open to criticism. (9)

2 Explain and analyse three important roles still played by the national party conventions. (9)

Section A (Comparative)

1 Explain and analyse three ways in which cultural theory could be used to study the differences between the elections and electoral systems of the USA and the UK. (9)

2 Explain and analyse three ways in which cultural theory could be used to study the party make-up of the US House of Representatives and the UK House of Commons. (9)

Section B (USA)

Should the Electoral College be abolished?

Recent elections have urgently demonstrated the lack of viability of the Electoral College. Not only have we seen the usual over-representation of the small states and the lack of opportunity for minor parties, but it's the reality of the candidate winning the election in the Electoral College having lost the popular vote which has loomed largest over American democracy. As two of the five elections between 2000 and 2016 have seen the popular vote loser win, it is clearly time to abolish the Electoral College. In 2000, George W. Bush won 271 Electoral College votes despite receiving over half-a-million votes less than Al Gore. As images of Supreme Court justices awarding the presidency to Bush were beamed throughout the world, the beacon of democracy looked rather more like a fading light. And then in 2016, Donald Trump received over 2.5 million fewer votes than Hillary Clinton yet won 304 Electoral College votes. In the same election, seven Electors acted as 'faithless Electors' — voting for someone other than their pledged candidate. Surely such a process should last no longer.

But for all its flaws, the Electoral College is not without its advantages. It usually guarantees that the president will have received the support of more than 50% of the voters — something it has achieved in 18 of the last 25 elections. It also preserves the voice of the small-population states — something that is even more important nowadays than it was when the system was devised in the 1780s. But the most compelling argument against its abolition is the absence of agreement about any better and more viable system to replace it. To abolish the Electoral College would require a constitutional amendment making abolition not only inadvisable but also impractical.

Adapted from Ben Clemson and Anthony J. Bennett, 'Is it now time to abolish the Electoral College?' *Politics Review*, Vol. 27, No. 2, November 2017.

Analyse, evaluate and compare the arguments in the above passage for and against the view that the Electoral College should be abolished. (25)

Section C (Comparative)

In your answer you should draw on material from across the whole range of your course of study in Politics.

1 'Money is too important and unregulated in US and UK general elections.' Analyse and evaluate this statement. (25)

2 'The first-past-the-post electoral system is the most significant determinant of elections in both the USA and the UK.' Analyse and evaluate this statement. (25)

Chapter 7

Parties and pressure groups
Political parties

> **Learning outcomes**
>
> Key questions answered in this section:
> - How are the two major parties organised?
> - What is the ideology of each of the major parties?
> - How do the two major parties compare in terms of policies?
> - What is the coalition of supporters for each party?
> - Does the USA still have a two-party system?
> - What role is played by third parties?
> - Are the US parties in a period of decline or renewal?
> - What are the significant comparisons between US and UK political parties?

Introduction

During one of my early visits to Washington DC back in 1980, I was attending a lunch to which I had been invited and got talking with Mike Barnes — a Democrat member of the House of Representatives. Barnes was in his first term representing the 8th District of Maryland, an area stretching from the northern suburbs of the capital towards the Pennsylvania state border. He was a moderately conservative Democrat and represented a generally upscale part of western Maryland.

I soon discovered that, upon learning that I was British, American politicians often have a tendency to try to display their knowledge of British politics — though that is not to say this knowledge is always accurate. After all, most Americans seem to think that the terms 'England' and 'Britain' are interchangeable, and that Belfast is in 'Ireland'. This occasion was no different, so when I asked Congressman Barnes how he would explain the difference between the Democratic and Republican parties, he was ready with his British comparison. 'Well, it's like this,' he said. 'We have the Republican Party that is rather like your Conservative Party, and then we have the Democratic Party that is rather like — your Conservative Party!'

Given the slightly mischievous smile he had on his face, I don't think I was meant to take him too literally. But he was making two related points about American political parties nearly 40 years ago. First, there were conservatives in both parties. And second, on a large number of issues, there was little to differentiate between the two major parties. Things had not changed all that much by the era of Bill Clinton in the 1990s. In was in 1997 that political commentator Mark Shields, writing in *The Washington Post*, stated that 'as of today, the country has two Republican parties, separated by the issue of abortion'.

But as we shall discover in this chapter, a great deal has changed in the 40 years since my conversation with Mike Barnes and in the 20 years since Mark Shields was writing his newspaper column. Indeed, the party political world in which they were talking and writing has simply ceased to exist.

Party organisation

Here we come almost full circle. Back in Chapter 2 we saw that one of the three key principles of the United States Constitution is federalism — a system of government by which political power is divided between a national government and state governments, each having their own areas of substantive jurisdiction. In other words, federalism is a decentralised form of government. If government is decentralised, political parties are likely to reflect that.

For most of the nineteenth and twentieth centuries American political parties were much more evident at the state and local levels than at the national level. With little ideological cohesion between the state organisations of the same party, being a Democrat or Republican meant little outside of the presidential election cycle. But during the last three decades of the last century, a number of factors led to the strengthening of national party structures at the expense of the state and local parties:

- New campaign finance laws meant that money flowed more to the national parties and the presidential candidates themselves rather than being raised locally.
- Television provided a medium through which candidates could appeal directly to voters — a role that state and local parties had traditionally played through rallies, whistle-stop tours and torchlight processions.

- The emergence of more sophisticated and widely available opinion polls allowed candidates to 'hear' what the voters were saying, without actually meeting them.
- The adoption of new technology allowed the national parties to target voters with political and fundraising messages in their homes through computerised direct mailing and, later, through social media.
- Parties became more ideologically cohesive and politics became more partisan, resulting in more centralised control of both the message and the messengers.
- National parties established systems to recruit and train state and local party candidates, offering them legal advice, media training, financial advice and analysis of voting trends, along with national advertising campaigns, especially during election cycles.

All this means that the organisational structures of the two main parties are today more 'top-down' than they were four decades ago when they were very clearly 'bottom-up'. That said, there is still a clear divide between the national and state parties. This can best be seen by asking the questions: 'Who is leader of the Republican Party?' and 'Who is leader of the Democratic Party?' The former question might elicit the answer of 'President Trump', but that is highly questionable. After all, most of the Republican Party hierarchy made it very clear throughout his election campaign that they did not want him even as their presidential nominee. And as we saw in Chapter 3, the president may be able to exercise little leadership in Congress. President Trump was elected as *president* in a nationwide election, not as party leader in an internal party election — like British prime ministers.

National party organisation

National committees

The only manifestations of permanent party structure at the national level are the national committees of each party — the Democratic National Committee (DNC) and the Republican National Committee (RNC). Both have offices in Washington DC. Each has a chair, normally elected by the members of the respective national committee, though by tradition incumbent presidents recommend the chair of their own national committee. After the 2016 elections, Donald Trump nominated Ronna Romney McDaniel — the niece of 2012 Republican presidential nominee Mitt Romney — to be the new RNC chair. Then in February 2017, the DNC elected former secretary of labor Tom Perez as its new chair, beating Representative Keith Ellison of Minnesota in what was seen as a victory for the Hillary Clinton wing of the party over the Bernie Sanders wing.

But these national party chairs are mostly anonymous party bureaucrats or former elected officials who are seldom in the public eye. The national committees raise money, hire staff and coordinate election strategy for their party's candidates for local, state and national office. They are also responsible for organising the national party convention that meets during the summer of each presidential election year (see Chapter 6).

It is when one looks at the membership of the respective national committees that one sees all too clearly that the national party is really nothing more than the coming together of the state parties. There is really no separate entity called the national party. The DNC is made up of the chair and vice-chair of each of the 50 state Democratic parties, plus a further 200 elected members apportioned to the state parties on the basis of state population. All DNC members are admitted as super-delegates to the Democratic national convention (see Chapter 6). The RNC consists of the chair of each state Republican party, plus two committee members from each state party — one man and one woman.

Congressional leadership and committees

At the national level, each party also has its congressional leadership (see Chapter 3) as well as committees to oversee elections to each house of Congress: the Democratic Senatorial Campaign Committee; the Democratic Congressional Campaign Committee; the National Republican Senatorial Committee; the National Republican Congressional Committee.

State and local party organisation

Everything else to do with political parties is at the state level where there is a bewildering variety of organisation, laws and customs, and considerable power is vested in state governors and big city mayors. There are state party committees (headed by the state party chair) as well as state party conventions. Below that exist the party committees at congressional district, county, city, ward and precinct levels.

Party ideology

Key term

Ideology A collectively held set of ideas and beliefs.

The names of the two major parties immediately suggest that they are not ideologically exclusive parties, for 'democracy' and 'republicanism' are two all-embracing ideologies, if ideologies they are. Some ideologies, such as fascism and socialism, are narrow in their compass, but this is not so with the two being considered here. Indeed, Hillary Clinton, who is a Democrat (i.e. a member of the Democratic Party), is also a republican, in that she believes in the principles of republican government. Likewise, Donald Trump, who is a Republican (i.e. a member of the Republican Party), is also a democrat, in that he believes in the principles of democratic government, or at least one hopes that he does. As recently as the period between 2001 and 2007, Trump identified with the Democratic Party and was personally very close to both Bill and Hillary Clinton.

Because the parties' names do not necessarily suggest an ideological colour, we find that commentators, and even politicians themselves, attach ideological labels ahead of the party names. Thus, there are 'conservative Democrats' and 'liberal Democrats'; 'conservative Republicans' and 'moderate Republicans'. George W. Bush ran his 2000 election campaign calling himself a 'compassionate conservative'. In the USA ideology and region are often linked. The South tends to be more conservative; the Northeast and the west coast tend to be more liberal or libertarian. Thus, for both parties to be viable in all regions of the country, they need to take on the ideological shades of the region. Southern Democrats such as Senator Bill Nelson of Florida tend to be more conservative than New England Democrats such as Senator Chris Murphy of Connecticut. Similarly, New England Republicans such as Senator Susan Collins of Maine are more liberal than southern Republicans such as Senator Richard Burr of North Carolina.

Growth of ideological differences

As we saw at the very beginning of this chapter, it used to be the conventional wisdom that there was very little ideological difference between the two major parties, that they were, in the famous phrase of Lord Bryce, 'like two bottles with different labels, both empty', or if you prefer Professor Clinton Rossiter: 'They are creatures of compromise, coalitions of interest in which principle is muted and often silenced.' When asked the question in 1972: 'Do you think there are any important differences in what the Republicans and Democrats stand for?' 44% said 'no' and 46% said 'yes'. As Figure 7.1 shows, the trend has been towards Americans seeing the parties as far more distinct, and this has accelerated since 2000, so that by 2012, 81% of respondents thought there were important differences between the two parties.

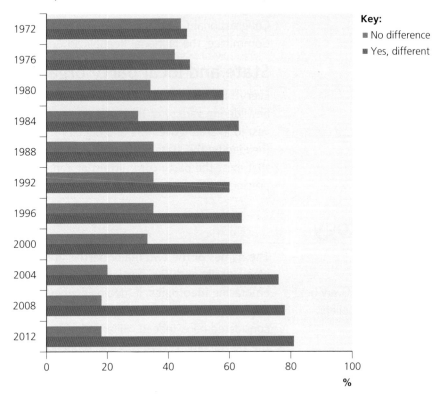

Source: data from www.electionstudies.org

Figure 7.1 Question: 'Do you think there are any important differences in what the Republicans and Democrats stand for?', 1972–2012

A similar change is discernible when one looks at the perceived ideological difference between the two parties by asking the question: 'Do you think one party is more conservative than the other?' The data in Table 7.1 show clearly that over the past three decades the percentage seeing the Republican Party as the more conservative has increased significantly, while the percentage seeing no difference in ideology between the parties has declined.

Table 7.1 Question: 'Is one party more conservative than the other?' — 1984 and 2012 compared

Answer	1984 (%)	2012 (%)
Yes, Republicans	53	73
Yes, Democrats	15	10
No: both the same	32	18

It is possible to suggest that the ideological pattern of Democrats — support for abortion and gay rights, opposition to prayer in state-run schools — is one that could be described as 'liberal'. Equally, one could suggest that the ideological pattern of Republicans — support for cutting taxes, support for the death penalty and opposing abortion rights — is one that could be described as 'conservative'.

Such ideological leanings can be clearly seen in the way Americans vote for the two major parties according to their declared ideological position (see Table 7.2).

Table 7.2 Voting by ideology in the 2016 election

Ideology	Percentage of all voters	Voted Republican (%)	Voted Democrat (%)
Liberal	26	10	84
Conservative	35	81	15

The Democrats and ideology

But the two major parties are not ideological monoliths. Not all Democrats can be correctly identified as liberals — especially those who live in the South or the Midwest. Many will be more likely to identify themselves as moderate Democrats or even conservative Democrats, though in the current era of hyper-partisanship, the number of people within the Democratic Party who call themselves moderates, centrists or conservatives has diminished. Certainly their presidential candidates in the last four election cycles — John Kerry, Barack Obama and Hillary Clinton — would not have attached such adjectives to their party label.

Many commentators saw the contest between Hillary Clinton and Bernie Sanders in the Democratic primaries in terms of ideology — with Sanders out on the left and Clinton appealing more to the centrist or moderate wing of the party. Indeed, Sanders usually talked of his challenge in such ideological terms, presenting what he called a 'democratic socialist alternative' — whatever that meant — to the safer, centrist and establishment-approved politics of the Democratic Party's elites. His campaign was often presented in terms of a 'movement' separating the 'Sandersista' from the Clinton centrists.

The trouble with this scenario is that it is very difficult to find much evidence for it in the primary exit poll data. Collectively, the exit polls showed liberal Democrats preferring Clinton over Sanders by 53% to 46%, while non-liberals preferred Clinton by 61% to 36%. The difference in vote share between the two ideological sub-groups thus stood at 8 percentage points for Clinton and 10 points for Sanders — much less than one might have expected. What the exit polls showed was that, rather than being a battle for the 'ideological soul of the Democratic Party', the Democratic primaries were part of a wider anti-establishment agenda that seemed dominant in both parties' primaries and in the general election.

The Republicans and ideology

Likewise in the Republican Party, not everyone can be correctly identified as conservatives — especially those who live in the Northeast or on the West Coast. Some will qualify their conservatism — hence labels such as 'social conservatives' for those who are conservative on social, moral and religious issues like abortion, same-sex marriage, women's rights and school prayer, but who may be more moderate on economic issues. These are Republicans who would have naturally gravitated towards the Moral Majority in the 1980s, and nowadays to what is loosely referred to as the **Christian right**.

Then there are those who would call themselves 'fiscal conservatives' and who joined the Tea Party movement to fight for a reduction of the national debt and the federal budget deficit, as well as a reduction in government spending and a lowering of federal taxes. There was also George W. Bush's 'compassionate conservatism' which sought to use traditional conservative beliefs in order to improve the lives of those who felt abandoned and neglected by government and

Key term

Christian right (or religious right) Conservative Christian groups, closely linked to Protestant evangelicals, seeking cultural and social changes favouring 'family values', pro-life policies, parental rights and prayer in public schools.

society. So-called 'moderate Republicans' are a dwindling breed as the party has become much more conservatively homogeneous in its ideology at a national level.

So what did the Republican primaries in 2016 tell us about the party's ideological stance? Was Trump leading an ideological battle within the Republican Party? Many commentators thought not. Indeed, during the campaign, Trump seemed an almost post-ideological candidate in many ways. He was not a conservative in the mould of Senator Ted Cruz or former House Speaker Newt Gingrich. He did not give glowing speeches about limited government or the sanctity of the Constitution. Indeed, he actually opposed such Republican shibboleths as free trade, Wall Street financiers and corporate executives who moved jobs abroad. He even wanted to protect entitlement programmes from budget cuts. This was all ideological heresy to many conservative Republicans.

But then neither was Trump a moderate or liberal Republican in the mould of Mitt Romney or John McCain, the party's two previous presidential nominees. He promised to appoint conservative judges to the Supreme Court, he courted leading evangelical leaders and constantly extolled his admiration for President Ronald Reagan. Trump's attraction to those who supported him had more to do with what he was *not* — a politician — than what he *was* in ideological terms. What the long-term future will be for the Republican Party of Trump's brand of 'America First' economic nationalism is still very much an unknown quantity. To utilise one of his own adjectives for the media, will Trump prove to be a fake Republican?

Party policies

It is certainly possible to discern some clear differences between the two major parties when it comes to policies. Table 7.3 shows the parties' stands on a number of high-profile policy issues. All these issues will be debated in any modern-day, national political campaign. This table needs to be read with an accompanying health warning: we are not, of course, suggesting that *all* Democrats oppose the death penalty or *all* Republicans support prayer in state-run schools, but we can say that, in general, *most* Democrats tend to oppose the death penalty and *most* Republicans tend to support school prayer. This can be seen in the positions taken by presidential candidates as well as in the voting patterns on these issues both in Congress and in the wider electorate.

Table 7.3 Differences between Democratic and Republican parties on key policies

Key policy	Democrats tend to	Republicans tend to
Increased spending on social welfare programmes	Support	Oppose
A 'get tough' policy on crime	Oppose	Support
Death penalty	Oppose	Support
Gun control	Support	Oppose
Cut federal taxes	Oppose	Support
Women's rights on abortion	Support	Oppose
High levels of defence spending	Oppose	Support
Gay rights, same-sex marriage	Support	Oppose
Stricter controls on immigration	Oppose	Support
Prayer in state-run schools	Oppose	Support
Strict environmental controls	Support	Oppose
'The federal government should do less'	Oppose	Support
'Obamacare'	Support	Oppose

Table 7.3 shows that the Democrats tend to be more progressive on social and moral issues, as well as on issues relating to law and order. They favour greater governmental intervention both in the economy and on social and welfare issues such as education and healthcare. Republicans, on the other hand, tend to focus more on individualism with government playing a much more limited role in the economy, as well as in social and moral issues. These differences can be seen in the extracts from the two parties' 2016 party platforms on some key issues (see Table 7.4).

Table 7.4 Selected party policies (2016 platforms) compared

Issue	Democrats	Republicans
Abortion	'Every woman should have access to quality reproductive healthcare services, including safe and legal abortion.' 'We will fight efforts to roll back the clock on women's health and reproductive rights.'	'We assert the sanctity of human life and affirm that the unborn child has a fundamental right to life which cannot be infringed.' 'We call for a permanent ban on federal funding and subsidies for abortion and healthcare plans that include abortion.'
Gender rights	'We will fight for comprehensive federal non-discrimination protections for all LGBT Americans.' Supported Supreme Court decision that upheld same-sex marriage as a constitutional right.	'Our laws and our government's regulations should recognise marriage as the union between one man and one woman and actively promote married family life as the basis of a stable and prosperous society.'
Crime	'We understand the disproportionate effects of crime, violence and incarceration on communities of colour.'	'Support mandatory prison sentences for gang crimes, violence or sexual offences against children, repeat drug dealers, rape, robbery and murder.'
Environment	'Climate change is an urgent threat and a defining challenge of our time.' 'Reduce greenhouse gas emissions more than 80% below 2005 levels by 2050.' 'We are committed to getting 50% of our electricity from clean energy sources within a decade.'	'We support the development of all forms of energy that are marketable in a free economy without subsidies including coal, oil, natural gas, nuclear power and hydropower.' 'We oppose any carbon tax.' 'The environment is too important to be left to radical environmentalists whose approach is based on shoddy science.'
Minimum wage	'We should raise the federal minimum wage to $15 an hour over time and index it [to inflation].'	The minimum wage is 'an issue that should be handled at state and local level'.
Wall Street	'We will vigorously implement, enforce and build on President Obama's financial reform law and will stop dead in its tracks every Republican effort to weaken it.'	Called banking regulations 'an excuse to establish unprecedented government control over the nation's financial markets'.
Taxation	Supported allowing the Bush tax cuts for the wealthiest to expire. Supported adopting the Buffett Rule so that no millionaire pays a smaller share of their income in taxes than do middle-class families.	Supported extending the Bush tax cuts and stopping taxes rising on income, interest, dividends and capital gains. Proposed three tax brackets on income ranging from 33% to 12%.
Medicare	'Believe that healthcare is a right not a privilege, and that our healthcare system should put people before profits.' Would 'fight any attempts by Republicans to privatise, "voucherise" or phase out Medicare'.	'Impose no changes for persons 55 or older. Give others the option of traditional Medicare or transition to a premium-support model designed to strengthen patient choice, promote cost-saving competition among providers.'
Healthcare	The Affordable Care Act 'has covered 20 million more Americans and ensured millions more will never be denied coverage because of pre-existing conditions'. Supported reducing cost of prescription drugs, combating drug and alcohol addiction and improving the treatment of those with mental health issues.	'Any honest agenda for improving healthcare must start with repeal of the dishonestly named Affordable Care Act. It weighs like the dead hand of the past on American medicine.' 'It must be removed and replaced with an approach based on genuine competition, patient choice, excellent care and timely access to treatment.'
Education	'Committed to making good public schools available to every child no matter where they live and at last making debt-free college a reality for all Americans.'	'The federal government should not be a partner...as the Constitution gives it no role in education.' 'Parents are a child's first and foremost educators.'

American political parties are best thought of as coalitions of interest. Those coalitions may be more narrowly drawn than they were three or four decades ago, but they still need to be coalitions in order to garner enough support from the electorate to win the presidency. So how do the parties' coalitions of supporters line up in the voting booth? Who voted for which party in the 2016 presidential election? Figure 7.2 shows the major data trends from the exit polls. From this one can see the outline of the Republican Party coalition of support in this particular election. But to get a more accurate picture, we will consider the parties' support under five headings: gender, race, class and education, geographic region, and religion.

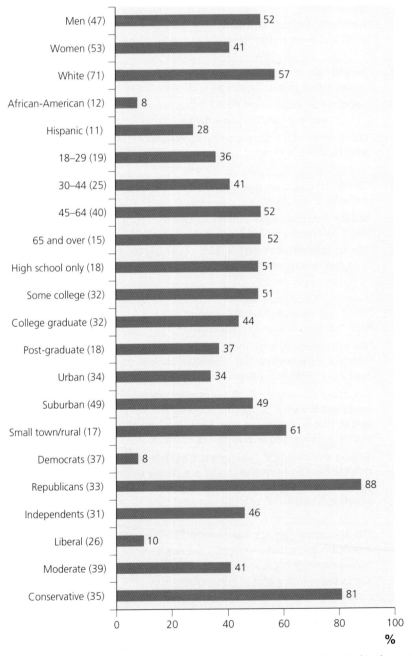

Note: Figures in brackets show percentage who voted in that category.
Source: Compiled from exit poll data at www.nytimes.com

Figure 7.2 Voter support for Donald Trump (Republican), 2016

Gender

Key term

Gender gap The gap
between the support given
to a candidate by women
and the support given to
the same candidate by
men.

In nine out of the ten elections between 1964 and 2000, women were
significantly more supportive of the Democrat candidate than men. This is what
we call the **gender gap**. In 2016 the gender gap for Trump was 11 points —
with 52% of men and 41% of women voting for the Republican candidate. This
was the widest gender gap for a Republican presidential candidate in over half a
century. The gender gap for Clinton was even wider at 13 points — with 54%
of women and 41% of men voting for her. Maybe her status as the first female
major-party presidential candidate and the perceived attitude of her opponent
towards women helped stretch that gap.

Indeed, Trump's attitude towards and treatment of women became a
prominent issue in the 2016 campaign, not only during the primaries, when he
made embarrassingly rude remarks about fellow Republican candidate Carly
Fiorina as well as the political commentator Megyn Kelly, but in the general
election as well. Just a month before Election Day, a videotape was released
into the public domain showing Trump bragging in the most vulgar terms about
kissing, groping, and trying to have sex with different women — even women
he knew to be married. 'When you're a star, they let you do it. You can do
anything,' Trump boasted. One might have expected the female vote to desert
him in droves. Exit poll data showed just 41% of women voters supporting
Trump — only 3 percentage points down from the 44% that voted for Romney
in 2012. But that 41% was the lowest level of support from women voters for
a Republican candidate in a two-party contest since Barry Goldwater's 38% in
1964 (see Figure 7.3). Among non-married women, Trump's support fell to 32%.

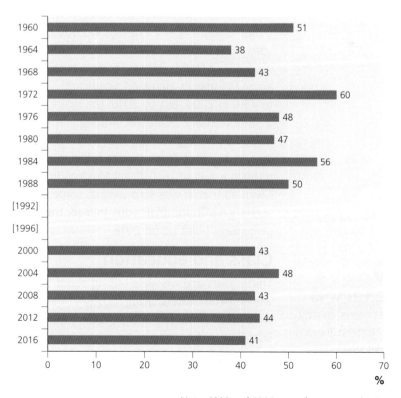

Note: 1992 and 1996 were three-party elections
Source: Compiled from exit poll data at www.nytimes.com

Figure 7.3 Support from women voters for Republican presidential candidates in
two-party elections, 1960–2016

The reason for the gender gap is often thought to be connected with policy differences between the two parties. In five major policy areas — abortion, defence, law and order, gun control and women's rights — the Democrats tend to take positions that are more favoured by women. Democrats are pro-choice on abortion, tend to favour lower levels of spending on defence, oppose capital punishment and support gun control. It was the Democrats who pushed — albeit unsuccessfully — for an Equal Rights Amendment to the Constitution protecting the civil rights of women.

Race

The most significant minority racial groups in the American electorate are African-Americans and Hispanics. In the ten elections between 1980 and 2016, African-Americans never gave less than 83% support to the Democrats. President Clinton was said to have a particular affinity with African-Americans during his presidency, and they were his most loyal group of supporters, especially during the difficult period of his impeachment and trial. With Barack Obama as the first African-American presidential candidate for a major party in 2008, the share of black people voting Democrat rose from 88% in 2004 to 95% in 2008. Black turnout was also up, accounting for 13% of the electorate. But with Hillary Clinton in 2016, black support for the Democrats fell back to 89%.

Hispanics are a growing group. According to the 2000 census, they formed 12% of the population, but by the 2010 census this figure had increased to over 16%. Furthermore, because they are a young group and a significant proportion are not yet of voting age, their full political importance is yet to show. The states where Hispanics make up more than 25% of the population include California, Nevada, Arizona, Texas and New Mexico. Hispanics are a disparate group — including those from Mexico, Puerto Rico and Cuba, as well as other Central American countries.

Bush's Republican campaign in 2000 made a significant pitch for the Hispanic vote. Bush himself speaks fluent Spanish. His brother, Jeb Bush, the former governor of Florida, is married to a Hispanic woman. The Republican vote among Hispanics increased significantly from 20% in 1996 to 31% in 2000 and to 43% in 2004. But by 2016, the figure was down to 28%, with Clinton holding a 38-percentage-point lead among Hispanic voters. Trump's cause was hardly helped by his aggressively nasty tone about Mexican immigrants, saying that 'they're bringing drugs, they're bringing crime, they're rapists', and promising to build a wall to keep illegal Mexican immigrants out of the United States. Given all that, it was surprising to some that more than a quarter of Hispanic voters gave Trump their vote. Indeed, the Hispanic Republican vote was even a percentage point up on 2012.

Class and education

Thirty years ago we were talking about Reagan Democrats. These were white, working-class voters, living mostly in the Northeast and the Midwest. They were often employed in blue-collar jobs in what is often referred to as the Rust Belt — a swathe of America's former industrial heartland stretching from eastern Iowa and southeastern Wisconsin, through northern Illinois, the lower peninsula of Michigan, the states of Indiana and Ohio, and then down from western New York to Pennsylvania and West Virginia. By 1980, these traditional Democrat voters were disillusioned with the economic malaise of President Jimmy Carter and were attracted by Ronald Reagan's economic plans and conservative agenda. They played a significant role in getting Reagan elected

Key term

Reagan Democrats White working-class voters, mostly living in the Northeast and Midwest, employed in blue collar jobs, who had been traditional Democrats but who supported Republican Ronald Reagan in 1980 and 1984.

in 1980 and in delivering his landslide re-election four years later, and even in electing Reagan's vice president, George H.W. Bush, in 1988. But during the next two decades, they tended to return to the Democratic Party, giving their support to both Bill Clinton and Barack Obama. Some of them, however, stayed in the Republican tent and would eventually join the Tea Party movement.

A derelict steel plant in Bethlehem, Pennsylvania — part of the Rust Belt

These were the voters to whom Donald Trump's campaign seemed to speak most directly in 2016 — not only in the Republican primaries, but then in the general election. Of those nine Rust Belt states listed above, Trump won the primaries in six of them, and even managed a respectable second-place finish in Ohio despite the fact that he was competing against the state's incumbent governor, John Kasich. In the general election, Trump won seven of these states, with their 86 Electoral College votes — including four that Obama had won both in 2008 and 2012. Indeed, in 2008, Obama had won Pennsylvania by 11 points, Wisconsin by 14 points and Michigan by 16 points, and yet Trump won all three in 2016.

Writing in 2016, Arlie Russell Hochschild drew attention to poorer and older white male Americans who 'suffer a higher than average death rate due to alcohol, drugs and even suicide'. She continued:

> Although life expectancy for nearly every group is rising, between 1990 and 2008 the life expectancy of older white men without high school diplomas has been shortened by three years — and truly, it seems, by despair...They also feel culturally marginalised: their views about abortion, gay marriage, gender roles, race, guns and the Confederate flag are held up to ridicule in the national media as backward. They've begun to feel a besieged minority.

These white, older, blue-collar voters — more likely to be men than women — were also characterised by being those whose education, for most at least, had finished when they graduated from high school, or even before that. They were not college graduates. Trump's message of bringing home American jobs, curbing illegal immigration, safeguarding America's borders from infiltration by people he claimed might be potential terrorists, and restoring a sense of national and civic pride — of 'making America great again' — was what they had been longing to hear for decades. And it was just these same voters with whom Hillary Clinton had failed to resonate — in her 2008 and 2016 primary campaigns, and in her general election campaign against Trump. What Figure 7.4 shows is how these groups flocked to support Trump — indeed, probably secured his election. Some 62% of white men, and 62% of white 45–64-year-olds voted for Trump, and white non-college men, who made up nearly one-sixth of the electorate, voted 71% for Trump and just 23% for Clinton.

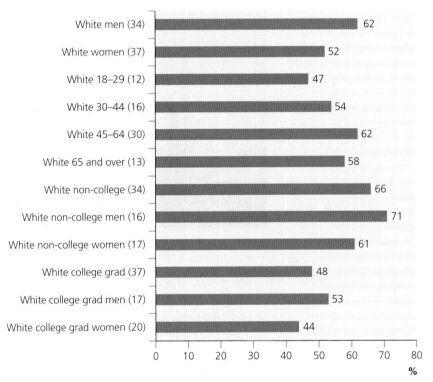

Note: Figures in brackets show percentage who voted in that category.
Source: Compiled from exit poll data at www.nytimes.com

Figure 7.4 Support from white voters for Donald Trump, 2016

Geographic region

There are two important trends when it comes to voting in relation to geographic region. First, the Northeast has become the new heartland of the Democratic Party. Gone are the days of the Democrats' 'solid South'. Now it is the 'solid Northeast'. In the seven elections from 1984 through to 2008, the Northeast gave the Democratic Party candidate his largest percentage of the vote. In 2012, the Democrats won every northeastern state, and in 2016 they won all bar Pennsylvania. But the bad news for the Democrats is that the Northeast is the one region that has a declining proportion of the nation's population. In 2016, Donald Trump broke through what had been called the 'Blue Wall' — a block of states in the upper Midwest and industrial Northeast that had voted solidly for the Democrats over a number of elections — when he won Iowa, Wisconsin and Michigan, as well as Pennsylvania.

Second, the South has moved from being 'solid' for Democrats to being very supportive of Republicans. This was shown most clearly when in 1996 the South was the only region in which the Democratic ticket of Clinton and Gore — both southerners — failed to beat the Republican ticket of Dole and Kemp, neither of whom was from the South. In 2000, the Republicans won every state in the South, including the Democrat nominee Al Gore's home state of Tennessee, and they did the same again in 2004. In 2008, Barack Obama managed to flip three southern states — Virginia, North Carolina and Florida — into the Democratic column. In 2012, the Republicans won back North Carolina, leaving Obama with just two southern states. In 2016, Hillary Clinton was left with only Virginia in her column from the South — and that mostly because she had chosen a Virginian, Tim Kaine, as her running-mate, though the state is trending more Democratic these days, as is neighbouring North Carolina.

The Democrats continue their hold on the West Coast — with California, Oregon and Washington lining up in the Democratic column in every election from 1992 to 2016. George H.W. Bush is the last Republican candidate to win a West Coast state when he won California back in 1988. Meanwhile, the Republicans have laid a similar stranglehold on a swathe of states running from Idaho through the Dakotas, Montana, Wyoming, Kansas and Missouri.

Urban versus rural

The 2016 election also revealed how America is more and more divided by community, with urban areas heavily supporting the Democrats while small towns and rural areas swung significantly to the Republicans. Whereas in 2012, Mitt Romney won small towns and rural areas by just 2 percentage points (50–48), in 2016 Trump won the same communities by 27 points (61–34). It was particularly in small town and rural communities that were slowly withering away, that Trump found his voice, and his message of 'Make America great again' resonated, especially with those white, older, blue-collar workers, in counties like Erie County, Pennsylvania, and Wayne County, Iowa, or Monroe and Adams counties in Ohio.

Donald Trump campaigns in Erie, Pennsylvania, August 2016

Take Wayne County, for example, in south-central Iowa. Its population is 99% white, but 14% are below the poverty level. It was home to nearly 12,000 back in 1950. Now it numbers just over 6,000. In 2012, it voted 55–43% for Romney over Obama, giving the Republican a 12-point victory. In 2016, Trump had a 46-point victory margin over Clinton, with 71% of the vote to Clinton's 25%.

When the economy went pear-shaped in 2008–09, many blue-collar, small town Americans felt that they had been made to carry most of the resulting financial hardship. President Obama boasted about having saved America from going over the fiscal cliff and claimed credit for the recovery. But politicians of both parties underestimated the degree of anger and pain in the nation — the degree to which the recovery had been only for a fortunate few while many more experienced stagnation or decline. As the protest chant went, 'Banks got bailed out, we got sold out.' Illegal immigration, globalisation, trade, corporate greed, their own decaying communities and bank bailouts all helped stoke the feelings of anger and resentment in many small town and rural communities — especially those east of the Missouri and Mississippi rivers.

Just after the 2016 election, Ronald Brownstein wrote in *The Atlantic* magazine that 'not since the election of 1920 has the cultural chasm between urban and non-urban America shaped the struggle over the country's direction as much as today' (Brownstein, 2016). Brownstein saw Trump's victory as 'an empire-strikes-back moment' for all those places that 'felt left behind in an increasingly diverse, post-industrial, and urbanised America'. This is likely to be one of the most watched stories as we approach the election of 2020.

Religion

In a country with a strict separation between church and state, it is perhaps surprising in the twenty-first century to find religion as an issue in deciding which party people vote for. But religion is, as we suggested earlier, closely linked with those social and moral issues that divide the parties.

Protestants and white evangelicals

Protestant Christianity is closely linked with the religious right, with social conservatism, with the Bible Belt — a line of southern states from Texas to southern and central Virginia. As Table 7.5 shows, Protestants are a staple support group for the Republican Party, giving it between 54 and 59% of their votes in each of the last five presidential elections. Within that group, white evangelicals provide even more solid support. Indeed, Donald Trump's 81% support among this group in 2016 was one of the highest levels of support enjoyed by a Republican presidential candidate, though this might have had more to do with their antipathy towards Hillary Clinton than their commitment to Donald Trump. One of the important issues in garnering this high level of support from white evangelicals is appointments to the Supreme Court. This group more than any other puts a high premium on the appointment of strict constructionist judges (see Chapter 5) who will hand down decisions in line with evangelicals' conservative social agenda.

Catholics

The support of Catholics traditionally went to the Democratic Party — with its strong link to European Catholicism among the immigrant communities, especially among Irish Americans in the Northeast. But since the 1970s, the support from Catholics for the Democratic Party has wavered because of the

Democrats' support for abortion, which runs contrary to the Catholic Church's official teaching. Thus devout and practising Catholics tend to be drawn to the Republican Party on this issue. As Table 7.5 shows, Democrats won the Catholic vote in three of the last five presidential elections, but not in 2016 when only 45% voted Democratic — the lowest figure in a two-party contest since 1984.

Table 7.5 Party support from selected religious groups, 2000–16

Year	Protestants (Republican %)	White evangelicals (Republican %)	Catholics D–R (%)
2000	56	–	49–47
2004	59	78	47–52
2008	54	74	54–45
2012	57	78	50–48
2016	58	81	45–52

Religious attendance

Another trend noted by pollsters over the past decade or so is the strong correlation between frequency of attendance at a religious service and party support. In 2016, of those voters who said they attended a religious service at least once a week, 56% voted Republican, while among those who said they never attended such services, the Republicans picked up just 31 to 62% for the Democrats. This again links with the stance of the parties on social and moral issues.

So, to summarise — and generalise — a typical Republican voter in 2016 was a regularly worshipping white Protestant male, who probably was not a graduate, and lived in the South or the Midwest, while the typical Democrat was a non-worshipping minority-race female, who had been to college, and lived either in the Northeast or on the West Coast.

The polarisation of American politics

As we have seen, the 1990s brought a seismic shift in American politics. Up to then, both parties included a wide ideological range from liberals to conservatives. But with the break-up of the old Solid South, southern conservative Democrats began to cross to the Republican Party, making the Republicans a far more ideologically conservative party and leaving the Democrats as a more homogeneous, liberal party. Commentators began to talk of a 50–50 nation, of Red America and Blue America — and of the Red–Blue divide. As the twenty-first century dawned, many states were becoming reliably Red (Republican) or Blue (Democrat).

- **Red America.** Red America was characterised as white, overwhelmingly Protestant (and specifically, evangelical) but often joined by practising Catholics (because of the abortion issue). It was wealthy, rural or suburban, and unmistakably conservative. In Red America, the majority of voters think that the federal government does too many things which would be better left to private businesses and individuals, and they tend to think that federal income tax should be cut, even if that means cuts in federally funded services. Red America is pro-life, pro-guns and pro-traditional marriage, and is opposed to Obamacare. Red America gets its news from the Fox News channel and listens to conservative talk radio featuring such hosts as Sean Hannity, Rush Limbaugh and Mark Levin. Red America loved George W. Bush but loathed the Clintons and Barack Obama.

■ **Blue America.** By contrast, Blue America, it is claimed, is racially a rainbow coalition of white, black, Asian and Hispanic Americans. Attending a place of worship on a regular basis is not all that important in Blue America. It tends to be wealthier, predominantly urban, and unmistakably liberal. In Blue America, the majority of voters think that the federal government should do more to solve problems, and they tend to think that federal income tax should be increased on the more wealthy in order to protect federally funded services. Blue America is pro-choice, favours gun control legislation, is pro same-sex marriage and is supportive of Obamacare. Blue America gets its news from CNN and watches *Saturday Night Live* on NBC. Blue America loved the Clintons and Barack Obama, loathed George W. Bush and hates Donald Trump. This is clearly illustrated in the statements quoted in Box 7.1.

Box 7.1

Polarised views of the Trump administration, February 2017

In early February 2017, PBS reporter William Brangham visited Bellville and South Austin — two counties in Texas. In Bellville, 80% had voted for Donald Trump while in South Austin two-thirds had voted for Hillary Clinton. Brangham asked residents a number of identical questions. Here are their answers to some of them.

Q1: How was election night for you?

Bellville resident Phil Oxley: 'It was great. I was on cloud nine. I was a Trump guy from day one.'	**South Austin resident Ishrat Kundawala:** 'Brutal, heart-breaking, devastating.'
Bellville resident Joyce Knolle: 'I was so excited when he won, because I just believe in everything that he says.'	**South Austin resident Krystle Papic:** 'If I were to have a nightmare that night, then my nightmare would be a reality, because I definitely didn't want Trump to win.'

Q2: What have you made of Trump's cabinet picks?

Bellville resident Neville Remmert: 'I love every one of them. I love Betsy DeVos. I hope she does something about education. I love Jeff Sessions. He's not a racist. It's just ridiculous.'	**Ishrat Kundawala:** 'I don't know how he could have picked more unqualified people to run things like the education department, or Rick Perry for energy.'

Q3: What's your view of [Trump's chief strategist] Steve Bannon?

Neville Remmert: 'I love Steve Bannon. I think he's great.'	**South Austin resident Phillip Yennerell:** 'He's the devil incarnate. Everything he stands for, I do not.'

Q4: What's your main source of news?

Neville Remmert: 'Fox News. I won't look at CNN. I get ill.'	**Ishrat Kundawala:** 'I would say, CNN.'

Source: www.pbs.org/newshour

In 2015, California socialist Arlie Russell Hochschild — a native of Blue America — wanted to better understand those who lived in Red America. So she went to live for a time in Louisiana, deep in Red America, and wrote a book of her experience — *Strangers in Their Own Land* (2016). Towards the start of the book, she writes of how different the social landscape was coming from Berkeley, California, to Lake Charles, Louisiana:

> Certain absences reminded me I was not at home. No *New York Times* at the newsstand, almost no organic produce in the grocery stores or farmers' markets, no foreign films in movie houses, few small cars, fewer petite sizes in clothing stores, fewer pedestrians speaking foreign languages into cell phones — indeed, fewer pedestrians. There were fewer yellow Labradors and more pit bulls or bulldogs. Forget bicycle lanes, color-coded recycling bins, or solar panels on roofs. In some cafes, virtually everything on the menu was fried. There were no questions before meals about gluten-free entrees, and dinner generally began with prayer.

Of course, these portraits are generalisations and, in part, caricatures. But they also contain a good deal of truth and show two starkly different Americas living as almost parallel universes. There are red states like Texas, South Carolina and Kansas and blue states such as California, Massachusetts and Oregon. Twenty-eight states have voted for the same party's candidate in all seven presidential elections between 1992 and 2016. Thirty-seven states have voted for the same party's candidate in the last five presidential elections. But, of course, states are not uniform. There are blue enclaves in Texas — like South Austin, for example — as well as red enclaves in California. But this polarisation of the country and of the parties is the most significant change to occur in American politics this century and it has huge implications for how American government and politics work today.

The two-party system

Evidence of a two-party system

A **two-party system** might be defined as one in which two major parties regularly win at least 80% of the popular vote in general elections, regularly win at least 90% of the seats in the legislature and alternately control the executive branch of government. If these criteria are used in the USA, then US politics is clearly a two-party system.

- **Popular vote.** As Table 7.6 shows, in the seven presidential elections between 1992 and 2016, the Democrats and Republicans accounted for more than 80% of the popular vote on every occasion. Indeed, in four of these seven elections, their combined vote exceeded 95%.
- **Seats in the legislature.** When it comes to seats in Congress, the picture is clearly that of a two-party system. Following the 2016 elections, only two members of the Senate—Bernie Sanders of Vermont and Angus King of Maine—had not been elected as either Democrats or Republicans. Sanders is the longest-serving independent member of Congress, having been elected to the House of Representatives in 1990 and then to the Senate in 2006. But although elected as an independent, he is opposed by only a Republican candidate at each election. And as was clear in the 2016 Democratic presidential primaries, Sanders is really a Democrat. King is a former independent governor of Maine and caucuses with the Democrats.
- **Control of the executive.** In the White House, every president since 1853 has been either a Democrat or a Republican. That is 42 straight

presidential elections won by the two major parties over more than a century-and-a-half.

Table 7.6 Combined Democratic and Republican party vote in presidential elections, 1992–2016

Year	Combined Democratic and Republican vote (%)
1992	81
1996	91
2000	97
2004	99
2008	99
2012	99
2016	94

■ **State government.** Even in terms of state government, the picture is the same. In January 2017, 49 of the 50 state governors were either Democrats or Republicans, the only exception being Bill Walker of Alaska, but he ran — unsuccessfully — as a Republican in 2010, and in 2014 merged his campaign with that of Democrat nominee Bryon Mallott, who became his running-mate.

Reasons for a two-party system

Three main factors explain the dominance of the two-party system in US politics:

■ **Electoral system.** The first-past-the-post electoral system makes life difficult for national third parties. As we shall see later on in this chapter, third-party support is usually widespread but shallow. They pick up a fraction of the vote in almost every state but under a winner-take-all system they receive no reward at all. A national third-party candidate on the ticket merely lowers the percentage of the vote needed by the major-party candidate to win the election.

■ **Broad party ideologies.** When the two major parties encompass such a wide ideological spectrum there is not much room left for any other parties to attract substantial support. The two major parties are ideologically all-embracing.

■ **Primary elections.** The phenomenon of primary elections helps to make the major parties more responsive to the electorate, minimising the need for protest voting. Protest votes often go to third parties.

A 50-party system?

Some analysts challenge the simple assumption that the USA has a two-party system and suggest that the USA has not a two-party system, but a 50-party system. The term 'two-party system' seems to convey the idea of two disciplined, centralised national parties with national leaders and national policy programmes. Although this description might be more appropriate now than it was two decades ago, parties in the USA are still essentially decentralised, state-based parties with no national leader in the accepted sense and no national policy programme — except maybe for four months of every fourth year when these state-based parties must unite in a presidential campaign.

Does the USA have a two-party system?

Yes

- All presidents since 1853 have been either Democrat or Republican.
- Democrats and Republicans combined regularly win over 95% of the vote in presidential elections.
- In January 2017, all 435 members of the House of Representatives were either Democrats or Republicans.
- In January 2017, 98 of 100 senators were either Democrats or Republicans.
- Leadership in Congress is organised by the two major parties.
- State politics is equally dominated by the two major parties.

No

- The USA has a 50-party system with individual state parties being autonomous and ideologically varied.
- Some states are virtually one-party states.
- Third parties have played a significant role in some elections.
- Many voters join 'groups' or 'movements' (e.g. Tea Party) rather than parties.
- Many Americans are self-described 'independents'.

The idea of a 50-party system reminds us that the Texas Republican Party is a very different creature from the Massachusetts Republican Party; that the California Democratic Party is a very different animal from the Georgia Democratic Party. This is the natural consequence of federalism and a country in which every election — even the presidential one — is a state-based election run largely under state laws by state officials.

Furthermore, even if the USA were thought to have a two-party system, the fact that political power in Washington is so often divided makes this less obvious. A two-party system is one in which the two major parties tend to *alternate* control of the levers of power, whereas in the USA, the two parties so often have their hands on the levers of power *at the same time* — one party controlling the White House and the other controlling one or both houses of Congress. As someone commented in the aftermath of the 2012 elections, 'The US is — for the moment at least — a two-party system with no-party rule.'

Third parties

Despite the domination of US politics by the Democrats and Republicans, third parties do exist. There are different types: national, regional and state-based; permanent and temporary; issues-based and ideological.

- The best-known national third parties are the Libertarian Party and the Green Party. The Libertarian Party presidential candidate Gary Johnson was on the ballot in all 50 states in the 2016 presidential election, while Green Party candidate Jill Stein was on the ballot in 44 states and was a write-in candidate in three more.
- Regional third parties have included Strom Thurmond's States Rights Party (founded 1948) and George Wallace's American Independent Party (founded 1968).
- The Green Party and the Libertarian Party are examples of permanent third parties, while the Reform Party and the American Independent Party are examples of temporary third parties.
- The Green Party and the Prohibition Party are both examples of issue-based third parties, while the Socialist Party and the Libertarian Party are examples of ideological third parties.

Impact of third parties

What the USA does not have are national, permanent third parties that regularly win a sizeable proportion of the votes in general elections. There are reasons for this. The status of third parties in US politics is something of a paradox: they are both unimportant and important. Their combined popular vote in 2012 was less than 2%, and just 6% in 2016. But their potential importance is shown in the fact that in three of the nine presidential elections between 1968 and 2000 it could be argued that a third party affected the outcome — in 1968, 1992 and 2000.

In the 2000 presidential election, Nader's 2.7% for the Green Party almost certainly cost Al Gore the presidency. In Florida, where Bush won by just 537 votes, Nader polled nearly 100,000 votes. In New Hampshire, where Bush won by just 7,000 votes, Nader had over 22,000 votes. And exit poll data suggested that at least half of those Nader voters would have been Gore voters — and the other half would probably not have voted at all had Nader not been on the ballot.

In the five sets of House elections between 2008 and 2016, the combined votes for third parties never exceeded 3.6% (2012), while in the Senate races during the same period third-party support averaged 4.5% with the highest figure being 6.6% in 2010. In those elections, the Green Party candidate won 9.4% in South Carolina, the Constitution Party won 5.7% in Utah, and the Libertarian Party won 5.4% in Indiana.

Gary Johnson, Libertarian Party candidate, 2016

Table 7.7 Third-party support in the 2016 presidential election

Candidate	Party	Popular votes	Popular vote (%)
Gary Johnson	Libertarian	4,489,233	3.27
Jill Stein	Green	1,457,222	1.06
Evan McMullin	Independent	728,860	0.53
Darrell Castle	Constitution	203,039	0.15

Activity

Go to the websites listed below, as well as using internet search engines, to find out information on the policies and ideology of three of the USA's most significant and enduring third parties:
- Constitution Party: **www.constitutionparty.com**
- Green Party: **www.gp.org**
- Libertarian Party: **www.lp.org**

Third-party difficulties

Third parties face five significant difficulties in their attempts to win votes in elections.

Electoral system

The electoral system is a first-past-the-post, winner-take-all system. All elections — whether for the presidency, Congress or state or local office — use this system, which makes life difficult for national third parties. Regional third parties can do well. In 1968 George Wallace won 45 Electoral College votes with 13% of the vote because his votes were concentrated in a small number of southern states. In 1992, Ross Perot won no Electoral College votes with 19% of the vote. Perot's votes, by contrast, were spread throughout the entire USA.

Ballot access laws

Third parties are disadvantaged by the states' ballot access laws. Laws in each state regulate how third-party candidates can qualify to get their name on the ballot. Some, such as those in Tennessee, are straightforward. Tennessee requires just 25 signatures on a petition. But other states, such as New York and California, are much more demanding. In New York, a third-party candidate must gain a certain number of signatures in every county in the state. In California, the number of signatures required is equal to 1% of the electorate in the state.

Lack of resources

People are understandably reluctant to give money to parties that they know are going to lose: this creates something of a 'catch 22' situation. Hence third parties cannot compete with the two main parties in terms of expenditure — on organisation, staff, media or get-out-the-vote operations.

Lack of media coverage

Third parties suffer from a lack of media coverage. News programmes do not think them sufficiently newsworthy. The parties can rarely afford the cost of making — let alone of airing — television commercials. Their candidates are usually barred from appearing in the televised debates. In 2016, only Trump and Clinton appeared in the three presidential debates. Both Gary Johnson and Jill Stein were excluded.

Co-optation

What if a third party, against all the odds, does well in pre-election opinion polls and even wins a significant number of votes on Election Day, as Ross Perot did in 1992? This success brings with it a final problem for a third party: the co-optation of its key policies by one or both of the major parties. It happened to Perot when both Democrat President Bill Clinton and the congressional Republicans adopted policies to deal with Perot's flagship policy — the federal budget deficit. By 2000 the federal budget was in surplus and the Reform Party's vote had fallen from 19% in 1992 to 0.4% in 2000.

Debate

Do third parties play any significant role in US politics?

Yes
- Ross Perot won 19% of the vote in 1992 and contributed to President Bush's defeat.
- The Green Party's 2.7% in 2000 contributed to Al Gore's defeat.
- Third parties can lose elections but win influence by changing the policies of one (or both) of the two major parties.
- Some states (e.g. Alaska, New York) have quite vibrant third parties which can play a significant role in state and local races.

No
- The two major parties dominate presidential elections.
- The two major parties control Congress.
- The two major parties control state politics.
- The two major parties will often co-opt the policies of successful third parties, thereby curtailing their electoral success (e.g. co-opting Perot's call for a balanced federal budget).

It is, however, important to ask: what are the aims of third parties? For in the case of Perot, one could argue that it was not to win the presidency, but to have a significant effect on the policy debate. In this, Perot scored a significant victory. Nader's ability to affect the outcome of the 2000 election is another case in point. It would therefore be inaccurate to write off all third-party candidates as failures. Although third parties often fail in electoral terms — they get few votes — they may, as in 2000, affect the outcome of the election both in certain states and possibly nationally, as well as the policy agendas of one or both of the two major parties.

Theories of party decline and renewal

Theories of party decline

It was David Broder who popularised the idea that US political parties were in serious decline. In 1972, he published a book with the ominous title *The Party's Over: The Failure of Politics in America*. The first three words of that title caught on as being shorthand for the demise of America's two major political parties. Then came Ruth Scott's volume *Parties in Crisis* (1979), followed five years later by Martin Wattenberg's *The Decline of American Political Parties*.

Broder's title has often been taken out of context, however. What he wrote was:

> It is called *The Party's Over* not in prophecy but in alarm. I am not predicting the demise of the Republicans or the Democrats. Party loyalties have been seriously eroded, the Democrat and Republican organisations weakened by years of neglect. But our parties are not yet dead…Whatever the fate of our political parties, for America the party *is* over.

There are three factors to consider regarding theories of party decline.

Candidate selection

The parties have lost control over presidential candidate selection (see Chapter 6). Whereas until the late 1960s, presidential candidates were largely selected by party bosses in smoke-filled rooms, now they are chosen largely by ordinary voters in presidential primaries. This is a significant loss of clout for the parties. Indeed, in 2016, both parties had much difficulty in controlling their presidential candidate selection process. The Democrats struggled to anoint their preferred candidate, Hillary Clinton, because of unexpectedly strong opposition from Bernie Sanders. Meanwhile, the Republican hierarchy lost complete control with the hostile takeover by Donald Trump.

Communication with voters

Parties have lost their traditional function as the communicator between politicians and the voters, and vice versa. Politicians who wished to communicate with the voters would do so through a party rally. The same party-organised function gave the voters a chance to communicate with politicians, either through a formal question-and-answer session, or by heckling. Today, politicians communicate their message largely through television, while voters 'speak back' to the politicians through opinion polls. The role of the party is cut out.

Emergence of 'movements'

The emergence of the Tea Party and Occupy 'movements' during the first decade or so of this century showed the extent to which many Americans are more prone to join a 'movement' than a traditional party. Each of these movements has sought to exert political influence on the Republican and Democratic parties respectively. Americans therefore seek to influence the parties more from without than from within. The extent to which the Tea Party movement managed to get its preferred candidates chosen in certain congressional races over the wishes of the Republican Party leadership was, some would suggest, yet another manifestation of the decline of political parties.

In 2016, Donald Trump talked of his campaign — both in the primaries and in the general election — as a movement rather than the activity of the Republican Party. The business tycoon's success in the Republican primaries was described by some commentators as a hostile takeover of the Republican Party, and to continue the metaphor he sealed the deal with his victory in November, despite vocal opposition from many within the Republican Party hierarchy, including the party's 2012 presidential nominee Mitt Romney and both the party's living presidents — George H.W. and George W. Bush. And the same claim of a 'movement' was made by Bernie Sanders during his campaign in the Democratic primaries the same year.

Theories of party renewal

Theories of party decline were popular in the 1970s and 1980s. More recently, however, many commentators have been arguing that US political parties are undergoing renewal. How can these theories of party renewal be supported?

Theories of party decline were exaggerated

It is probably the case that the theories of party decline were exaggerated. Parties might be less important than they used to be, but they still play a significant role in US politics. Both parties could echo the words of Mark Twain: 'The report of my death was an exaggeration.' The death of the Republican Party was reported following the Watergate affair and Nixon's resignation; its candidate was back in the White House in just over six years. The death of the Democratic Party was reported following the leftward shift of the party in the 1960s, 1970s and 1980s, but the party was resurrected by the New Democrat model of the Clinton–Gore ticket in 1992. And when all is said and done, the two major parties controlled the White House, Congress and the vast majority of state governorships throughout the entire twentieth century.

Nationalisation of campaigns

Party renewal has been seen in moves towards the nationalising of electoral campaigns. This was especially true of the Republican Party in the midterm elections of 1994 and 2002. In 1994, the Republicans campaigned around a ten-point policy programme called the *Contract with America*. The brainchild of Congressman Newt Gingrich, this national policy document was supported by nearly all Republican House candidates in that election. It promised that, under a Republican-controlled Congress, votes would be held within the first 100 days of such a Congress on ten policy issues of interest to conservative voters, such as a constitutional amendment providing for a balanced budget and congressional term limits.

Newt Gingrich with House Republicans at a *Contract with America* rally on Capitol Hill, 1995

Then, in 2002, the Republicans launched another successful nationalised midterm election, resulting in the White House gaining seats in both houses of Congress in a midterm election for the first time since 1934. The Democrats followed suit in the 2006 midterm elections with their 'Six for 06' agenda, which accompanied their retaking control of both houses of Congress after 12 years in the minority. Four years later, the Republicans published their *Pledge to America* in advance of the 2010 midterm elections, which listed the policies they would bring to the floor in the 112th Congress (2011–12) if they won control of either or both houses.

Increased partisanship in Congress

A final pointer to party renewal came with increased levels of partisanship in Congress. If parties were declining in importance, a decline in partisanship could be anticipated. After all, if parties no longer matter, why should their members continually disagree? But as we saw in Chapter 3, partisanship has increased significantly in Congress over the past decade or so and shows no signs of abating anytime soon.

Current conflicts within the parties

The Democrats

As the dust settled after the 2016 election cycle, the Democrats were in poor shape. Whatever President Obama's legacy would be, leaving the Democratic Party in a stronger state than when he found it in 2009 would not be one of his achievements. It is in a decidedly weaker state — in the White House, Congress, the governors' mansions and the state legislatures.

- **White House.** Obama's Democrats lost the White House, and the fact that their candidate won the popular vote by nearly 3 million votes will offer little comfort. It is the Electoral College that counts.
- **Congress.** In 2009, the Democrats effectively controlled 58 seats in the Senate and 255 in the House. Eight years later, they had just 48 votes in the Senate and 194 in the House, and were the minority party in both

houses. In those eight years they had lost 10 seats in the Senate and 61 in the House.

- **State governorships.** As President Obama entered office, the Democrats controlled 29 of the 50 state governorships. Eight years later, they held just 16 — that was 13 governorships lost in just eight years.
- **State legislatures.** Here the picture was just as bleak. In 2009, Democrats controlled 61 of the 98 partisan state legislative houses (Nebraska has a non-partisan unicameral legislature). By 2017, they controlled just 31 — a loss of 30 state legislative houses in just eight years. And in terms of seats in state legislatures, the Democrats held 4,082 (56%) of the state legislative seats in 2009, but only 3,135 (43%) by 2017 — a loss of nearly a thousand seats in eight years.

In 2009, the Democrats had overall control of 18 states, in which they controlled both legislative houses and the governorship; the Republicans controlled only 10, with the remaining 21 being split. By 2017, the Democrats had overall control of just 7 states while the Republicans controlled 24. Those 7 Democratic states consisted of three on the Atlantic coast (Delaware, New York and Rhode Island), three on the Pacific Coast (Washington, Oregon and California) plus Hawaii. That was the extent of the party's power at state level — its lowest level of control since 1925.

The Democrats will doubtless see much soul searching before the next presidential election as to why they are in their current state. Doubtless some on the left of the party will be arguing for a more left-of-centre, radical approach, stressing such issues as income equality, the benefits of carefully controlled but benevolent immigration, and civil rights and liberties for racial and gender groups. Others will try to appeal to what they hope will become a growing number of disenchanted Trump voters, especially among the white working class who deserted the party in droves during the Obama years.

These disagreements played out in a somewhat rancorous contest in early 2017 to decide who would chair the Democratic National Committee, pitting establishment figures who wanted to try to work with President Trump on issues of mutual interest such as public works schemes, against those who wanted to take the fight to Trump and his supporters. Before the vote, Bernie Sanders issued a statement asking, 'Do we stay with a failed, status quo approach or do we go forward with a fundamental restructuring of the Democratic Party?' Sanders continued: 'I say we go forward and create a grassroots party which speaks for working people and is prepared to stand up to the top 1%.' The result — the election of Tom Perez as DNC chair — was, in Sanders' phrase, a victory for the 'failed status quo approach' — as had been the choice of the party's presidential candidate the previous year.

The Republicans

After the election of Barack Obama in 2008, the Tea Party movement grew out of the dissatisfaction with Obama's response to the banking collapse and economic meltdown on Wall Street. The Tea Party stood for a strict adherence to the Constitution, limited government, reducing the size and scope of the federal government, reducing federal taxes and reducing the national debt and the federal budget deficit. It also vehemently opposed Obama's healthcare reforms. Working through the Republican Party, it was instrumental in getting congressional candidates selected for the 2010 midterm elections who reflected their views. Once elected — mainly to the House — they then formed the Freedom Caucus, which became pretty much the de facto controller of the agenda of the House of Representatives. And one could argue that in some ways it was the Tea Party that gave birth to Donald Trump in 2016. But what this meant was that, despite being a winning party that year, it was still a party in conflict.

As a result, for a winning party, the Republicans will have a surprising amount of soul searching of their own to do. How will traditional and religious conservatives adapt to the Donald Trump version of Republican ideology? What will the party do regarding the free trade versus protectionism debate? What about the internationalist versus the 'America first' debate? What about immigration and healthcare? Because the party establishment failed to resolve these issues in the run-up to the 2016 elections, there are still a surprisingly large number of unresolved issues within the governing party. How will the Trump White House cope with the party's leadership in Congress, and vice versa? And internally, will the party attempt further to reshape its candidate selection processes? Conflicts are inevitable as the balance of power changes between different factions and tendencies within the party.

Comparing US and UK parties

Campaign finance and party funding

Both the United States and the United Kingdom have faced issues concerning campaign finance and party funding. In both countries this has often surfaced as a result of financial scandals relating either to electioneering or to one of the two major parties. So in the USA there was Watergate in the 1972 presidential election, and then 'Chinagate' during the 1996 campaign. Congress answered with legislation. Yet the amount of money associated with elections, parties and associated political groups continued to mushroom and the $1 billion election was soon to become a common occurrence.

In the UK, there have been frequent allegations of party funding scandals. The Conservatives allege that Labour is in the pockets of the big unions, while Labour accuses the Conservatives of being the poodles of big business — simply because each party is so dependent on these groups for funding their activities. And as in the USA, some changes have occurred. In 2000, the Electoral Commission was created by the Political Parties, Elections and Referendums Act. But, according to Jones and Norton (2014), even after that had been around for more than a decade, a report on party finance by the Committee on Standards in Public Life found that 85% of the Labour Party's income came from trade union donations and that 51% of all Conservative Party income was coming from institutions or individuals based in the City of London. And in 2012, the chief executive of the independent Electoral Reform Society wrote that 'the most recent in a long line of party funding scandals made it clear that it is big business and rich donors — not voters — who's opinions count' (Electoral Reform Society, 2012).

So the pattern goes something like this: scandal over election and party funding leads to widespread concern; widespread concern leads to changes in the law. But then something else occurs: parties, groups and individuals often find ways around the new regulations. And then in the USA there is a fourth stage to this: are the new laws and regulations constitutional? Thus, as we saw in Chapter 5, the United

States Supreme Court has handed down a number of important decisions, the effect of which has been to weaken the laws that Congress has passed.

State funding

Both countries have tried state funding as a way of trying to solve campaign and party funding problems. In the USA, the 1970s saw the introduction of federal matching funds, and these funds played an important role in presidential campaigns for some three decades. In the UK, there was the introduction of Short money and Cranborne money — state money paid to opposition parties to help them cover the administrative costs associated with their role of scrutinising the government. But in neither country has significant state funding of political parties been adopted and this is where the debate is to be had.

Debate

Should state funding for political parties be introduced?

Yes

- It would end parties' dependence on wealthy donors, corporations and labour groups, and thus avoid the perception that such donors are able to buy influence over a party's policies.
- It would enable parties to better perform their important functions in a democracy — organising opinion, representing the people, creating policy priorities, etc.
- It would fill the significant gap created by the dramatic decline in party membership.
- It would lead to greater transparency in party finances.
- It would help to equalise the financial resources between political parties — especially advantageous to minor parties.
- It would make it easier to limit spending.
- It might lead to greater public engagement with parties if funding were linked to turnout at elections.

No

- It would reinforce the financial advantage of the two major parties, especially under first-past-the-post electoral systems.
- It would further increase the disconnect and perceived distance between the parties and ordinary voters.
- It would move political parties away from being regarded as part of civil society and towards being seen as part of the apparatus of the state.
- It would diminish belief in the principle that citizens' participation in politics ought to be voluntary.
- It would lead to objections from citizens who would see their tax money going to parties which they not only do not support, but whose policies they may strongly oppose.
- It would allow parties to have a dependable source of income without the need to pursue policies more in tune with the needs and wishes of voters.
- It would merely reinforce the parties' role in a democracy, which is increasingly seen as something of an anachronism by many voters — especially that now many voters gain their political information not from parties but from the internet and social media.

In terms of the three theoretical approaches, the issue of party funding could be interpreted in line with two of them. First, one could see this in a structural sense. Structures create relationships within institutions, and within political parties the relationships between the party establishment on the one hand and the party members and donors on the other hand may go some way to account for the ways in which parties wish to operate. Second, one could see this in a rational choice sense. The hierarchy of major parties will almost certainly be happy with the status quo; third and minor parties are more likely to favour change. Each favours the funding method that benefits their own party. Hence, the American Libertarian Party and the UK Liberal Democrats, plus the Green Party in both countries, are more likely to favour state funding.

Party systems

The United States

Theories of party systems tend to distinguish between three overlapping formats: dominant-party systems; two-party systems; multiparty systems. The dominant-party system may be applicable to politics within a few of the states of the USA. This would refer to states such as Wyoming or Massachusetts in which, respectively, the Republicans or the Democrats win almost every election, be it presidential, congressional, state or local. It might also refer to certain UK constituencies where one party has such a stranglehold that it is constantly winning the parliamentary seat and constantly winning any elections for local office too.

But when comparing the party systems of the USA and the UK, the other two formats need to come into play. According to Caramani (2011), a two-party system is one in which 'two fairly equally balanced large parties dominate the party system and alternate in power'. This describes the United States' political system. Whether in the White House, the two houses of Congress, the governors' mansions or the state legislatures of most states, the Democrats and Republicans do 'alternate in power', as Caramani puts it. True, we saw earlier in this chapter that if one digs deeper, one can see different, state-based manifestations of these two parties. But essentially America has — and has pretty much always had — a two-party system in which third parties attract very small proportions of the vote and rarely win office at any level of government.

The United Kingdom

The difficulty arises when we try to characterise the party system in the UK. Were we looking at the UK half-a-century ago or more, the two-party label would be equally apt with the Conservatives and Labour alternating in government and alternating in control of the House of Commons, with that chamber being dominated by the members of those two parties and just a handful of members from other parties. In 1955, the two major parties won 96% of the votes and only two other parties won seats in the House of Commons (see Figure 7.5). But following the 2015 election, the combined Conservative and Labour vote was just 67% and there were 11 parties represented in the House of Commons. Yet there was no change in the electoral system during this period. So what caused these significant changes?

The answer lies in the cultural and structural changes that occurred in the UK during those six decades — principally the increase in support for nationalist parties. In 1955, there were nationalist parties in Wales and Northern Ireland but they accounted for only 1% of the national vote between them. The Unionist vote in Northern Ireland was included in the Conservative vote — the Conservative and Unionist Party as it was then titled. The Liberals (as they were then) won only 3% of the national vote. By 2015, six of the eight new parties in the Commons were nationalist parties from Scotland, Wales and Northern Ireland, plus UKIP, and the unionist parties in Northern Ireland which had split away from the Conservatives in the 1970s. Nationalism in Scotland, Wales and Northern Ireland, spurred on by the era of devolution in the closing decades of the last century, changed the UK party system from a two-party system into one that is difficult to categorise.

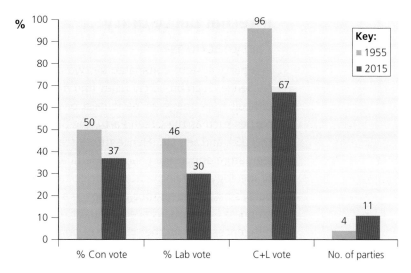

Figure 7.5 Representation of the two major parties in the UK House of Commons: 1955 and 2015 compared

In terms of control of the executive branch, it is still a two-party system with Labour and the Conservatives still alternating control. But the party system in Parliament and in the country is a hybrid multiparty system in a considerable state of rapid change. After the 2005 election, the Liberal Democrats had 62 MPs, but ten years later they had just 10. After the 2010 election, the SNP had just 6 seats; five years later they had 56. After the 1997 election, Labour had 418 seats, but 18 years later they had just 232. The British party system — whatever label one uses to describe it — is clearly in a state of flux.

Changing cultures in the UK

Until relatively recently, the USA and the UK both had the same electoral systems and very similar party systems. Why then do they now have such different party systems although there has been no change in the electoral system at the national level? The answer is to be found in the changing cultures within the United Kingdom. First there were the troubles in Northern Ireland, which boosted support for nationalist parties in the province and split off the unionists from the Conservative Party. Then came devolution in Scotland and Wales and the increase in support for the nationalist parties in both countries. Third came the debate about the status of the UK in the European Union, which gave rise to UKIP and its surge of support as a referendum on the issue approached and was then won by the Leave campaign. Furthermore, the structure of the UK has changed with the ending of direct rule in Northern Ireland, and the creation of the Welsh Assembly and the Scottish Parliament in the closing years of the last century. The structure will change again as Britain exits the EU and would change yet again were Scotland ever to vote for independence from the UK.

Meanwhile, in the United States, no such cultural or structural changes have taken place. In Washington, the party system works under a structure that allows one party to control the presidency while at the same time the other party controls Congress. Hence, as Duncan Watts (2008) explains, 'the British-style divide between government and opposition is absent'. Another institutional factor in creating the current party system in the USA is the nature of the presidency — the ultimate prize in American politics — which can be won only by parties that enjoy broad, national support.

Internal party unity

Party factions

In a party system dominated by two major parties, party unity is often a challenge. Such broad churches find maintaining internal unity much more difficult than one issue, nationalist or purely ideological (or ideologically pure) parties such as the Green Party, the SNP or the Socialist Party — in both the USA and the UK. Hence the existence of party factions — both in the legislature and in the country. Members of these factions stress certain strands of ideology, certain traditions, or certain policies over others. All believe in the party's biggest ideas, but perhaps in a different priority order and with different emphases — perhaps even different methods to achieve them. And these differences may be the product of an era (such as Reaganites or Thatcherites), or of ideology (neo-conservatives or compassionate conservatives), or of traditionalists versus modernists (Old Labour versus New Labour).

Party factions can be constructive — providing new ideas and policies — or they can be destructive as members of different intra-party factions struggle for control and indulge in party in-fighting. Party factions tend to resemble the shifting patterns of sand on a beach. As the tide of ideas — and elections — washes over the party, and as different issues present themselves on the national agenda, factions appear and disappear, morphing into new allegiances and groupings — each with some catchy new name. Hence, the world of party factions in the USA and the UK is the world of Blue Dogs, the Tea Party, Momentum, Fresh Start, Bright Blue or the Freedom Caucus (see Table 7.8). Some might be formal membership groups, while others might be just loose coalitions of the like-minded. Some might exist only among professional politicians, while others exist only at the grassroots. Some may exist at both levels. Some may exist for only short periods of time; others last for decades.

Table 7.8 Examples of US and UK party factions

USA	Democrats	Republicans
	Blue Dog conservative liberal libertarian progressive	Christian Right (Neo-)conservative moderate Freedom Caucus Tea Party
UK	**Labour**	**Conservatives**
	New Labour Momentum Compass Group Blue Labour Labour for the Common Good	Cornerstone one-nation Conservatives Conservative Voice Thatcherite Bright Blue

Aims of party factions

So what are the aims and functions of party factions? Here are eight to consider:

- To accentuate certain policies (e.g. income equality, free trade/protectionism, low taxes, moral issues)
- To focus on a particular aspect of ideology (e.g. conservative Democrats, liberal Democrats, hard left, libertarians)

- To reflect geographic, ethnic, economic, generational, religious or ideological groups within the party (e.g. southern Democrats, Christian Right, one-nation Conservatives)
- To widen voter appeal (e.g. Tea Party, Momentum)
- To extol the party 'greats' of a previous era (e.g. Reaganites, Thatcherites, Bennites)
- To offer diversity within a party that stresses unity
- To offer personal support and encouragement to those politicians/voters of a similar view
- To challenge the party establishment (e.g. Freedom Caucus, New Labour, Tea Party, Momentum)

Effect of factions on voting intentions

The existence of party factions can affect people's voting intentions in elections. If factions are destructive and the party as a whole appears disunited, then this may become a negative issue in an election. For example, the Republicans appeared divided in 1992 when President George H.W. Bush, an establishment, country club Republican — fiscally conservative, but more moderate on social issues — fell out with paleo-conservative Pat Buchanan, who was more in tune with social and religious conservatives within the party. Likewise, there were negatives for the Democrats in 2016 in the fight between the Hillary Clinton and Bernie Sanders wings of the party. During the Trump presidency, one can expect there to be a battle for the soul of the conservative movement within the Republican Party between the congressional wing of the party, the Steve Bannon and Breitbart News wing and the so-called Alt-Right. Polling evidence suggests that voters are reluctant to vote for divided, factionalised parties. The midterm elections of 2018 may test that principle for the Republican Party under Donald Trump.

The same has been true for the two major British parties — for the Conservatives dividing into factions over Europe, and Labour into factions between traditionalists and modernisers, New Labour versus Momentum. When factions are truly destructive, party splits occur, as was seen in the UK Labour Party in the 1980s with the departure of the social democrat faction of the party to form the SDP, which would eventually morph into the Liberal Democrats. There is also the danger that party factions can be led by people who think of the organisation more as a 'movement' of protest than as a 'party' of government.

Effect of factions on party membership and principles

But factions within a party can be constructive, keeping people within the party who otherwise might leave the party — either for the other major party, or for a third party. So, for example, the Blue Dog faction within the Democratic Party played an important role during the first decade-and-a-half of this century in keeping conservatives within the party — both politicians and voters. The same was true of the Tea Party movement for the Republican Party during the Obama years. And the same is true of the one-nation conservatism faction within the UK Tory party during the era when Thatcherism was the majority grouping within the party. It is also true that what is a party faction one moment can quickly become the party leadership the next. Take, for example, the switch from faction to leadership of the Trump America First,

Bernie Sanders addresses a rally in Salt Lake City, Utah, March 2016

Alt-Right Republicans, and the quick change from leadership to faction of David Cameron's Notting Hill, metropolitan elite within the UK Conservative Party following his replacement as party leader and prime minister by Theresa May in 2016.

Finally, in an era when the accusation is often made that modern political parties are ideologically and philosophically lightweight, factions can keep ideological and philosophical principles alive, even allowing them to return to majority favour as the political climate changes. These issues concerning internal party unity can be understood as an outworking of structural factors — the relationships within parties, as well as between the party establishment and its grassroots membership — but also in terms of rational choice analysis as both politicians and members pursue policies and priorities that advance the political goals they seek.

Party policies

In comparing the policies of the two major parties in each country, the danger is to suggest simplistically that the Democrats' policies match those of Labour as two left-of-centre parties, while the Republicans' match those of the Conservatives as two right-of-centre parties. But those two claims mask essential differences, which are best seen by remembering how each of the parties evolved.

- Unlike the Democratic Party in the USA, the British Labour Party came out of the trade union movement and has been a truly socialist party for most of its life. Despite cheap jibes to the contrary by disgruntled Republicans during the Obama years, the Democratic Party is not and never has been a socialist party. Culturally, the appeal of socialism within the USA has never been widespread and for decades had to compete with the fear of communism and talk of a Red Scare.

■ Similarly, the Conservative Party came out of British nineteenth-century politics as a party dominated by the landed aristocracy and the established church. Nothing resembles that in the history of the Republican Party, which was born out of the Civil War.

Such cultural differences have left very distinct marks on all four parties, making it dangerous to offer simple parallels of left and right.

Policy agreements

That said, there are policy areas where the left–right divide does provide a match between the US Republicans and the UK Conservatives, as well as between the US Democrats and the UK Labour Party. Let us consider each in turn. There are a number of policy areas in which the Republicans and the Conservatives are in broad agreement:

■ Both dislike 'big government'.
■ Both favour low taxation when the economy permits.
■ Both talk of being strong on law and order.
■ Both stress high levels of defence spending.
■ Both talk more about equality of opportunity than equality of results.

Equally, there are a number of policy areas in which the Democrats and Labour are in broad agreement:

■ Both put great stress on the rights of minorities — gender, racial, sexual orientation, etc.
■ Both stress the rights of workers.
■ Both favour 'green' environmental policies.
■ Both want equality of opportunity, leading to equality of results.
■ Both favour high levels of government spending on health, welfare and education.
■ Both tend to favour higher levels of taxation on the more wealthy to fund services for the less well-off.

Policy differences

But it is also important to realise that, ideologically, the centre of gravity in American party politics is further to the right than it is in British party politics. What this means is that, broadly speaking, the Republicans sit well to the right of the Conservatives, and the Democrats sit to the right of Labour — certainly Old Labour, and certainly Jeremy Corbyn's Labour Party. Indeed, as Table 7.12 shows, in some policy areas the UK Conservative Party has more in common with the Democrats than with the Republicans. Like the Democrats, the UK Conservatives oppose the death penalty, support same-sex marriage and support a central government-run healthcare system. The Republicans support the death penalty, oppose same-sex marriage and opposed Obamacare as overly centralised. And on the issues of abortion, renewable energy and the role of central government in education, while the UK Conservatives may not be as far to the left as the Democrats, they are certainly not as far to the right as Republicans.

Table 7.9 Selected policy comparisons between US and UK major parties

Policy	UK Labour tends to	US Democrats tend to	UK Conservatives tend to	US Republicans tend to
Abortion	Support	Support	Support but with limits; seen as a conscience issue	Oppose
Death penalty	Oppose	Oppose	Oppose	Support
Same-sex marriage	Support	Support	Support	Oppose
Renewable energy	Support	Support	Support but with limits	Oppose
National healthcare	Support	Support	Support	Oppose
Role of central government in education	Support	Support	Support but with limits	Oppose

Third and minor parties

The data in Tables 7.10 and 7.11 show that, whereas support for third parties in US elections — be they presidential or congressional — is minimal, support for third parties in UK parliamentary, local and European elections has been substantial, with third parties winning up to a third of votes in parliamentary and local elections, and over half the votes in the last three sets of UK-wide European elections. Of course, the European elections were conducted under a proportional voting system, but why are third parties so much stronger in the UK than in the USA even in first-past-the-post elections? There are five principal reasons:

■ The issues that UK third parties reflect are mostly those associated with the four constituent parts of the UK — England (UKIP, with some support elsewhere as well), Scotland (SNP), Wales (Plaid Cymru) and Northern Ireland (the unionist parties, the SDLP and Sinn Féin). The culture and history of the UK affects its party structures.

■ On the issue of Britain's relationship with the European Union — the UKIP issue — both the major parties were taking a mainly pro-EU stance, forcing those opposed to the EU to make the only rational choice of seeking a

Table 7.10 Share of vote for third parties in the USA, 2008–16

Year	Presidential election (%)	House elections (%)	Senate elections (%)
2008	1.4	4.2	3.6
2010	–	3.4	6.6
2012	1.7	3.6	4.2
2014	–	3.3	4.5
2016	6.1	2.9	3.8

Table 7.11 Share of vote for third parties in the UK, 1997–2015

Parliamentary (%)	Local (%)	European Parliament (%)
1997: 26.2	2012: 31	1994: 30.6
2001: 27.6	2013: 46	1999: 36.2
2005: 32.4	2014: 40	2004: 50.7
2010: 34.9	2015: N/A	2009: 56.6
2015: 32.7	2016: 34	2014: 52.5

third party. The USA has no such issues drawing votes away from its major parties.

- Minor parties in the USA face significant problems because of the central position that the presidential election holds in the structure of American politics. On only four occasions in the twentieth century — 1912, 1948, 1968 and 1992 — did a third party manage to mount a serious challenge in the presidential race. There has been no such challenge in the past quarter-of-a-century.
- The structures of the major parties in the USA are more flexible and responsive than their UK counterparts. The use of the direct primary makes the major US parties more responsive to ordinary voters, who therefore see less reason to seek out third parties for a protest vote in the general election. One can see how primary voters can change the policies and priorities of a major party by the way in which Republican primary voters transformed their own party by selecting Donald Trump as its presidential candidate in 2016.
- Finally, elections in the USA are so much more expensive and organisation on a national scale is so much more challenging than in the UK. This again makes it very difficult for third parties to compete in national elections.

Pressure groups

Learning outcomes

Key questions answered in this section:
- How does pluralism explain the theoretical basis of pressure group activity?
- What types of pressure group exist in the USA?
- What are the main functions of pressure groups?
- What methods do pressure groups use?
- What power and impact do they have?
- What are the arguments for and against pressure groups?
- What are the significant comparisons between US and UK pressure groups?

Key term

Pressure group An organised interest group in which members hold similar beliefs and actively pursue ways to influence government.

Pressure groups are regarded as having important implications for a modern democracy. Through them, citizens can participate in the political process between elections. They can also use their membership of them to pressurise all three branches of the federal government — the legislature (Congress), the executive (the president and the bureaucracy), and the judiciary (headed by the Supreme Court). In a country like the United States, with a participatory tradition and an open form of government, pressure groups seem to take on added importance. They benefit from numerous access points within the political system — places where their influence can be brought to bear. They also benefit from a weak and fragmented party system and from election campaigns that are often issue based rather than merely party based.

Pluralism

The Founding Fathers, meeting in Philadelphia in the summer of 1787, did not talk about pressure groups. They weren't contacted by powerful firms from

K Street — the street in Washington DC around which today's lobbying firms congregate. But they did talk a lot about 'factions' in the society they were trying to organise and govern. And 'factions' to the likes of James Madison would probably have been an anathema. What Madison called 'the causes of faction' were, to him, a threat to a stable and secure democracy. But they were also 'sown in the nature of man'. Madison worried that groups would more likely oppress than liberate and therefore believed that the aim of all right-thinking people should be to 'cure the mischiefs of faction'.

The theoretical basis of pressure group activity is to be found in what political theorists call **pluralism**. Pluralism has been written about and debated by a host of eminent political philosophers through the years. In *The Governmental Process*, published in 1951, David Truman claimed that politics could be understood only by studying the way different groups interacted with one another. In the 1960s, it was Robert Dahl's study of local politics in New Haven, Connecticut, that became the classic study of pluralism in the USA. His famous book, *Who Governs?*, was written as an answer to another classic of political science, C. Wright Mills' *The Power Elite* (1956).

Mills had argued that the United States was ruled by a small governing elite — wealthy and powerful individuals — and that, as a consequence, ordinary Americans had little real control over how they were governed or who governed them. Dahl, on the other hand, claimed that US society was based not on **elitism** but on pluralism. In three critical areas — political party nominations, urban redevelopment and public education — Dahl claimed that widely differing groups of ordinary Americans were both active and influential. Dahl's theory was that democracy was not so much a theory about '50% plus 1' as a 'process in which there is a high probability that an active and legitimate group in the population can make itself heard effectively at some crucial stage in the process of making decisions'. Hence, to Dahl, democracy was all about compromise — compromise between competing groups.

Key term

> **Pluralism** A theory that political power does not rest simply with the electorate or the governing elite, but is distributed among groups representing widely different interests.

Key term

> **Elitism** A theory that political power rests with a small group who gain power through wealth, family status or intellectual superiority.

Types of pressure group

Pressure groups are quite different from political parties. Whereas political parties seek to win control of government, pressure groups seek to influence those who have control of government.

Pressure groups vary considerably in size, wealth and influence. In the United States they operate at all levels of government — federal, state and local — and seek to bring their influence to bear on all three branches of government. As a result there are numerous typologies of pressure groups. First of all, one can divide pressure groups into two broad categories: sectional groups and causal groups (see Table 7.12).

Table 7.12 Types of pressure group

Sectional groups	Causal groups
Business/trade groups	Single-interest groups
Labour unions and agricultural groups	Ideological groups
Professional groups	Policy groups
Intergovernmental groups	Think-tanks

Chapter 7 Parties and pressure groups

Sectional groups

Sectional pressure groups seek to represent their own section or group within society. In this first category, therefore, are business and trade groups such as the American Business Conference, the National Association of Manufacturers and the National Automobile Dealers Association. Of great importance are the US Chamber of Commerce, which represents thousands of different businesses across the nation, and the labour unions, most of which represent a particular trade, such as the United Auto Workers or the Teamsters representing truck drivers.

The American Federation of Labor–Congress of Industrial Organizations (AFL–CIO) is the US equivalent of the British Trades Union Congress. Not only industry has such groups: there are sectional groups representing the interests of America's agriculture, such as the American Farm Bureau Federation, the National Farmers' Union and Associated Milk Producers Incorporated.

Alternatively, Americans might join a group that represents individuals with a common gender, ethnic, religious or social characteristic, such as the National Organization for Women (NOW), the National Association for the Advancement of Colored People (NAACP), the Christian Coalition of America, or the American Association of Retired Persons (AARP). Sectional groups also include **professional groups**, such as the American Medical Association, the National Education Association and the American Bar Association. Then there are intergovernmental pressure groups — those that lobby one level of government on behalf of another, such as the National Governors' Conference.

Causal groups

Causal pressure groups campaign for a particular cause or issue. Americans like to join groups, but they are selective. They are more likely than, for example, their European counterparts to join social, charitable, civic, political and religious groups, although they are less likely to join trade unions.

On the whole, however, Americans join, subscribe, write, phone, petition, protest and march more than the citizens of most nation-states. The causal groups they join may be **single-interest groups**, such as the National Rifle Association (NRA), Mothers Against Drunk Driving (MADD), or the National Abortion and Reproductive Rights Action League (NARAL). Equally, they might join an ideological group, such as the American Conservative Union, People for the American Way, or the American Civil Liberties Union (ACLU). These can also be referred to as **policy groups**: for instance, Common Cause, Friends of the Earth, or the Sierra Club.

Think-tanks could be seen as another type of causal group and they are especially numerous in the United States. Think-tanks conduct research, write reports, write articles for publication in leading broadsheet newspapers, publish journals and books, organise conferences and give evidence to congressional committees. Most have a particular ideological slant. On the liberal side come the Institute for Policy Studies and the Brookings Institution. On the conservative side are the Heritage Foundation and the American Enterprise Institute.

Key term

Professional group A pressure group organised to promote the interest of a profession or business.

Key term

Single-interest group or policy group A pressure group created in response to a specific issue in order to promote policies that the group desires concerning that issue.

331

Pressure groups perform five basic functions, although not all pressure groups perform all these functions.

Representation

Pressure groups may perform a representative function. They are a means whereby US citizens can have their views represented and their grievances articulated. They are an important link between the public and the politician, the governed and the government. They provide a channel of easy access through which ordinary citizens can voice their opinions. For many Americans, pressure groups will be the most important way in which their strongest-held views are represented. One's senator or representative, for example, will have many calls upon their representative roles — a great variety of constituents, their political party and the administration being three of the most important. But through a pressure group, women, African-Americans, gun owners, business people, environmentalists, Christians, farmers or retired persons can have their views represented in all three branches of government at the federal, state and local levels.

Citizen participation

Pressure groups increase the opportunities for ordinary citizens to participate in the decision-making process between elections. In the USA, political participation is seen as a virtue. True, elections occur more frequently in the USA than they do in the UK. But when all is said and done, Election Day is merely one day in a year — or, with a primary, maybe two days in a year. Many Americans seek far greater, more frequent participation in the democratic process. Pressure groups also offer an opportunity to participate in a specific policy area — pro-guns, anti-abortion, pro-environment or anti-war, or whatever policy or issue a particular citizen feels deeply about.

Public education

Pressure groups attempt to educate public opinion, warning people of the possible dangers if issues are not addressed, as well as the likely effects of decisions made by the government. As Jeffrey Berry and Clyde Wilcox (2007) comment:

> With their advocacy efforts, publications and publicity campaigns, pressure groups can make people better aware of both policy problems and proposed solutions.

Agenda building

Pressure groups may perform the function of agenda building. In so doing they attempt to influence the agendas of political parties, legislators and bureaucrats to give priority to their members' interests. They may attempt to bring together different parts of US society — for example, business groups, religious groups, state governments and professional organisations — to achieve a common interest. An example given by Berry and Wilcox is of the manufacturers and distributors of CDs, DVDs and computer software working together to get governments to pay attention to the problem of piracy of such goods. As a result of such coordinated agenda building, China promised to close down factories that were illegally duplicating American goods.

Programme monitoring

Pressure groups may scrutinise and hold government to account in the implementation of policies, to try to ensure that promises are fulfilled, policies delivered and regulations enforced. After the passage of the Bipartisan Campaign Reform Act in 2002 — commonly known as the McCain–Feingold Act — the Campaign Finance Institute commissioned a set of studies by scholars on the law's impact on the funding of campaigns. As a result of such monitoring, pressure groups such as the National Rifle Association (NRA) and the American Civil Liberties Union (ACLU) will sometimes bring cases to the state and federal courts, asking the judicial branch of government to monitor the effects of legislation. It was the ACLU that brought the first legal challenges to President Trump's executive order placing a 90-day ban on entry into the United States from seven predominantly Muslim countries during the first weeks of his presidency.

ACLU legal observer at Dulles Airport outside Washington following President Trump's ban on travel from designated Muslim-majority countries, January 2017

Methods used by pressure groups

Pressure groups use several methods in fulfilling their functions.

Electioneering and endorsement

Since the campaign finance reforms of the 1970s, considerable changes have taken place in the role of pressure groups and political fundraising. The reforms limited the amount that any pressure group could give to a candidate in a federal election. What the reforms encouraged, therefore, was the setting up of political action committees (PACs) and Super PACs that could make such donations (see Chapter 6). A PAC is an organisation whose purpose is to raise and then give campaign funds to candidates for political office.

Pressure groups also actively support or oppose presidential and congressional candidates on the basis of the candidates' positions on the policy areas of concern to them. In 2016, the pro-life group the National Right to Life endorsed Donald Trump while the pro-choice group NARAL endorsed Hillary Clinton.

Table 7.13 The 'dirty dozen' list, 2016

Candidate	Party	Race	Incumbent/challenger	State/district	Election outcome
Darryl Glenn	R	**Senate**	**Challenger**	**Colorado**	**Defeated**
Mike Coffman	R	House	Incumbent	Colorado 6	Elected
David Jolly	R	House	Incumbent	Florida 13	Elected
Jason Lewis	R	House	Open race	Minnesota 2	Elected
Joe Heck	R	**Senate**	**Open race**	**Nevada**	**Defeated**
Cresent Hardy	R	**House**	**Incumbent**	**Nevada 4**	**Defeated**
Richard Burr	R	Senate	Incumbent	North Carolina	Elected
Rob Portman	R	Senate	Incumbent	Ohio	Elected
Pat Toomey	R	Senate	Incumbent	Pennsylvania	Elected
Will Hurd	R	House	Incumbent	Texas 23	Elected
Donald Trump	R	President	Challenger	–	Elected
Ron Johnson	R	Senate	Incumbent	Wisconsin	Elected

Websites offered candidate comparisons in crucial congressional races so that voters could clearly see the differences between those candidates being endorsed and those being opposed.

Every two years, the League of Conservation Voters (LCV) publishes its 'dirty dozen' list — the 12 candidates with what they regard as the worst record on environmental conservation. Its 'dirty dozen' list for the 2016 elections included eight members of Congress — four from each house (see Table 7.13). But the LCV's record was far from impressive with only three of its dirty dozen defeated, including only one incumbent. Clearly being on this list in 2016 was not as damning as one might have thought. The LCV's record in previous election cycles had been more impressive.

Lobbying

Perhaps the most effective method of lobbying is the provision of accurate, detailed, up-to-date information to those who need it. Legislators and bureaucrats are busy people who have many demands made upon their limited time and resources. Legislators, in particular, must appear knowledgeable about and take positions on a bewildering number of policy issues. Pressure groups are often the only source of information.

In order to facilitate this method of operation, pressure groups maintain offices in Washington DC, state capitals and other major cities. This allows them to be on hand to lobby members of the federal, state and local government. The presence of lobbyists in Washington DC itself is almost overwhelming and is often referred to as the 'K Street corridor', named after the street in the capital on which the offices of many lobbyists are located. Others are located on streets nearby.

Some of the most notable lobbying firms in Washington are built around former presidential aides and cabinet officers whose visibility and experience helps to attract clients, especially those who need to lobby the executive branch of government. There is, for example, the Podesta Group, started by John Podesta, who is a former White House chief of staff to President Bill Clinton and also served in the Obama White House, with headquarters just five blocks east of the White House at 10th and G Streets.

> **Activity**
>
> - Go to the website **www.opensecrets.org/lobby/** to find information on lobbying spending and numbers of lobbyists.
> - Click on 'Top Lobbying Firms' to see (by year) which firms were the top spenders.
> - Using the internet, Google some of these firms to find out more about their background, activities and locations.

Voting cues and scorecards

Pressure groups also provide legislators with voting cues. Liberal Democrats look to such groups as the AFL–CIO, the NAACP and Americans for Democratic Action (ADA) to provide reassurance that they are taking the right stand on a particular issue. Conservative Republicans find the American Conservative Union (ACU), Americans for Constitutional Action (ACA) and the US Chamber of Commerce equally helpful. Pressure groups such as ADA, the AFL–CIO and the ACU publish regular ratings of legislators, showing how often — or how rarely — a particular legislator has supported policy positions in line with the views of that particular group.

When the AFL–CIO published its Senate Scorecard for the first session of the 114th Congress (2015), it ranked each senator on how they had voted on what the AFL–CIO regarded as 14 key votes during that year. At the approval end of the scale, 22 senators — all Democrats — had 100% ratings, having voted in agreement with the AFL–CIO position on all 14 votes. These included Charles Schumer of New York and Al Franken of Minnesota. The lowest rating was zero — for Republicans Ben Sasse of Nebraska and Bob Corker of Tennessee.

Organising grassroots activities

Grassroots activities by members are often thought to be the most effective of pressure groups' methods, especially when these activities are aimed directly at legislators or policy-makers. Such grassroots activities may include the organisation of a social media or phone 'blitz' on Congress, the White House or a government department. However, knowing that members of Congress pay little attention to the arrival of such communications, pressure groups encourage their members to frame their own written and verbal protests. There are even firms that exist to orchestrate mail, e-mail and telephone blitzes.

Marches and demonstrations are sometimes aimed at state and federal court houses, where other forms of lobbying are inappropriate. Whenever the United States Supreme Court delivers a judgement on a controversial issue such as abortion, school prayers, capital punishment, gun control or minority rights, the pavement outside the Supreme Court building in Washington DC is filled with people from pressure groups representing the opposing sides of the argument.

The power of pressure groups

Pressure groups are big business. The total federal lobbying revenue in 2016 amounted to just over of $3.1 billion. And that sum includes only that income which must be disclosed under federal law. On top of that, clients spent at least hundreds of millions of dollars more on grassroots lobbying, public relations, consulting, strategic advice and many other forms of lobbying that make up the Washington lobbying sector. It is hardly surprising, therefore, that pressure groups have had a significant impact in a number of policy areas.

Environmental protection

Towards the end of the nineteenth century, when both industrialisation and 'westward expansion' were well under way, the matter of environmental conservation became important. This is when the Sierra Club was formed. It was followed in the early twentieth century by the Wilderness Society and the National Wildlife Federation. Such groups have been behind the push towards stricter laws for environmental protection and will doubtless be at the forefront of opposition to the Trump administration's attempts to scale back on environmental protection laws.

Women's rights

Groups such as the League of Women Voters and the National Organization for Women pushed — unsuccessfully — for the passage of an Equal Rights Amendment to the Constitution during the 1970s and 1980s. They have remained very active in US politics, campaigning on such issues as equal pay and job opportunities for women. In addition, they have been involved in the debate over attempting to root out sexual harassment in the workplace, with some high-profile cases in the US military.

Women's groups have also been deeply involved in moves to try to increase the number of women being elected to Congress. The pressure group EMILY's List — an acronym for '**E**arly **M**oney **I**s **L**ike **Y**east' — supports female candidates early in the election process so that they will be able to demonstrate their ability to raise money later on in the electoral cycle and win seats.

Abortion rights

Both the pro-choice and pro-life lobbies have been active in US politics during the past four to five decades. Since the 1973 *Roe* v *Wade* decision by the Supreme Court, pro-choice pressure groups have fought to preserve the constitutional right of women to have an abortion, whereas pro-life groups have fought to have it both narrowed and overturned. Most recently, they have been involved in the debate over the practice of so-called partial birth abortions. When Congress initially tried to ban such types of abortion, President Clinton vetoed the bills, once in 1996 and again in 1997. And in 2000, the Supreme Court refused to allow states to ban this type of abortion. But once George W. Bush had signed a partial birth abortion ban into law, the Supreme Court, in 2007, upheld the ban. In pursuing their respective agendas, both sides in the debate have lobbied the Senate over presidential judicial appointments, most especially those to the Supreme Court.

Gun control

The National Rifle Association (NRA) is arguably one of the most powerful pressure groups in US politics, with a membership of some 3 million. It was formed in 1871 as a group dedicated to teaching Americans how to use guns. Since the 1960s, however, it has been influential in stopping what it sees as encroachment on citizens' rights to own and use legal firearms. It seeks to uphold the strictest interpretation of the Second Amendment right to 'keep and bear arms'. It also works to oppose tougher gun control laws put forward at any level of government. The NRA opposed the Brady Bill and the assault weapons ban, as well as laws requiring background checks on those purchasing guns and the mandatory sale of trigger locks with handguns. It played a significant role in the Supreme Court case of *District of Columbia* v *Heller* in 2008 and became involved in the national debate on gun control following the killing of 20 children and 6 teachers by a 20-year-old gunman at Sandy Hook Elementary School in Newtown, Connecticut, in December 2012.

Tom Mauser (right), father of a Columbine High School shooting victim, at a protest outside the NRA convention

The debate below shows some comments made by members of Congress about the influence of the NRA in the immediate aftermath of the cinema shootings in Aurora, Colorado, in July 2012. Gun control and gun rights featured prominently in the 2016 election cycle, coming as it did after more horrifying episodes of mass shootings in Dallas, San Bernardino, Orlando and Charleston.

Debate

How much influence does the NRA have on the gun control debate in Congress?

Democrat members of Congress

- 'The NRA has been effective in ensuring that there has been relatively little gun control debate in recent years.'
- 'They "own" Congress.'
- 'Thanks to the NRA, you can't even discuss the issue in a rational way, let alone pass commonsense gun control measures.'
- 'The NRA "owns" the Republican Party.'
- 'Right now, a very large number of members are afraid to upset the NRA.'

Republican members of Congress

- 'Few if any interest groups are in the same league as the NRA. They are well funded, they have a committed and active grassroots network, and members of Congress both fear and respect them as a political force.'
- 'The NRA has influence because the majority of Americans agree with their principles.'
- 'The NRA is the best single-issue lobby group in politics, bar none.'
- 'Their membership is vast and deep and protecting our constitutional rights is an important advocacy.'

Source: 'Congressional insiders poll', *National Journal*, 28 July 2012

Economic inequality

The collapse in the banking and finance sectors which began in America during the latter years of the presidency of George W. Bush gave rise to the international Occupy movement to pressure governments to address the specific issue of economic inequality. The first protest to receive the full focus of the media was the occupation of Zuccotti Park in New York City on 17 September 2011 by the Occupy Wall Street movement. Within a month, similar protests had sprung up in each of the 50 states as well as a well-publicised protest in Washington DC.

The movement became known initially through its slogan — 'We are the 99%' — a reference to the concentration of wealth among the top 1% of income earners. It was initially seen as something of a democratic awakening, not only in the United States but worldwide. There is no doubt that in the early weeks of the protests, the Occupy movement drove a good deal of the substance of public and political debate. The Obama administration, the Democratic Party leadership and the American labour union movement initially all showed some interest in and sympathy for the core beliefs and objectives of the movement. Some in America saw it as the left's answer to the Tea Party movement, but its influence was far less significant.

The impact of pressure groups on government

Impact on Congress

Pressure groups seek to influence the way House and Senate members vote. They do this by a number of methods.

Lobbying members of Congress

Pressure groups make direct contact with members of Congress as well as senior members of their staff. Visit the website of almost any pressure group and you will find directions as to how to contact your members of Congress along with regular updates on the current state of relevant legislation going through Congress.

Lobbying congressional committees

They also make contact with the relevant congressional committees — especially those who chair or are ranking minority members on those committees. As we saw in Chapter 3, Congress does most of its work in committees — specifically the standing committees. So it is no surprise that most of the work of legislative lobbyists is directed at committees. Standing committees have significant power to amend legislation which they consider during the legislative process. This provides pressure groups with one of their most valuable access points into the legislative process. One lobbyist commented:

> You have to start at the bottom. You have to start at the subcommittee level. If you wait until the bill gets to the floor [of the House or the Senate], your efforts will very seldom work.

Because the membership of congressional committees is relatively small — about 16 in the Senate, and 40 in the House of Representatives — and also fairly constant, lobbyists find it easy to build a close working relationship with the members of the particular policy-specific committees in which they are interested. Indeed, it soon becomes two-way traffic: not only do lobbyists contact members of Congress to lobby for their policy position, but members of Congress contact lobbyists as a source of information and support. Committee staff are another target of pressure group activity. Staff members are often more accessible than their bosses. Berry and Wilcox (2007) quote a lobbyist for a large manufacturer as saying: 'If you have a [committee] staff member on your side, it might be a lot better than talking to the member of Congress.' Pressure groups will also target standing committee oversight hearings, as shown in Table 7.14.

Table 7.14 Examples of pressure group activity in Congress

Committee	Hearing	Pressure group witnesses
Senate Judiciary Committee	Protecting Older Americans from Financial Exploitation, 29 June 2016	Joseph Marquart, Member, AARP Iowa Executive Council
House Judiciary Committee	State of Religious Liberty in America, 16 February 2017	Kim Colby, Director, Christian Legal Society's Center for Law and Religious Freedom

Organising constituents

Pressure groups attempt to organise constituents to write to, telephone, e-mail or visit their member of Congress to express either support for or opposition to a certain policy. This is most likely to occur just before a high-profile committee hearing, floor debate or final passage vote. In January 2016, for example, a united cross-sector set of over 1,500 pressure groups representing, among others, organised labour and environmental groups, organised a joint letter-writing campaign urging Congress to oppose the Trans-Pacific Partnership (TPP). 'As you would expect from a deal negotiated behind closed doors with hundreds of corporate advisers, the TPP would reward a handful of well-connected elites at the expense of our economy, environment and public health,' said Arthur Stamoulis, the executive director of Citizens Trade Campaign, which organised the campaign.

Publicising voting records and endorsing candidates

As we saw earlier, pressure groups publicise the voting records of House and Senate members, sometimes offering their own rankings. At election time they endorse supportive and oppose non-supportive incumbents by fundraising and media advertising.

> ### Activity
>
> 1 Visit the Vote Smart website at **www.votesmart.org**.
>   - At the bottom of the home page, click on 'Interest Groups'.
>   - In the 'Issue' window, choose a policy issue (e.g. civil liberties and civil rights)
>   - You will then be offered a range of interest groups.
>   - Click on an interest group (e.g. American Civil Liberties Union)
>   - You will then see a description of the group and their latest ratings of members of Congress and/or the group's endorsement of candidates in recent elections.
> 2 Go to the website of the American Conservative Union (ACU) at **acuratings. conservative.org**.
>   - Click on 'Federal Legislative Ratings'.
>   - Use the search filter for year, chamber and state.
>   By looking at the ACLU and ACU ratings, you will be able to compare the ratings by a liberal and a conservative pressure group.
> 3 Go to the website **www.aflcio.org**.
>   - At the bottom of the page, click on 'Legislative Voting Records'.
>   - Click on 'Full Senate Scorecard' to compare senators' current voting records as ranked by the AFL-CIO.

Impact on the executive

Pressure groups seek to maintain strong ties with relevant executive departments, agencies and regulatory commissions. This is especially the case when it comes to the regulatory work of the federal government — regulations, for example, regarding health and safety at work, business, the transport and communications industries, and the environment. Problems can emerge when regulatory bodies are thought to have too cosy a relationship with the particular group that they are meant to be regulating. Are they acting as 'watchdogs' or 'lapdogs'?

Edward Ashbee and Nigel Ashford (1999) identify another close link, between producer groups — such as companies, labour unions or small business federations — and relevant government departments and agencies seeking protection, funding, subsidies or price guarantee mechanisms.

Impact on the judiciary

Pressure groups take a lively interest in the nominations the president makes to the federal courts, especially those to the US Supreme Court. As we have seen, nominations to the courts are for life and the Supreme Court has very significant power, for example to interpret the Constitution and declare acts of Congress unconstitutional, thereby affecting the everyday life of ordinary Americans. The American Bar Association evaluates the professional qualifications of nominees and their evaluation can play a significant role in the confirmation process conducted by the Senate.

Pressure groups can hope to influence the courts by offering *amicus curiae* briefings. Through these, pressure groups have an opportunity to present their views to the court in writing before oral arguments are heard. Pressure groups have used this method to great effect in recent decades, in such areas as the civil rights of racial minorities, abortion and First Amendment rights. Here are some examples of pressure group activities in the courts:

■ One of the most active pressure groups in the courts is the American Civil Liberties Union (ACLU). In 2005, the ACLU was at the Supreme Court in the case of *McCreary* v *ACLU*, in which the Court ruled that a display of the Ten Commandments in a Kentucky courthouse was unconstitutional.

Activity

- Go to the website of the American Civil Liberties Union (ACLU) at **www.aclu.org**.
- Click on 'Defending our rights'.
- Click on 'Court Battles' or 'Supreme Court Cases' to see examples of ACLU activity in the federal courts.
- You can also navigate this website to see other information about ACLU:
    - Issues
    - About
    - Take Action

■ A much lower-profile pressure group, Parents Involved in Community Schools (PICS), brought a landmark case to the Supreme Court in 2007, *PICS* v *Seattle School District*, in which the Court declared it unconstitutional to assign students to public (i.e. state-run) schools solely for the purpose of achieving racial balance.

- In 2008, the National Rifle Association played a significant role in the landmark case of *District of Columbia* v *Heller*, in which the Supreme Court declared Washington DC's ban on handguns to be unconstitutional.
- In 2012, it was the National Federation of Independent Business (NFIB) that brought the landmark legal challenge to President Obama's healthcare reform — Obamacare — the case making it all the way to the Supreme Court.
- In 2017, ACLU was back at the Supreme Court again, fighting a gender discrimination case concerning transgender student rights in Virginia, in *Gloucester County School Board* v *G.G.*

Arguments for pressure groups

The arguments in favour of pressure groups tend to follow the functions they may usefully perform, as discussed above:

- They provide legislators and bureaucrats with useful information and act as a sounding board for legislators at the policy formulation stage in the legislative process.
- They bring some kind of order to the policy debate, aggregating views and channelling the wishes of the clients and members whom they seek to represent.
- They broaden the opportunities for participation in a democracy.
- They can increase levels of accountability both for Congress and for the executive branch.
- They increase opportunities for representation between elections, as well as offering opportunities for minority views to be represented that would be lost in the big tent of political parties.
- They enhance the two fundamental rights of freedom of speech and freedom of association.

The US political process is one that is conducive to pressure group activity. There are many access points in the democratic process where pressure groups can have their say. This is especially the case in Congress, where the decentralisation of power, the autonomy of committees, and the lack of strict party discipline when it comes to voting, all make Congress an institution that is far more open to persuasion by pressure groups than most national legislatures. The number of access points is merely increased by the federal division of powers, which allows many important decisions to be made in the host of state and local governments across the USA.

Arguments against pressure groups

But pressure groups can come in for something of a bad press. Do they enhance democracy? Are they a 'good thing' or merely a 'necessary evil'? Several arguments are made against the activities of pressure groups.

The revolving-door syndrome

Many pressure groups work through hired lobbyists employed by lobbying firms — many based in Washington DC — whose full-time job is to lobby government. There is nothing inherently wrong with that. A criticism that can be made, however, is that a high proportion of these professional lobbyists are former members of Congress or former congressional staff members. This is what is known as the **revolving-door syndrome**: people walk out of the political door, so to speak, perhaps having just been defeated in an election, but immediately re-enter the political world as a Washington lobbyist. Federal law forbids former public officials from taking up a job as a lobbyist within a year of leaving public office, but after that year has elapsed, the traffic through the revolving door from public official to professional lobbyist is quite heavy.

Critics argue that this constitutes an abuse of public service. People exploit their knowledge of and contacts within Congress or the executive branch of government in order to further the interests of their pressure group clients and in so doing make large sums of money for themselves. It is alleged that serving politicians may favour particular group interests because they are hoping for a job representing that interest, should they lose their public office. According to Craig Holman, a government affairs lobbyist for Public Citizen, the revolving-door syndrome has two fundamental problem areas:

> First, you have to wonder what lawmakers are giving in exchange for their potentially lucrative employment, and second, once they leave office, are they exploiting their relationships in office for profitable gain?

The iron-triangle syndrome

The **iron triangle** is a term used to describe a strong relationship that many commentators of US politics see existing between pressure groups and the relevant congressional committees on the one hand and the relevant government department or agency on the other. This cosy relationship — the term 'cosy triangle' is sometimes used — guarantees policy outcomes to the benefit of all three parties involved. One example is what might be called the veterans' iron triangle. On one side of the triangle would be veterans' groups such as the Vietnam Veterans of America, the Disabled American Veterans, the Veterans of Foreign Wars and the American Legion. On another side would be the Veterans' Affairs committees of the House and the Senate. The Department of Veterans' Affairs would constitute the third side of this particular iron triangle. Such an iron triangle can become so powerful that it constitutes almost its own sub-government. This is particularly the case in such policy areas as agriculture and national defence.

The iron triangle is linked with the revolving-door syndrome. A Pentagon general might, after the lawful waiting period, end up as a lobbyist for a missile manufacturer. Similarly, a former staff member from the Senate Armed Services Committee might get a job lobbying for a defence contractor.

The existence of these iron triangles raises the question of whether pressure group activities are compatible with a pluralist society. A pluralist society is one in which political resources such as money, expertise and access to both government and the mass media are spread widely and are in the hands of many diverse individuals and groups. In contrast, many see pressure groups as fostering an elitist view of society in which the aforementioned political resources are in the hands, not of the many, but of the few.

Inequality of groups

Defenders of pressure groups would have us believe that at the very least pressure groups operate within a series of 'competing elites'. They see US politics as a system in which pressure groups, along with political parties, bureaucrats, business people, trade unions, the media, educators, lawyers and so on, compete

The National Rifle Association headquarters, Fairfax, Virginia

for influence over those who make policy. They would argue that, because each group represents the interests of its own clients, this is entirely compatible with a democratic society. Such an argument is associated with those on the right of the political spectrum.

Those on the left criticise pressure groups because they see this 'competition' as being one that is often unequal. As early as the 1950s, President Eisenhower warned against what he saw as the power of the 'military-industrial complex'. At around the same time, the noted American political philosopher C. Wright Mills continued this theme in his 1956 book *The Power Elite*.

There are a number of policy areas in which pressure groups representing the opposing sides of the argument are clearly unequal — for example, the area of the environment. Many would argue that the resources of big business often outweigh the resources of the environmental protectionists. In the policy area of gun control, a battle between the National Rifle Association on the one hand and Handgun Control Inc. on the other is clearly unequal. In the debate over health issues and tobacco smoking, the resources of one side have traditionally outweighed the resources of the other.

Special interests versus the public interest

A criticism levelled at pressure groups is that they tend to put the interests of a small group before the interests of society as a whole. The pressure groups that represent various ethnic groups within American society are a good example — the National Association for the Advancement of Colored People (NAACP), the American Jewish Congress, the Indian American Center for Public Awareness, the Organization of Chinese Americans and the National Association for Hispanic Health, to name but a few. Critics see this as pressure groups adding to a splintering, or 'atomisation', of US society.

Pressure groups tend to accentuate 'me' rather than 'we'. They spend too much time fighting for their special interest and little time working for the wider public interest. Provided their client group is satisfied, they rarely consider the implications for society as a whole. They can also lead to group stereotyping, by making it appear as if all blacks, or all Jews, or all Latinos — or women, or teachers, or airline pilots, or whoever — think the same way and want the same policy outcomes. Some would argue that part of the reason for the criticism heaped upon Supreme Court nominee Clarence Thomas in 1991 was that he was a *conservative* black who did not fit the group-think of liberal politics as espoused by the NAACP and most other black pressure groups.

Buying political influence

The late Senator Edward Kennedy once famously remarked that America has 'the finest Congress that money can buy'. You have to 'pay to play'. But what do lobbyists get for their money? The short answer for the critics of pressure groups is 'a disproportionate level of influence'. Elizabeth Drew (1996) claimed that lobbyists acting on behalf of business corporations wrote legislation for members of Congress. She quoted a *Washington Post* story that a lobbyist for the energy and petrochemical industries wrote the first draft of a bill during that Congress and that lobbyists working for a group called Project Relief were given a Capitol Hill office to use as a 'war room' during an energy debate showdown. Meanwhile, *The New York Times* was reporting a story that a bill to weaken the Clean Water Act was written by a taskforce of lobbyists representing groups such as the Chemical Manufacturers Association and International Paper.

Advantages and disadvantages

Pressure groups

Advantages
- Provide legislators and bureaucrats with useful information
- Act as a sounding board during policy formulation
- Provide order, priorities and aggregation in political debate
- Broaden opportunities for participation both during and between elections
- Can increase levels of accountability for legislators and executive branch members
- Increase opportunities for representing minority interests
- Enhance freedom of speech and freedom of association — two basic democratic rights

Disadvantages
- Revolving-door syndrome
- Iron-triangle relationships
- Inequality between groups leading to unfair representation of some views
- Concentration on 'special interest' at the expense of 'public interest'
- Over-influence of money
- Some methods used by groups are undemocratic

Using direct action

A final criticism levelled at pressure groups is their use of direct action, which is deemed by others to be inappropriate. This criticism is raised whenever pressure groups use what most consider unacceptable levels of violence to pursue their political agenda. In recent years, direct action has been associated with pro- and anti-abortion groups, environmentalists, anti-capitalist groups and groups of the extreme right pursuing their anti-government agenda. Violence — even

Black Lives Matter demonstration, New York City, 2017

shootings, bombings and murders — conducted around abortion clinics by 'pro-life' groups hit the headlines in the 1990s. When the Occupy movement turned violent in some American cities, support quickly evaporated among the ordinary citizenry. The group Black Lives Matter has also trodden a narrow path between peaceful protest and violence.

Box 7.2

***Fortune* magazine's top ten most influential pressure groups in America (2014)**

1   National Rifle Association (NRA)
2   US Chamber of Commerce
3   American Medical Association
4   American Association of Retired Persons (AARP)
5   Americans for Prosperity
6   MoveOn.org
7   American Israel Public Affairs Committee
8   American Federation of Labor-Congress of Industrial Organizations (AFL-CIO)
9   National Abortion and Reproductive Rights Action League (NARAL)
10 National Association for the Advancement of Colored People (NAACP)

Activity

- Use an internet search engine to find out the web addresses for the *Fortune* magazine top ten pressure groups in America listed in Box 7.2.
- Find out what are the goals of some of the groups, the size of their membership, how they operate, etc. to use as examples in your essays.

Comparing US and UK pressure groups

As we have seen, pressure groups operate through a variety of methods: electioneering, endorsing, lobbying and organising grassroots activities. A case can certainly be made that, because of the institutional structure of American politics and government, pressure groups in the USA have more opportunity for influence than do their counterparts in the UK.

Electioneering and endorsing

In terms of electioneering and endorsing, there are simply far more elective posts in the USA than in the UK. This is clear even at the federal level. In the USA, there is a four-yearly direct election for the president and vice president. There is no comparable election in the UK. In the USA, both houses of Congress are directly elected. In the UK, only the House of Commons is elected. In the USA, the House of Representatives is elected every two years. In the UK, the House of Commons is elected at least every five years. In all these elections in the USA — presidential and congressional — there is also the possibility of holding direct primaries. In the UK, only party members have a say in candidate selection.

Then in the USA, there are all the elections at state levels — governors, lieutenant governors, state legislators — of which there is nothing on a comparable scale in the UK, except for elections to the devolved legislatures in Scotland, Wales and Northern Ireland. All this means that US pressure groups have far more opportunities for influence than do their UK counterparts for these structural reasons.

Trade unions and business

In the UK, most Labour MPs have some formal link — either through membership or donations — to a trade union. For example, well over half of Labour MPs in the Parliament elected in 2015 had links with the super-union Unite. Indeed, before the election, Unite had a campaign to secure safe Labour seats for candidates affiliated to it. Many business groups and corporations maintain strong financial links with the Conservative Party. Given the very high levels of incumbency in US congressional elections, American pressure groups give their money overwhelmingly to incumbents, not to no-hope challengers. Business and organised labour gravitate towards the Republican and Democratic parties respectively.

The fact that the UK Labour Party was born out of the trade union movement means that the way labour groups organise and operate in the UK is quite different from how they operate and organise in the USA. In both countries, labour and trade union membership is down from its peaks in the 1970s. In the UK, for example, trade union membership fell from 13 million in 1979 to just over 7 million by 2000, and is now under 6 million. In the USA, labour unions peaked in the 1950s. But American unions never managed to unionise anywhere near the proportion of the workforce which their British counterparts achieved. True, the AFL-CIO — the US equivalent of the British TUC — has more affiliated members than any other pressure group except for the AARP. But millions of American workers belong to unions which are not affiliated to the AFL-CIO. Figures from 2000 show that in the UK 29% of employees were members of a trade union whereas in the USA that figure was just 13%. This has significant implications for workers' lobbying power.

Lobbying

In terms of lobbying, again important structural differences open up more opportunities for pressure groups in the USA than in the UK.

Legislature

In terms of lobbying of the legislature, groups in the UK will be aware that the British Parliament is a much more controlled and disciplined body — largely controlled by the executive and under the discipline of political parties — than the US Congress, over which the executive branch has little or no control, and in which parties have at least traditionally been less able to operate in a highly disciplined fashion. And as Rod Hague and Martin Harrop (2010) observe:

> In the United States, most [pressure] groups have learned that the surest route to the hearts of members of Congress is through their constituents. Therefore groups follow a dual strategy: going public and going Washington.

Unlike the US Congress, the UK Parliament has not traditionally proved to be a happy hunting ground for pressure groups. As Malcolm Walles (1988) explains:

> Operating, as they usually do, under the tight constraints imposed by party whips, MPs are rarely swayed by the pleadings of groups if questions of a party political nature are involved. They may occasionally be persuaded to raise a question in the House, perhaps to pursue a point which is embarrassing to their leaders: rarely will they go to the extent of voting for 'the group' as opposed to 'the party' line.

In recent years, with the House of Lords coming more into the focus of political debate, the unelected chamber has become more the focus of pressure group activity, as peers are not whipped to toe the party line to the same extent as their Commons counterparts.

Executive

The dominance of the government in UK politics means that most UK pressure group activity is focused on the executive branch. Policy-specific pressure groups tend to focus their fire on the appropriate government department in much the same way as their American counterparts focus on the appropriate congressional committee — as well as the executive department or agency. This structural difference — the separation of powers and checks and balances in the USA, as opposed to the fusion of powers and the dominance of the government in the UK — is the most important factor that affects the different ways pressure groups operate in the two countries.

Judiciary

There is a significant difference in lobbying in the USA and the UK because of the difference in political importance of the two judiciaries. As Watts (2008) points out: 'In countries in which the constitution provides the courts with a formal role of judicial review, activists will use the courts more readily.' It is clear that this method of lobbying is much more established in the USA than in the UK. One way in which this is shown is the time, money and energy that groups in the USA spend in lobbying the state and federal courts, given the power and influence of the judiciary in both levels of government. Moreover, pressure groups in the USA have a long and distinguished history of lobbying the Supreme Court and of being a major player in some landmark decisions — on equal rights for racial minorities, abortion, religious freedoms and freedom of speech, to mention just four. It clearly makes sense for pressure groups to aim their fire at courts that have wide-ranging powers to challenge federal and state law.

But in the UK, where the courts — even the new UK Supreme Court — must operate within a constitutional structure dominated by the doctrine of parliamentary sovereignty, and which lacks a codified, entrenched constitution, there is no such tradition of lobbying of the judiciary. With the arrival on the scene of the new UK Supreme Court, pressure groups in Britain may see new opportunities for lobbying, but because the UK Supreme Court does not have the political clout of its namesake in Washington, the balance will doubtless remain much the same.

Grassroots activity

Groups on both sides of the Atlantic will continue to see organising grassroots activities as an important method of influence. In the UK, where political parties are seen as more disciplined and dominant, this often means organising activities to influence one of the two major parties. In the USA, where parties are a looser federation of state parties, influence will be more aimed at the branches of government themselves. In both countries, pressure groups will seek to gain influence in the mass media through the organisation of grassroots activities.

What determines success?

In both systems, pressure group success will be determined largely by the same factors:

- size of membership
- amount of money available
- the group's strategic position in the political system
- the balance of public opinion
- strength of countervailing group(s)
- attitude of the administration (US) / government (UK)
- ability to access the media

But as Malcolm Walles (1988) correctly observed, 'Pressure groups are successful largely to the extent that those who control the authority of the state allow them to be successful.' In neither Washington nor Westminster does political power reside ultimately in pressure groups or their activities, and their success or failure depends in large part 'upon the ability of the duly constituted authorities to stand up to them, and upon their ability to make rational decisions after adequate consideration of all relevant information'. Therefore the answer to those who worry about the power and influence that pressure groups have in either system is not necessarily to weaken the groups, but to strengthen the institutions of government which they try to bend to their will.

References

Ashbee, E. and Ashford, N., *US Politics Today*, Manchester University Press, 1999.

Berry, J.M. and Wilcox, C., *The Interest Group Society*, Pearson Longman, 2007.

Broder, D., *The Party's Over: The Failure of Politics in America*, Harper and Row, 1972.

Brownstein, R., 'How the election revealed the divide between city and country', *The Atlantic*, 17 November 2016.

Caramani, D., *Comparative Politics*, Oxford University Press, 2011.

Drew, E., *Showdown: The Struggle between the Gingrich Congress and the Clinton White House*, Simon and Schuster, 1996.

Electoral Reform Society, 'British voters abandon democracy', www.electoralreform.org.uk, 25 April 2012.

Hague, R. and Harrop, M., *Comparative Government and Politics: An Introduction* (8th edn), Palgrave Macmillan, 2010.

Hochschild, A.R., *Strangers in Their Own Land: Anger and Mourning on the American Right*, The New Press, 2016.

Jones, B. and Norton, P., *Politics UK* (8th edn), Routledge, 2014.

Scott, R.K., *Parties in Crisis: Party Politics in America*, Wiley, 1979.

Walles, M., *British and American Systems of Government*, Philip Allan, 1988.

Wattenberg, M.P., *The Decline of American Political Parties*, Harvard University Press, 1984.

Watts, D., *US/UK Government and Politics: A Comparative Guide*, Manchester University Press, 2008.

Further reading

Ashbee, E., 'US pressure groups: why are some more successful than others?' *Politics Review*, Vol. 23, No. 2, November 2013.

Ashbee, E., 'US pressure groups: are they more powerful than political parties?' *Politics Review*, Vol. 25, No. 1, September 2015.

Bennett, A.J., 'US political parties: why are they so different?' *Politics Review*, Vol. 23, No. 1, September 2013.

Bennett, A.J., 'Just how polarised is America?' *US Government & Politics: Annual Update 2015*, Hodder, 2015, Chapter 2.

Bennett, A.J., 'Which is healthier — the Democrats or the Republicans?' *US Government & Politics: Annual Update 2016*, Hodder, 2016, Chapter 1.

Brown, S. and Gallop, N., 'Should political parties be funded by the state?' *Politics Review*, Vol. 24, No. 3, February 2015.

Rathbone, M., 'Pressure groups: do they strengthen pluralist democracy?' *Politics Review*, Vol. 25, No. 2, November 2015.

Singh, R., 'US politics parties: the source of dysfunction in US government?' *Politics Review*, Vol. 25, No. 2, November 2015.

The first place to go online for information on US political parties is www.politics1.com and click on 'Political Parties'. This will give you information on both the major parties and third parties.

The two major parties each have a website: www.democrats.org and www.gop.com.

Exam focus

Edexcel

Section A (Comparative)

1 Examine the ways in which the party systems in the USA and the UK differ. (12)

2 Examine the ways in which the party policies of the US Republican Party differ from those of the UK Conservative Party. (12)

3 Examine the factors that enhance the power of pressure groups in both the USA and the UK. (12)

4 Examine the ways in which pressure groups lobby the judiciary in both the USA and the UK. (12)

Section B (Comparative)

In your answer you must consider the relevance of at least one comparative theory.

1 Analyse the differences in party funding in the USA and the UK. (12)

2 Analyse the differences in the opportunities for lobbying for pressure groups in the US Congress and the UK Parliament. (12)

Section C (USA)

In your answer you must consider the stated view and the alternative to this view in a balanced way.

1 Evaluate the extent to which the USA has a two-party system. (30)

2 Evaluate the extent to which gender, geographic region, and class and education played a significant role in the way people voted in the 2016 presidential election. (30)

3 Evaluate the extent to which pressure groups perform useful functions in US politics. (30)

4 Evaluate the extent to which pressure groups have made a significant impact in the policy areas of abortion and gun control. (30)

AQA

Section A (USA)

1 Explain and analyse three ways in which class and education played a significant role in the 2016 elections. (9)

2 Explain and analyse three ways in which third parties can play an important role in US elections. (9)

3 Explain and analyse three ways in which pressure groups can enhance democracy in the USA. (9)

4 Explain and analyse three ways in which pressure groups can seek to influence Congress. (9)

Section A (Comparative)

1 Explain and analyse three ways in which cultural theory could be used to study party systems in the USA and the UK. (9)

2 Explain and analyse three ways in which structural theory could be used to study lobbying in the USA and the UK. (9)

Section B (USA)

The party system in the USA

So what kind of party system exists in the USA? The conventional answer is that the USA has a two-party system. Every president elected since 1852 has been either a Democrat or a Republican. Even political outsiders like Dwight Eisenhower and Donald Trump have to be adopted as a major party candidate in order to win the White House. The overwhelming number of members of Congress, and state governors and legislators, are either Democrats or Republicans — and even the few that aren't are either renegade members or members in all but name. Congress is organised on a two-party structure with majority and minority parties in each chamber. And as for the voters, they overwhelmingly cast their ballots for Democrats or Republicans. In the last six presidential elections, the two major parties have always garnered more than 90% of the popular vote — and in three of them around 99% of the vote.

But there is another view. To call the USA a two-party political system is to presume that the Democratic and Republican parties are national, centralised parties with powerful national leaders and overriding national party programmes. Nothing could be further from the truth — even in an era of increased partisanship. Both national parties are essentially amalgams of their 50 state parties and party power — like political power — is decentralised within a federal structure. The Democratic Party of California has little in common with the Democratic Party of Mississippi; the Republican Party of Massachusetts has little in common with the Republican Party of Alabama. And in three elections since 1968, third parties have played a significant role in determining the result.

Analyse, evaluate and compare the arguments in the above passage for and against the view that the USA has a two-party system. (25)

Section C (Comparative)

In your answer you should draw on material from across the whole range of your course of study in Politics.

1 'The party systems in the USA and the UK are largely dictated by the electoral system.' Analyse and evaluate this statement. (25)

2 'The case for state funding of political parties is self-evident in both the USA and the UK.' Analyse and evaluate this statement. (25)

3 'Pressure groups play a much more important role in lobbying the legislature in the USA than in the UK.' Analyse and evaluate this statement. (25)

4 'Pressure group success in the USA and the UK is largely determined by money.' Analyse and evaluate this statement. (25)

Presidents of the USA

1	George Washington	1789–97	Federalist
2	John Adams	1797–1801	Federalist
3	Thomas Jefferson	1801–09	Democratic-Republican
4	James Madison	1809–17	Democratic-Republican
5	James Monroe	1817–25	Democratic-Republican
6	John Quincy Adams	1825–29	Democratic-Republican
7	Andrew Jackson	1829–37	Democrat
8	Martin Van Buren	1837–41	Democrat
9	William Harrison*	1841	Whig
10	John Tyler	1841–45	Whig
11	James Polk	1845–49	Democrat
12	Zachary Taylor*	1849–50	Whig
13	Millard Fillmore	1850–53	Whig
14	Franklin Pierce	1853–57	Democrat
15	James Buchanan	1857–61	Democrat
16	Abraham Lincoln*	1861–65	Republican
17	Andrew Johnson	1865–69	Republican
18	Ulysses Grant	1869–77	Republican
19	Rutherford Hayes	1877–81	Republican
20	James Garfield*	1881	Republican
21	Chester Arthur	1881–85	Republican
22	Grover Cleveland	1885–89	Democrat
23	Benjamin Harrison	1889–93	Republican
24	Grover Cleveland	1893–97	Democrat
25	William McKinley*	1897–1901	Republican
26	Theodore Roosevelt	1901–09	Republican
27	William Taft	1909–13	Republican
28	Woodrow Wilson	1913–21	Democrat
29	Warren Harding*	1921–23	Republican
30	Calvin Coolidge	1923–29	Republican
31	Herbert Hoover	1929–33	Republican
32	Franklin Roosevelt*	1933–45	Democrat
33	Harry Truman	1945–53	Democrat
34	Dwight Eisenhower	1953–61	Republican
35	John Kennedy*	1961–63	Democrat
36	Lyndon Johnson	1963–69	Democrat
37	Richard Nixon†	1969–74	Republican
38	Gerald Ford	1974–77	Republican

39	Jimmy Carter	1977–81	Democrat
40	Ronald Reagan	1981–89	Republican
41	George H.W. Bush	1989–93	Republican
42	Bill Clinton	1993–2001	Democrat
43	George W. Bush	2001–09	Republican
44	Barack Obama	2009–17	Democrat
45	Donald Trump	2017–	Republican

*Died in office †Resigned

The Constitution of the USA

We the People of the United States, in Order to form a more perfect Union, establish Justice, insure domestic Tranquility, provide for the common defence, promote the general Welfare, and secure the Blessings of Liberty to ourselves and our Posterity, do ordain and establish this Constitution for the United States of America.

Article I

Section 1

All legislative Powers herein granted shall be vested in a Congress of the United States, which shall consist of a Senate and House of Representatives.

Section 2

1 The House of Representatives shall be composed of Members chosen every second Year by the People of the several States, and the Electors in each State shall have the Qualifications requisite for Electors of the most numerous Branch of the State Legislature.

2 No Person shall be a Representative who shall not have attained to the Age of twenty five Years, and been seven Years a Citizen of the United States, and who shall not, when elected, be an Inhabitant of that State in which he shall be chosen.

3 Representatives and direct Taxes shall be apportioned among the several States which may be included within this Union, according to their respective Numbers, which shall be determined by adding to the whole Number of free Persons, including those bound to Service for a Term of Years, and excluding Indians not taxed, three fifths of all other Persons. The actual Enumeration shall be made within three Years after the first Meeting of the Congress of the United States, and within every subsequent Term of ten Years, in such Manner as they shall by Law direct. The Number of Representatives shall not exceed one for every thirty Thousand, but each State shall have at Least one Representative; and until such enumeration shall be made, the State of New Hampshire shall be entitled to chuse three, Massachusetts eight, Rhode Island and Providence Plantations one, Connecticut five, New York six, New Jersey four, Pennsylvania eight, Delaware one, Maryland six, Virginia ten, North Carolina five, South Carolina five and Georgia three.

4 When vacancies happen in the Representation from any State, the Executive Authority thereof shall issue Writs of Election to fill such Vacancies.

5 The House of Representatives shall chuse their Speaker and other Officers; and shall have the sole Power of Impeachment.

Section 3

1   The Senate of the United States shall be composed of two Senators from each State, chosen by the Legislature thereof, for six Years; and each Senator shall have one Vote.

2   Immediately after they shall be assembled in Consequence of the first Election, they shall be divided as equally as may be into three Classes. The Seats of the Senators of the first Class shall be vacated at the Expiration of the second Year, of the second Class at the Expiration of the fourth Year, and of the third Class at the Expiration of the sixth Year, so that one third may be chosen every second Year; and if Vacancies happen by Resignation, or otherwise, during the Recess of the Legislature of any State, the Executive thereof may make temporary Appointments until the next Meeting of the Legislature, which shall then fill such Vacancies.

3   No person shall be a Senator who shall not have attained to the Age of thirty Years, and been nine Years a Citizen of the United States, and who shall not, when elected, be an Inhabitant of that State for which he shall be chosen.

4   The Vice President of the United States shall be President of the Senate, but shall have no Vote, unless they be equally divided.

5   The Senate shall chuse their other Officers, and also a President pro tempore, in the absence of the Vice President, or when he shall exercise the Office of President of the United States.

6   The Senate shall have the sole Power to try all Impeachments. When sitting for that Purpose, they shall be on Oath or Affirmation. When the President of the United States is tried, the Chief Justice shall preside: And no Person shall be convicted without the Concurrence of two thirds of the Members present.

7   Judgment in Cases of Impeachment shall not extend further than to removal from Office, and disqualification to hold and enjoy any Office of honor, Trust or Profit under the United States: but the Party convicted shall nevertheless be liable and subject to Indictment, Trial, Judgment and Punishment, according to Law.

Section 4

1   The Times, Places and Manner of holding Elections for Senators and Representatives, shall be prescribed in each State by the Legislature thereof; but the Congress may at any time by Law make or alter such Regulations, except as to the Place of Chusing Senators.

2   The Congress shall assemble at least once in every Year, and such Meeting shall be on the first Monday in December, unless they shall by Law appoint a different Day.

Section 5

1   Each House shall be the Judge of the Elections, Returns and Qualifications of its own Members, and a Majority of each shall constitute a Quorum to do Business; but a smaller number may adjourn from day to day, and may be authorized to compel the Attendance of absent Members, in such Manner, and under such Penalties as each House may provide.

2   Each House may determine the Rules of its Proceedings, punish its Members for disorderly Behavior, and, with the Concurrence of two thirds, expel a Member.

3   Each House shall keep a Journal of its Proceedings, and from time to time publish the same, excepting such Parts as may in their Judgment require Secrecy; and the Yeas and Nays of the Members of either House on any question shall, at the Desire of one fifth of those Present, be entered on the Journal.

4   Neither House, during the Session of Congress, shall, without the Consent of the other, adjourn for more than three days, nor to any other Place than that in which the two Houses shall be sitting.

Section 6

1   The Senators and Representatives shall receive a Compensation for their Services, to be ascertained by Law, and paid out of the Treasury of the United States. They shall in all Cases, except Treason, Felony and Breach of the Peace, be privileged from Arrest during their Attendance at the Session of their respective Houses, and in going to and returning from the same; and for any Speech or Debate in either House, they shall not be questioned in any other Place.

2   No Senator or Representative shall, during the Time for which he was elected, be appointed to any civil Office under the Authority of the United States which shall have been created, or the Emoluments whereof shall have been increased during such time; and no Person holding any Office under the United States, shall be a Member of either House during his Continuance in Office.

Section 7

1   All bills for raising Revenue shall originate in the House of Representatives; but the Senate may propose or concur with Amendments as on other Bills.

2   Every Bill which shall have passed the House of Representatives and the Senate, shall, before it become a Law, be presented to the President of the United States; If he approve he shall sign it, but if not he shall return it, with his Objections to that House in which it shall have originated, who shall enter the Objections at large on their Journal, and proceed to reconsider it. If after such Reconsideration two thirds of that House shall agree to pass the Bill, it shall be sent, together with the Objections, to the other House, by which it shall likewise be reconsidered, and if approved by two thirds of that House, it shall become a Law. But in all such Cases the Votes of both Houses shall be determined by Yeas and Nays, and the Names of the Persons voting for and against the Bill shall be entered on the Journal of each House respectively. If any Bill shall not be returned by the President within ten Days (Sundays excepted) after it shall have been presented to him, the Same shall be a Law, in like Manner as if he had signed it, unless the Congress by their Adjournment prevent its Return, in which Case it shall not be a Law.

3   Every Order, Resolution, or Vote to which the Concurrence of the Senate and House of Representatives may be necessary (except on a question of Adjournment) shall be presented to the President of the United States; and before the Same shall take Effect, shall be approved by him, or being disapproved by him, shall be repassed by two thirds of the Senate and House of Representatives, according to the Rules and Limitations prescribed in the Case of a Bill.

Section 8

1 The Congress shall have Power To lay and collect Taxes, Duties, Imposts and Excises, to pay the Debts and provide for the common Defence and general Welfare of the United States; but all Duties, Imposts and Excises shall be uniform throughout the United States;

2 To borrow money on the credit of the United States;

3 To regulate Commerce with foreign Nations, and among the several States, and with the Indian Tribes;

4 To establish an uniform Rule of Naturalization, and uniform Laws on the subject of Bankruptcies throughout the United States;

5 To coin Money, regulate the Value thereof, and of foreign Coin, and fix the Standard of Weights and Measures;

6 To provide for the Punishment of counterfeiting the Securities and current Coin of the United States;

7 To establish Post Offices and Post Roads;

8 To promote the Progress of Science and useful Arts, by securing for limited Times to Authors and Inventors the exclusive Right to their respective Writings and Discoveries;

9 To constitute Tribunals inferior to the supreme Court;

10 To define and punish Piracies and Felonies committed on the high Seas, and Offenses against the Law of Nations;

11 To declare War, grant Letters of Marque and Reprisal, and make Rules concerning Captures on Land and Water;

12 To raise and support Armies, but no Appropriation of Money to that Use shall be for a longer Term than two Years;

13 To provide and maintain a Navy;

14 To make Rules for the Government and Regulation of the land and naval Forces;

15 To provide for calling forth the Militia to execute the Laws of the Union, suppress Insurrections and repel Invasions;

16 To provide for organizing, arming, and disciplining the Militia, and for governing such Part of them as may be employed in the Service of the United States, reserving to the States respectively, the Appointment of the Officers, and the Authority of training the Militia according to the discipline prescribed by Congress;

17 To exercise exclusive Legislation in all Cases whatsoever, over such District (not exceeding ten Miles square) as may, by Cession of particular States, and the acceptance of Congress, become the Seat of the Government of the United States, and to exercise like Authority over all Places purchased by the Consent of the Legislature of the State in which the Same shall be, for the Erection of Forts, Magazines, Arsenals, dock-Yards, and other needful Buildings; And

18 To make all Laws which shall be necessary and proper for carrying into Execution the foregoing Powers, and all other Powers vested by this Constitution in the Government of the United States, or in any Department or Officer thereof.

Section 9

1 The Migration or Importation of such Persons as any of the States now existing shall think proper to admit, shall not be prohibited by the Congress prior to the Year one thousand eight hundred and eight, but a tax or duty

may be imposed on such Importation, not exceeding ten dollars for each Person.

2   The Privilege of the Writ of Habeas Corpus shall not be suspended, unless when in Cases of Rebellion or Invasion the public Safety may require it.

3   No Bill of Attainder or ex post facto Law shall be passed.

4   No Capitation, or other direct, Tax shall be laid, unless in Proportion to the Census or Enumeration herein before directed to be taken.

5   No Tax or Duty shall be laid on Articles exported from any State.

6   No Preference shall be given by any Regulation of Commerce or Revenue to the Ports of one State over those of another: nor shall Vessels bound to, or from, one State, be obliged to enter, clear, or pay Duties in another.

7   No Money shall be drawn from the Treasury, but in Consequence of Appropriations made by Law; and a regular Statement and Account of the Receipts and Expenditures of all public Money shall be published from time to time.

8   No Title of Nobility shall be granted by the United States: And no Person holding any Office of Profit or Trust under them, shall, without the Consent of the Congress, accept of any present, Emolument, Office, or Title, of any kind whatever, from any King, Prince or foreign State.

Section 10

1   No State shall enter into any Treaty, Alliance, or Confederation; grant Letters of Marque and Reprisal; coin Money; emit Bills of Credit; make any Thing but gold and silver Coin a Tender in Payment of Debts; pass any Bill of Attainder, ex post facto Law, or Law impairing the Obligation of Contracts, or grant any Title of Nobility.

2   No State shall, without the Consent of the Congress, lay any Imposts or Duties on Imports or Exports, except what may be absolutely necessary for executing its inspection Laws: and the net Produce of all Duties and Imposts, laid by any State on Imports or Exports, shall be for the Use of the Treasury of the United States; and all such Laws shall be subject to the Revision and Controul of the Congress.

3   No State shall, without the Consent of Congress, lay any duty of Tonnage, keep Troops, or Ships of War in time of Peace, enter into any Agreement or Compact with another State, or with a foreign Power, or engage in War, unless actually invaded, or in such imminent Danger as will not admit of delay.

Article II

Section 1

1   The executive Power shall be vested in a President of the United States of America. He shall hold his Office during the Term of four Years, and, together with the Vice-President chosen for the same Term, be elected, as follows:

2   Each State shall appoint, in such Manner as the Legislature thereof may direct, a Number of Electors, equal to the whole Number of Senators and Representatives to which the State may be entitled in the Congress: but no Senator or Representative, or Person holding an Office of Trust or Profit under the United States, shall be appointed an Elector.

3   The Electors shall meet in their respective States, and vote by Ballot for two persons, of whom one at least shall not libe an Inhabitant of the same State with themselves. And they shall make a List of all the Persons voted for, and of the Number of Votes for each; which List they shall sign and certify, and transmit sealed to the Seat of the Government of the United States, directed to the President of the Senate. The President of the Senate shall, in the Presence of the Senate and House of Representatives, open all the Certificates, and the Votes shall then be counted. The Person having the greatest Number of Votes shall be the President, if such Number be a Majority of the whole Number of Electors appointed; and if there be more than one who have such Majority, and have an equal Number of Votes, then the House of Representatives shall immediately chuse by Ballot one of them for President; and if no Person have a Majority, then from the five highest on the List the said House shall in like Manner chuse the President. But in chusing the President, the Votes shall be taken by States, the Representation from each State having one Vote; a quorum for this Purpose shall consist of a Member or Members from two thirds of the States, and a Majority of all the States shall be necessary to a Choice. In every Case, after the Choice of the President, the Person having the greatest Number of Votes of the Electors shall be the Vice President. But if there should remain two or more who have equal Votes, the Senate shall chuse from them by Ballot the Vice-President.

4   The Congress may determine the Time of chusing the Electors, and the Day on which they shall give their Votes; which Day shall be the same throughout the United States.

5   No person except a natural born Citizen, or a Citizen of the United States, at the time of the Adoption of this Constitution, shall be eligible to the Office of President; neither shall any Person be eligible to that Office who shall not have attained to the Age of thirty-five Years, and been fourteen Years a Resident within the United States.

6   In Case of the Removal of the President from Office, or of his Death, Resignation, or Inability to discharge the Powers and Duties of the said Office, the same shall devolve on the Vice President, and the Congress may by Law provide for the Case of Removal, Death, Resignation or Inability, both of the President and Vice President, declaring what Officer shall then act as President, and such Officer shall act accordingly, until the Disability be removed, or a President shall be elected.

7   The President shall, at stated Times, receive for his Services, a Compensation, which shall neither be increased nor diminished during the Period for which he shall have been elected, and he shall not receive within that Period any other Emolument from the United States, or any of them.

8   Before he enter on the Execution of his Office, he shall take the following Oath or Affirmation:

"I do solemnly swear (or affirm) that I will faithfully execute the Office of President of the United States, and will to the best of my Ability, preserve, protect and defend the Constitution of the United States."

Section 2

1   The President shall be Commander in Chief of the Army and Navy of the United States, and of the Militia of the several States, when called into the actual Service of the United States; he may require the Opinion, in writing,

of the principal Officer in each of the executive Departments, upon any subject relating to the Duties of their respective Offices, and he shall have Power to Grant Reprieves and Pardons for Offences against the United States, except in Cases of Impeachment.

2   He shall have Power, by and with the Advice and Consent of the Senate, to make Treaties, provided two thirds of the Senators present concur; and he shall nominate, and by and with the Advice and Consent of the Senate, shall appoint Ambassadors, other public Ministers and Consuls, Judges of the supreme Court, and all other Officers of the United States, whose Appointments are not herein otherwise provided for, and which shall be established by Law: but the Congress may by Law vest the Appointment of such inferior Officers, as they think proper, in the President alone, in the Courts of Law, or in the Heads of Departments.

3   The President shall have Power to fill up all Vacancies that may happen during the Recess of the Senate, by granting Commissions which shall expire at the End of their next Session.

Section 3

He shall from time to time give to the Congress Information of the State of the Union, and recommend to their Consideration such Measures as he shall judge necessary and expedient; he may, on extraordinary Occasions, convene both Houses, or either of them, and in Case of Disagreement between them, with Respect to the Time of Adjournment, he may adjourn them to such Time as he shall think proper; he shall receive Ambassadors and other public Ministers; he shall take Care that the Laws be faithfully executed, and shall Commission all the Officers of the United States.

Section 4

The President, Vice President and all civil Officers of the United States, shall be removed from Office on Impeachment for, and Conviction of, Treason, Bribery, or other high Crimes and Misdemeanors.

Article III

Section 1

The judicial Power of the United States, shall be vested in one supreme Court, and in such inferior Courts as the Congress may from time to time ordain and establish. The Judges, both of the supreme and inferior Courts, shall hold their Offices during good Behaviour, and shall, at stated Times, receive for their Services a Compensation, which shall not be diminished during their Continuance in Office.

Section 2

1   The judicial Power shall extend to all Cases, in Law and Equity, arising under this Constitution, the Laws of the United States, and Treaties made, or which shall be made, under their Authority; to all Cases affecting Ambassadors, other public Ministers and Consuls; to all Cases of admiralty and maritime Jurisdiction; to Controversies to which the United States shall be a Party; to Controversies between two or more States; between a State and Citizens of another State; between Citizens of different States; between

Citizens of the same State claiming Lands under Grants of different States, and between a State, or the Citizens thereof, and foreign States, Citizens or Subjects.

2   In all Cases affecting Ambassadors, other public Ministers and Consuls, and those in which a State shall be Party, the supreme Court shall have original Jurisdiction. In all the other Cases before mentioned, the supreme Court shall have appellate Jurisdiction, both as to Law and Fact, with such Exceptions, and under such Regulations as the Congress shall make.

3   The Trial of all Crimes, except in Cases of Impeachment, shall be by Jury; and such Trial shall be held in the State where the said Crimes shall have been committed; but when not committed within any State, the Trial shall be at such Place or Places as the Congress may by Law have directed.

Section 3

1   Treason against the United States, shall consist only in levying War against them, or in adhering to their Enemies, giving them Aid and Comfort. No Person shall be convicted of Treason unless on the Testimony of two Witnesses to the same overt Act, or on Confession in open Court.

2   The Congress shall have power to declare the Punishment of Treason, but no Attainder of Treason shall work Corruption of Blood, or Forfeiture except during the Life of the Person attainted.

Article IV

Section 1

Full Faith and Credit shall be given in each State to the public Acts, Records, and judicial Proceedings of every other State. And the Congress may by general Laws prescribe the Manner in which such Acts, Records and Proceedings shall be proved, and the Effect thereof.

Section 2

1   The Citizens of each State shall be entitled to all Privileges and Immunities of Citizens in the several States.

2   A Person charged in any State with Treason, Felony, or other Crime, who shall flee from Justice, and be found in another State, shall on demand of the executive Authority of the State from which he fled, be delivered up, to be removed to the State having Jurisdiction of the Crime.

3   No Person held to Service or Labour in one State, under the Laws thereof, escaping into another, shall, in Consequence of any Law or Regulation therein, be discharged from such Service or Labour, But shall be delivered up on Claim of the Party to whom such Service or Labour may be due.

Section 3

1   New States may be admitted by the Congress into this Union; but no new States shall be formed or erected within the Jurisdiction of any other State; nor any State be formed by the Junction of two or more States, or parts of States, without the Consent of the Legislatures of the States concerned as well as of the Congress.

2   The Congress shall have Power to dispose of and make all needful Rules and Regulations respecting the Territory or other Property belonging to the

United States; and nothing in this Constitution shall be so construed as to Prejudice any Claims of the United States, or of any particular State.

Section 4

The United States shall guarantee to every State in this Union a Republican Form of Government, and shall protect each of them against Invasion; and on Application of the Legislature, or of the Executive (when the Legislature cannot be convened) against domestic Violence.

Article V

The Congress, whenever two thirds of both Houses shall deem it necessary, shall propose Amendments to this Constitution, or, on the Application of the Legislatures of two thirds of the several States, shall call a Convention for proposing Amendments, which, in either Case, shall be valid to all Intents and Purposes, as part of this Constitution, when ratified by the Legislatures of three fourths of the several States, or by Conventions in three fourths thereof, as the one or the other Mode of Ratification may be proposed by the Congress; Provided that no Amendment which may be made prior to the Year One thousand eight hundred and eight shall in any Manner affect the first and fourth Clauses in the Ninth Section of the first Article; and that no State, without its Consent, shall be deprived of its equal Suffrage in the Senate.

Article VI

1   All Debts contracted and Engagements entered into, before the Adoption of this Constitution, shall be as valid against the United States under this Constitution, as under the Confederation.
2   This Constitution, and the Laws of the United States which shall be made in Pursuance thereof; and all Treaties made, or which shall be made, under the Authority of the United States, shall be the supreme Law of the Land; and the Judges in every State shall be bound thereby, any Thing in the Constitution or Laws of any State to the Contrary notwithstanding.
3   The Senators and Representatives before mentioned, and the Members of the several State Legislatures, and all executive and judicial Officers, both of the United States and of the several States, shall be bound by Oath or Affirmation, to support this Constitution; but no religious Test shall ever be required as a Qualification to any Office or public Trust under the United States.

Article VII

The Ratification of the Conventions of nine States, shall be sufficient for the Establishment of this Constitution between the States so ratifying the Same.
Done in Convention by the Unanimous Consent of the States present the Seventeenth Day of September in the Year of our Lord one thousand seven hundred and Eighty seven and of the Independence of the United States of America the Twelfth.

Amendments to the Constitution

Amendment I (1791)

Congress shall make no law respecting an establishment of religion, or prohibiting the free exercise thereof; or abridging the freedom of speech, or of the press; or the right of the people peaceably to assemble, and to petition the Government for a redress of grievances.

Amendment II (1791)

A well regulated Militia, being necessary to the security of a free State, the right of the people to keep and bear Arms, shall not be infringed.

Amendment III (1791)

No Soldier shall, in time of peace be quartered in any house, without the consent of the Owner, nor in time of war, but in a manner to be prescribed by law.

Amendment IV (1791)

The right of the people to be secure in their persons, houses, papers, and effects, against unreasonable searches and seizures, shall not be violated, and no Warrants shall issue, but upon probable cause, supported by Oath or affirmation, and particularly describing the place to be searched, and the persons or things to be seized.

Amendment V (1791)

No person shall be held to answer for a capital, or otherwise infamous crime, unless on a presentment or indictment of a Grand Jury, except in cases arising in the land or naval forces, or in the Militia, when in actual service in time of War or public danger; nor shall any person be subject for the same offence to be twice put in jeopardy of life or limb; nor shall be compelled in any criminal case to be a witness against himself, nor be deprived of life, liberty, or property, without due process of law; nor shall private property be taken for public use, without just compensation.

Amendment VI (1791)

In all criminal prosecutions, the accused shall enjoy the right to a speedy and public trial, by an impartial jury of the State and district wherein the crime shall have been committed, which district shall have been previously ascertained by law, and to be informed of the nature and cause of the accusation; to be confronted with the witnesses against him; to have compulsory process for obtaining witnesses in his favor, and to have the Assistance of Counsel for his defence.

Amendment VII (1791)

In Suits at common law, where the value in controversy shall exceed twenty dollars, the right of trial by jury shall be preserved, and no fact tried by a jury, shall be otherwise re-examined in any Court of the United States, than according to the rules of the common law.

Amendment VIII (1791)

Excessive bail shall not be required, nor excessive fines imposed, nor cruel and unusual punishments inflicted.

Amendment IX (1791)

The enumeration in the Constitution, of certain rights, shall not be construed to deny or disparage others retained by the people.

Amendment X (1791)

The powers not delegated to the United States by the Constitution, nor prohibited by it to the States, are reserved to the States respectively, or to the people.

Amendment XI (1798)

The Judicial power of the United States shall not be construed to extend to any suit in law or equity, commenced or prosecuted against one of the United States by Citizens of another State, or by Citizens or Subjects of any Foreign State.

Amendment XII (1804)

The Electors shall meet in their respective states, and vote by ballot for President and Vice-President, one of whom, at least, shall not be an inhabitant of the same state with themselves; they shall name in their ballots the person voted for as President, and in distinct ballots the person voted for as Vice-President, and they shall make distinct lists of all persons voted for as President, and of all persons voted for as Vice-President, and of the number of votes for each, which lists they shall sign and certify, and transmit sealed to the seat of the government of the United States, directed to the President of the Senate.

The President of the Senate shall, in the presence of the Senate and House of Representatives, open all the certificates and the votes shall then be counted.

The person having the greatest Number of votes for President, shall be the President, if such number be a majority of the whole number of Electors appointed; and if no person have such majority, then from the persons having the highest numbers not exceeding three on the list of those voted for as President, the House of Representatives shall choose immediately, by ballot, the President. But in choosing the President, the votes shall be taken by states, the representation from each state having one vote; a quorum for this purpose shall consist of a member or members from two-thirds of the states, and a majority of all the states shall be necessary to a choice. And if the House of Representatives shall not choose a President whenever the right of choice shall devolve upon them, before the fourth day of March next following, then the Vice-President shall act as President, as in the case of the death or other constitutional disability of the President.

The person having the greatest number of votes as Vice-President, shall be the Vice-President, if such number be a majority of the whole number of Electors appointed, and if no person have a majority, then from the two highest numbers on the list, the Senate shall choose the Vice-President; a quorum for the purpose shall consist of two-thirds of the whole number of Senators, and a majority of the whole number shall be necessary to a choice. But no person constitutionally ineligible to the office of President shall be eligible to that of Vice-President of the United States.

Amendment XIII (1865)

1. Neither slavery nor involuntary servitude, except as a punishment for crime whereof the party shall have been duly convicted, shall exist within the United States, or any place subject to their jurisdiction.
2. Congress shall have power to enforce this article by appropriate legislation.

Amendment XIV (1865)

1. All persons born or naturalized in the United States, and subject to the jurisdiction thereof, are citizens of the United States and of the State wherein they reside. No State shall make or enforce any law which shall abridge the privileges or immunities of citizens of the United States; nor shall any State deprive any person of life, liberty, or property, without due process of law; nor deny to any person within its jurisdiction the equal protection of the laws.
2. Representatives shall be apportioned among the several States according to their respective numbers, counting the whole number of persons in each State, excluding Indians not taxed. But when the right to vote at any election for the choice of electors for President and Vice-President of the United States, Representatives in Congress, the Executive and Judicial officers of a State, or the members of the Legislature thereof, is denied to any of the male inhabitants of such State, being twenty-one years of age, and citizens of the United States, or in any way abridged, except for participation in rebellion, or other crime, the basis of representation therein shall be reduced in the proportion which the number of such male citizens shall bear to the whole number of male citizens twenty-one years of age in such State.
3. No person shall be a Senator or Representative in Congress, or elector of President and Vice-President, or hold any office, civil or military, under the United States, or under any State, who, having previously taken an oath, as a member of Congress, or as an officer of the United States, or as a member of any State legislature, or as an executive or judicial officer of any State, to support the Constitution of the United States, shall have engaged in insurrection or rebellion against the same, or given aid or comfort to the enemies thereof. But Congress may by a vote of two-thirds of each House, remove such disability.
4. The validity of the public debt of the United States, authorized by law, including debts incurred for payment of pensions and bounties for services in suppressing insurrection or rebellion, shall not be questioned. But neither the United States nor any State shall assume or pay any debt or obligation incurred in aid of insurrection or rebellion against the United States, or any claim for the loss or emancipation of any slave; but all such debts, obligations and claims shall be held illegal and void.
5. The Congress shall have power to enforce, by appropriate legislation, the provisions of this article.

Amendment XV (1870)

1. The right of citizens of the United States to vote shall not be denied or abridged by the United States or by any State on account of race, color, or previous condition of servitude.
2. The Congress shall have power to enforce this article by appropriate legislation.

Amendment XVI (1913)

The Congress shall have power to lay and collect taxes on incomes, from whatever source derived, without apportionment among the several States, and without regard to any census or enumeration.

Amendment XVII (1913)

1   The Senate of the United States shall be composed of two Senators from each State, elected by the people thereof, for six years; and each Senator shall have one vote. The electors in each State shall have the qualifications requisite for electors of the most numerous branch of the State legislatures.
2   When vacancies happen in the representation of any State in the Senate, the executive authority of such State shall issue writs of election to fill such vacancies: Provided, That the legislature of any State may empower the executive thereof to make temporary appointments until the people fill the vacancies by election as the legislature may direct.
3   This amendment shall not be so construed as to affect the election or term of any Senator chosen before it becomes valid as part of the Constitution.

Amendment XVIII (1919: repealed by Amendment XXI, 1933)

1   After one year from the ratification of this article the manufacture, sale, or transportation of intoxicating liquors within, the importation thereof into, or the exportation thereof from the United States and all territory subject to the jurisdiction thereof for beverage purposes is hereby prohibited.
2   The Congress and the several States shall have concurrent power to enforce this article by appropriate legislation.
3   This article shall be inoperative unless it shall have been ratified as an amendment to the Constitution by the legislatures of the several States, as provided in the Constitution, within seven years from the date of the submission hereof to the States by the Congress.

Amendment XIX (1920)

1   The right of citizens of the United States to vote shall not be denied or abridged by the United States or by any State on account of sex.
2   Congress shall have power to enforce this article by appropriate legislation.

Amendment XX (1933)

1   The terms of the President and Vice President shall end at noon on the 20th day of January, and the terms of Senators and Representatives at noon on the 3d day of January, of the years in which such terms would have ended if this article had not been ratified; and the terms of their successors shall then begin.
2   The Congress shall assemble at least once in every year, and such meeting shall begin at noon on the 3d day of January, unless they shall by law appoint a different day.
3   If, at the time fixed for the beginning of the term of the President, the President elect shall have died, the Vice President elect shall become President. If a President shall not have been chosen before the time fixed for the beginning of his term, or if the President elect shall have failed to qualify, then the Vice President elect shall act as President until a President shall have qualified; and the Congress may by law provide for the case wherein neither a President elect nor a Vice President elect shall have

qualified, declaring who shall then act as President, or the manner in which one who is to act shall be selected, and such person shall act accordingly until a President or Vice President shall have qualified.

4　The Congress may by law provide for the case of the death of any of the persons from whom the House of Representatives may choose a President whenever the right of choice shall have devolved upon them, and for the case of the death of any of the persons from whom the Senate may choose a Vice President whenever the right of choice shall have devolved upon them.

5　Sections 1 and 2 shall take effect on the 15th day of October following the ratification of this article.

6　This article shall be inoperative unless it shall have been ratified as an amendment to the Constitution by the legislatures of three-fourths of the several States within seven years from the date of its submission.

Amendment XXI (1933)

1　The eighteenth article of amendment to the Constitution of the United States is hereby repealed.

2　The transportation or importation into any State, Territory, or possession of the United States for delivery or use therein of intoxicating liquors, in violation of the laws thereof, is hereby prohibited.

3　The article shall be inoperative unless it shall have been ratified as an amendment to the Constitution by conventions in the several States, as provided in the Constitution, within seven years from the date of the submission hereof to the States by the Congress.

Amendment XXII (1951)

1　No person shall be elected to the office of the President more than twice, and no person who has held the office of President, or acted as President, for more than two years of a term to which some other person was elected President shall be elected to the office of the President more than once. But this Article shall not apply to any person holding the office of President, when this Article was proposed by the Congress, and shall not prevent any person who may be holding the office of President, or acting as President, during the term within which this Article becomes operative from holding the office of President or acting as President during the remainder of such term.

2　This article shall be inoperative unless it shall have been ratified as an amendment to the Constitution by the legislatures of three-fourths of the several States within seven years from the date of its submission to the States by the Congress.

Amendment XXIII (1961)

1　The District constituting the seat of Government of the United States shall appoint in such manner as the Congress may direct: A number of electors of President and Vice President equal to the whole number of Senators and Representatives in Congress to which the District would be entitled if it were a State, but in no event more than the least populous State; they shall be in addition to those appointed by the States, but they shall be considered, for the purposes of the election of President and Vice President, to be electors appointed by a State; and they shall meet in the District and perform such duties as provided by the twelfth article of amendment.

2 The Congress shall have power to enforce this article by appropriate legislation.

Amendment XXIV (1964)

1 The right of citizens of the United States to vote in any primary or other election for President or Vice President, for electors for President or Vice President, or for Senator or Representative in Congress, shall not be denied or abridged by the United States or any State by reason of failure to pay any poll tax or other tax.

2 The Congress shall have power to enforce this article by appropriate legislation.

Amendment XXV (1967)

1 In case of the removal of the President from office or of his death or resignation, the Vice President shall become President.

2 Whenever there is a vacancy in the office of the Vice President, the President shall nominate a Vice President who shall take office upon confirmation by a majority vote of both Houses of Congress.

3 Whenever the President transmits to the President pro tempore of the Senate and the Speaker of the House of Representatives his written declaration that he is unable to discharge the powers and duties of his office, and until he transmits to them a written declaration to the contrary, such powers and duties shall be discharged by the Vice President as Acting President.

4 Whenever the Vice President and a majority of either the principal officers of the executive departments or of such other body as Congress may by law provide, transmit to the President pro tempore of the Senate and the Speaker of the House of Representatives their written declaration that the President is unable to discharge the powers and duties of his office, the Vice President shall immediately assume the powers and duties of the office as Acting President.

Thereafter, when the President transmits to the President pro tempore of the Senate and the Speaker of the House of Representatives his written declaration that no inability exists, he shall resume the powers and duties of his office unless the Vice President and a majority of either the principal officers of the executive department or of such other body as Congress may by law provide, transmit within four days to the President pro tempore of the Senate and the Speaker of the House of Representatives their written declaration that the President is unable to discharge the powers and duties of his office. Thereupon Congress shall decide the issue, assembling within forty-eight hours for that purpose if not in session. If the Congress, within twenty-one days after receipt of the latter written declaration, or, if Congress is not in session, within twenty-one days after Congress is required to assemble, determines by two-thirds vote of both Houses that the President is unable to discharge the powers and duties of his office, the Vice President shall continue to discharge the same as Acting President; otherwise, the President shall resume the powers and duties of his office.

Amendment XXVI (1971)

1   The right of citizens of the United States, who are eighteen years of age or older, to vote shall not be denied or abridged by the United States or by any State on account of age.

2   The Congress shall have power to enforce this article by appropriate legislation.

Amendment XXVII (1992)

No law varying the compensation for the services of the Senators and Representatives, shall take effect until an election of Representatives shall have intervened.

Index

Note: **bold** page numbers indicate key terms.

A

abortion
  Gonzales v *Carhart* 195–96
  party policies compared 258, 301
  pressure groups 227, 336
  Roe v *Wade* 194–95
  Supreme Court decisions 194–97
  Whole Woman's Health v *Hellerstedt* 196–97
acceptance speech **259–60**
accountability 165–66
  and recall elections 287
activism, judicial **186–87**
the administration 93
affirmative action **213–15**
  arguments for and against 217
  evaluating success of 218
  future of 219–20
  and public opinion 218–19
  and the Supreme Court 215–17
Affordable Care Act ('Obamacare') 44, 46, 81, 144, 191, 199, 301
African-Americans 304
  and affirmative action 214, 219, 220
  in the cabinet 121, 223
  in Congress 222
  congressional membership 61–62
  in executive branch 222
  voting rights 220–21
age
  of cabinet members 122
  and death penalty 194
agenda building, pressure groups 332
amendments to the Constitution 22–26, 39, 363–75

American Civil Liberties Union (ACLU) 228, 333, 340, 341
amicus curiae (court briefings) 228, 340
annual budget submission by president 113–14
appointments (recruitment)
  cabinet 119–22, 223
  confirmation of presidential 71
  confirming by Senate 64–65
  confirming vice president 66
  judicial 115, 165, 178–85, 206–07
  recess 150–51, 201–02
  vice president 66
approval ratings of president 160–61
  following a crisis 162
Articles of Confederation **6**, 37
Articles of the Constitution 20–21, 354–62

B

balanced cabinet 121–22
balanced ticket **254**
bicameralism 95, 104, 105
Bill of Rights 24–26
  interpretation by Supreme Court 189–94
bills *see* legislative process
Bipartisan Campaign Reform Act (2002) 262, 263
bipartisanship **35**
black voters 221
Blue America 310
Blue Dog Coalition 99
brokered convention **256**
budget process, OMB 134
budget submission by president 113–14
Bush, George W. (2001–09) 155
  the Bush Doctrine 157–58

federalism under 40–42
busing of school children **214**

C

the cabinet **118**
  assessment of 126–27
  balanced 121–22
  historical background 118–19
  meetings 122–26
  minority representation in 223
  pools of recruitment 119–21
  US-UK comparison 167–68
capital punishment 177
Carter, Jimmy (1977-81) 11, 123, 124, 267
Catholics
  Congress members 63
  Democratic party support 308–09
caucuses **240**
  congressional 98–99
  early 242–43
  low turnout 247
  timing of 241
  voter unrepresentativeness 250
causal pressure groups 331
chairpersons of standing committees 73–74
chairs of standing committees, seniority rule 73–74
checks and balances **28–29**
  check by president on Congress 29–30
  checks by Congress on courts 34
  checks by Congress on president 30–33, 159
  checks by courts on Congress 34
  checks by courts on president 34, 159–60
  checks by president on courts 30
  consequences for politics 35